D1385377

Better Homes and Gardens®

quick
quicker
quickest

350 delicious meals ready in 20, 30, or 40 minutes!

WILEY

John Wiley & Sons, Inc.

Meredith Corporation

Editor: Jessica Saari Christensen

Contributing Editor: Janet Figg

Recipe Testing: Better Homes and
Gardens Test Kitchen

John Wiley & Sons, Inc.

Publisher: Natalie Chapman

Associate Publisher: Jessica Goodman

Executive Editor: Anne Ficklen

Editor: Adam Kowit

Senior Production Editor:
Amy Zarkos

Cover Design: Suzanne Sunwoo

Design: Tai Blanche

Layout: Indianapolis
Composition Services

Manufacturing Manager: Tom Hyland

Better Homes and Gardens®

Test Kitchen

Our seal assures you that every recipe in
Quick, Quicker, Quickest has been tested
in the Better Homes and Gardens® Test
Kitchen. This means that each recipe is
practical and reliable and meets our high
standards of taste appeal. We guarantee
your satisfaction with this book for as
long as you own it.

For general information on our other products and services or for technical
support, please contact our Customer Care Department within the United States
at (877) 762-2974, outside the United States at (317) 572-3993 or fax (317) 572-4002.

Wiley also publishes its books in a variety of electronic formats. Some content
that appears in print may not be available in electronic books. For more
information about Wiley products, visit our web site at www.wiley.com.

Library of Congress Cataloging-in-Publication Data:

Quick quicker quickest : 350 delicious meals ready in 20, 30, or 40 minutes! /
by Better homes and gardens.
    p. cm.
  At head of title: Better homes and gardens
  Includes index.
  ISBN 978-0-470-54638-3 (pbk.)
  1. Quick and easy cookery. I. Better homes and gardens. II. Title:
Better homes and gardens.
  TX833.5.Q5355 2010
  641.5'55--dc22

                  2009045468

ISBN: 978-0-470-54638-3

Printed in the United States of America

10 9 8 7 6 5 4 3 2 1

CONTENTS

Dinner is back!

Between Monday night soccer practice and Wednesday night ballet lessons, family life can be very hectic—sometimes even a little frantic! After working all day, driving the kids around, and running all your errands, finding time to whip together a home-cooked meal may seem like a daunting task. But stop . . . and take a deep breath.

Meals at home are possible. No matter how much or how little time you have to put good food on the table for your family, there's a recipe here for you. You'll find three sections in this book, each tailor-made to fit your time constraints. Our first section includes the quickest recipes ever—ready in 20 minutes or less. Our second section keeps it simple with meals that can be created in 30 minutes. And our final section gives you over a hundred 40-minute options for when time is a little easier to find.

Quick, Quicker, Quickest was designed just for you—the time-crunched grown-ups who are juggling everything but also know the importance of home-cooked meals for themselves and their families. These recipes were designed to be not only irresistible, but also healthful and super-convenient to prepare. So go ahead—enjoy dinner again!

Stocking the Pantry

In each of the recipes, we've included a shopping list and a pantry list. The former are things you might need to pick up at the grocery store, while the latter includes items you probably have in your kitchen. Before you start, here are the absolute basics you should keep on hand—with them, dinner is never far away!

Essential pantry foods

All-purpose flour

Baking powder and soda

Balsamic vinegar

Barbecue sauce

Bottled hot pepper sauce

Bottled salad dressing (Italian, ranch)

Bread

Cayenne pepper

Chili powder

Cider vinegar

Cornstarch

Crushed red pepper

Dried basil

Dried Italian seasoning

Dried oregano

Dried pasta (spaghetti, angel hair, elbow macaroni, orzo, small shell macaroni)

Dried thyme

Fine dry bread crumbs

Garlic bulbs or bottled minced garlic

Garlic salt

Ground black pepper

Ground cinnamon

Ground cumin

Honey

Ketchup

Maple syrup

Mayonnaise (light or regular)

Mustard (Dijon and yellow)

Nonstick cooking spray

Oil (cooking, olive, vegetable)

Peanut butter

Rice (white and brown)

Salt

Shortening

Soy sauce

Sugar (granulated and brown)

Worcestershire sauce

Essential refrigerator items

Butter (margarine)

Eggs

Milk

Orange juice

Once you've got the basics tucked away in the cupboards, stock up on some other commonly used foods. Mix and match from each category and you'll never be without dinner again!

Other pantry foods

Canned beans

Canned chicken, beef, and vegetable broth

Canned coconut milk

Canned diced tomatoes

Canned soup

Canned tuna or salmon

Corn muffin mix

Curry powder

Dried egg or ramen noodles

Flour or corn tortillas

Instant rice (white or brown)

Jars of gravy

Jelly and/or jams

Nuts (peanuts, almonds, walnuts)

Panko (Japanese-style) bread crumbs

Pasta sauce

Pesto

Pickles

Pizza sauce

Pouches of cooked rice

Quick-cooking couscous

Salsa

Stewed tomatoes (plain, Mexican-style, and Italian-style)

Stir-fry or hoisin sauces

Other refrigerator and freezer items

Beef stir-fry strips

Cheese (cheddar, feta, Parmesan)

Chicken breasts

Cream cheese and flavored cream cheese spreads

Dairy sour cream

Deli meats (ham, roast beef, turkey)

Frozen bread or bread dough

Frozen vegetables

Ground beef

Plain yogurt

Pork chops

Refrigerated pasta

Shredded cheese

Sliced bacon

Sliced cheese

Other produce

Broccoli

Carrots

Celery

Cucumbers

Green beans

Mushrooms

Onions

Packages of mixed salad greens

Potatoes

Shredded cabbage with carrot (coleslaw mix)

Sweet peppers

Sweet potatoes

Yellow summer squash

Zucchini

20 minute

meals

Quick Thai **Chicken**

Start to Finish: **20 minutes**

- **4 skinless, boneless chicken breast halves**
- **1 tablespoon cooking oil**
- **¾ cup unsweetened coconut milk**
- **¼ cup peanut butter**
- **¼ teaspoon ground ginger**
- **¼ teaspoon ground black pepper**
- **4 green onions, cut into 1-inch pieces**
- **¼ cup honey-roasted peanuts, coarsely chopped**

1 In a large skillet cook chicken in hot oil over medium heat for 8 to 12 minutes or until no longer pink (170°F), turning occasionally to brown evenly. Remove chicken from skillet; cover to keep warm.

2 In a small bowl whisk together coconut milk, peanut butter, ginger, and pepper; set aside. Add green onions to skillet. Cook and stir about 2 minutes or until tender. Stir in coconut milk mixture. Cook and stir until bubbly. Spoon over chicken; sprinkle with peanuts.

Makes 4 servings

Nutrition facts per serving: 415 cal., 25 g total fat (11 g sat. fat), 82 mg chol., 192 mg sodium, 8 g carbo., 2 g dietary fiber, 39 g protein.

Shopping list:
- 4 skinless, boneless chicken breast halves
- 1 14-ounce can unsweetened coconut milk
- 1 small container ground ginger
- 1 bunch green onions
- 1 8-ounce container honey-roasted peanuts

Pantry list:
Cooking oil

Peanut butter

Ground black pepper

20 minutes

Skillet **Chicken**

Start to Finish: **20 minutes**

4 **skinless, boneless chicken breast halves**

1 **10.75-ounce can condensed golden mushroom soup**

¾ **cup reduced-sodium chicken broth**

½ **of an 8-ounce tub cream cheese with chive and onion**

8 **ounces angel hair pasta or thin spaghetti, cooked and drained**

1 Place each chicken breast half, boned side up, between two pieces of plastic wrap. Pound lightly until ¼ inch thick. Discard plastic wrap.

2 Heat a large nonstick skillet over medium-high heat for 1 minute. Add chicken and cook about 4 minutes or until no longer pink (170°F), turning once. (If necessary, cook half the chicken at a time.) Remove chicken from skillet; keep warm.

3 Add soup, broth, and cream cheese to the hot skillet. Cook and stir over medium heat until combined and mixture is heated through. Serve chicken and sauce over hot cooked pasta.

Makes 4 servings

Nutrition facts per serving: 520 cal., 14 g total fat (8 g sat. fat), 113 mg chol., 906 mg sodium, 51 g carbo., 2 g dietary fiber, 43 g protein.

Shopping list:

4 skinless, boneless chicken breast halves

1 10.75-ounce can condensed golden mushroom soup

1 14-ounce can reduced-sodium chicken broth

1 8-ounce tub cream cheese with chive and onion

Pantry list:

Angel hair pasta

Chicken Veronique

Start to Finish: **20 minutes**

- 4   **skinless, boneless chicken breast halves**
- ¼   **teaspoon salt**
- ¼   **teaspoon ground black pepper**
- ¼   **cup butter**
- 1   **cup seedless red grapes, halved**
- 3   **tablespoons sherry vinegar or red wine vinegar**
- ¼   **teaspoon dried thyme, crushed**

1   Sprinkle chicken with salt and pepper. In a large skillet cook chicken in 2 tablespoons of the hot butter over medium-high heat for 8 to 10 minutes or until no longer pink (170°F), turning once. Transfer to a serving platter; keep warm.

2   For sauce, add the remaining 2 tablespoons butter, grapes, vinegar, and thyme to the hot skillet. Cook and stir until slightly thick, loosening any brown bits on bottom of skillet. Serve sauce over chicken.

Makes 4 servings

Nutrition facts per serving: 301 cal., 15 g total fat (8 g sat. fat), 115 mg chol., 348 mg sodium, 7 g carbo., 0 g dietary fiber, 33 g protein.

20 minutes

Shopping list:

4 skinless, boneless chicken breast halves

1 small bag seedless red grapes

1 small bottle sherry vinegar

Pantry list:

Salt

Ground black pepper

Butter

Dried thyme

Chicken Tossed Salad

Start to Finish: **20 minutes**

4   skinless, boneless chicken breast halves

1   tablespoon olive oil

¼   teaspoon garlic-pepper blend

8   cups torn mixed salad greens

1   medium yellow or red sweet pepper, cut into bite-size strips

1   medium tomato, cut into wedges

½   cup bottled reduced-calorie salad dressing (such as berry or roasted garlic vinaigrette or Parmesan-basil Italian)

¼   cup crumbled feta cheese

¼   cup purchased croutons

1 Brush chicken with oil; sprinkle with garlic-pepper. In a medium nonstick skillet cook chicken over medium heat for 12 to 15 minutes or until no longer pink (170°F). Slice chicken into bite-size strips. Set aside.

2 In a large serving bowl toss greens, sweet pepper, and tomato; add dressing and toss to coat. Top with chicken, feta cheese, and croutons.

Makes 4 servings

Nutrition facts per serving: 277 cal., 12 g total fat (2 g sat. fat), 74 mg chol., 536 mg sodium, 12 g carbo., 3 g dietary fiber, 29 g protein.

Shopping list:
4 skinless, boneless chicken breast halves

1 small container garlic-pepper blend

1 10-ounce package mixed salad greens

1 medium yellow sweet pepper

1 medium tomato

1 8-ounce bottle reduced-calorie salad dressing

1 4-ounce package feta cheese

1 6-ounce box croutons

Pantry list:
Olive oil

20 minutes

Lemon-Tarragon Chicken Toss

Start to Finish: **20 minutes**

- 6 ounces dried fettuccine or linguine
- 2 cups broccoli or cauliflower florets
- ½ cup reduced-sodium chicken broth
- 3 tablespoons lemon juice
- 1 tablespoon honey
- 2 teaspoons cornstarch
- ¼ teaspoon ground white pepper
- 12 ounces skinless, boneless chicken breasts, cut into bite-size strips
- 2 teaspoons olive oil or cooking oil
- ½ cup shredded carrot
- 1 tablespoon snipped fresh tarragon or ½ teaspoon dried tarragon, crushed

  Lemon slices, halved (optional)

1 Cook pasta according to package directions, adding broccoli for the last 4 minutes of cooking. Drain.

2 Meanwhile, in a small bowl combine broth, lemon juice, honey, cornstarch, and white pepper; set aside.

3 In a large nonstick skillet cook and stir chicken in hot oil for 3 to 4 minutes or until no longer pink. Stir cornstarch mixture; add to skillet. Cook and stir until thick and bubbly. Add carrot and tarragon; cook for 1 minute more.

4 To serve, spoon chicken mixture over pasta. If desired, garnish with lemon slices.

Makes 4 servings

Nutrition facts per serving: 320 cal., 4 g total fat (1 g sat. fat), 49 mg chol., 143 mg sodium, 43 g carbo., 3 g dietary fiber, 27 g protein.

Shopping list:

- 1 8-ounce package dried fettuccine
- 1 head fresh broccoli
- 1 14-ounce container reduced-sodium chicken broth
- 1 lemon
- 1 small container ground white pepper
- 12 ounces skinless, boneless chicken breasts
- 1 small package shredded carrot
- 1 small package fresh tarragon

Pantry list:

Honey

Cornstarch

Olive oil

20 minutes

Caribbean **Chicken**

Start to Finish: **20 minutes**

1 ½ cups quick-cooking brown rice

1 pound chicken breast tenderloins

¼ teaspoon salt

⅛ to ¼ teaspoon cayenne pepper

1 teaspoon roasted peanut oil or cooking oil

1 medium sweet potato, peeled, halved lengthwise, and thinly sliced

1 small banana pepper, seeded and chopped

¾ cup unsweetened pineapple juice

1 teaspoon cornstarch

2 unripe bananas, quartered lengthwise and cut into ¾-inch pieces

1 Prepare rice according to package directions.

2 Meanwhile, season chicken with salt and cayenne pepper. In a large skillet cook chicken in hot oil over medium heat for 3 to 4 minutes or until brown, turning once. Add sweet potato slices and banana pepper. Cook and stir for 5 to 6 minutes more.

3 In a small bowl stir together unsweetened pineapple juice and cornstarch. Add to skillet. Cook, stirring gently, until bubbly. Add banana pieces. Cook and stir for 2 minutes more. Serve over rice.

Makes 4 servings

Nutrition facts per serving: 335 cal., 4 g total fat (1 g sat. fat), 66 mg chol., 244 mg sodium, 47 g carbo., 5 g dietary fiber, 30 g protein.

Shopping list:

1 8-ounce package quick-cooking brown rice

1 pound chicken breast tenderloins

1 small bottle roasted peanut oil

1 medium sweet potato

1 small banana pepper

1 6-ounce can unsweetened pineapple juice

2 unripe bananas

Pantry list:

Salt

Cayenne pepper

Cornstarch

20 minutes

Stir-Fry **Chicken and Rice**

Start to Finish: **10 minutes**

1   **8.8-ounce pouch cooked brown or white rice**

½   **cup frozen peas**

1   **pound chicken breast tenderloins, halved crosswise**

1   **tablespoon cooking oil**

¼   **cup bottled stir-fry sauce**

1   **2-ounce package oven-roasted sliced almonds**

1 Stir peas into rice pouch. Heat in microwave according to package directions.

2 Meanwhile, in a large skillet cook and stir chicken in hot oil over medium-high heat for 2 to 3 minutes or until no longer pink. Stir rice mixture into skillet. Stir in stir-fry sauce; heat through. Sprinkle with almonds.

Makes 4 servings

Nutrition facts per serving: 311 cal., 9 g total fat (1 g sat. fat), 66 mg chol., 453 mg sodium, 25 g carbo., 2 g dietary fiber, 31 g protein.

Shopping list:

1 10-ounce package frozen peas

1 pound chicken breast tenders

1 8-ounce bottle stir-fry sauce

1 2-ounce package oven-roasted sliced almonds

Pantry list:

Brown rice

Cooking oil

20 minutes

Hawaiian Sweet and Sour Chicken

Start to Finish: **20 minutes**   Oven: **350°F**

- 2 **tablespoons slivered almonds**
- 1 **tablespoon cooking oil**
- 1 **medium carrot, thinly bias-sliced**
- 1 **medium green sweet pepper, cut into bite-size strips**
- 4 **green onions, bias-sliced**
- 12 **ounces chicken breast tenderloins, halved crosswise**
- 1 **8- to 10-ounce bottle sweet and sour sauce**
- 1 **8-ounce can pineapple chunks (juice pack), drained**
- 1 **8.8-ounce pouch cooked long-grain rice**

1 Preheat oven to 350°F. Spread almonds in a single layer in a shallow baking pan. Bake for 5 to 10 minutes or until golden brown, stirring once or twice; set aside.

2 Meanwhile, heat oil in a wok or large skillet over medium-high heat. Add carrot; cook and stir for 2 minutes. Add sweet pepper; cook and stir for 2 minutes. Add green onions; cook and stir for 1 minute more or until vegetables are crisp-tender. Remove vegetables from skillet.

3 Add chicken to hot wok (add more oil if needed). Cook and stir for 3 to 4 minutes or until chicken is no longer pink. Return vegetables to wok. Add sweet and sour sauce and drained pineapple. Heat through.

4 Prepare rice according to package directions. Serve chicken mixture with rice; top with toasted almonds.

Makes 4 servings

Nutrition facts per serving: 390 cal., 8 g total fat (1 g sat. fat), 49 mg chol., 263 mg sodium, 51 g carbo., 3 g dietary fiber, 23 g protein.

Shopping list:
- 1 2-ounce package slivered almonds
- 1 1-pound package carrots
- 1 medium green sweet pepper
- 1 bunch green onions
- 12 ounces chicken breast tenderloins
- 1 8- to 10-ounce bottle sweet and sour sauce
- 1 8-ounce can pineapple chunks (juice pack)
- 1 8.8-ounce pouch cooked long-grain rice

Pantry list:
Cooking oil

Southwestern **Cobb Salad** *(See photo on page 129.)*

Start to Finish: **20 minutes**

1 **10-ounce package chopped hearts of romaine**

1 **6-ounce package refrigerated cooked Southwestern chicken breast strips**

1 **15-ounce can black beans, rinsed and drained**

1 **cup halved grape or cherry tomatoes**

1 **cup lime-flavored or plain tortilla chips, coarsely broken (about 1 ounce)**

2 **medium avocados, peeled, pitted, and sliced**

1 **11-ounce can whole kernel corn with sweet peppers, drained**

½ **cup shredded Mexican-style four-cheese blend**

½ **cup thinly sliced red onion**

½ **cup bottled spicy ranch salad dressing***

Spread romaine on a large serving platter. Arrange chicken, beans, tomatoes, tortilla chips, sliced avocado, corn, cheese, and onion in rows over the lettuce. Serve with dressing.

Makes 6 servings

Nutrition facts per serving: 363 cal., 22 g total fat (5 g sat. fat), 33 mg chol., 880 mg sodium, 32 g carbo., 9 g dietary fiber, 17 g protein.

*Test Kitchen Tip: If you can't find spicy ranch salad dressing, mix ½ cup ranch salad dressing with 2 tablespoons barbecue sauce.

Shopping list:

1 10-ounce package chopped hearts of romaine

1 17-ounce package refrigerated cooked Southwestern chicken breast strips

1 15-ounce can black beans

1 pint grape tomatoes

1 13-ounce bag lime-flavored tortilla chips

2 medium avocados

1 11-ounce can whole kernel corn with sweet peppers

1 8-ounce package shredded Mexican-style four-cheese blend

1 small red onion

1 16-ounce bottle spicy ranch salad dressing

20 minutes

Chicken Lettuce Wraps

Start to Finish: **20 minutes**

- **2 6-ounce packages refrigerated cooked chicken breast strips**
- **2 cups shredded cabbage with carrot (coleslaw mix)**
- **1 8-ounce can sliced water chestnuts, drained**
- **2 green onions, cut up**
- **2 tablespoons snipped fresh cilantro**
- **⅓ cup Asian sweet chili sauce or bottled stir-fry sauce**
- **1 tablespoon lime juice**
- **8 leaves Bibb or green leaf lettuce**

1 In a food processor combine about half of the chicken, coleslaw mix, water chestnuts, green onions, and cilantro; cover and process with several on/off turns until finely chopped. Transfer to a large skillet. Repeat with remaining chicken, coleslaw mix, water chestnuts, green onions, and cilantro. Add chili sauce and lime juice to mixture in skillet. Cook and stir over medium heat until heated through.

2 If necessary, cut veins from large lettuce leaves. Spoon chicken mixture onto lettuce leaves; roll up.

Makes 4 servings

Nutrition facts per serving: 219 cal., 3 g total fat (2 g sat. fat), 60 mg chol., 1,073 mg sodium, 22 g carbo., 5 g dietary fiber, 23 g protein.

Shopping list:

- 2 6-ounce packages refrigerated cooked chicken breast strips
- 1 16-ounce package shredded cabbage with carrot (coleslaw mix)
- 1 8-ounce can sliced water chestnuts
- 1 bunch green onions
- 1 bunch cilantro
- 1 bottle Asian sweet chili sauce
- 1 lime
- 1 head Bibb lettuce

20 minutes

Chicken Club Sandwiches with Avocado Spread

Start to Finish: **15 minutes**

1 **medium avocado**

1 **tablespoon lime juice**

Salt and ground black pepper

4 **potato rolls, individual ciabatta rolls, or hamburger buns, split and toasted**

1 **6-ounce package refrigerated Southwestern cooked chicken breast strips***

8 **slices packaged ready-to-serve cooked bacon**

1 **small tomato, thinly sliced**

Peel and pit avocado. In a medium bowl mash avocado with a fork. Stir in lime juice. Season to taste with salt and pepper. Spread avocado mixture on cut side of roll tops. On roll bottoms layer chicken breast strips, bacon, and tomato. Add roll tops.

Makes 4 servings

Nutrition facts per serving: 280 cal., 12 g total fat (3 g sat. fat), 38 mg chol., 892 mg sodium, 27 g carbo., 5 g dietary fiber, 17 g protein.

***Note:** For a warm sandwich, heat chicken according to package directions. Assemble as above.

Shopping list:

1 medium avocado

1 lime

1 package potato rolls or hamburger buns

1 6-ounce package refrigerated Southwestern chicken breast strips

1 2.1-ounce package ready-to-serve cooked bacon

1 small tomato

Pantry list:

Salt

Ground black pepper

Cajun Chicken **Tortellini**

Start to Finish: **20 minutes**

- 1 **20-ounce package refrigerated three-cheese tortellini**
- 1 **small red onion, cut into thin wedges**
- 1 **medium yellow sweet pepper, cut into bite-size strips**
- 1 **tablespoon olive oil**
- 2 **6-ounce packages refrigerated cooked chicken breast strips**
- 1 **10-ounce container refrigerated Alfredo pasta sauce**
- 1 **teaspoon Cajun seasoning**

1 Prepare tortellini according to package directions; drain and return to pan.

2 Meanwhile, in a large skillet cook onion and sweet pepper in hot oil over medium heat for 5 to 7 minutes or until tender, stirring occasionally. Stir in chicken, pasta sauce, and Cajun seasoning. Heat through. Add to tortellini; toss to coat.

Makes 6 servings

Nutrition facts per serving: 574 cal., 22 g total fat (19 g sat. fat), 109 mg chol., 1,417 mg sodium, 64 g carbo., 4 g dietary fiber, 43 g protein.

Shopping list:

1 20-ounce package refrigerated three-cheese tortellini

1 small red onion

1 medium yellow sweet pepper

2 6-ounce packages refrigerated cooked chicken breast strips

1 10-ounce container refrigerated Alfredo pasta sauce

1 small jar Cajun seasoning

Pantry list:

Olive oil

20

minutes

Bistro-Style Chicken and Roasted Pepper Sandwiches

Start to Finish: **20 minutes**

1 ½ **cups mesclun or other mixed spring salad greens**

½ **of a 7-ounce jar roasted red sweet peppers, drained and cut into strips (about ½ cup)**

1 **tablespoon white wine vinegar**

2 **teaspoons olive oil**

2 **7-inch Italian flat breads (focaccia)**

1 **6-ounce package refrigerated cooked chicken breast strips**

2 **slices provolone or mozzarella cheese**

1 In a small bowl toss together mesclun, roasted sweet peppers, vinegar, and 1 teaspoon of the oil. Set aside.

2 Lightly brush the focaccia with the remaining 1 teaspoon oil. Place focaccia, oil sides up, on the unheated rack of a broiler pan or on a baking sheet. Broil 4 to 5 inches from the heat for 1 to 2 minutes or until lightly toasted.

3 Top focaccia with mesclun mixture, chicken, and cheese. Broil for 1 to 2 minutes more or until cheese melts and chicken is warm.

Makes 2 servings

Nutrition facts per serving: 468 cal., 20 g total fat (9 g sat. fat), 80 mg chol., 1,367 mg sodium, 41 g carbo., 5 g dietary fiber, 35 g protein.

Shopping list:

1 8-ounce package mesclun

1 7-ounce jar roasted red sweet peppers

1 bottle white wine vinegar

2 7-inch Italian flat breads

1 6-ounce package refrigerated cooked chicken breast strips

1 6-ounce package sliced provolone cheese

Pantry list:

Olive oil

Bavarian **Quesadillas**

Start to Finish: **20 minutes**   Oven: **300°F**

4 **9- to 10-inch flour tortillas**

  Nonstick cooking spray

¼ **cup spicy brown mustard**

1½ **cups shredded Swiss cheese**

1 **6-ounce package refrigerated cooked chicken breast strips**

1 **medium Granny Smith apple, cored and sliced**

1 **teaspoon caraway seeds**

1 Coat one side of each tortilla with cooking spray; place, coated sides down, on a work surface lined with waxed paper. Spread tortillas with mustard. Top half of each tortilla with cheese, chicken, apple slices, and caraway seeds. Fold tortillas in half, pressing gently.

2 Heat a very large skillet over medium heat for 1 minute. Cook quesadillas two at a time over medium heat for 4 to 6 minutes or until light brown, turning once. Keep warm in a 300°F oven. Repeat with remaining quesadillas. Cut into wedges to serve.

Makes 4 servings

Nutrition facts per serving: 511 cal., 21 g total fat (11 g sat. fat), 73 mg chol., 1,065 mg sodium, 48 g carbo., 3 g dietary fiber, 30 g protein.

Shopping list:
1 package 9- to 10-inch flour tortillas

1 12-ounce bottle spicy brown mustard

1 8-ounce package shredded Swiss cheese

1 6-ounce package refrigerated cooked chicken breast strips

1 medium Granny Smith apple

1 small container caraway seeds

Pantry list:
Nonstick cooking spray

20 minutes

Alfredo Chicken **Pita Pizzas**

Start to Finish: 20 minutes   Oven: 450°F

4   **large pita bread rounds**

½   **cup refrigerated Alfredo pasta sauce**

1   **6-ounce package refrigerated cooked chicken breast strips**

½   **cup roasted red sweet peppers, cut into thin strips**

¼   **cup sliced green onions**

1   **cup finely shredded Italian blend cheeses**

Preheat oven to 450°F. Place pita bread rounds on a large baking sheet. Bake for 6 to 8 minutes or until light brown. Spread tops of pitas with Alfredo pasta sauce. Top with chicken breast strips, roasted sweet peppers, green onions, and cheese. Bake for 6 to 8 minutes more or until cheese melts and toppings are heated through.

Makes 4 servings

Nutrition facts per serving: 387 cal., 15 g total fat (8 g sat. fat), 65 mg chol., 1,123 mg sodium, 39 g carbo., 2 g dietary fiber, 24 g protein.

20 minutes

Shopping list:

1 package pita bread rounds

1 10-ounce package refrigerated Alfredo pasta sauce

1 6-ounce package refrigerated cooked chicken breast strips

1 7-ounce jar roasted red sweet peppers

1 bunch green onions

1 8-ounce package finely shredded Italian blend cheeses

Quick Chicken and **Tortellini Soup**

Start to Finish: **15 minutes**

- **2 cups milk**
- **1 10.75-ounce can condensed cream of chicken with herbs soup**
- **1 10.5-ounce can condensed chicken broth**
- **1 9-ounce package refrigerated cheese tortellini**
- **1 6-ounce package refrigerated oven-roasted chicken breast strips**
- **1 cup purchased coarsely shredded fresh carrot or coarsely shredded carrot**

In a 4-quart Dutch oven whisk together milk, cream of chicken soup, and chicken broth until smooth. Cook over high heat just until boiling, stirring frequently. Stir in tortellini, chicken, and carrot. Reduce heat. Simmer, covered, for 5 to 6 minutes or until tortellini is tender, stirring occasionally.

Makes 4 servings

Nutrition facts per serving: 404 cal., 12 g total fat (4 g sat. fat), 78 mg chol., 1,742 mg sodium, 45 g carbo., 2 g dietary fiber, 28 g protein.

Shopping list:

- 1 10.75-ounce can condensed cream of chicken with herbs soup
- 1 10.5 ounce can condensed chicken broth
- 1 9-ounce package refrigerated cheese tortellini
- 1 6-ounce package refrigerated oven-roasted chicken breast strips
- 1 10-ounce package coarsely shredded fresh carrot

Pantry list:

Milk

Wasatch **Mountain Chili** *(See photo on page 130.)*

Start to Finish: **15 minutes**

- 1 **medium onion, chopped (½ cup)**
- 1 **tablespoon cooking oil**
- 1 **15- to 16-ounce can hominy, drained**
- 1 **15- to 16-ounce can Great Northern beans, rinsed and drained**
- 1 **14-ounce can reduced-sodium chicken broth**
- 1 **9-ounce package frozen cooked chicken breast strips**
- ¼ **cup lime juice**
- 2 **tablespoons chopped fresh cilantro**
- ¼ **teaspoon ground cumin**
- ¼ **teaspoon ground black pepper**
- ½ **cup shredded Colby and Monterey Jack cheese, Monterey Jack, or cheddar cheese (2 ounces)**
- **Bottled green salsa (optional)**
- **White corn tortilla chips (optional)**
- **Fresh cilantro leaves (optional)**

In a large saucepan cook onion in hot oil over medium heat for 3 minutes. Stir in hominy, beans, chicken broth, frozen chicken, lime juice, cilantro, cumin, and pepper. Cover and bring to boiling over high heat, stirring occasionally. Serve topped with cheese and, if desired salsa, tortilla chips, and fresh cilantro.

Makes 4 servings

Nutrition facts per serving: 434 cal., 14 g total fat (5 g sat. fat), 58 mg chol., 1,001 mg sodium, 48 g carbo., 9 g dietary fiber, 31 g protein.

Shopping list:
- 1 medium onion
- 1 15- to 16-ounce can hominy
- 1 15- to 16-ounce can Great Northern beans
- 1 14-ounce can reduced-sodium chicken broth
- 1 9-ounce package frozen cooked chicken breast strips
- 1 mall bottle lime juice
- 1 bunch fresh cilantro
- 1 8-ounce package shredded Colby and Monterey Jack cheese

Pantry list:
Cooking oil

Ground Cumin

Ground black pepper

20 minutes

Chicken Tenders Parmesan

Start to Finish: **20 minutes**   Oven: **425°F**

- 1 **12-ounce package frozen cooked, breaded chicken breast tenders**
- 1 **cup bottled marinara sauce**
- ½ **cup shredded Italian blend cheeses**
- 2 **tablespoons snipped fresh basil (optional)**

Preheat oven to 425°F. Place chicken tenders in a 2-quart square baking dish. Top with marinara sauce and cheese. Bake for 15 minutes or until hot and bubbly. If desired, sprinkle with fresh basil.

Makes 4 servings

Nutrition facts per serving: 279 cal., 14 g total fat (4 g sat. fat), 35 mg chol., 863 mg sodium, 23 g carbo., 2 g dietary fiber, 17 g protein.

Shopping list:

- 1 12-ounce package frozen cooked, breaded chicken breast tenders
- 1 26-ounce jar marinara sauce
- 1 8-ounce package shredded Italian blend cheeses
- 1 bunch fresh basil

Asian Chicken Salad

Start to Finish: **20 minutes**

- 1 **purchased roasted chicken**
- 1 **16-ounce package shredded cabbage with carrot (coleslaw mix)**
- 1 **cup snow peas, trimmed and halved crosswise**
- 1 **medium red or yellow sweet pepper, cut into thin strips**
- 1/3 **cup bias-sliced green onions**
- 2/3 **cup bottled toasted sesame salad dressing or other Asian-flavored salad dressing**
- 1/2 **cup packaged garlic ginger or wasabi ranch crisp wonton strips or toasted sliced almonds**

1 Remove skin and bones from chicken; discard skin and bones. Shred 3 cups of meat. Place any remaining meat in a covered storage container and chill for up to 3 days for another use.

2 In a very large serving bowl combine chicken, coleslaw mix, snow peas, sweet pepper, and green onions. Add dressing and toss to coat. Top with wonton crisps.

Makes 6 servings

Nutrition facts per serving: 337 cal., 13 g total fat (2 g sat. fat), 93 mg chol., 406 mg sodium, 16 g carbo., 3 g dietary fiber, 36 g protein.

20 minutes

Shopping list:
- 1 purchased roasted chicken
- 1 16-ounce package shredded cabbage with carrot (coleslaw mix)
- 4 ounces snow peas
- 1 medium red or yellow sweet pepper
- 1 bunch green onions
- 1 16-ounce bottle Asian toasted sesame salad dressing
- 1 3.5-ounce package garlic ginger crisp wonton strips

Chicken Pesto Pasta

Start to Finish: **20 minutes**

- 1 **9-ounce package refrigerated fettuccine**
- ¼ **cup pine nuts**
- 1 **purchased roasted chicken**
- 1 **medium onion, cut into thin wedges**
- 1 **tablespoon olive oil**
- 1 **medium zucchini, halved lengthwise and sliced**
- 1 **8-ounce package button mushrooms, quartered**
- 1 **7-ounce container refrigerated basil pesto**

1 Prepare fettuccine according to package directions; drain. Snip through pasta with clean kitchen shears to make shorter lengths.

2 Meanwhile, in a very large skillet cook pine nuts over medium heat for 2 to 3 minutes or until golden brown, stirring occasionally. Remove from skillet; set aside. Remove 2 cups of meat from chicken and coarsely chop. Reserve remaining chicken for another use.

3 In the same skillet cook onion in hot oil until softened. Add zucchini and mushrooms; cook for 5 minutes or until vegetables are tender, stirring frequently. Stir in chicken and heat through.

4 Stir in pasta and pesto until coated. Sprinkle with pine nuts.

Makes 4 servings

Nutrition facts per serving: 663 cal., 42 g total fat (5 g sat. fat), 103 mg chol., 661 mg sodium, 48 g carbo., 3 g dietary fiber, 29 g protein.

Shopping list:

- 1 9-ounce package refrigerated fettuccine
- 1 1.5-ounce package pine nuts
- 1 purchased roasted chicken
- 1 medium onion
- 1 medium zucchini
- 1 8-ounce package button mushrooms
- 1 7-ounce container refrigerated basil pesto

Pantry list:

Olive oil

Southern **Chicken Salad**

Start to Finish: **20 minutes**

½ cup dairy sour cream

¼ cup white wine vinegar

3 to 4 tablespoons Dijon-style mustard

2 cloves garlic, minced

½ teaspoon salt

¼ teaspoon ground black pepper

6 cups torn mixed salad greens

½ cup lightly packed small fresh mint leaves

2 tablespoons shredded fresh basil or marjoram leaves

4 slices Texas toast or large slices sourdough bread, toasted

2 to 4 tablespoons honey butter

1 purchased roasted chicken, quartered*

4 medium peaches or nectarines, pitted and sliced

1 For dressing, in a small bowl whisk together sour cream, vinegar, mustard, garlic, salt, and pepper; set aside.

2 In a large bowl toss together greens, mint, and basil. Spread each toast slice with honey butter and place 1 slice on each of 4 plates. Top each with some of the greens. Arrange chicken and peaches on top of greens. Drizzle with dressing.

Makes 4 servings

Nutrition facts per serving: 677 cal., 36 g total fat (13 g sat. fat), 218 mg chol., 965 mg sodium, 37 g carbo., 3 g dietary fiber, 52 g protein.

*Note: Chicken can be warm or chilled.

Shopping list:

1 8-ounce carton dairy sour cream

1 bottle white wine vinegar

1 7-ounce package mixed salad greens

1 package fresh mint

1 small package fresh basil

4 slices Texas toast

1 small container honey butter

1 purchased roasted chicken

4 medium peaches

Pantry list:

Dijon-style mustard

Garlic

Salt

Ground black pepper

20 minutes

Tortellini and Cheese

Start to Finish: 20 minutes

- 1 **9-ounce package refrigerated cheese tortellini**
- 1 **cup frozen peas or snow peas**
- 1 **8-ounce tub cream cheese spread with garden vegetables or chive and onion**
- ½ **cup milk**
- 1 **9-ounce package frozen chopped cooked chicken breast**

1 In a large saucepan cook tortellini according to package directions. Place frozen peas in colander. Drain hot pasta over vegetables to thaw; return pasta-vegetable mixture to pan.

2 Meanwhile, in a small saucepan combine cream cheese and milk; heat and stir until cheese melts. Heat chicken according to package directions.

3 Stir cheese sauce into cooked pasta mixture. Cook and gently stir until heated through. Spoon into individual serving bowls. Top with chicken.

Makes 4 servings

Nutrition facts per serving: 505 cal., 26 g total fat (15 g sat. fat), 130 mg chol., 525 mg sodium, 32 g carbo., 2 g dietary fiber, 32 g protein.

Shopping list:
- 1 9-ounce package refrigerated cheese tortellini
- 1 10-ounce package frozen peas
- 1 8-ounce tub cream cheese spread with garden vegetables
- 1 9-ounce package frozen chopped cooked chicken breast

Pantry list:
Milk

Cabbage and Chicken with Sesame Dressing

Start to Finish: 20 minutes   **Oven: 375°F**

¼ cup slivered almonds

¼ cup bottled Italian salad dressing

1 tablespoon soy sauce

1 teaspoon toasted sesame oil

⅛ to ¼ teaspoon crushed red pepper

3 cups packaged shredded cabbage with carrot (coleslaw mix)

1 9-ounce package frozen diced cooked chicken breast, thawed

2 tablespoons snipped fresh cilantro

1 head Boston or Bibb lettuce, separated into leaves

1 Preheat oven to 375°F. Place almonds on a baking sheet. Bake for 5 to 7 minutes or until toasted. Meanwhile, for dressing, in a small bowl combine salad dressing, soy sauce, sesame oil, and crushed red pepper. Set aside.

2 In a large bowl toss together coleslaw mix, chicken, and cilantro. Drizzle with dressing; toss lightly to coat.

3 Line 4 plates with lettuce leaves. Divide chicken mixture among plates. Sprinkle with almonds.

Makes 4 servings

Nutrition facts per serving: 180 cal., 10 g total fat (1 g sat. fat), 34 mg chol., 700 mg sodium, 7 g carbo., 2 g dietary fiber, 17 g protein.

20 minutes

Shopping list:

1 2.25-ounce package slivered almonds

1 8-ounce bottle toasted sesame oil

1 16-ounce package shredded cabbage with carrot (coleslaw mix)

1 9-ounce package frozen diced cooked chicken breast

1 bunch fresh cilantro

1 head Boston or Bibb lettuce

Pantry list:

Bottled Italian salad dressing

Soy sauce

Crushed red pepper

Minestrone in Minutes

Start to Finish: **10 minutes**

1 **18- to 19-ounce can ready-to-serve minestrone soup**

½ **of a 9-ounce package frozen chopped cooked chicken breast, thawed (1 cup)**

½ **teaspoon bottled roasted minced garlic**

1 **cup fresh baby spinach leaves**

2 **tablespoons finely shredded Parmesan cheese**

1 In a large saucepan combine soup, cooked chicken, and garlic. Cook over medium heat until heated through.

2 Add spinach leaves; stir just until wilted. Heat through. Sprinkle individual servings with Parmesan cheese.

Makes 2 servings

Nutrition facts per serving: 233 cal., 7 g total fat (3 g sat. fat), 35 mg chol., 1,243 mg sodium, 26 g carbo., 8 g dietary fiber, 17 g protein.

Shopping list:
1 18- to 19-ounce can ready-to-serve minestrone soup

1 9-ounce package frozen chopped cooked chicken breast

1 10-ounce package fresh baby spinach leaves

1 3-ounce package finely shredded Parmesan cheese

Pantry list:
Bottled minced roasted garlic

20 minutes

Dill Chicken Wraps

Start to Finish: **20 minutes**

- 4 **10-inch flour tortillas**
- ¼ **cup dairy sour cream dill-flavor dip**
- ½ **cup fresh spinach leaves**
- 8 **ounces sliced cooked chicken breast**
- 2 **dill pickle spears, quartered lengthwise**
- 4 **ounces smoked Gouda or mozzarella cheese, shredded (1 cup)**

1 Wrap tortillas in plain white paper towels. Microwave on 100% power (high) for 1 minute.

2 Spread each tortilla with 1 tablespoon of the dip. Top with spinach leaves and chicken. Arrange pickle spears lengthwise down the center of each tortilla; sprinkle with cheese.

3 Tightly roll up tortillas; secure with wooden picks, if necessary. If desired, cut rolls in half.

Makes 4 wraps

Nutrition facts per wrap: 363 cal., 16 g total fat (8 g sat. fat), 88 mg chol., 666 mg sodium, 24 g carbo., 1 g dietary fiber, 28 g protein.

20 minutes

Shopping list:

- 1 14-ounce package flour tortillas
- 1 8-ounce container dairy sour cream dill-flavor dip
- 1 5-ounce package fresh spinach
- 8 ounces sliced smoked cooked chicken breast
- 1 16-ounce jar dill pickle spears
- 4 ounces smoked Gouda cheese

Chicken Salad **Sandwiches**

Start to Finish: **20 minutes**

¼ **cup mango chutney**

2 **tablespoons mayonnaise or salad dressing**

1 **teaspoon curry powder**

2 **cups cubed, cooked chicken or turkey**

1 **cup seedless red grapes, halved**

¼ **cup sliced or slivered almonds, toasted**

4 **croissants, split, or 6-inch pita bread rounds, halved crosswise**

Lettuce leaves

Cut up any large pieces of chutney. In a medium bowl combine chutney, mayonnaise, and curry powder. Stir in chicken, grapes, and almonds. Line each croissant with lettuce; top with chicken salad mixture.

Makes 4 servings

Nutrition facts per serving: 501 cal., 26 g total fat (9 g sat. fat), 103 mg chol., 566 mg sodium, 41 g carbo., 3 g dietary fiber, 26 g protein.

Shopping list:

1 15.25-ounce jar mango chutney

1 small container curry powder

1 8-ounce package cubed, cooked chicken

1 small bunch seedless red grapes

1 2-ounce package sliced almonds

4 croissants

1 head lettuce

Pantry list:

Mayonnaise

Chicken Tostadas

Start to Finish: **20 minutes**

8 **tostada shells**

½ **cup dairy sour cream**

1 **cup purchased fruit salsa**

1½ **cups finely chopped, cooked chicken**

1 **cup shredded Monterey Jack cheese with jalapeño peppers (4 ounces)**

1 Spread one side of each tostada shell with 1 tablespoon sour cream, spreading to edges. Spread 2 tablespoons salsa evenly on top of sour cream on each tostada. Top each with 3 tablespoons chopped chicken and 2 tablespoons shredded cheese.

2 Place 4 of the tostadas on a large cookie sheet. Place on rack of a broiler pan. Broil 4 to 5 inches for 1 to 1½ minutes or until cheese melts. Repeat with remaining tostadas. Serve warm.

Makes 4 servings

Nutrition facts per serving: 511 cal., 26 g total fat (12 g sat. fat), 89 mg chol., 488 mg sodium, 42 g carbo., 4 g dietary fiber, 27 g protein.

Shopping list:

8 tostada shells

1 8-ounce carton dairy sour cream

1 8-ounce jar fruit salsa

1 16-ounce package chopped, cooked chicken

1 4-ounce package shredded Monterey Jack cheese with jalapeño peppers

20 minutes

Honey-Cranberry Turkey

Start to Finish: **20 minutes**

- **2 turkey breast tenderloins, halved horizontally (about 1 ¼ pounds)**
- **Salt and ground black pepper**
- **1 tablespoon butter**
- **½ cup whole cranberry sauce**
- **1 tablespoon honey**
- **½ teaspoon finely shredded lemon peel**
- **1 tablespoon lemon juice**

1 Sprinkle turkey with salt and pepper. In a very large skillet cook turkey in hot butter over medium-high heat for 12 to 15 minutes or until no longer pink (170°F), turning once. Transfer to a serving platter; reserve drippings in skillet. Cover turkey to keep warm.

2 Stir cranberry sauce, honey, lemon peel, and lemon juice into reserved drippings in skillet. Cook and stir until heated through. Spoon over turkey.

Makes 4 servings

Nutrition facts per serving: 252 cal., 4 g total fat (2 g sat. fat), 96 mg chol., 246 mg sodium, 18 g carbo., 0 g dietary fiber, 35 g protein.

Shopping list:

2 turkey breast tenderloins

1 16-ounce can whole cranberry sauce

1 lemon

Pantry list:

Salt

Ground black pepper

Butter

Honey

Italian **Turkey Burgers**

Start to Finish: **20 minutes**

- 1 **pound uncooked ground turkey**
- 2 **teaspoons dried Italian seasoning, crushed**
- ½ **cup shredded mozzarella cheese (2 ounces)**
- ¼ **cup mayonnaise or salad dressing**
- 2 **tablespoons refrigerated basil pesto**
- 4 **hamburger buns, split and toasted, if desired**
- 1 **small tomato, thinly sliced**

1 In a medium bowl combine ground turkey and Italian seasoning. Shape into four ½-inch-thick patties (use wet hands, if necessary). Lightly grease the rack of an indoor electric grill or grill pan. Preheat grill or grill pan. Place patties on the grill rack or in pan. If using a grill with a cover, close the lid. Grill for 5 to 7 minutes for a covered grill or 9 to 12 minutes for an uncovered grill or grill pan, turning once, or until no longer pink (165°F). Remove burgers to a plate. Top hot burgers with cheese and let stand, covered with foil, for 1 to 2 minutes or until cheese melts.

2 Meanwhile, in a small bowl combine mayonnaise and pesto. Spread mixture on cut sides of hamburger buns. Top bun bottoms with turkey burgers and sliced tomatoes. Add bun tops.

Makes 4 servings

Nutrition facts per serving: 467 cal., 28 g total fat (7 g sat. fat), 106 mg chol., 550 mg sodium, 24 g carbo., 1 g dietary fiber, 29 g protein.

20 minutes

Shopping list:
- 1 pound uncooked ground turkey
- 1 8-ounce package shredded mozzarella cheese
- 1 7-ounce container refrigerated basil pesto
- 1 package hamburger buns
- 1 small tomato

Pantry list:
Dried Italian seasoning
Mayonnaise

Turkey Chili with a Twist

Start to Finish: **20 minutes**

12 ounces uncooked bulk turkey Italian sausage or uncooked ground turkey

2 15-ounce cans chili beans with chili gravy

1 cup bottled salsa with lime

1 15-ounce can golden hominy, drained

$\frac{2}{3}$ cup water

$\frac{1}{3}$ cup sliced green onions

In a large saucepan cook turkey sausage until brown. Stir in undrained chili beans, salsa, hominy, and the water. Heat through. Sprinkle with green onions.

Makes 4 to 5 servings

Nutrition facts per serving: 470 cal., 11 g total fat (3 g sat. fat), 45 mg chol., 1,897 mg sodium, 64 g carbo., 16 g dietary fiber, 28 g protein.

Shopping list:

12 ounces uncooked bulk turkey Italian sausage

2 15-ounce cans chili beans with chili gravy

1 8-ounce jar salsa

1 15-ounce can golden hominy

1 bunch green onions

20 minutes

Deli Sandwich Stacks

Start to Finish: 20 minutes

- ½ of a 4-ounce container semisoft cheese with garlic and herb
- 2 tablespoons honey mustard
- ¼ teaspoon lemon-pepper seasoning
- 6 slices marble rye, cracked wheat, or seven-grain bread
- 2 small roma tomatoes, thinly sliced
- ⅓ cup sliced banana peppers, well drained
- 1 cup loosely packed fresh spinach leaves or 4 lettuce leaves
- 4 thin slices Colby or Monterey Jack cheese
- 4 ounces thinly sliced cooked turkey breast
- 4 ounces sliced cooked turkey ham

1 In a small bowl combine semisoft cheese, honey mustard, and lemon-pepper seasoning. Spread mixture evenly on one side of 4 of the bread slices.

2 Divide tomatoes, banana peppers, spinach, and cheese evenly among spread sides of the 4 bread slices. Top 2 stacks with turkey breast and 2 stacks with turkey ham. Arrange the stacks with turkey ham on top of the stacks with turkey breast. Add remaining 2 bread slices. Cut stacks in half.

Makes 4 servings

Nutrition facts per serving: 361 cal., 15 g total fat (8 g sat. fat), 77 mg chol., 861 mg sodium, 30 g carbo., 4 g dietary fiber, 25 g protein.

Shopping list:

- 1 4-ounce container semisoft cheese with garlic and herb
- 1 4-ounce jar honey mustard
- 1 small container lemon-pepper seasoning
- 1 loaf marble rye bread
- 2 small roma tomatoes
- 1 large banana pepper
- 1 10-ounce package fresh spinach leaves
- 1 8-ounce package sliced Colby cheese
- 4 ounces thinly sliced turkey breast
- 4 ounces thinly sliced turkey ham

Thanksgiving **Club Sandwich** *(See photo on page 130.)*

Start to Finish: **15 minutes**

8 slices firm-texture marble rye bread or multigrain bread, toasted

4 leaves leaf lettuce

8 ounces sliced cooked turkey breast

8 slices packaged ready-to-serve cooked bacon

2 ounces white cheddar cheese, sliced

4 thin slices red onion, halved

½ cup whole cranberry sauce

   Fresh whole cranberries (optional)

   Sweet Potato Fries* (optional)

Top 4 of the bread slices with lettuce, turkey, bacon, cheese, and onion. Top with cranberry sauce and remaining 4 bread slices. If desired, garnish toothpicks skewered with whole fresh cranberries.

Makes 4 servings

Nutrition facts per serving: 404 cal., 14 g total fat (6 g sat. fat), 55 mg chol., 1,297 mg sodium, 43 g carbo., 2 g dietary fiber, 26 g protein.

*Kitchen Tip: If you have a few extra minutes, these fries take 25 minutes to make, but are a crispy, crunchy, delicious side for these sandwiches. Otherwise, simply reheat some frozen fries.

*Sweet Potato Fries:

Cut 2 large sweet potatoes into wedges. Toss wedges with 1 tablespoon olive oil, 2 teaspoons salt, and 1 teaspoon freshly cracked black pepper. Arrange in a single layer on a large baking sheet. Bake in a 425°F oven for 25 minutes or until brown, turning once.

Shopping list:

1 loaf firm-textured marble rye bread

1 head green leaf lettuce

8 ounces sliced cooked turkey breast

1 2-ounce package ready-to-eat cooked bacon

2 ounces white cheddar cheese

1 medium red onion

1 16-ounce can whole cranberry sauce

20
minutes

Grilled Turkey-Apricot Sandwiches

Start to Finish: **20 minutes**

3 tablespoons apricot preserves

2 tablespoons Dijon-style mustard

8 slices whole grain bread

8 ounces sliced cooked turkey breast

4 slices Muenster cheese

¼ cup butter, softened

In a small bowl combine preserves and mustard. Spread or brush mustard mixture on one side of each slice of bread. Top spread sides of four of the bread slices with turkey and Muenster cheese. Top with remaining four bread slices, spread side down. Spread a plain side of each bread stack with butter. Place sandwiches, butter side down, in a very large skillet or on a griddle over medium heat. Carefully spread unbuttered bread with butter. Cook for 2 to 3 minutes on each side or until brown and cheese melts.

Makes 4 servings

Nutrition facts per serving: 471 cal., 21 g total fat (11 g sat. fat), 75 mg chol., 1,238 mg sodium, 42 g carbo., 8 g dietary fiber, 26 g protein.

Shopping list:

1 12-ounce jar apricot preserves

1 loaf whole grain bread

8 ounces sliced cooked turkey breast

1 6- to 8-ounce package sliced Muenster cheese

Pantry list:

Dijon-style mustard

Butter

20 minutes

Smoked Turkey Chuck Wagon Soup

Start to Finish: **20 minutes**

- 2 **14-ounce cans reduced-sodium chicken broth**
- 1 **15-ounce can white hominy, drained**
- 1 **11-ounce can condensed tomato rice soup**
- 2 **cups chopped smoked turkey**
- ½ **cup chopped yellow sweet pepper**
- ⅓ **cup bottled salsa**
- 1 **teaspoon ground cumin**
- 1 ½ **cups crushed tortilla chips (about 2 ½ ounces)**

  Dairy sour cream (optional)

1 In a large saucepan combine chicken broth, hominy, tomato rice soup, turkey, sweet pepper, salsa, and cumin. Bring to boiling; reduce heat. Simmer, uncovered, about 5 minutes or until sweet pepper is tender.

2 Ladle into soup bowls. Top with tortilla chips and, if desired, sour cream.

Makes 4 servings

Nutrition facts per serving: 318 cal., 10 g total fat (2 g sat. fat), 38 mg chol., 2,013 mg sodium, 39 g carbo., 5 g dietary fiber, 20 g protein.

Shopping list:
2 14-ounce cans reduced-sodium chicken broth

1 15-ounce can white hominy

1 11-ounce can condensed tomato rice soup

1 12-ounce package chopped smoked turkey

1 small yellow sweet pepper

1 8-ounce jar salsa

1 small bag tortilla chips

Pantry list:
Ground cumin

Steak with Creamy Mushrooms

Start to Finish: **20 minutes**

4 **beef tenderloin steaks, cut ¾ inch thick (about 1 pound total)**

Salt and ground black pepper

1 **tablespoon olive oil**

3 **cups sliced fresh mushrooms (about 8 ounces)**

¼ **cup seasoned beef broth**

¼ **cup whipping cream**

1 Sprinkle steaks lightly with salt and pepper. In a large skillet cook steaks in hot oil over medium-high heat for 7 to 9 minutes or to desired doneness (145°F for medium-rare or 160°F for medium), turning once halfway through cooking. Transfer steaks to a serving platter; keep warm.

2 In the same skillet cook and stir mushrooms over medium-high heat for 4 to 5 minutes or until tender. Stir in broth and cream. Cook and stir over medium-high heat for 2 minutes. Season sauce to taste with additional salt and pepper. Spoon mushroom mixture over steaks.

Makes 4 servings

Nutrition facts per serving: 279 cal., 19 g total fat (7 g sat. fat), 90 mg chol., 189 mg sodium, 3 g carbo., 1 g dietary fiber, 26 g protein.

Shopping list:

4 beef tenderloin steaks

1 8-ounce package sliced fresh mushrooms

1 14-ounce can seasoned beef broth

1 8-ounce carton whipping cream

Pantry list:

Salt

Ground black pepper

Olive oil

20 minutes

Herb-Horseradish Steaks

Start to Finish: **20 minutes**

- **2 12- to 14-ounce beef top loin steaks, cut 1 inch thick**
- **Salt and ground black pepper**
- **2 tablespoons prepared horseradish**
- **1 tablespoon Dijon-style mustard**
- **2 teaspoons snipped fresh Italian (flat-leaf) parsley**
- **1 teaspoon snipped fresh thyme**
- **Broiled cherry tomatoes (optional)**
- **Broiled sweet pepper strips (optional)**

1 Preheat broiler. Season steaks with salt and pepper. Place steaks on the unheated rack of a broiler pan. Broil 4 inches from heat for 7 minutes. Meanwhile, combine horseradish, mustard, parsley, and thyme.

2 Turn steaks. Broil for 8 to 9 minutes more for medium doneness (160°F). The last 1 minute of broiling, spread steaks with horseradish mixture. If desired, serve with tomatoes and peppers.

Makes 4 servings

Nutrition facts per serving: 284 cal., 15 g total fat (6 g sat. fat), 84 mg chol., 351 mg sodium, 1 g carbo., 0 g dietary fiber, 33 g protein.

✶Test Kitchen Tip: Steaks also may be grilled directly over medium coals for the same amount of time.

Shopping list:
- 2 12- to 14-ounce beef top loin steaks
- 1 8-ounce bottle prepared horseradish sauce
- 1 bunch fresh Italian (flat-leaf) parsley
- 1 package fresh thyme

Pantry list:
- Salt
- Ground black pepper
- Dijon-style mustard

20 minutes

Jamaican **Jerk Steak**

Start to Finish: 20 minutes

4 boneless beef top loin steaks, cut 1 inch thick (about 2 ½ pounds)

1 tablespoon cooking oil

1 tablespoon Jamaican jerk seasoning

1 large mango, peeled, seeded, and chopped

¼ cup finely chopped red onion

¼ cup snipped fresh cilantro

1 jalapeño pepper, seeded and finely chopped*

½ teaspoon finely shredded lime peel

1 tablespoon lime juice

½ teaspoon ground cumin

¼ teaspoon salt

1 Trim fat from steaks. Brush steaks with oil; sprinkle with jerk seasoning. Heat a nonstick grill pan (or lightly coat a grill pan with nonstick cooking spray) over medium-high heat until very hot. Add steaks; reduce heat to medium and cook for 12 to 15 minutes (145°F for medium rare or 160°F for medium doneness), turning once. (For an electric indoor grill, preheat grill according to manufacturer's directions. Grill steaks to desired doneness. For a covered grill, allow 4 to 6 minutes for medium-rare or 6 to 8 minutes for medium; for an uncovered grill allow 8 to 12 minutes for medium-rare or 12 to 15 minutes for medium doneness.)

2 Meanwhile, for salsa, in a medium bowl combine mango, onion, cilantro, jalapeño pepper, lime peel, lime juice, cumin, and salt. Serve salsa with steaks.

Makes 4 servings

Nutrition facts per serving: 607 cal., 34 g total fat (13 g sat. fat), 167 mg chol., 542 mg sodium, 10 g carbo., 1 g dietary fiber, 62 g protein.

*Note: Because hot chile peppers, such as jalapeños, contain volatile oils that can burn your skin and eyes, avoid direct contact with chiles as much as possible. When working with chile peppers, wear plastic or rubber gloves. If your bare hands do touch chile peppers, wash your hands well with soap and water.

Shopping list:

4 boneless beef top loin steaks

1 small container Jamaican jerk seasoning

1 large mango

1 red onion

1 bunch cilantro

1 jalapeño pepper

1 lime

Pantry list:

Cooking oil

Ground cumin

Salt

20 minutes

Steaks with Pan Sauce

Start to Finish: **20 minutes**

- 5 **tablespoons cold butter**
- 2 **beef steaks, such as top loin, ribeye, or tenderloin, cut about ¾ inch thick**
- ⅓ **cup dry red wine or apple juice**
- ¼ **cup reduced-sodium beef broth**
- 2 **tablespoons finely chopped shallots or 1 clove garlic, minced**
- 1 **tablespoon whipping cream (no substitutes)**
  Salt
  Ground white pepper

1 In a large skillet melt 1 tablespoon of the butter over medium-high heat (if possible do not use a nonstick skillet). Reduce heat to medium. Add steaks and cook about 6 minutes or until medium rare (145°F), turning once. Transfer steaks to a platter; cover tightly with foil to keep warm (steaks will continue to cook as they stand). Drain fat from skillet.

2 Add wine, broth, and shallots to the hot skillet. Using a wire whisk, stir and scrape the bottom of the pan to remove browned bits. Continue to cook over medium heat about 3 to 4 minutes or until liquid is reduced to about 2 tablespoons. Reduce heat to medium low.

3 Stir in cream. Stir in remaining 2 tablespoons butter, 1 tablespoon at a time, whisking until butter melts and sauce thickens slightly. Season to taste with salt and white pepper. Serve sauce at once over steaks.

Makes 2 servings

Nutrition facts per serving: 599 cal., 52 g total fat (28 g sat. fat), 163 mg chol., 325 mg sodium, 3 g carbo., 0 g dietary fiber, 23 g protein.

Shopping list:

- 2 beef steaks
- 1 bottle dry red wine
- 1 14-ounce can reduced-sodium beef broth
- 1 package shallots
- 1 8-ounce carton whipping cream
- 1 small container ground white pepper

Pantry list:

Butter

Salt

20 minutes

Tomato-Herb Steak

Start to Finish: 20 minutes

- 2 beef top loin steaks, cut ¾ inch thick
- Salt and ground black pepper
- Nonstick cooking spray
- ½ cup sliced green onions
- 2 teaspoons snipped fresh basil or 1 teaspoon dried basil, crushed
- 1 cup chopped tomato

1 Cut steaks in half; season with salt and pepper. Lightly coat a large heavy skillet with cooking spray. Heat skillet over medium-high heat. Add steaks and reduce heat to medium; cook for 5 to 10 minutes or to desired doneness, (145°F for medium rare or 160°F for medium), turning once. Remove steaks and keep warm.

2 Add green onions and dried basil (if using) to drippings in skillet. Cook about 2 minutes or until onions are tender. Stir in tomato and fresh basil (if using). Serve over steaks. Sprinkle lightly with salt.

Makes 4 servings

Nutrition facts per serving: 219 cal., 11 g total fat (4 g sat. fat), 66 mg chol., 207 mg sodium, 3 g carbo., 1 g dietary fiber, 26 g protein.

20 minutes

Shopping list:
2 beef top loin steaks
1 bunch green onions
1 package fresh basil
1 large tomato

Pantry list:
Salt
Ground black pepper
Nonstick cooking spray

Beef-Broccoli **Noodle Bowl**

Start to Finish: **20 minutes**

- 8 ounces packaged beef stir-fry strips
- 1 tablespoon cooking oil
- 2 teaspoons grated fresh ginger or bottled minced ginger
- 3 cloves garlic, minced
- 2 14-ounce cans beef broth
- 2 tablespoons reduced-sodium soy sauce
- 2 teaspoons rice vinegar
- 2 cups broccoli florets
- 1 ½ cups packaged fresh julienne carrots
- 1 3-ounce package ramen noodles (any flavor)

In a large saucepan cook beef strips in hot oil until brown. Stir in ginger and garlic, cook 1 minute more. Add beef broth, soy sauce, and vinegar. Bring to boiling; reduce heat. Add broccoli and carrots. Simmer, covered, for 3 minutes or until crisp-tender. Break ramen noodles into smaller pieces (discard spice packet). Add noodles to saucepan. Simmer, uncovered, for 3 minutes or until noodles and vegetables are tender.

Makes 4 servings

Nutrition facts per serving: 262 cal., 11 g total fat (1 g sat. fat), 24 mg chol., 1,066 mg sodium, 22 g carbo., 3 g dietary fiber, 19 g protein.

Shopping list:
- 1 8-ounce package beef stir-fry strips
- 1 piece fresh ginger
- 2 14-ounce cans beef broth
- 1 10-ounce bottle reduced-sodium soy sauce
- 1 10-ounce bottle rice vinegar
- 1 bunch broccoli
- 1 10-ounce package fresh julienne carrots
- 1 3-ounce package ramen noodles

Pantry list:
Cooking oil

Garlic

Asian-Style **Beef Soup**

Start to Finish: **15 minutes**

3 **14-ounce cans beef broth**

1 **16-ounce package loose-pack frozen broccoli stir-fry vegetables**

3 **tablespoons teriyaki sauce**

2 **teaspoons grated fresh ginger or $\frac{1}{2}$ teaspoon ground ginger**

1 **9-ounce package frozen cooked seasoned beef strips, thawed and cut up, or 2 cups chopped cooked beef**

In a large saucepan bring beef broth to boiling. Stir in frozen vegetables, teriyaki sauce, and ginger. Return to boiling; reduce heat. Simmer, covered, for 3 to 5 minutes or until vegetables are tender. Stir in beef strips; heat through.

Makes 4 servings

Nutrition facts per serving: 177 cal., 6 g total fat (2 g sat. fat), 41 mg chol., 1,885 mg sodium, 10 g carbo., 2 g dietary fiber, 21 g protein.

20 minutes

Shopping list:

3 14-ounce cans beef broth

1 16-ounce package loose-pack frozen broccoli stir-fry vegetables

1 8-ounce jar teriyaki sauce

1 piece fresh ginger

1 9-ounce package frozen cooked seasoned beef strips

Beef-Vegetable Stew

Start to Finish: **20 minutes**

- 2 **cups water**
- 1 **10.75-ounce can condensed golden mushroom soup**
- 1 **10.75-ounce can condensed tomato soup**
- ½ **cup dry red wine or beef broth**
- 2 **cups chopped cooked roast beef**
- 1 **16-ounce package frozen sugar snap stir-fry vegetables or one 16-ounce package frozen cut broccoli**
- ½ **teaspoon dried thyme, crushed**

1 In a 4-quart Dutch oven combine the water, mushroom soup, tomato soup, and wine. Stir in beef, frozen vegetables, and thyme.

2 Cook over medium heat until bubbly, stirring frequently. Continue cooking, uncovered, for 4 to 5 minutes or until vegetables are crisp-tender, stirring occasionally.

Makes 5 servings

Nutrition facts per serving: 304 cal., 10 g total fat (4 g sat. fat), 56 mg chol., 852 mg sodium, 24 g carbo., 4 g dietary fiber, 23 g protein.

Shopping list:
1 10.75-ounce can condensed golden mushroom soup

1 10.75-ounce can condensed tomato soup

1 bottle dry red wine

1 17-ounce package refrigerated cooked roast beef

1 16-ounce package frozen sugar snap stir-fry vegetables

Pantry list:
Dried thyme

20 minutes

Horseradish **Beef Wraps**

Start to Finish: **10 minutes**

⅓ cup mayonnaise

1 tablespoon prepared horseradish

4 9- to 10-inch flour tortillas

8 ounces sliced cooked roast beef

4 slices Swiss cheese

⅔ cup shredded lettuce

¼ cup shredded radishes

In a small bowl stir together mayonnaise and horseradish. Spread mixture on one side of each tortilla. Top with beef, cheese, lettuce, and radishes. Tightly roll up each tortilla. Serve wraps at once or, if desired, wrap in plastic wrap and refrigerate for up to 4 hours.

Makes 4 servings

Nutrition facts per serving: 455 cal., 28 g total fat (9 g sat. fat), 59 mg chol., 967 mg sodium, 25 g carbo., 1 g dietary fiber, 22 g protein.

20 minutes

Shopping list:

1 8-ounce jar prepared horseradish

1 package 9- to 10-inch flour tortillas

8 ounces thinly sliced cooked roast beef

1 6-ounce package sliced Swiss cheese

1 package shredded lettuce

1 bunch radishes

Pantry list:

Mayonnaise

Beef and Tapenade Focaccia Sandwiches

Start to Finish: **15 minutes**

1 **10-inch round or square focaccia**

½ **of an 8-ounce tub cream cheese spread with chive and onion**

½ **cup purchased black olive tapenade**

1 **pound thinly sliced deli roast beef**

2 **medium tomatoes, thinly sliced**

2 **or 3 romaine leaves**

Cut focaccia in half horizontally. Spread bottom half with cream cheese spread and then with tapenade. Top with roast beef, tomatoes, and romaine leaves. Add top half of focaccia. Cut into 6 wedges or rectangles. Secure portions with wooden skewers.

Makes 6 sandwiches

Nutrition facts per sandwich: 467 cal., 23 g total fat (8 g sat. fat), 53 mg chol., 1,450 mg sodium, 37 g carbo., 4 g dietary fiber, 23 g protein.

Shopping list:

1 10-inch round focaccia

1 8-ounce tub cream cheese spread with chive and onion

1 8-ounce container black olive tapenade

1 pound thinly sliced deli roast beef

2 medium tomatoes

1 head romaine lettuce

20 minutes

Pronto **Taco Salad**

Start to Finish: **20 minutes**

1   **5.6-ounce package baked crisp tortilla salad shells (4)**

1   **18-ounce package taco sauce with seasoned ground beef**

4   **cups packaged shredded iceberg lettuce**

4   **ounces Monterey Jack cheese with jalapeño peppers, shredded (1 cup)**

1   **large tomato, chopped**

Bottled spicy ranch salad dressing*

1 Prepare salad shells according to package directions. Heat meat mixture according to package directions.

2 Divide lettuce among taco shells. Top with meat mixture, cheese, and tomato. Drizzle with spicy ranch dressing.

Makes 4 servings

Nutrition facts per serving: 655 cal., 45 g total fat (15 g sat. fat), 73 mg chol., 1,269 mg sodium, 39 g carbo., 3 g dietary fiber, 24 g protein.

*Test Kitchen Tip: If you can't find spicy ranch salad dressing, mix ½ cup ranch salad dressing with 2 tablespoons barbecue sauce.

Shopping list:

1 5.6-ounce package baked crisp tortilla salad shells

1 18-ounce package taco sauce with seasoned ground beef

1 10-ounce package shredded iceberg lettuce

1 8-ounce piece Monterey Jack cheese with jalapeño peppers

1 large tomato

1 16-ounce bottle spicy ranch salad dressing

20 minutes

Stuffed Peppers Mole

Start to Finish: **20 minutes**

- **4** small or 2 large sweet peppers
- **1** 8.8-ounce pouch cooked Spanish-style rice or long-grain and wild rice
- **10** to 12 ounces cooked ground beef crumbles or 2 cups cooked ground beef
- **½** cup frozen whole kernel corn
- **3** tablespoons purchased mole sauce*
- **2** tablespoons water
- **½** cup shredded Mexican cheese blend or shredded cheddar cheese (2 ounces)
- Salt and ground black pepper
- **2** tablespoons snipped fresh cilantro

1 Cut tops off small sweet peppers or halve large peppers lengthwise. Remove membranes and seeds. In a 4-quart Dutch oven cook peppers in boiling water for 3 minutes. Remove peppers; drain, cut sides down, on paper towels.

2 For filling, in a saucepan combine rice, beef, corn, mole sauce, and water. Cook, uncovered, over medium heat until heated through, stirring frequently. Remove from heat; stir in cheese. Place peppers, cut sides up, on platter. Sprinkle with salt and black pepper. Spoon filling into peppers. Sprinkle with cilantro.

Makes 4 servings

Nutrition facts per serving: 360 cal., 15 g total fat (7 g sat. fat), 75 mg chol., 732 mg sodium, 29 g carbo., 3 g dietary fiber, 28 g protein.

*Note: If you can't find mole sauce, substitute ¼ cup enchilada sauce and omit the 2 tablespoons water.

Shopping list:

- 4 small sweet peppers
- 1 8.8-ounce pouch cooked Spanish-style rice
- 10 to 12 ounces cooked ground beef crumbles
- 1 8.75-ounce can whole kernel corn
- 1 9-ounce bottle mole sauce
- 1 8-ounce package Mexican cheese blend
- 1 bunch cilantro

Pantry list:

Salt

Ground black pepper

Ciabatta with Meatballs and Greens

Start to Finish: **15 minutes**

⅓ cup olive oil

¼ cup lemon juice

1 bunch Italian (flat-leaf) parsley, large stems removed

2 cloves garlic

Salt and ground black pepper

1 16- to 18-ounce package frozen cooked Italian-style meatballs, thawed

6 ciabatta rolls, split and toasted

½ of a small head romaine lettuce, cut-up or torn

1 In a food processor or blender combine oil, lemon juice, parsley, and garlic; cover and process until finely chopped. Add salt and pepper to taste.

2 Transfer parsley mixture to a large skillet; add meatballs and cook, covered, over medium heat until heated through, stirring and spooning sauce over meatballs occasionally.

3 Place 1 ciabatta roll, toasted side up, on each of 6 plates. Top with shredded romaine. Remove meatballs from skillet with a slotted spoon; place on romaine. Drizzle with parsley mixture. Top with remaining roll halves.

Makes 6 servings

Nutrition facts per serving: 534 cal., 31 g total fat (10 g sat. fat), 49 mg chol., 1,002 mg sodium, 43 g carbo., 6 g dietary fiber, 20 g protein.

20 minutes

Shopping list:

1 lemon

1 bunch Italian (flat-leaf) parsley

1 16- to 18-ounce package frozen cooked Italian-style meatballs

1 head romaine lettuce

6 ciabatta rolls

Pantry list:

Olive oil

Garlic

Salt

Ground black pepper

Monster **Meatball Sub** *(See photo on page 130.)*

Start to Finish: 20 minutes

1   16-ounce package barbecue sauce with seasoned meatballs

1   loaf French bread

4   ounces sliced provolone cheese

⅓   cup thinly sliced red onion

1   small tomato, chopped

1   Preheat broiler. Heat meatballs according to package directions.

2   Cut bread in half horizontally, cutting to but not through to one side, so that the bread opens up like a book. Hollow out insides of bread halves, leaving 1-inch shells; set excess bread aside for another use. Place loaf, cut side up, on a baking sheet. Top bottom side of loaf with cheese slices.

3   Broil 4 to 5 inches from the heat for 2 to 3 minutes or until cheese melts and bread is lightly toasted.

4   With a slotted spoon, remove meatballs from sauce and place on bottom half of the loaf. Sprinkle with red onion and tomato. Close loaf and cut in slices to serve. If desired, serve with remaining barbecue sauce.

Makes 6 servings

Nutrition facts per serving: 450 cal., 15 g total fat (7 g sat. fat), 32 mg chol., 1,122 mg sodium, 60 g carbo., 2 g dietary fiber, 22 g protein.

Shopping list:

1   16-ounce package barbecue sauce with seasoned meatballs

1   loaf French bread

1   6-ounce package sliced provolone cheese

1   red onion

1   small tomato

20 minutes

Spicy Reuben Melts

Start to Finish: **20 minutes**

8 slices rye bread, toasted

8 ounces sliced corned beef or pastrami

½ cup sauerkraut, rinsed and drained

12 bottled pepperoncini salad peppers, sliced

4 slices Swiss cheese

¼ cup bottled thousand island salad dressing

Preheat broiler. Place 4 bread slices on a baking sheet. Top the bread slices with corned beef, sauerkraut, pepperoncini, and cheese. Broil 4 to 5 inches from the heat for 2 minutes or until cheese melts. Spread salad dressing on remaining 4 bread slices. Place bread, dressing side down, on top of broiled sandwiches.

Makes 4 servings

Nutrition facts per serving: 394 cal., 17 g total fat (6 g sat. fat), 55 mg chol., 2,056 mg sodium, 38 g carbo., 5 g dietary fiber, 24 g protein.

Shopping list:
1 16-ounce loaf rye bread

8 ounces thinly sliced corned beef or pastrami

1 14-ounce can sauerkraut

1 16-ounce jar pepperoncini salad peppers

1 8-ounce package sliced Swiss cheese

1 16-ounce bottle thousand island salad dressing

20 minutes

Balsamic **Pork Medallions**

Start to Finish: **15 minutes**

- 2 **cups sliced fresh mushrooms**
- 2 **cups small broccoli florets, chopped broccoli raab, or chopped broccolini**
- 2 **tablespoons butter**
- 12 **ounces pork tenderloin**

    Salt and ground black pepper

- 2 **ounces prosciutto, cut into bite-size strips**
- ¼ **cup balsamic vinegar**
- 1 **tablespoon packed brown sugar**

1 In a large skillet cook mushrooms and broccoli in 1 tablespoon hot butter over medium-high heat about 3 minutes or until crisp-tender, stirring occasionally. Remove vegetables from skillet; set aside.

2 Meanwhile, trim fat from pork; cut pork into ½-inch slices. Sprinkle pork with salt and pepper. Add to skillet and cook in remaining 1 tablespoon hot butter for 4 to 6 minutes or until juices run clear (160°F), turning once.

3 Add prosciutto, vinegar, brown sugar, and vegetables to skillet, heat through.

Makes 4 servings

Nutrition facts per serving: 240 cal., 10 g total fat (5 g sat. fat), 80 mg chol., 551 mg sodium, 12 g carbo., 2 g dietary fiber, 25 g protein.

Shopping list:

- 1 8-ounce package sliced fresh mushrooms
- 1 head broccoli
- 12 ounces pork tenderloin
- 2 ounces prosciutto

Pantry list:

Butter

Salt

Ground black pepper

Balsamic vinegar

Brown sugar

Pork Medallions with Cranberry-Fig Chutney

Start to Finish: **20 minutes**

½ cup fresh cranberries or ¼ cup canned whole cranberry sauce

¼ cup apple juice or apple cider

2 tablespoons snipped dried figs

1 tablespoon packed brown sugar or granulated sugar

½ teaspoon snipped fresh rosemary or ¼ teaspoon dried rosemary, crushed

Salt

Ground black pepper

6 ounces pork tenderloin

2 teaspoons cooking oil

1 For chutney, in a small heavy saucepan stir together cranberries, apple juice, figs, sugar, and rosemary. Bring to boiling; reduce heat. Simmer, uncovered, for 5 to 8 minutes or until chutney is desired consistency, stirring occasionally. Season to taste with salt and pepper; set aside.

2 Meanwhile, trim fat from pork. Cut meat into six pieces. Press each piece with palm of your hand to make an even thickness. In a large nonstick skillet cook pork in hot oil over medium-high heat for 2 to 3 minutes or until juices run clear (160°F), turning once. Serve pork with chutney.

Makes 2 servings

Nutrition facts per 2 ½ ounces pork + ¼ cup chutney: 227 cal., 7 g total fat (1 g sat. fat), 55 mg chol., 185 mg sodium, 23 g carbo., 3 g dietary fiber, 18 g protein.

Shopping list:

1 12-ounce package fresh cranberries

1 5-ounce can apple juice

1 9-ounce package dried figs

1 package fresh rosemary

6 ounces pork tenderloin

Pantry list:

Brown sugar

Salt

Ground black pepper

Cooking oil

Asian Pork Soup

Start to Finish: **20 minutes**

- **12** **ounces lean boneless pork, cut into thin bite-size strips**
- **1** **tablespoon cooking oil**
- **2** **cups sliced fresh mushrooms**
- **2** **cloves garlic, minced**
- **3** **14-ounce cans reduced-sodium chicken broth**
- **2** **tablespoons dry sherry**
- **2** **tablespoons reduced-sodium soy sauce**
- **2** **teaspoons grated fresh ginger or ¹⁄₂ teaspoon ground ginger**
- **¹⁄₄** **teaspoon crushed red pepper**
- **2** **cups thinly sliced Chinese (napa) cabbage**
- **1** **green onion, thinly sliced**

1 In a large saucepan cook pork strips in hot oil for 2 to 3 minutes or until slightly pink in center. Remove from pan; set aside. Add mushrooms and garlic to saucepan; cook until tender.

2 Stir in broth, sherry, soy sauce, ginger, and crushed red pepper. Bring to boiling. Stir in meat, cabbage, and green onion; heat through.

Makes 6 servings

Nutrition facts per serving: 142 cal., 6 g total fat (2 g sat. fat), 31 mg chol., 690 mg sodium, 4 g carbo., 1 g dietary fiber, 16 g protein.

Shopping list:

- 12 ounces lean boneless pork
- 1 8-ounce package sliced fresh mushrooms
- 3 14-ounce cans reduced-sodium chicken broth
- 1 small bottle dry sherry
- 1 10-ounce bottle reduced-sodium soy sauce
- 1 piece fresh ginger
- 1 small head Chinese (napa) cabbage
- 1 bunch green onions

Pantry list:

Cooking oil

Garlic

Crushed red pepper

20 minutes

Pork Medallions on Green Beans

Start to Finish: **20 minutes**

1 **1- to 1 ½-pound honey-mustard marinated pork tenderloin**

1 **tablespoon butter**

1 **9-ounce package frozen French-cut green beans, thawed**

1 **teaspoon dried dillweed**

1 **teaspoon lemon juice**

1 Cut tenderloin into ¼-inch slices. In a 12-inch skillet cook pork in hot butter over medium heat for 4 to 6 minutes or until juices run clear (160°F), turning once. Remove meat from skillet, reserving drippings in skillet. Keep warm.

2 Add green beans and dill to drippings in skillet. Cook and stir for 3 to 4 minutes or until beans are tender. Stir in lemon juice. Transfer beans to a serving platter. Serve pork on top of green beans.

Makes 4 servings

Nutrition facts per serving: 187 cal., 8 g total fat (4 g sat. fat), 53 mg chol., 549 mg sodium, 7 g carbo., 2 g dietary fiber, 21 g protein.

20 minutes

Shopping list:

1 1- to 1½-pound honey-mustard marinated pork tenderloin

1 9-ounce package frozen French-cut green beans

1 small container dried dillweed

1 lemon

Pantry list:

Butter

Jamaican-Style Pork

Start to Finish: **20 minutes**

1 **16-ounce package frozen peppers and onion stir-fry vegetables**

1 **tablespoon cooking oil**

12 **ounces pork strips for stir-frying**

2 **to 3 teaspoons Jamaican jerk seasoning**

½ **cup plum sauce**

Soy sauce (optional)

Peanuts (optional)

2 **cups hot cooked rice or pasta**

1 In a wok or skillet cook and stir frozen vegetables in hot oil over medium-high heat for 5 to 7 minutes or until vegetables are crisp-tender. Remove from wok.

2 Toss pork strips with jerk seasoning; add to wok. Add more oil if necessary. Cook and stir for 2 to 5 minutes or until pork is no longer pink.

3 Add plum sauce to wok; return vegetables. Gently toss to coat; heat through. If desired, season with soy sauce and sprinkle with peanuts. Serve over rice.

Makes 4 servings

Nutrition facts per serving: 357 cal., 9 g total fat (2 g sat. fat), 54 mg chol., 405 mg sodium, 45 g carbo., 2 g dietary fiber, 22 g protein.

*Test Kitchen Tip: If your supermarket doesn't sell pork strips, cut them from pork loin.

Shopping list:

1 16-ounce package frozen stir-fry vegetables

12 ounces pork strips for stir-frying

1 small container Jamaican jerk seasoning

1 5.5-ounce bottle plum sauce

Pantry list:

Cooking oil

Rice

Curry Pork Stir Fry

Start to Finish: 20 minutes

- 2 6-ounce boneless pork top loin chops, cut into thin bite-size strips
- 1 tablespoon cooking oil
- 1 medium onion, chopped (½ cup)
- 1 medium red sweet pepper, coarsely chopped (¾ cup)
- 2 teaspoons curry powder
- 1 teaspoon bottled minced ginger or ½ teaspoon ground ginger
- ¼ teaspoon salt
- 1 14-ounce can unsweetened coconut milk
- 1 tablespoon cornstarch
- 1 cup frozen peas
- ¼ cup golden raisins
- 1 tablespoon lime juice (optional)
- 1 8.8-ounce pouch cooked long-grain rice

1 In a large skillet cook pork strips in hot oil over medium-high heat for 3 to 5 minutes or until brown, stirring occasionally. Remove meat from skillet. Add onion, sweet pepper, curry powder, ginger, and salt to skillet. Cook about 5 minutes or until vegetables are crisp-tender, stirring frequently. Add additional cooking oil if necessary.

2 Meanwhile, in a medium bowl whisk together coconut milk and cornstarch. Add to vegetable mixture in skillet. Cook and stir until thick and bubbly. Cook and stir for 2 minutes more. Stir in meat, peas, raisins, and, if desired, lime juice. Heat through.

3 Meanwhile, prepare rice according to package directions. Serve pork mixture over rice.

Makes 4 servings

Nutrition facts per serving: 520 cal., 28 g total fat (19 g sat. fat), 47 mg chol., 253 mg sodium, 41 g carbo., 4 g dietary fiber, 25 g protein.

Shopping list:
- 2 6-ounce boneless pork top loin chops
- 1 medium onion
- 1 medium red sweet pepper
- 1 small container curry powder
- 1 4-ounce bottle minced fresh ginger
- 1 14-ounce can unsweetened coconut milk
- 1 10-ounce package frozen peas
- 1 15-ounce package golden raisins
- 1 8.8-pouch cooked long-grain rice

Pantry list:
Cooking oil

Salt

Cornstarch

20 minutes

Fruity Pork Fajitas

Start to Finish: **20 minutes**

- 8 ounces boneless pork top loin chops, cut into thin strips
- 1 small red onion, cut into thin wedges
- 1 medium Anaheim or poblano pepper, stemmed, seeded, and finely chopped*
- 1 tablespoon cooking oil
- 1 ½ cups frozen peach slices, thawed
- 1 teaspoon ground coriander
- ¼ teaspoon salt
- ¼ teaspoon ground black pepper
- 4 7- to 8-inch flour tortillas
  Bottled peach or pineapple salsa
  Dairy sour cream
  Lime wedges

In a large skillet cook pork strips, onion, and Anaheim pepper in hot oil over medium-high heat for 4 minutes or until meat is no longer pink and vegetables are tender. Add peaches, coriander, salt, and black pepper. Cook and stir until heated through. Use a slotted spoon to serve in flour tortillas with peach salsa, sour cream, and lime wedges.

Makes 4 servings

Nutrition facts per serving: 295 cal., 11 g total fat (4 g sat. fat), 36 mg chol., 389 mg sodium, 33 g carbo., 3 g dietary fiber, 16 g protein.

*Note: Because hot chile peppers, such as poblano and Anaheim peppers, contain volatile oils that can burn your skin and eyes, avoid direct contact with chiles as much as possible. When working with chile peppers, wear plastic or rubber gloves. If your bare hands do touch chile peppers, wash your hands well with soap and water.

Shopping list:
- 8 ounces boneless pork top loin chops
- 1 small red onion
- 1 medium Anaheim pepper
- 1 16-ounce package frozen peach slices
- 1 small container ground coriander
- 1 package 7- to 8-inch flour tortillas
- 1 16-ounce jar peach or pineapple salsa
- 1 8-ounce carton dairy sour cream
- 1 lime

Pantry list:
Cooking oil

Salt

Ground black pepper

Quick **Mu Shu Pork**

Start to Finish: **20 minutes**

12 ounces boneless pork top loin chops, cut into thin strips

1 tablespoon cooking oil

1 8-ounce package sliced button mushrooms

½ cup bias-sliced green onions

4 cups packaged shredded cabbage with carrot (coleslaw mix)

2 tablespoons soy sauce

1 teaspoon toasted sesame oil

⅛ teaspoon crushed red pepper

8 7- to 8-inch flour tortillas, warmed

Bottled hoisin or plum sauce

1 In a large skillet cook pork strips in hot oil over medium-high heat for 4 to 5 minutes or until no longer pink. Remove meat from skillet. Add mushrooms and green onions to skillet; cook for 3 minutes or until softened. Add coleslaw mix and cook about 1 minute until wilted. Return meat to skillet. Add soy sauce, sesame oil, and crushed red pepper. Heat through.

2 Serve pork mixture with warm tortillas and bottled hoisin sauce.

Makes 4 servings

Nutrition facts per serving: 412 cal., 14 g total fat (3 g sat. fat), 47 mg chol., 1,066 mg sodium, 43 g carbo., 4 g dietary fiber, 26 g protein.

Shopping list:

12 ounces boneless pork top loin chops

1 8-ounce package sliced button mushrooms

1 bunch green onions

1 16-ounce package shredded cabbage with carrot (coleslaw mix)

1 12.7-ounce bottle sesame oil

1 package 7- to 8-inch flour tortillas

1 8.5-ounce bottle hoisin sauce

Pantry list:

Cooking oil

Soy sauce

Crushed red pepper

20 minutes

Cowboy Bowls

Start to Finish: **20 minutes**

- 1 24-ounce package refrigerated mashed potatoes
- 1 17- to 18-ounce package refrigerated cooked shredded pork with barbecue sauce
- 1 15- to 16-ounce can chili beans in chili gravy
- 1 cup frozen whole kernel corn
- ½ cup chopped red sweet pepper
- ¼ cup finely chopped onion
- ½ cup shredded cheddar cheese (2 ounces)

1 Heat mashed potatoes according to package directions.

2 Meanwhile, in a medium saucepan combine pork with sauce, undrained chili beans, corn, sweet pepper, and onion. Heat through. Transfer mashed potatoes to 4 shallow bowls. Top each bowl with pork mixture; sprinkle with cheese.

Makes 4 servings

Nutrition facts per serving: 600 cal., 21 g total fat (7 g sat. fat), 76 mg chol., 1,125 mg sodium, 74 g carbo., 8 g dietary fiber, 31 g protein.

Shopping list:

- 1 24-ounce package refrigerated mashed potatoes
- 1 17- to 18-ounce package refrigerated cooked shredded pork with barbecue sauce
- 1 15- to 16-ounce can chili beans in chili gravy
- 1 10-ounce package frozen whole kernel corn
- 1 small red sweet pepper
- 1 small onion
- 1 8-ounce package shredded cheddar cheese

Pork Chops with **Pear-Maple Sauce**

Start to Finish: **20 minutes**

- 4 **boneless pork loin chops, cut ¾ inch thick (about 1 pound)**
- ½ **teaspoon salt**
- ½ **teaspoon ground black pepper**
- 1 **tablespoon olive oil**
- ¼ **cup butter**
- 3 **tablespoons pure maple syrup or maple-flavor syrup**
- 3 **tablespoons peach, apricot, or plum preserves or jam**
- ½ **teaspoon dried basil, crushed**
- 3 **medium pears, cored and thinly sliced**

1 Trim fat from chops. Sprinkle chops with salt and pepper. In a large skillet cook chops in hot oil over medium-high heat for 8 to 12 minutes or until juices run clear (160°F), turning once. Remove chops from skillet; cover to keep warm.

2 For sauce, in the same skillet melt butter over medium heat. Stir in maple syrup, peach preserves, and basil. Add pears. Cook, covered, about 3 minutes or just until the pears are tender and heated through, occasionally spooning sauce over pears. Serve chops with pears and sauce.

Makes 4 servings

Nutrition facts per serving: 495 cal., 23 g total fat (11 g sat. fat), 108 mg chol., 437 mg sodium, 40 g carbo., 4 g dietary fiber, 32 g protein.

20 minutes

Shopping list:

4 boneless pork loin chops

1 8- or 10-ounce jar peach preserves

3 medium pears

Pantry list:

Salt

Ground black pepper

Olive oil

Butter

Maple syrup

Dried basil

Pork with Cranberries and Sweet Potatoes

Start to Finish: **20 minutes**

- 4 boneless pork loin chops, cut ¾ inch thick (about 1 pound)
- Salt and ground black pepper
- Nonstick cooking spray
- 1 17-ounce can vacuum-packed sweet potatoes
- 1 tablespoon butter
- 1 cup orange juice
- ¼ cup dried cranberries

1 Trim fat from chops. Sprinkle chops lightly with salt and pepper. Lightly coat an unheated large skillet with cooking spray. Heat skillet over medium-high heat. Add chops; cook for 8 to 12 minutes or until juices run clear (160°F), turning once. Transfer chops to a serving platter; cover to keep warm.

2 Meanwhile, place sweet potatoes in a medium saucepan. Mash with a potato masher. Stir in butter. Cook and stir over medium heat until potatoes are heated through. If desired, season with additional salt and pepper.

3 Add orange juice and cranberries to skillet. Bring to boiling; reduce heat. Simmer, uncovered, about 7 minutes or until liquid is reduced by half. Spoon sauce over chops. Serve with sweet potatoes.

Makes 4 servings

Nutrition facts per serving: 341 cal., 8 g total fat (4 g sat. fat), 78 mg chol., 226 mg sodium, 38 g carbo., 3 g dietary fiber, 27 g protein.

Shopping list:
- 4 boneless pork loin chops
- 1 17-ounce can vacuum-packed sweet potatoes
- 1 3-ounce package dried cranberries

Pantry list:
- Salt
- Ground black pepper
- Nonstick cooking spray
- Butter
- Orange juice

20 minutes

Pork with Berry-Dressed Greens

Start to Finish: **20 minutes**

- 2 boneless pork loin chops, cut ¾ inch thick (about 12 ounces total)
- ¼ teaspoon salt
- ¼ teaspoon ground ginger
- ⅛ teaspoon ground black pepper
- 1 teaspoon cooking oil
- 1 teaspoon bottled minced garlic or 2 cloves garlic, minced
- ½ cup fresh sugar snap peas
- ⅓ cup sliced fresh mushrooms
- ⅔ cup bottled reduced-fat raspberry vinaigrette salad dressing
- ½ cup fresh raspberries
- 8 cups torn fresh spinach and/or romaine or torn mixed salad greens

1 Trim fat from chops. Sprinkle both sides of chops with salt, ginger, and pepper. In a large nonstick skillet cook chops in hot oil over medium heat for 8 to 12 minutes or until juices run clear (160°F), turning once. Remove chops from skillet, reserving drippings. Cover chops; keep warm.

2 In the same skillet cook and stir garlic in reserved drippings for 30 seconds. Add sugar snap peas and mushrooms. Pour vinaigrette dressing over all. Cover and cook for 2 to 3 minutes or until heated through. Remove from heat. Gently stir in raspberries; set aside and keep warm.

3 Divide spinach evenly among 4 dinner plates. Thinly slice chops. Arrange meat on spinach. Pour warm raspberry mixture over all.

Makes 4 servings

Nutrition facts per serving: 248 cal., 12 g total fat (2 g sat. fat), 46 mg chol., 617 mg sodium, 12 g carbo., 7 g dietary fiber, 21 g protein.

Shopping list:
- 2 boneless pork loin chops
- 1 small container ground ginger
- 2 ounces fresh sugar snap peas
- 1 8-ounce package sliced fresh mushrooms
- 1 8-ounce bottle reduced-fat raspberry vinaigrette
- 1 pint fresh raspberries
- 1 10-ounce package fresh spinach

Pantry list:
Salt

Ground black pepper

Cooking oil

Bottled minced garlic

20 minutes

Smoked Pork Chops with Spiced Cream

Start to Finish: **15 minutes**

6   cooked smoked boneless pork loin chops

1   teaspoon ground coriander

½   teaspoon ground ginger

½   teaspoon ground cinnamon

¼   teaspoon ground cumin

¼   teaspoon cayenne pepper

   Dash ground mace

1   tablespoon butter

¼   cup whipping cream

1   tablespoon dairy sour cream

1 Trim fat from chops. In a small bowl combine coriander, ginger, cinnamon, cumin, cayenne pepper, and mace. Remove ¼ teaspoon of the spice mixture; set aside. Rub remaining spice mixture on both sides of chops.

2 In a very large skillet cook chops in hot butter over medium heat for 8 to 10 minutes or until hot, turning once.

3 Meanwhile, in a small mixing bowl beat whipping cream with a rotary beater or wire whisk until soft peaks form (tips curl). Fold in sour cream and reserved ¼ teaspoon spice mixture.

4 Serve chops with whipped cream mixture.

Makes 6 servings

Nutrition facts per serving: 193 cal., 12 g total fat (6 g sat. fat), 80 mg chol., 1,313 mg sodium, 1 g carbo., 0 g dietary fiber, 20 g protein.

Shopping list:

6 cooked smoked boneless pork loin chops

1 small container ground coriander

1 small container ground ginger

1 small container mace

1 8-ounce carton whipping cream

1 8-ounce carton dairy sour cream

Pantry list:

Ground cinnamon

Ground cumin

Cayenne pepper

Butter

Ham Slice with Mustard Sauce

Start to Finish: **20 minutes**

- 1 **1- to 1 ¼-pound cooked boneless center-cut ham slice, cut 1 inch thick**
- 1 **tablespoon butter**
- ¼ **cup chicken broth**
- ¼ **cup dairy sour cream**
- 2 **tablespoons horseradish mustard or Dijon-style mustard**
- 1 **tablespoon chopped green onions**

1 In a very large skillet cook ham in hot butter over medium heat for 14 to 16 minutes or until heated through, turning once halfway through cooking. Transfer to a serving platter; keep warm.

2 Reduce heat to low. Add broth to skillet. Cook until bubbly, stirring to loosen any brown bits on bottom of skillet. Add sour cream, mustard, and green onion to skillet. Cook and stir over low heat until heated through (do not boil). Serve sauce with ham.

Makes 4 servings

Nutrition facts per serving: 246 cal., 16 g total fat (6 g sat. fat), 78 mg chol., 1,636 mg sodium, 6 g carbo., 2 g dietary fiber, 20 g protein.

20 minutes

Shopping list:
- 1 1- to 1 ¼-pound cooked boneless center-cut ham slice
- 1 14-ounce can chicken broth
- 1 8-ounce carton dairy sour cream
- 1 6-ounce bottle horseradish mustard
- 1 bunch green onions

Pantry list:
Butter

Ham-and-Potato-**Stuffed Peppers**

Start to Finish: **15 minutes**

- **2** **medium green sweet peppers**
- **1** **pint deli potato salad**
- **1** **cup diced cooked ham**
- **½** **cup frozen whole kernel corn, thawed**
- **1** **to 2 tablespoons dill pickle relish**

1 Cut sweet peppers in half; remove stems, seeds, and membranes. In a large saucepan cook pepper halves in boiling water for 3 minutes. Drain. Put pepper halves in bowl of ice water to chill.

2 Meanwhile, stir together potato salad, ham, corn, and pickle relish. Invert pepper halves onto paper towels to drain. Spoon potato mixture into pepper halves.

Makes 4 servings

Nutrition facts per serving: 280 cal., 14 g total fat (3 g sat. fat), 106 mg chol., 1,229 mg sodium, 23 g carbo., 3 g dietary fiber, 12 g protein.

Shopping list:
2 medium green sweet peppers

1 pint deli potato salad

1 8-ounce package diced cooked ham

1 10-ounce package frozen whole kernel corn

1 jar dill pickle relish

20 minutes

Ham and Cheese **Wraps**

Start to Finish: **20 minutes**

4   **9- to 10-inch flour tortillas**

⅓   **cup honey mustard**

8   **ounces thinly sliced cooked ham**

4   **slices Swiss or cheddar cheese**

2   **medium tomatoes, thinly sliced**

1 ½   **cups shredded lettuce**

½   **cup thinly sliced radishes or shredded carrot**

Spread one side of each tortilla with honey mustard. Top with ham, Swiss cheese, tomato slices, lettuce, and radishes. Tightly roll up each tortilla. If desired, cut in half to serve.

Makes 4 servings

Nutrition facts per serving: 470 cal., 18 g total fat (8 g sat. fat), 58 mg chol., 1,269 mg sodium, 51 g carbo., 4 g dietary fiber, 26 g protein.

Shopping list:

1 package 9- to 10-inch flour tortillas

1 9-ounce bottle honey mustard

8 ounces thinly sliced cooked ham

1 6-ounce package sliced Swiss cheese

2 medium tomatoes

1 head leaf lettuce

1 bunch radishes

20 minutes

Super Sub *(See photo on page 130.)*

Start to Finish: **20 minutes**

1 **loaf baguette-style whole grain or regular French bread, split in half horizontally**

¼ **cup bottled Italian salad dressing**

4 **leaves leaf lettuce**

6 **ounces thinly sliced cooked ham**

6 **ounces sliced salami**

6 **slices Swiss or provolone cheese**

3 **thin slices red onion, separated into rings (optional)**

1 **large tomato, thinly sliced**

6 **sweet cherry peppers**

Lay bread on a work surface, cut side up. Drizzle cut sides of bread with salad dressing. Arrange lettuce leaves on bottom half, tearing to fit. Layer ham, salami, and Swiss cheese on lettuce. Top with onion rings, if desired, and tomato slices. Add top half of bread. Attach peppers to the top of the loaf with decorative sandwich picks. Cut into 6 portions.

Makes 6 servings

Nutrition facts per serving: 503 cal., 21 g total fat (9 g sat. fat), 66 mg chol., 1,620 mg sodium, 49 g carbo., 3 g dietary fiber, 32 g protein.

Shopping list:
1 loaf baguette-style French bread
1 head leaf lettuce
1 6-ounce package thinly sliced cooked ham
1 8-ounce package salami
1 6-ounce package sliced Swiss cheese
1 red onion
1 large tomato
1 16-ounce jar whole sweet cherry peppers

Pantry list:
Bottled Italian salad dressing

Kielbasa, Rice, and **Bean Salad**

Start to Finish: **20 minutes**

12 ounces cooked, smoked Polish sausage (kielbasa), halved lengthwise and sliced ½ inch thick

1 14.8-ounce pouch cooked long-grain rice

3 cups packaged fresh baby spinach

1 15-ounce can cannellini beans, rinsed and drained

1 cup grape or cherry tomatoes, halved

½ cup chopped yellow sweet pepper

⅓ cup chopped red onion

½ cup bottled red wine vinaigrette or Italian salad dressing with cheese

1 In a large skillet cook and stir kielbasa just until heated through. Meanwhile, prepare rice according to package directions.

2 In a large bowl combine spinach, beans, tomatoes, sweet pepper, and onion. Add kielbasa, rice, and salad dressing; stir until combined.

Makes 6 servings

Nutrition facts per serving: 421 cal., 25 g total fat (8 g sat. fat), 25 mg chol., 904 mg sodium, 38 g carbo., 5 g dietary fiber, 15 g protein.

Shopping list:

1 16-ounce cooked, smoked Polish sausage (kielbasa)

1 14.8-ounce pouch cooked long-grain rice

1 5- to 6-ounce package fresh baby spinach

1 15-ounce can cannellini beans

1 pint grape tomatoes

1 yellow sweet pepper

1 red onion

1 16-ounce bottle red wine vinaigrette

Lamb Chops with Tomato Topping

Start to Finish: **20 minutes**

8 **lamb loin chops, cut 1 inch thick**

Salt and ground black pepper

1 **8.8-ounce pouch cooked long-grain rice**

4 **medium roma tomatoes, chopped**

4 **green onions, cut into 1-inch pieces**

1 **tablespoon snipped fresh oregano**

1 **tablespoon balsamic vinegar**

1 Preheat broiler. Season chops with salt and pepper. Place chops on the unheated rack of a broiler pan. Broil 4 inches from the heat for 12 to 14 minutes for medium-rare (145°F), turning once halfway through broiling.

2 Meanwhile, microwave rice according to package directions. In a food processor combine tomatoes, green onions, and oregano; process with on/off turns until coarsely chopped. Transfer to bowl; stir in vinegar. Season with salt and pepper. Arrange chops on rice; top with tomato mixture.

Makes 4 servings

Nutrition facts per serving: 273 cal., 7 g total fat (2 g sat. fat), 70 mg chol., 153 mg sodium, 26 g carbo., 3 g dietary fiber, 25 g protein.

Shopping list:
8 lamb loin chops

1 8.8-ounce pouch cooked long-grain rice

4 medium roma tomatoes

1 bunch green onions

1 package fresh oregano

Pantry list:
Salt

Ground black pepper

Balsamic vinegar

Rosemary-Garlic **Lamb Chops**

Start to Finish: **20 minutes**

- **8** **lamb rib chops, cut 1 inch thick (about 2 pounds)**
- **1** **tablespoon snipped fresh rosemary**
- **2** **cloves garlic, minced, or 1 teaspoon bottled minced garlic**
- **Salt and ground black pepper**
- **1** **tablespoon olive oil**

1 Trim fat from chops. Rub rosemary and garlic over both sides of chops; sprinkle with salt and pepper. If desired, cover chops with plastic wrap and let stand for 15 minutes.

2 In a nonstick skillet heat oil over medium-high heat. Add chops and reduce heat to medium. Cook for 9 to 11 minutes or until done (160°F), turning once halfway through cooking. If chops brown too quickly, reduce heat to medium-low.

Makes 4 servings

Nutrition facts per serving: 198 cal., 12 g total fat (4 g sat. fat), 64 mg chol., 216 mg sodium, 1 g carbo., 0 g dietary fiber, 20 g protein.

Shopping list:

6 lamb rib chops

1 small container fresh rosemary

Pantry list:

Garlic

Salt

Ground black pepper

Olive oil

20 minutes

Indian Lamb Burgers

Start to Finish: **20 minutes**

- 1 **pound lean ground lamb**
- 1 **tablespoon snipped fresh mint or 1 teaspoon dried mint, crushed**
- 2 **teaspoons garam masala**
- 4 **hamburger buns, split and toasted**
- ¼ **cup mango chutney**
- ½ **cup shredded cucumber**
- 4 **thin tomato slices**

1 In a large bowl combine lamb, mint, and garam masala. Shape into four ¾-inch-thick patties.

2 On a grill pan or indoor electric grill cook patties for 12 to 15 minutes or until no longer pink (160°F), turning once. If using a covered grill, cook for 5 to 7 minutes.

3 Serve burgers on buns. Top with chutney, cucumber, and tomato slices.

Makes 4 servings

Nutrition facts per serving: 490 cal., 29 g total fat (12 g sat. fat), 83 mg chol., 405 mg sodium, 32 g carbo., 1 g dietary fiber, 24 g protein.

Shopping list:
- 1 pound ground lamb
- 1 bunch fresh mint
- 1 small container garam masala
- 1 package hamburger buns
- 1 9-ounce jar mango chutney
- 1 cucumber
- 1 tomato

20 minutes

Fish with **Tomato Sauce**

Start to Finish: **20 minutes**

1 ½ **pounds fresh or frozen white fish fillets, ½ to 1 inch thick**

¼ **teaspoon salt**

⅛ **teaspoon ground black pepper**

2 **cups packaged sliced fresh mushrooms**

1 **tablespoon cooking oil**

1 **14.5-ounce can Italian-style stewed tomatoes, undrained**

1 **10.75-ounce can condensed tomato bisque soup**

⅛ **teaspoon ground black pepper**

⅓ **cup finely shredded Parmesan cheese**

Hot cooked pasta

1 Thaw fish, if frozen. Rinse fish; pat dry with paper towels. If necessary, cut fish into 6 serving-size pieces. Measure thickness of fish. Place fish on the greased unheated rack of a broiler pan. Turn under any thin portions to make uniform thickness. Sprinkle with salt and ⅛ teaspoon pepper.

2 Broil about 4 inches from the heat until fish flakes when tested with a fork. (Allow 4 to 6 minutes per ½-inch thickness of fish. If fillets are 1 inch thick, turn once halfway through broiling.)

3 Meanwhile, for sauce, in a medium saucepan cook mushrooms in hot oil until tender. Stir in undrained tomatoes, tomato bisque soup, and ⅛ teaspoon pepper. Cook and stir over medium heat until heated through.

4 Spoon sauce over fish fillets. Sprinkle with Parmesan cheese. Serve with hot cooked pasta.

Makes 6 servings

Nutrition facts per serving: 415 cal., 14 g total fat (6 g sat. fat), 71 mg chol., 1,218 mg sodium, 35 g carbo., 2 g dietary fiber, 37 g protein.

Shopping list:

1½ pounds fresh or frozen fish fillets

1 8-ounce package sliced fresh mushrooms

1 14.5-ounce can Italian-style stewed tomatoes

1 10.75-ounce can condensed tomato bisque soup

1 7-ounce container shredded Parmesan cheese

1 8-ounce package desired pasta

Pantry list:

Salt

Ground black pepper

Cooking oil

Tilapia with Almond Browned Butter

Start to Finish: **20 minutes**

- 3 cups snow peas, trimmed
- 4 4- to 5-ounce fresh skinless tilapia or other firm white fish fillets
- Salt and ground black pepper
- 1 teaspoon all-purpose flour
- 1 tablespoon olive oil
- 2 tablespoons butter
- ¼ cup coarsely chopped almonds
- 1 tablespoon snipped fresh parsley

1 In a large saucepan bring lightly salted water to boiling. Add snow peas. Cook for 2 minutes. Drain and set aside.

2 Meanwhile, rinse fish; pat dry with paper towels. Season fish on one side with salt and pepper; sprinkle with flour. Measure thickness of fish. In a large skillet cook fish, flour side up, in hot oil over medium-high heat for 4 to 6 minutes per ½ inch thickness of fish or until fish flakes when tested with a fork, turning once halfway through cooking. (If necessary, cook fish half at a time.) Arrange peas on a serving platter; place fish on top of peas.

3 Reduce heat to medium. Add butter to skillet. When butter begins to melt, stir in almonds. Cook for 30 to 60 seconds or until butter melts and nuts are lightly toasted (do not let butter burn). Spoon butter mixture over fish fillets. Sprinkle with parsley.

Makes 4 servings

Nutrition facts per serving: 266 cal., 15 g total fat (5 g sat. fat), 71 mg chol., 210 mg sodium, 7 g carbo., 3 g dietary fiber, 24 g protein.

Shopping list:
- 6 ounces fresh snow pea pods
- 4 4- to 5-ounce skinless fresh tilapia fillets
- 1 2-ounce package almonds
- 1 bunch fresh parsley

Pantry list:
- Salt
- Ground black pepper
- All-purpose flour
- Olive oil
- Butter

Salmon with **Red Cabbage** *(See photo on page 131.)*

Start to Finish: **20 minutes**

- 4 **5-ounce fresh or frozen skinless salmon fillets**
- ¼ **cup balsamic vinegar**
- ⅛ **teaspoon salt**
- ¼ **teaspoon ground black pepper**
- ¼ **cup purchased basil pesto**
- 6 **cups coarsely shredded red cabbage**
- 2 **green onions, bias-sliced**

1 Preheat broiler. Thaw salmon, if frozen. Rinse fish; pat dry with paper towels. Place salmon fillets on the greased unheated rack of a broiler pan. Measure thickness of fish. Brush salmon with 1 tablespoon of the balsamic vinegar; sprinkle with salt and pepper. Broil 4 to 5 inches from heat for 4 to 6 minutes per ½-inch thickness or until salmon flakes when tested with a fork.

2 Meanwhile, in a bowl whisk together remaining vinegar and pesto until combined. Remove 2 tablespoons pesto mixture. Add cabbage to pesto mixture in bowl; toss to coat.

3 To serve, place cabbage mixture on plate; top with salmon. Drizzle with reserved pesto mixture. Sprinkle with green onion slices.

Makes 4 servings

Nutrition facts per serving: 329 cal., 16 g total fat (3 g sat. fat), 83 mg chol., 354 mg sodium, 14 g carbo., 3 g dietary fiber, 31 g protein.

20 minutes

Shopping list:
4 5-ounce fresh or frozen skinless salmon fillets

1 8-ounce container basil pesto

1 head red cabbage

1 bunch green onions

Pantry list:
Balsamic vinegar

Salt

Ground black pepper

Wasabi-Glazed Salmon with Edamame Rice Salad

Start to Finish: **20 minutes**

- **4 5- to 6-ounce fresh skinless salmon fillets**
- **2 tablespoons sesame ginger liquid meat marinade**
- **½ teaspoon wasabi powder**
- **1 cup frozen sweet soybeans (edamame)**
- **1 8.8-ounce pouch cooked long-grain rice**
- **2 tablespoons rice vinegar**
- **2 tablespoons salad oil**
- **1 teaspoon honey**
- **1 teaspoon soy sauce**
- **½ teaspoon ground ginger**
- **⅓ cup bias-sliced green onions**

1 Preheat broiler. Rinse fish; pat dry with paper towels. Measure thickness of fish.

2 Place fish fillets on the greased unheated rack of a broiler pan, tucking under any thin edges. Broil 4 inches from the heat for 4 to 6 minutes per ½-inch thickness of fish or until fish flakes when tested with a fork. (If fillets are 1 inch or more thick, carefully turn once halfway through broiling.) In a small bowl combine sesame ginger marinade and wasabi powder. Brush on salmon the last 2 minutes of broiling.

3 Meanwhile, cook edamame according to package directions; set aside. Prepare rice according to package directions; set aside. In a screwtop jar combine rice vinegar, salad oil, honey, soy sauce, and ginger. Cover and shake well.

4 In a medium bowl combine edamame, rice, green onions, and dressing. Toss to combine. Serve with salmon.

Makes 4 servings

Nutrition facts per serving: 482 cal., 25 g total fat (4 g sat. fat), 84 mg chol., 467 mg sodium, 28 g carbo., 2 g dietary fiber, 33 g protein.

Shopping list:

- 4 5- to 6-ounce fresh skinless salmon fillets
- 1 12-ounce bottle sesame ginger liquid meat marinade
- 1 small container wasabi powder
- 1 12-ounce package frozen sweet soybeans (edamame)
- 1 8.8-ounce pouch cooked long-grain rice
- 1 10-ounce bottle rice vinegar
- 1 small container ground ginger
- 1 bunch green onions

Pantry list:

Salad oil

Honey

Soy sauce

20 minutes

Lemon-Garlic Trout

Start to Finish: **20 minutes**

4 **5- to 6-ounce skinless trout, catfish, or tilapia fillets**

Salt and ground black pepper

½ **teaspoon dried thyme, crushed**

3 **cloves garlic, thinly sliced**

2 **tablespoons butter**

1 **tablespoon olive oil**

¼ **cup sliced almonds**

1 **teaspoon finely shredded lemon peel**

2 **tablespoons lemon juice**

1 Rinse fish; pat dry with paper towels. Measure thickness of fish. Sprinkle fish with salt, pepper, and thyme.

2 In a very large skillet cook garlic in hot butter and oil over medium heat for 30 seconds. Add fish. Cook about 4 to 6 minutes per ½-inch thickness of fish or until fish flakes when tested with a fork, turning once. Remove fish from skillet; keep warm.

3 Add almonds to skillet and cook, stirring frequently, about 2 minutes or until golden brown. Carefully add lemon peel and lemon juice to skillet, stirring to combine. Spoon almond mixture over fish.

Makes 4 servings

Nutrition facts per serving: 316 cal., 20 g total fat (7 g sat. fat), 99 mg chol., 237 mg sodium, 3 g carbo., 1 g dietary fiber, 31 g protein.

20 minutes

Shopping list:

4 5- to 6-ounce fresh trout, catfish, or tilapia fillets

1 2.25-ounce package sliced almonds

1 lemon

Pantry list:

Salt

Ground black pepper

Dried thyme

Garlic

Butter

Olive oil

Cuban Broiled Snapper

Start to Finish: **20 minutes**

1 **pound fresh or frozen skinless red snapper fillets, ½ to ¾ inch thick**

Salt and ground black pepper

2 **tablespoons butter, melted**

¾ **cup soft bread crumbs (1 slice)**

2 **tablespoons snipped fresh Italian (flat-leaf) parsley**

1 **teaspoon finely shredded orange peel (optional)**

1 **tablespoon orange juice**

1 **clove garlic, minced**

¼ **teaspoon dried oregano, crushed**

¼ **teaspoon ground black pepper**

⅛ **teaspoon salt**

1 Thaw fish, if frozen. Preheat broiler. Rinse fish; pat dry with paper towels. Cut fish into 4 serving-size portions. Measure thickness of the fish. Place fish on the greased unheated rack of a broiler pan. Tuck under any thin edges. Sprinkle lightly with salt and pepper. Brush 2 teaspoons of the butter over the fish.

2 Broil fish 4 inches from the heat for 4 to 6 minutes per ½-inch thickness or until fish flakes when tested with a fork.

3 Meanwhile, combine remaining butter, bread crumbs, parsley, orange peel, if desired, orange juice, garlic, oregano, ¼ teaspoon pepper, and ⅛ teaspoon salt. Spoon mixture over fish; broil 1 to 2 minutes more or until topping is light golden.

Makes 4 servings

Nutrition facts per serving: 187 cal., 8 g total fat (4 g sat. fat), 58 mg chol., 315 mg sodium, 4 g carbo., 0 g dietary fiber, 24 g protein.

Shopping list:

1 pound fresh or frozen skinless red snapper fillets

1 bunch fresh Italian (flat-leaf) parsley

1 orange

Pantry list:

Salt

Ground black pepper

Butter

Bread

Garlic

Dried oregano

Cajun Catfish and Rice

Start to Finish: **20 minutes**

- 4 **6-ounce fresh catfish fillets, about ½ inch thick**
- 3 **to 4 teaspoons blackened seasoning**
- ⅔ **cup fine dry bread crumbs**
- 3 **tablespoons olive oil**
- 1 **medium onion, chopped (½ cup)**
- 1 **medium red or yellow sweet pepper, chopped (¾ cup)**
- 2 **cloves garlic, minced**
- 1 **8.8-ounce pouch cooked roasted-chicken-flavored rice**

1 Rinse fish; pat dry with paper towels. Sprinkle fish with 2 to 3 teaspoons of the blackened seasoning. Place bread crumbs in a shallow dish. Coat both sides of fish with bread crumbs.

2 In a very large skillet cook fish fillets in 2 tablespoons of the hot oil over medium-low to medium heat about 6 to 8 minutes or until golden brown and fish flakes when tested with a fork, carefully turning once. Remove from skillet and keep warm.

3 Add onion, sweet pepper, garlic, and remaining 1 tablespoon oil to skillet. Cook and stir until vegetables are tender. Meanwhile, prepare rice according to package directions. Stir rice and remaining 1 teaspoon blackened seasoning into vegetable mixture; heat through. Serve fish with rice.

Makes 4 servings

Nutrition facts per serving: 506 cal., 6 g total fat (5 g sat. fat), 80 mg chol., 904 mg sodium, 36 g carbo., 2 g dietary fiber, 32 g protein.

Shopping list:
- 4 6-ounce fresh catfish fillets
- 1 3-ounce jar blackened seasoning
- 1 medium onion
- 1 medium red or yellow sweet pepper
- 1 8.8-ounce pouch cooked roasted-chicken-flavored rice

Pantry list:
Fine dry bread crumbs

Olive oil

Garlic

20 minutes

Fried Catfish Salad

Start to Finish: 20 minutes   Oven: **350°F**

- ½ **cup coarsely chopped pecans**
- 1 **pound fresh catfish fillets**
- 1 **tablespoon Cajun seasoning**
- ¼ **cup cornmeal**
- ¼ **cup all-purpose flour**
- ¼ **cup cooking oil**
- ½ **cup bottled ranch salad dressing**
- ½ **teaspoon bottled hot pepper sauce**
- 1 **5- to 8-ounce package mixed salad greens**
- 1 **large tomato, cut into thin wedges**
- 1 **medium red or yellow sweet pepper, cut into bite-size strips**

1 Preheat oven to 350°F. Place pecans in a shallow baking pan. Bake for 5 to 10 minutes or until golden brown; set aside.

2 Meanwhile, rinse fish; pat dry with paper towels. Cut fillets into 1-inch strips. Toss catfish strips with 2 teaspoons of the Cajun seasoning. In a small dish combine cornmeal and flour. Coat catfish strips with cornmeal mixture.

3 In a large skillet cook catfish strips, half at a time, in hot oil over medium heat about 2 to 3 minutes per side or until golden brown and fish flakes when tested with a fork. Remove from skillet.

4 In a small bowl combine ranch salad dressing, remaining Cajun seasoning, and hot pepper sauce.

5 On a serving platter combine salad greens, tomato, sweet pepper, and pecans. Top with catfish strips. Drizzle with dressing.

Makes 4 servings

Nutrition facts per serving: 587 cal., 47 g total fat (7 g sat. fat), 63 mg chol., 443 mg sodium, 22 g carbo., 4 g dietary fiber, 22 g protein.

Shopping list:
- 1 4-ounce package pecan halves
- 1 pound catfish fillets
- 1 small container Cajun seasoning
- 1 5- to 8-ounce package mixed salad greens
- 1 large tomato
- 1 medium sweet pepper

Pantry list:
- Cornmeal
- All-purpose flour
- Cooking oil
- Bottled ranch salad dressing
- Bottled hot pepper sauce

20 minutes

Easy Cajun **Fish Soup**

Start to Finish: **20 minutes**

12 ounces fresh or frozen sea bass, cod, or orange roughy fillets

4 cups assorted stir-fry vegetables from salad bar or produce department or one 16-ounce package frozen loose-pack stir-fry vegetables

4 cups reduced-sodium chicken broth

2 teaspoons Cajun seasoning

1 14.5-ounce can diced tomatoes, undrained

1 Thaw fish, if frozen. Rinse fish; pat dry with paper towels. Cut fish into 1-inch pieces; set aside.

2 In a large saucepan combine vegetables, chicken broth, and Cajun seasoning. Bring to boiling; reduce heat. Simmer, covered, for 3 to 5 minutes or until vegetables are crisp-tender. Stir in fish and undrained tomatoes. Return to boiling; reduce heat. Simmer, covered for 2 to 3 minutes or until fish flakes when tested with a fork.

Makes 4 servings

Nutrition facts per serving: 157 cal., 2 g total fat (0 g sat. fat), 35 mg chol., 968 mg sodium, 12 g carbo., 3 g dietary fiber, 21 g protein.

20 minutes

Shopping list:

12 ounces fresh or frozen sea bass

4 cups assorted stir-fry vegetables

3 14-ounce cans reduced-sodium chicken broth

1 small container Cajun seasoning

1 14.5-ounce can diced tomatoes

Mexican Fish Soup

Start to Finish: **15 minutes**

- 2 **14-ounce cans chicken broth**
- 1 **14.5-ounce can diced tomatoes and green chiles, undrained**
- 1 **11-ounce can whole kernel corn with sweet peppers, drained**
- 1 **fresh jalapeño pepper, seeded and finely chopped***
- 1 **teaspoon ground cumin**
- 12 **ounces fresh skinless firm white fish (such as cod or halibut), cut into bite-size pieces**
- 1 **tablespoon snipped fresh cilantro**
- 1 **tablespoon lime juice**

    Coarsely crushed tortilla chips with lime (optional)

In a large saucepan combine broth, undrained tomatoes, corn, jalapeño pepper, and cumin. Bring to boiling. Add fish. Return to boiling; reduce heat. Simmer, uncovered, for 3 minutes or until fish flakes when tested with a fork. Stir in cilantro and lime juice. If desired, top each serving with tortilla chips.

Makes 4 servings

Nutrition facts per serving: 172 cal., 1 g total fat (0 g sat. fat), 39 mg chol., 1,572 mg sodium, 21 g carbo., 4 g dietary fiber, 20 g protein.

*Note: Because hot chile peppers, such as jalapeños, contain volatile oils that can burn your skin and eyes, avoid direct contact with chiles as much as possible. When working with chile peppers, wear plastic or rubber gloves. If your bare hands do touch chile peppers, wash your hands well with soap and water.

Shopping list:

- 2 14-ounce cans chicken broth
- 1 14.5-ounce can diced tomatoes and green chiles
- 1 11-ounce can whole kernel corn with sweet peppers
- 1 fresh jalapeño pepper
- 12 ounces firm white fish
- 1 bunch cilantro
- 1 lime

Pantry list:

Ground cumin

20 minutes

Orange-Onion Glazed **Swordfish**

Start to Finish: **20 minutes**

1 **pound fresh or frozen swordfish steaks, cut 1 inch thick**

¼ **teaspoon salt**

¼ **teaspoon coarsely ground black pepper**

Nonstick cooking spray

1 **tablespoon butter**

1 **large onion, thinly sliced and separated into rings**

½ **cup orange juice**

1 **tablespoon snipped fresh basil or 1 teaspoon dried basil, crushed**

1 Thaw fish, if frozen. Rinse fish; pat dry with paper towels. Cut fish into 4 serving-size pieces. Sprinkle fish with salt and pepper.

2 Lightly coat a large skillet with cooking spray. Heat skillet over medium-high heat. Add swordfish to skillet. Cook, covered, about 12 minutes or until fish flakes when tested with a fork, turning once. Remove fish from skillet; keep warm.

3 Add butter to hot skillet. Cook and stir onion in hot butter until tender. Carefully stir in orange juice and basil. Bring to boiling; reduce heat. Simmer, uncovered, for 1 to 2 minutes or until most of the liquid has evaporated. Spoon onion mixture over fish.

Makes 4 servings

Nutrition facts per serving: 191 cal., 7 g total fat (3 g sat. fat), 51 mg chol., 280 mg sodium, 7 g carbo., 1 g dietary fiber, 23 g protein.

20 minutes

Shopping list:

1 pound fresh or frozen swordfish steaks

1 large onion

1 package fresh basil

Pantry list:

Salt

Ground black pepper

Nonstick cooking spray

Butter

Orange juice

Lemon-Pepper Tuna Caesar Salad

Start to Finish: **20 minutes**

- **4** **6-ounce fresh tuna steaks, cut 1 inch thick**
- **1** **tablespoon lemon-pepper seasoning**
- **1** **9- to 10-ounce package chopped hearts of romaine**
- **½** **cup finely shredded Parmesan cheese**
- **½** **cup bottled Caesar salad dressing**
- **2** **cups Caesar salad croutons**

1 Rinse fish; pat dry with paper towels. Sprinkle both sides of fish with lemon-pepper seasoning. Lightly grease the rack of an indoor electric grill or grill pan. Heat grill or grill pan. Place fish on grill rack. If using a covered grill, close lid. Grill until fish flakes when tested with a fork. For a covered grill, allow 4 to 6 minutes. For an uncovered grill or grill pan, allow 8 to 12 minutes, gently turning fish once. Break tuna steaks into large chunks.

2 On a serving platter combine hearts of romaine and Parmesan cheese. Add dressing and toss to coat. Top with tuna chunks and croutons.

Makes 4 servings

Nutrition facts per serving: 514 cal., 30 g total fat (7 g sat. fat), 72 mg chol., 958 mg sodium, 12 g carbo., 1 g dietary fiber, 46 g protein.

Shopping list:

- 4 6-ounce fresh tuna steaks
- 1 small container lemon-pepper seasoning
- 1 9- to 10-ounce package chopped hearts of romaine
- 1 6-ounce package finely shredded Parmesan cheese
- 1 16-ounce bottle Caesar salad dressing
- 1 package Caesar salad croutons

20 minutes

Broiled Halibut with Dijon Cream

Start to Finish: **20 minutes**

4   **fresh or frozen halibut steaks, cut 1 inch thick**

1 ½   **teaspoons Greek-style seasoning blend**

¼   **teaspoon coarsely ground black pepper**

¼   **cup dairy sour cream**

2   **tablespoons mayonnaise**

1   **tablespoon Dijon-style mustard**

1   **tablespoon milk**

½   **teaspoon dried oregano, crushed**

1 Thaw fish, if frozen. Preheat broiler. Rinse fish; pat dry with paper towels. Place fish on the greased unheated rack of a broiler pan. Sprinkle both sides of fish with Greek-style seasoning and pepper.

2 Broil 4 inches from the heat for 8 to 12 minutes or until fish flakes when tested with a fork, turning once halfway through broiling.

3 Meanwhile, for sauce, in a small bowl combine sour cream, mayonnaise, mustard, milk, and oregano. Serve fish with sauce.

Makes 4 servings

Nutrition facts per serving: 168 cal., 5 g total fat (2 g sat. fat), 42 mg chol., 300 mg sodium, 4 g carbo., 0 g dietary fiber, 24 g protein.

20 minutes

Shopping list:

4 fresh or frozen halibut steaks

1 small container bottle Greek-style seasoning blend

1 8-ounce carton dairy sour cream

Pantry list:

Ground black pepper

Mayonnaise

Dijon-style mustard

Milk

Dried oregano

Fish Sandwiches with Spicy Tartar Sauce

Start to Finish: **20 minutes**

1   **11-ounce package frozen baked breaded fish sticks (18)**

¼   **cup mayonnaise**

1   **tablespoon dill or sweet pickle relish**

1   **tablespoon finely chopped onion**

1   **teaspoon Creole mustard or spicy brown mustard**

¼   **teaspoon bottled hot pepper sauce**

4   **or 5 hamburger buns, split and toasted**

1   **cup purchased shredded iceberg lettuce**

¼   **cup purchased shredded carrot**

Bake fish sticks according to package directions. Meanwhile, in a small bowl combine mayonnaise, pickle relish, onion, mustard, and hot pepper sauce. Divide fish sticks among hamburger buns. Top with mayonnaise mixture, lettuce, and carrot.

Makes 4 or 5 servings

Nutrition facts per serving: 356 cal., 15 g total fat (3 g sat. fat), 24 mg chol., 683 mg sodium, 41 g carbo., 1 g dietary fiber, 12 g protein.

Shopping list:

1 11-ounce package frozen baked breaded fish sticks

1 8-ounce jar dill pickle relish

1 onion

1 5.25-ounce jar Creole mustard

1 package hamburger buns

1 10-ounce package shredded iceberg lettuce

1 10-ounce package shredded carrots

Pantry list:

Mayonnaise

Bottled hot pepper sauce

No-Bake **Tuna and Noodles** *(See photo on page 132.)*

Start to Finish: **20 minutes**

8 ounces dried wagon wheel or medium shell macaroni

¼ to ½ cup milk

1 6.5-ounce container or two 4-ounce containers light semisoft cheese with cucumber and dill or garlic and herb

1 12.25-ounce can solid white tuna, drained and broken into chunks

Salt and ground black pepper

1 In a saucepan cook pasta in lightly salted water, according to package directions. Drain and return to pan.

2 Add ¼ cup of the milk and the cheese to the pasta. Cook and stir over medium heat until cheese melts and pasta is coated, adding additional milk as needed to make a creamy consistency. Gently stir in tuna; heat through. Season to taste with salt and pepper.

Makes 4 servings

Nutrition facts per serving: 417 cal., 10 g total fat (7 g sat. fat), 66 mg chol., 552 mg sodium, 45 g carbo., 2 g dietary fiber, 33 g protein.

Shopping list:

1 8-ounce package dried wagon wheel macaroni

1 6.5-ounce container light semisoft cheese with cucumber and dill

1 12.25-ounce can solid white tuna

Pantry list:

Milk

Salt

Ground black pepper

Tuna Salad with a Twist

Start to Finish: **15 minutes**

1   **12-ounce can chunk white tuna, drained and broken into chunks**

⅓   **cup bottled creamy Italian salad dressing**

⅓   **cup chopped green sweet pepper**

2   **bagels (such as sesame seed, poppy seed, garlic, or plain), split**

4   **slices provolone, Swiss, or mozzarella cheese (about 4 ounces total)**

8   **red and/or yellow cherry tomatoes, halved or quartered, or 4 tomato slices**

1   Preheat broiler. In a medium bowl combine tuna, salad dressing, and sweet pepper. Set aside. Place bagel halves, cut side up, on the unheated rack of a broiler pan. Broil 4 to 5 inches from the heat for 1 minute or until toasted.

2   Place a cheese slice on each bagel half. Spoon tuna mixture over cheese slice. Broil for 2 to 4 minutes or until cheese melts. Top with tomatoes.

Makes 4 servings

Nutrition facts per serving: 385 cal., 19 g total fat (7 g sat. fat), 55 mg chol., 1,094 mg sodium, 23 g carbo., 1 g dietary fiber, 31 g protein.

Shopping list:

1 12-ounce can chunk white tuna

1 8-ounce bottle creamy Italian salad dressing

1 small green sweet pepper

2 bagels

1 8-ounce package sliced provolone cheese

1 pint cherry tomatoes

20 minutes

Tuna Salad **Pockets**

Start to Finish: **15 minutes**

- 1 **12-ounce can solid white tuna, drained**
- ¼ **cup finely chopped onion**
- ¼ **cup thinly sliced celery**
- ¼ **cup shredded carrot**
- 1 **tablespoon capers, rinsed and drained**
- 2 **tablespoons olive oil**
- 2 **tablespoons lime juice**
- 1 **tablespoon Dijon-style mustard**
- 1 **tablespoon white wine vinegar**
- 1 ½ **cups torn mixed salad greens**
- 2 **large whole wheat pita bread rounds, halved crosswise**

1 In a medium bowl combine tuna, onion, celery, carrot, and capers; set aside. For vinaigrette, in a small screw-top jar combine olive oil, lime juice, mustard, and vinegar. Cover and shake well to combine. Pour vinaigrette over tuna mixture; toss gently to combine. Add greens; toss gently to combine.

2 Place a pita bread half on each of 4 plates. Top with tuna mixture.

Makes 4 servings

Nutrition facts per serving: 272 cal., 10 g total fat (2 g sat. fat), 36 mg chol., 659 mg sodium, 22 g carbo., 3 g dietary fiber, 24 g protein.

20 minutes

Shopping list:

- 1 12-ounce can solid white tuna
- 1 small onion
- 1 bunch celery
- 1 10-ounce package shredded carrot
- 1 3.5-ounce jar capers
- 1 8-ounce bottle lime juice
- 1 8-ounce bottle white wine vinegar
- 1 8-ounce package mixed salad greens
- 1 package large whole wheat pita bread rounds

Pantry list:

Olive oil

Dijon-style mustard

Mexican Tuna Melt

Start to Finish: **20 minutes**

- 2 **6-ounce cans chunk white tuna, drained**
- ¼ **cup mayonnaise or salad dressing**
- 2 **tablespoons toasted pumpkin seeds (pepitas)* or dry roasted sunflower seeds**
- ½ **teaspoon finely shredded lime peel**
- 1 **tablespoon lime juice**
- 1 **tablespoon finely chopped red onion**
- 1 **teaspoon finely chopped chipotle peppers in adobo sauce (optional)****
- 8 **slices whole wheat bread**
- 4 **ounces Monterey Jack cheese with jalapeño peppers, shredded**
- 1 **small tomato, thinly sliced**
- 1 **cup packaged shredded lettuce**

Preheat broiler. In a medium bowl combine tuna, mayonnaise, pumpkin seeds, lime peel, lime juice, onion, and, if desired, chipotle. Place 4 of the bread slices on a baking sheet. Spread the tuna mixture on the bread slices. Top with cheese. Broil 4 to 5 inches from the heat for 1 ½ to 3 minutes or until cheese melts. Top with tomato slices, lettuce, and remaining bread slices.

Makes 4 servings

Nutrition facts per serving: 467 cal., 26 g total fat (9 g sat. fat), 73 mg chol., 883 mg sodium, 24 g carbo., 4 g dietary fiber, 36 g protein.

*Note: To toast pumpkin seeds, spread seeds in a shallow baking pan; bake in a 350°F oven for 7 to 10 minutes or until toasted. Cool.

**Note: Because hot peppers, such as chipotles, contain volatile oils that can burn your skin and eyes, avoid direct contact with chiles as much as possible. When working with chile peppers, wear plastic or rubber gloves. If your bare hands do touch chile peppers, wash your hands well with soap and water.

Shopping list:
- 2 6-ounce cans chunk white tuna
- 1 6-ounce package pumpkin seed (pepitas)
- 1 lime
- 1 red onion
- 1 7-ounce can chipotle peppers in adobo sauce
- 1 loaf whole wheat bread
- 1 8-ounce piece Monterey Jack cheese with jalapeño peppers
- 1 small tomato
- 1 10-ounce package shredded iceberg lettuce

Pantry list:
Mayonnaise

Curried Tuna on Biscuits

Start to Finish: **20 minutes**

- 3 **tablespoons butter**
- 3 **tablespoons all-purpose flour**
- 2 **to 3 teaspoons curry powder**
- ¼ **teaspoon salt**
- 2 **cups milk**
- 1 **12-ounce can chunk white tuna, drained**
- 1 **cup frozen peas**
- ½ **cup purchased coarsely shredded fresh carrot**
- 4 **frozen baked biscuits for microwave**

1 In a large saucepan melt butter over medium heat. Stir in flour, curry powder, and salt. Cook and stir for 30 seconds. Add milk all at once. Cook and stir until thick and bubbly; cook and stir 1 minute more. Stir in tuna, peas, and carrot; cook and stir until heated through.

2 Meanwhile, heat biscuits according to package directions. Serve tuna mixture over split biscuits.

Makes 4 servings

Nutrition facts per serving: 494 cal., 23 g total fat (10 g sat. fat), 68 mg chol., 1,208 mg sodium, 39 g carbo., 3 g dietary fiber, 31 g protein.

Shopping list:

1 small container curry powder

1 12-ounce can chunk white tuna

1 9- to 10-ounce package frozen peas

1 16-ounce package coarsely shredded fresh carrot

1 16-ounce package freezer-to-microwave baked biscuits

Pantry list:

Butter

All-purpose flour

Salt

Milk

20 minutes

Shrimp Pasta Diavolo

Start to Finish: 20 minutes

- 1 **9-ounce package refrigerated linguine**
- 12 **ounces medium fresh shrimp, peeled and deveined**
- 1 **medium onion, cut into thin wedges**
- 3 **cloves garlic, minced**
- ¼ **teaspoon crushed red pepper**
- 2 **tablespoons olive oil**
- 1 **14.5-ounce can diced tomatoes, undrained**
- ½ **cup torn fresh basil**
- 2 **cups fresh baby spinach**
- ½ **cup finely shredded Parmesan cheese**

1 Cook linguine according to package directions. Drain pasta and transfer to a very large bowl; set aside. Rinse shrimp; pat dry with paper towels.

2 Meanwhile, in a large skillet cook onion, garlic, and crushed red pepper in hot oil until tender. Stir in tomatoes. Bring to boiling; reduce heat. Simmer, uncovered, for 3 minutes. Add shrimp to skillet; cover and simmer for 3 minutes or until shrimp are opaque. Add shrimp mixture to pasta. Stir in basil and spinach. Top each serving with Parmesan cheese.

Makes 4 servings

Nutrition facts per serving: 412 cal., 13 g total fat (4 g sat. fat), 204 mg chol., 528 mg sodium, 44 g carbo., 4 g dietary fiber, 30 g protein.

Shopping list:

- 1 9-ounce package refrigerated linguine
- 12 ounces medium fresh shrimp
- 1 medium onion
- 1 14.5-ounce can diced tomatoes
- 1 bunch fresh basil
- 1 5- to 6-ounce package fresh baby spinach
- 1 6-ounce package finely shredded Parmesan cheese

Pantry list:

Olive oil

Garlic

Crushed red pepper

20 minutes

Seared Shrimp in Garlic Butter

Start to Finish: **20 minutes**

1 ½ **pounds fresh or frozen peeled, deveined medium shrimp**

3 **cloves garlic, minced**

2 **tablespoons butter**

2 **tablespoons dry white wine or chicken broth**

1 **tablespoon snipped fresh chives or parsley (optional)**

⅛ **teaspoon salt**

1 Thaw shrimp, if frozen. Rinse shrimp; pat dry with paper towels.

2 In a very large skillet cook and stir garlic in 1 tablespoon of the butter over medium-high heat until butter melts. Add shrimp. Cook for 1 to 3 minutes or until shrimp are opaque, stirring frequently.

3 Remove shrimp from skillet and transfer to a serving platter. Add wine and remaining butter to the skillet. Cook and stir to loosen any browned bits. Pour over shrimp. Sprinkle with chives, if desired, and salt.

Makes 4 servings

Nutrition facts per serving: 241 cal., 9 g total fat (4 g sat. fat), 274 mg chol., 366 mg sodium, 3 g carbo., 0 g dietary fiber, 35 g protein.

Shopping list:

1½ pounds fresh or frozen medium shrimp

1 bottle dry white wine

1 bunch fresh chives

Pantry list:

Garlic

Butter

Salt

20 minutes

Shrimp and Spinach Scrambled Eggs

Start to Finish: **20 minutes**

- 8 ounces fresh or frozen peeled, deveined shrimp
- 8 eggs
- ½ cup milk
- ¼ teaspoon salt
- ¼ teaspoon ground black pepper

  Nonstick cooking spray
- 2 ½ cups fresh baby spinach
- 1 5-ounce container semisoft cheese with garlic and herb, crumbled

1 Thaw shrimp, if frozen. Rinse shrimp; pat dry with paper towels. Halve shrimp lengthwise; set aside.

2 In a medium bowl beat together eggs, milk, salt, and pepper with a fork or rotary beater; set aside.

3 Lightly coat a large nonstick skillet with cooking spray. Heat skillet over medium heat. Add shrimp and spinach to skillet; cook and stir for 2 to 3 minutes or until shrimp are opaque.

4 Pour egg mixture into skillet. Cook over medium heat, without stirring, until mixture begins to set on the bottom and around edges. With a spatula or a large spoon, lift and fold the partially cooked egg mixture so the uncooked portion flows underneath. Continue cooking over medium heat for 2 to 3 minutes or until egg mixture is cooked through but is still glossy and moist.

5 Remove from heat immediately; sprinkle with cheese. Let stand 3 to 4 minutes or until cheese melts.

Makes 4 servings

Nutrition facts per serving: 343 cal., 23 g total fat (11 g sat. fat), 525 mg chol., 228 mg sodium, 4 g carbo., 2 g dietary fiber, 25 g protein.

Shopping list:

8 ounces fresh or frozen shrimp

1 5- to 6-ounce package fresh baby spinach

1 5-ounce container semisoft cheese with garlic and herb

Pantry list:

Eggs

Milk

Salt

Ground black pepper

Nonstick cooking spray

20 minutes

Asian Hot and Sour **Shrimp Soup**

Start to Finish: **20 minutes**

2　**14-ounce cans chicken broth**

¼　**cup rice vinegar**

2　**tablespoons soy sauce**

2　**teaspoons Asian chili sauce**

1　**cup thinly sliced shiitake or button mushrooms**

½　**cup bias-sliced green onions**

12　**ounces fresh peeled, deveined shrimp**

1　**8-ounce can sliced bamboo shoots, drained**

1　**egg, lightly beaten**

In a large saucepan combine broth, vinegar, soy sauce, chili sauce, mushrooms, and green onions. Bring to boiling; reduce heat. Simmer, uncovered, for 2 minutes. Rinse shrimp; pat dry with paper towels. Add shrimp and bamboo shoots to saucepan. Return to boiling. Simmer 1 minute or until shrimp are almost opaque. Pour egg into the soup in a steady stream, stirring a few times to create shreds.

Makes 4 servings

Nutrition facts per serving: 166 cal., 3 g total fat (1 g sat. fat), 184 mg chol., 1,489 mg sodium, 11 g carbo., 1 g dietary fiber, 21 g protein.

Shopping list:

2　14-ounce cans chicken broth

1　10-ounce bottle rice vinegar

1　17-ounce bottle Asian chili sauce

4　ounces shiitake mushrooms

1　bunch green onions

12　ounces fresh shrimp

1　8-ounce can sliced bamboo shoots

Pantry list:

Soy sauce

Egg

Orange-Avocado Crab Salad Sandwich

Start to Finish: **20 minutes**

- **1 pint deli crab salad**
- **½ teaspoon finely shredded orange peel**
- **½ cup chopped, sectioned, peeled orange**
- **½ cup chopped avocado**
- **4 croissants, split, or 8 slices brioche**
- **1 cup shredded lettuce**

In a medium bowl combine crab salad, orange peel, orange, and avocado. Spoon crab salad into croissants; top with shredded lettuce.

Makes 4 servings

Nutrition facts per serving: 482 cal., 30 g total fat (9 g sat. fat), 111 mg chol., 919 mg sodium, 34 g carbo., 4 g dietary fiber, 19 g protein.

20 minutes

Shopping list:
1 pint deli crab salad
1 orange
1 avocado
4 bakery croissants
1 10-ounce package shredded iceberg lettuce

Seafood Omelet with Avocado Salsa

Start to Finish: **20 minutes**

1 **medium avocado, halved, seeded, peeled, and chopped**

1 **tablespoon finely chopped red onion**

1 **tablespoon snipped fresh cilantro**

1 **tablespoon lime juice**

 Salt and ground black pepper

8 **eggs**

½ **cup water**

¼ **cup chopped green onions (2)**

¼ **teaspoon salt**

¼ **teaspoon ground black pepper**

¼ **teaspoon cayenne pepper**

4 **tablespoons butter**

1 **6-ounce can crabmeat, drained, flaked, and cartilage removed, or one 7-ounce package frozen peeled, cooked tiny shrimp, thawed and patted dry**

1 For avocado salsa, in a medium bowl combine avocado, red onion, cilantro, lime juice, and salt and pepper to taste.

2 In a large bowl combine eggs, the water, green onions, ¼ teaspoon salt, ¼ teaspoon black pepper, and cayenne pepper. Beat with a fork until combined but not frothy. Heat an 8-inch nonstick skillet with flared sides over medium-high heat until skillet is hot.

3 Add 1 tablespoon of the butter to skillet. When butter melts, add ½ cup of the egg mixture; lower heat to medium. Using a spatula, stir egg mixture gently but continuously until mixture resembles small pieces of cooked egg surrounded by liquid egg. Stop stirring. Cook 30 to 60 seconds more or until egg mixture is set but shiny.

4 Spoon one-fourth of the crab across center of eggs. With a spatula lift and fold edge of the omelet about one-third of the way toward the center. Remove from heat. Fold the opposite edge toward the center; transfer to a warm plate. Repeat with remaining butter, egg mixture, and filling. Serve immediately with avocado salsa.

Makes 4 servings

Nutrition facts per serving: 373 cal., 29 g total fat (10 g sat. fat), 493 mg chol., 665 mg sodium, 6 g carbo., 3 g dietary fiber, 22 g protein.

20 minutes

Shopping list:
1 medium avocado
1 small red onion
1 bunch fresh cilantro
1 8-ounce bottle lime juice

1 bunch green onions
1 6-ounce can crabmeat

Pantry list:
Salt
Ground black pepper

Eggs
Cayenne pepper
Butter

Seared Scallops with **Ginger Sauce**

Start to Finish: **15 minutes**

1 **pound fresh or frozen sea scallops**

4 **teaspoons butter**

⅓ **cup chicken broth**

¼ **cup frozen pineapple-orange juice concentrate, thawed**

1 **teaspoon grated fresh ginger**

1 Thaw scallops, if frozen. Rinse scallops; pat dry with paper towels. In a large skillet cook scallops in hot butter over medium-high heat for 2 to 3 minutes or until scallops are opaque, stirring frequently. Remove scallops from skillet; keep warm.

2 For sauce, add chicken broth, juice concentrate, and ginger to skillet. Bring to boiling. Boil, uncovered, until sauce is reduced by about half. Spoon over scallops.

Makes 4 servings

Nutrition facts per serving: 168 cal., 5 g total fat (3 g sat. fat), 48 mg chol., 311 mg sodium, 10 g carbo., 0 g dietary fiber, 19 g protein.

Shopping list:
1 pound fresh or frozen sea scallops

1 14-ounce can chicken broth

1 6-ounce can frozen pineapple-orange juice concentrate

1 piece fresh ginger

Pantry list:
Butter

Red Bean Stew

Start to Finish: **20 minutes**

2/3 cup chopped red onion

3 cloves garlic, minced

1 teaspoon cooking oil

1 cup water

2 tablespoons tomato paste

1 tablespoon snipped fresh cilantro

1 teaspoon snipped fresh oregano or 1/4 teaspoon dried oregano, crushed

1/2 teaspoon adobo seasoning*

1 15-ounce can red kidney beans, rinsed and drained

2 cups hot cooked brown rice

In a large skillet cook onion and garlic in hot oil over medium heat about 5 minutes or until onion is tender. Carefully add the water, tomato paste, cilantro, oregano, and adobo seasoning. Stir in beans. Bring to boiling; reduce heat. Cook and stir over medium heat for 5 to 10 minutes or until soup thickens slightly, mashing beans slightly while stirring. Serve stew with rice.

Makes 4 servings

Nutrition facts per serving: 220 cal., 2 g total fat (0 g sat. fat), 0 mg chol., 427 mg sodium, 44 g carbo., 8 g dietary fiber, 11 g protein.

*Test Kitchen Tip: Look for this seasoning blend at a market that specializes in Hispanic foods.

Shopping list:

1 small red onion

1 6-ounce can tomato paste

1 bunch fresh cilantro

1 package fresh oregano

1 small container adobo seasoning

1 15-ounce can red kidney beans

Pantry list:

Garlic

Cooking oil

Brown rice

20 minutes

Polenta and **Black Beans** *(See photo on page 134.)*

Start to Finish: 20 minutes

3 cups water

1 cup yellow cornmeal

1 cup water

½ teaspoon salt

1 15-ounce can black beans, rinsed and drained

1 14.5-ounce can diced tomatoes, undrained

1 cup bottled salsa with cilantro or other salsa

¾ cup shredded Mexican-style four-cheese blend (3 ounces)

1 For polenta, in a large saucepan bring the 3 cups water to boiling. In a medium bowl combine cornmeal, the 1 cup water, and salt. Stir cornmeal mixture slowly into the boiling water. Cook and stir until mixture comes to boiling. Reduce heat to low. Cook for 5 to 10 minutes or until mixture is thick, stirring occasionally. (If mixture is too thick, stir in additional water.)

2 Meanwhile, in a large skillet combine beans, undrained tomatoes, and salsa. Bring mixture to boiling; reduce heat. Simmer, uncovered, for 10 minutes, stirring frequently. Stir ½ cup of the cheese into the polenta. Divide polenta among 4 shallow bowls. Top with the bean mixture and sprinkle with the remaining cheese.

Makes 4 servings

Nutrition facts per serving: 311 cal., 8 g total fat (4 g sat. fat), 19 mg chol., 751 mg sodium, 49 g carbo., 8 g dietary fiber, 15 g protein.

Shopping list:

1 24-ounce package yellow cornmeal

1 15-ounce can black beans

1 14.5-ounce can diced tomatoes

1 8-ounce jar salsa

1 8-ounce package shredded Mexican-style four-cheese blend

Pantry list:

Salt

Black Bean and Corn **Quesadillas**

Start to Finish: **20 minutes**

2 cups shredded Mexican-style four-cheese blend (8 ounces)

8 8-inch flour tortillas

1½ cups purchased black bean and corn salsa

1 medium avocado, seeded, peeled, and chopped

Dairy sour cream

1 Sprinkle ¼ cup cheese over half of each tortilla. Top with 1 tablespoon salsa. Divide avocado among tortillas. Fold tortillas in half, pressing gently.

2 Heat a large skillet over medium-high heat for 2 minutes; reduce heat to medium. Cook quesadillas, two at a time, for 2 to 3 minutes or until light brown and cheese melts, turning once. Remove quesadillas from skillet; place on a baking sheet. Keep warm in a 300°F oven. Repeat with remaining quesadillas. Cut quesadillas into wedges. Serve with sour cream and remaining salsa.

Makes 4 servings

Nutrition facts per serving: 512 cal., 33 g total fat (14 g sat. fat), 55 mg chol., 940 mg sodium, 38 g carbo., 4 g dietary fiber, 18 g protein.

Shopping list:

1 16-ounce package shredded Mexican-style four-cheese blend

1 package 8-inch flour tortillas

1 16-ounce jar black bean and corn salsa

1 medium avocado

1 8-ounce carton dairy sour cream

Vegetable-Hummus Wrap

Start to Finish: **20 minutes**

1 **large portobello mushroom (5 to 6 ounces)**

1 **small zucchini, chopped**

½ **cup chopped red sweet pepper**

½ **cup chopped sweet onion or red onion**

½ **teaspoon salt**

¼ **teaspoon ground black pepper**

1 **tablespoon olive oil**

1 **7- to 8-ounce carton desired flavor hummus (such as roasted red pepper, spicy three pepper, black olive, or roasted garlic)**

4 **9- to 10-inch flour tortillas**

¼ **cup purchased finely shredded Parmesan cheese**

1 Remove stem and scrape out mushroom gills. Cut mushroom into bite-size strips. In a very large skillet cook mushroom, zucchini, sweet pepper, onion, salt, and black pepper in oil over medium-high heat for 5 to 8 minutes or until vegetables are crisp-tender, stirring occasionally.

2 Meanwhile, spread hummus evenly on tortillas. Sprinkle with Parmesan cheese. Top with cooked vegetables. Roll up tortillas. Cut in half to serve.

Makes 4 servings

Nutrition facts per serving: 400 cal., 14 g total fat (3 g sat. fat), 4 mg chol., 847 mg sodium, 56 g carbo., 6 g dietary fiber, 12 g protein.

Shopping list:

1 large portobello mushroom

1 small zucchini

1 small red sweet pepper

1 sweet onion

1 7- to 8-ounce carton desired flavor hummus

1 package 9- to 10-inch flour tortillas

1 8-ounce package shredded Parmesan cheese

Pantry list:

Salt

Ground black pepper

Olive oil

20 minutes

Bean Burritos with Lime Mayonnaise *(See photo on page 133.)*

Start to Finish: **20 minutes**

4   **9- to 10-inch flour tortillas**

1   **16-ounce can refried beans**

¼   **cup salsa**

¼   **cup mayonnaise**

½   **teaspoon finely shredded lime peel**

1   **tablespoon lime juice**

2   **cups shredded leaf or iceberg lettuce**

½   **cup cherry tomatoes, quartered**

2   **ounces Monterey Jack cheese with jalapeño peppers, shredded (½ cup)**

1 Place tortillas between paper towels. Microwave on 100% power (high), for 20 to 30 seconds to heat through.

2 Meanwhile, in a small saucepan combine refried beans and salsa. Cook over medium heat until heated through, stirring frequently.

3 In a medium bowl combine mayonnaise, lime peel, and lime juice. Add lettuce and tomato; toss to coat.

4 Spoon about ½ cup of the bean mixture onto each tortilla just below the center. Top each with 2 tablespoons cheese and about ⅓ cup lettuce mixture. Fold bottom edge of each tortilla up and over the filling. Fold opposite sides in and over filling. Roll up from the bottom.

Makes 4 servings

Nutrition facts per serving: 414 cal., 19 g total fat (6 g sat. fat), 29 mg chol., 992 mg sodium, 47 g carbo., 9 g dietary fiber, 15 g protein.

20 minutes

Shopping list:

1 package 9- to 10-inch flour tortillas

1 16-ounce can refried beans

1 8-ounce jar salsa

1 lime

1 16-ounce package shredded lettuce

1 pint cherry tomatoes

1 8-ounce piece Monterey Jack with jalapeño peppers

Pantry list:

Mayonnaise

Spicy Thai **Peanut Noodles**

Start to Finish: **20 minutes**

- 1 **9-ounce package refrigerated linguine**
- 1 **cup packaged fresh julienne or shredded carrots**
- 1 **medium red or yellow sweet pepper, seeded and cut into thin strips**
- ½ **of a medium cucumber, seeded and cut into thin strips**
- ⅓ **cup bias-sliced green onions**
- ⅓ **cup torn fresh basil**
- 1 **11.5-ounce bottle peanut sauce**
- ⅓ **cup dry roasted peanuts**

1 Cook linguini according to package directions; drain. Rinse under cold running water until chilled; drain again. If desired, snip pasta with clean kitchen scissors to make shorter lengths.

2 In a large bowl toss together drained pasta, carrots, sweet pepper, cucumber, green onions, and basil. Add peanut sauce and toss to coat. Sprinkle with peanuts.

Makes 4 servings

Nutrition facts per serving: 496 cal., 20 g total fat (4 g sat. fat), 68 mg chol., 1,288 mg sodium, 62 g carbo., 4 g dietary fiber, 16 g protein.

Shopping list:

- 1 9-ounce package refrigerated linguine
- 1 10-ounce package fresh julienne carrot
- 1 medium red sweet pepper
- 1 medium cucumber
- 1 bunch green onions
- 1 bunch fresh basil
- 1 11.5-ounce bottle peanut sauce
- 1 8-ounce jar dry roasted peanuts

20minutes

Vegetable **Tortellini**

Start to Finish: **20 minutes**

- 2 **9-ounce packages spinach-cheese tortellini**
- 1 **medium onion, cut into thin wedges**
- 1 **medium red sweet pepper, coarsely chopped (¾ cup)**
- 1 **tablespoon olive oil**
- 1 **8-ounce package button mushrooms, sliced**
- 1 **26- to 28-ounce can or jar four-cheese pasta sauce**
- 4 **cups fresh baby spinach**
- ½ **cup finely shredded Parmesan cheese**

1 Cook tortellini according to package directions; drain and return to saucepan.

2 Meanwhile, in a large skillet cook onion and sweet pepper in hot oil over medium heat until softened. Add mushrooms and cook until vegetables are tender. Stir in pasta sauce; bring to boiling. Add to drained tortellini along with spinach; cook over medium heat until spinach just wilts. Serve immediately. Sprinkle servings with Parmesan cheese.

Makes 4 or 5 servings

Nutrition facts per serving: 727 cal., 21 g total fat (9 g sat. fat), 97 mg chol., 1,563 mg sodium, 104 g carbo., 11 g dietary fiber, 32 g protein.

Shopping list:

2 9-ounce packages refrigerated spinach-cheese tortellini

1 medium onion

1 medium red sweet pepper

1 8-ounce package button mushrooms

1 26- to 28-ounce can or jar four-cheese pasta sauce

1 5- to 6-ounce package fresh baby spinach

1 6-ounce package finely shredded Parmesan cheese

Pantry list:

Olive oil

Easy Cheesy Macaroni

Start to Finish: **20 minutes**

- 8 **ounces dried penne, rotini, or gemelli**
- 2 **cups loose-pack frozen cauliflower, broccoli, and carrots**
- 1 **10-ounce container refrigerated light Alfredo pasta sauce**
- ¼ **cup milk**
- 1 **cup shredded cheddar cheese (4 ounces)**
- ½ **cup finely shredded Parmesan cheese**
- ¼ **cup chopped walnuts, toasted**

1 In a 4-quart Dutch oven cook pasta according to package directions, adding frozen vegetables for the last 4 minutes of cooking; drain well. Return to Dutch oven; cover and keep warm.

2 Meanwhile, in a medium saucepan combine Alfredo sauce and milk; heat and stir just until bubbly. Gradually add cheddar and Parmesan cheeses, stirring until melted. Add cheese mixture to pasta mixture in Dutch oven; stir to coat. Heat through. Top with toasted walnuts.

Makes 4 servings

Nutrition facts per serving: 586 cal., 28 g total fat (15 g sat. fat), 70 mg chol., 1,054 mg sodium, 57 g carbo., 3 g dietary fiber, 26 g protein.

Shopping list:
- 1 8-ounce package dried penne
- 1 16-ounce package loose-pack frozen cauliflower, broccoli, and carrots
- 1 10-ounce container refrigerated light Alfredo sauce
- 1 8-ounce package shredded cheddar cheese
- 1 4-ounce package shredded Parmesan cheese
- 1 2-ounce package chopped walnuts

Pantry list:
Milk

Vegetable **Fried Rice**

Start to Finish: **20 minutes**

- 1 **teaspoon toasted sesame oil or cooking oil**
- 2 **eggs, lightly beaten**
- ⅓ **cup rice vinegar**
- ¼ **cup soy sauce**
- ⅛ **teaspoon ground ginger**
- ⅛ **teaspoon crushed red pepper**
- 1 **cup sliced fresh mushrooms**
- 1 **teaspoon bottled minced garlic**
- 1 **tablespoon cooking oil**
- 2 **8.8-ounce pouches cooked long-grain rice**
- ½ **cup loose-pack frozen peas**
- 1 **2-ounce jar diced pimientos, drained**
- ¼ **cup chopped peanuts (optional)**

1 In a large skillet heat sesame oil over medium heat. Add half of the egg, lifting and tilting the skillet to form a thin layer (egg may not completely cover the bottom of the skillet). Cook about 1 minute or until set. Invert skillet over a baking sheet to remove cooked egg; cut into strips and set aside. Repeat with remaining egg.

2 In a small bowl stir together vinegar, soy sauce, ginger, and crushed red pepper; set aside.

3 In the same skillet cook mushrooms and garlic in hot oil over medium-high heat about 3 minutes or until mushrooms are tender. Stir in vinegar mixture. Stir in rice, peas, and pimientos. Cook and stir about 2 minutes or until heated through and liquid is nearly evaporated. Stir in egg strips. If desired, sprinkle servings with chopped peanuts.

Makes 4 servings

Nutrition facts per serving: 314 cal., 10 g total fat (1 g sat. fat), 106 mg chol., 999 mg sodium, 45 g carbo., 3 g dietary fiber, 10 g protein.

Shopping list:
- 1 8-ounce bottle toasted sesame oil
- 1 10-ounce bottle rice vinegar
- 1 5-ounce bottle soy sauce
- 1 small container ground ginger
- 1 8-ounce package sliced fresh mushrooms
- 1 8.8-ounce pouches cooked long-grain rice
- 1 10-ounce package frozen peas
- 1 2-ounce jar diced pimientos

Pantry list:
Eggs

Crushed red pepper

Cooking oil

Bottled minced garlic

Indian Lentils and Rice

Start to Finish: **20 minutes**

- 1 **medium onion, chopped (½ cup)**
- 2 **teaspoons garam masala**
- 1 **tablespoon cooking oil**
- 2 **cups bite-size cauliflower florets**
- 1 **medium carrot, bias-sliced**
- 1 **cup water**
- 1 **17.3-ounce package refrigerated steamed lentils or one 15-ounce can lentils, rinsed and drained***
- 1 **8.8-ounce pouch cooked long-grain rice**
- 1 **cup frozen peas**
- ⅓ **cup golden raisins**
  Salt and ground black pepper

1 In a very large skillet cook onion and garam masala in hot oil over medium heat for 5 minutes or until onion is tender. Add cauliflower, carrot, and water. Bring to boiling; reduce heat. Simmer, covered, for 5 minutes or until tender.

2 Stir in lentils, rice, peas, and raisins. Cook and stir until heated through and water is absorbed. Season to taste with salt and pepper.

Makes 4 to 6 servings

Nutrition facts per serving: 373 cal., 6 g total fat (0 g sat. fat), 0 mg chol., 510 mg sodium, 65 g carbo., 14 g dietary fiber, 17 g protein.

*Note: If refrigerated steamed lentils are not available, in a large saucepan combine 8 ounces lentils and 2 ½ cups water. Bring to boiling; reduce heat. Simmer, covered, 30 minutes or until tender.

Shopping list:
- 1 medium onion
- 1 small container garam masala
- 1 head cauliflower
- 1 package carrots
- 1 17.3-ounce package refrigerated steamed lentils
- 1 8.8-oz. pouch cooked long-grain rice
- 1 9- to 10-ounce package frozen peas
- 1 15-ounce package golden raisins

Pantry list:
- Cooking oil
- Salt
- Ground black pepper

Italian Vegetable Pesto Pizza

Start to Finish: **20 minutes**   Oven: **450°F**

1 **12-inch Italian bread shell (Boboli)**

⅓ **cup refrigerated basil pesto**

2 **medium roma tomatoes, thinly sliced**

½ **cup chopped yellow sweet pepper**

¼ **cup pitted kalamata olives, halved**

1 **cup shredded Italian blend cheeses**

Preheat oven to 450°F. Place bread shell on a baking sheet. Spread bread shell with pesto. Top with tomatoes, sweet pepper, olives, and cheese. Bake for 10 to 12 minutes or until cheese melts.

Makes 4 servings

Nutrition facts per serving: 566 cal., 28 g total fat (4 g sat. fat), 32 mg chol., 1,072 mg sodium, 59 g carbo., 1 g dietary fiber, 25 g protein.

20 minutes

Shopping list:

1 12-inch Italian bread shell (Boboli)

1 7-ounce carton refrigerated basil pesto

2 medium roma tomatoes

1 medium yellow sweet pepper

1 6-ounce jar pitted kalamata olives

1 8-ounce package shredded Italian blend cheeses

Mexican Vegetable **Sandwich**

Start to Finish: **20 minutes**

⅓ **cup mayonnaise**

2 **to 3 teaspoons finely chopped chipotle peppers in adobo sauce***

2 **teaspoons lime juice**

4 **French rolls, split and toasted, if desired**

2 **4-ounce cans whole green chiles, drained**

1 **medium avocado, halved, seeded, peeled, and sliced**

1 **medium tomato, sliced**

¼ **cup thinly sliced red onion**

4 **slices Monterey Jack cheese**

1 In a small bowl combine mayonnaise, chipotle, and lime juice.

2 Spread both sides of each roll with mayonnaise mixture. Split whole chiles so they lay flat. Top bottom half of each roll with green chiles, avocado, tomato, red onion, and Monterey Jack cheese. Add top halves of rolls.

Makes 4 servings

Nutrition facts per serving: 420 cal., 30 g total fat (9 g sat. fat), 32 mg chol., 722 mg sodium, 27 g carbo., 5 g dietary fiber, 12 g protein.

*Note: Because hot chile peppers, such as chipotles, contain volatile oils that can burn your skin and eyes, avoid direct contact with chiles as much as possible. When working with chile peppers, wear plastic or rubber gloves. If your bare hands do touch chile peppers, wash your hands well with soap and water.

Shopping list:

1 7-ounce can chipotle peppers in adobo sauce

1 lime

1 package French rolls

2 4-ounce cans whole green chiles

1 medium avocado

1 medium tomato

1 red onion

1 6-ounce package sliced Monterey Jack cheese

Pantry list:

Mayonnaise

20 minutes

Veggie-and-Cheese-Filled **Focaccia**

Start to Finish: **20 minutes**

⅓ **cup mayonnaise or salad dressing**

2 **tablespoons honey mustard**

1 **8- to 10-inch tomato or onion focaccia bread, halved horizontally**

1 **cup lightly packed fresh spinach leaves**

6 **ounces dilled Havarti cheese, very thinly sliced**

1 **16-ounce jar pickled mixed vegetables, drained and chopped**

In a small bowl stir together mayonnaise and honey mustard. Spread mayonnaise mixture over bottom half of focaccia. Top with spinach leaves and half of the cheese. Spoon vegetables over; top with remaining cheese. Add bread top. Cut into quarters.

Makes 4 servings

Nutrition facts per serving: 364 cal., 32 g total fat (2 g sat. fat), 67 mg chol., 1,251 mg sodium, 10 g carbo., 0 g dietary fiber, 10 g protein.

20 minutes

Shopping list:

1 8-ounce jar mayonnaise

1 8-ounce bottle honey mustard

1 8- to 10-inch tomato focaccia bread

1 5-ounce package fresh spinach leaves

1 8-ounce package dilled Havarti cheese

1 16-ounce jar pickled mixed vegetables

Pantry list:

Mayonnaise

Apple-Brie Grilled Sandwiches

Start to Finish: **20 minutes**

- 1 **medium sweet onion, cut into thin wedges**
- 1 **tablespoon cooking oil**
- 2 **tablespoons apple jelly**
- 1 **5-ounce package soft-style spreadable Brie cheese***
- 8 **slices whole grain bread**
- 1 **medium Granny Smith apple, cored and thinly sliced**
- ¼ **cup butter, softened**

1 In a large skillet cook onions in hot oil over medium heat until very tender and beginning to brown. Transfer onions to a small bowl and stir in apple jelly. Snip onions into smaller pieces, if desired.

2 Spread Brie on half of the bread slices. Top with apple slices and onion mixture. Add remaining bread slices.

3 Spread top slices of bread with half of the butter. In a very large skillet over medium heat place sandwiches, butter side down. Carefully spread unbuttered bread with remaining butter. Cook for 4 to 6 minutes or until cheese melts and bread browns, turning once.

Makes 4 servings

Nutrition facts per serving: 484 cal., 28 g total fat (14 g sat. fat), 66 mg chol., 529 mg sodium, 44 g carbo., 9 g dietary fiber, 19 g protein.

*Note: If you can't find soft-style spreadable Brie, thinly slice regular Brie and place on the bread slice; carefully spread slices together.

Shopping list:
1 medium sweet onion

1 12-ounce jar apple jelly

1 5-ounce package soft-style spreadable Brie cheese

1 loaf whole grain bread

1 medium Granny Smith apple

Pantry list:
Cooking oil

Butter

Potato-Bar Cheese Soup

Start to Finish: **20 minutes**

1 ½ **cups bite-size broccoli florets**

2 **tablespoons water**

1 **24-ounce package refrigerated mashed potatoes**

3 **cups milk**

1 ½ **cups shredded cheddar cheese**

Dairy sour cream, sliced green onion, chopped tomato, and/or shredded cheddar cheese (optional)

1 In a 1-quart baking dish combine broccoli and water. Microwave, covered, on 100% power (high) for 5 to 8 minutes or until crisp-tender, rearranging or stirring once.

2 In a large saucepan stir together mashed potatoes and milk. Bring to simmering. Stir in 1 ½ cups cheese until melted. Stir in broccoli; heat through. If desired, top servings with sour cream, green onions, tomato, and/or additional cheddar cheese.

Makes 4 servings

Nutrition facts per serving: 408 cal., 20 g total fat (11 g sat. fat), 59 mg chol., 605 mg sodium, 34 g carbo., 2 g dietary fiber, 21 g protein.

20 minutes

Shopping list:

1 bunch broccoli

1 24-ounce package refrigerated mashed potatoes

1 8-ounce package shredded cheddar cheese

Pantry list:

Milk

30 minute meals

Panfried Italian **Chicken Parmesan**

Start to Finish: **25 minutes**

- 8 ounces dried linguine or fettuccini
- 1 egg
- 1 tablespoon cooking oil
- ½ teaspoon salt
- ¼ teaspoon coarsely ground black pepper
- ½ cup panko (Japanese-style bread crumbs)
- ¼ cup grated Parmesan cheese
- 1 teaspoon dried Italian seasoning, crushed
- 4 skinless, boneless chicken breast halves

  Salt and ground black pepper

  2 tablespoons cooking oil

  1 cup prepared marinara sauce

  Grated Parmesan cheese (optional)

1 Prepare pasta according to package directions; drain.

2 Meanwhile, in a shallow dish whisk together egg, 1 tablespoon oil, salt, and pepper; set aside. In another shallow dish combine panko, ¼ cup Parmesan cheese, and Italian seasoning. Sprinkle chicken lightly with salt and pepper. Dip each chicken breast half in the egg mixture and then in the bread crumb mixture to coat.

3 In large skillet cook chicken in 2 tablespoons hot oil over medium-high heat for 8 to 12 minutes or until no longer pink (170°F), turning once. (If chicken browns too quickly, reduce heat to medium.)

4 Meanwhile, place marinara sauce in microwave-safe dish. Heat on high for 1 minute or until hot. Spoon about ¼ cup sauce on each chicken breast. If desired, sprinkle with additional Parmesan cheese. Serve with hot cooked pasta.

Makes 4 servings

Nutrition facts per serving: 456 cal., 17 g total fat (4 g sat. fat), 175 mg chol., 807 mg sodium, 31 g carbo., 1 g dietary fiber, 42 g protein.

Shopping list:
- 1 16-ounce package dried linguine
- 1 8-ounce package panko (Japanese-style bread crumbs)
- 1 4-ounce package grated Parmesan cheese
- 4 skinless boneless chicken breast halves
- 1 14-ounce jar marinara sauce

Pantry list:
- Egg
- Cooking oil
- Salt
- Ground black pepper
- Dried Italian seasoning

30 minutes

Caramelized Onion and Cherry Chicken

Start to Finish: **30 minutes**

4 **skinless, boneless chicken breast halves**

Salt and ground black pepper

2 **tablespoons cooking oil**

1 **large onion, thinly sliced**

¼ **cup water**

2 **tablespoons packed brown sugar**

2 **tablespoons dried sweet cherries**

1 **14.8-ounce pouch cooked long-grain white rice**

Sliced green onions

1 Season the chicken with salt and pepper. In a large skillet cook chicken in hot oil for 4 minutes, turning once. Add onions to skillet. Cook and stir for 4 minutes more or until onions are tender, turning the chicken to brown evenly. Stir in the water, brown sugar, and cherries. Cook and stir for 4 minutes or until cherries are plump, cooking liquid is slightly thick and chicken is no longer pink (170°F).

2 Meanwhile, prepare rice according to package directions. Serve chicken and onion mixture with rice. Sprinkle with sliced green onions.

Makes 4 servings

Nutrition facts per serving: 446 cal., 11 g total fat (1 g sat. fat), 82 mg chol., 243 mg sodium, 47 g carbo., 2 g dietary fiber, 36 g protein.

Shopping list:
4 boneless, skinless chicken breast halves

1 large onion

1 3-ounce package sweetened dried cherries

1 14.8-ounce pouch cooked long-grain white rice

1 bunch green onions

Pantry list:
Salt

Ground black pepper

Cooking oil

Brown sugar

Panfried Chicken Breasts with Orange Sauce

Start to Finish: 30 minutes

- 4 **skinless, boneless chicken breast halves**
- 4 **tablespoons butter**
- ½ **teaspoon finely shredded orange peel**
- 3 **tablespoons orange juice**
- 2 **tablespoons golden raisins or raisins**
- 2 **teaspoons packed brown sugar**

  Hot cooked rice or pasta

1 In a large skillet cook chicken in 1 tablespoon of the butter over medium-high heat for 12 minutes or until chicken is no longer pink (170°F), turning once. (Reduce heat if necessary to keep chicken from overbrowning.) Transfer chicken to a serving platter; cover and keep warm.

2 Add remaining butter to the skillet. Stir in orange peel, orange juice, raisins and brown sugar. Cook and stir over medium heat about 2 minutes or until slightly thick. Add chicken to skillet to heat through. Serve with hot cooked rice or pasta.

Makes 4 servings

Nutrition facts per serving: 391 cal., 14 g total fat (8 g sat. fat), 113 mg chol., 478 mg sodium, 30 g carbo., 1 g dietary fiber, 35 g protein.

Shopping list:

4 skinless, boneless chicken breast halves

1 orange

1 11-ounce package golden raisins

Pantry list:

Butter

Brown sugar

Rice or pasta

Mediterranean **Pizza Skillet** *(See photo on page 134.)*

Start to Finish: **30 minutes**

3 **skinless, boneless chicken breast halves, cut into ¾-inch pieces**

2 **cloves garlic, minced**

2 **tablespoons olive oil**

4 **roma tomatoes, chopped**

1 **14-ounce can artichoke hearts, drained and quartered**

1 **2.25-ounce can sliced pitted ripe olives, drained**

½ **teaspoon dried Italian seasoning, crushed**

¼ **teaspoon freshly ground black pepper**

2 **cups romaine lettuce or hearty mesclun, chopped**

1 **cup crumbled feta cheese (4 ounces)**

⅓ **cup fresh basil leaves, shredded or torn**

Crusty Italian or French bread, sliced

In a large skillet cook and stir chicken and garlic in hot oil over medium-high heat until chicken is brown. Stir in tomatoes, artichokes, olives, seasoning, and pepper. Bring to boiling; reduce heat. Simmer, covered, for 10 minutes or until chicken is no longer pink (170°F). Top with lettuce and cheese. Cook, covered, for 1 to 2 minutes more or until lettuce starts to wilt. Sprinkle with basil. Serve on or with bread.

Makes 4 servings

Nutrition facts per serving: 395 cal., 17 g total fat (6 g sat. fat), 82 mg chol., 1,003 mg sodium, 27 g carbo., 6 g dietary fiber, 33 g protein.

Shopping list:

3 skinless, boneless chicken breast halves

4 roma tomatoes

1 14-ounce can artichoke hearts

1 2.25-ounce can sliced pitted ripe olives

1 head romaine lettuce

1 4-ounce package feta cheese

1 small package fresh basil leaves

1 loaf Italian bread

Pantry list:

Garlic

Olive oil

Dried Italian seasoning

Ground black pepper

30 minutes

Maple Chicken **Fettuccine**

Start to Finish: **30 minutes**

10 ounces dried
    fettuccine

 5 skinless, boneless
    chicken breast halves

    Salt and ground
    black pepper

 1 tablespoon olive oil

 1 16-ounce package
    frozen sweet pepper
    and onion stir-fry
    vegetables

¾ cup chicken broth

 1 tablespoon cornstarch

 1 teaspoon snipped
    fresh rosemary

⅛ teaspoon ground
    black pepper

¼ cup maple syrup

1 Cook pasta according to package directions. Drain; set aside and keep warm.

2 Meanwhile, season chicken with salt and black pepper. In a very large skillet cook chicken in hot oil over medium heat for 10 to 12 minutes or until no longer pink (170°F), turning once. Remove chicken from skillet; keep warm.

3 Increase heat to medium-high. Add vegetable blend to skillet; cook and stir for 6 to 8 minutes or until vegetables are crisp-tender.

4 In a small bowl stir together broth, cornstarch, rosemary, and ⅛ teaspoon black pepper. Add to skillet. Cook and stir until thick and bubbly. Cook and stir 1 minute more. Stir in maple syrup.

5 Arrange hot pasta on 5 dinner plates or shallow bowls. Top with chicken. Spoon peppers and sauce over chicken.

Makes 5 servings

Nutrition facts per serving: 466 cal., 6 g total fat (1 g sat. fat), 79 mg chol., 285 mg sodium, 60 g carbo., 2 g dietary fiber, 40 g protein.

Shopping list:

1 12-ounce package
   dried fettuccine

5 skinless, boneless chicken
   breast halves

1 16-ounce package frozen
   sweet pepper and onion
   stir-fry vegetables

1 14-ounce can chicken broth

1 package fresh rosemary

Pantry list:

Salt

Ground black pepper

Olive oil

Cornstarch

Maple syrup

30 minutes

Lemon Chicken Stir-Fry

Start to Finish: 25 minutes

1 **pound skinless, boneless chicken breast halves**

¾ **cup chicken broth**

3 **tablespoons lemon juice**

1 **tablespoon cornstarch**

1 **tablespoon soy sauce**

1 **16-ounce package frozen stir-fry vegetables (any blend)**

2 **tablespoons cooking oil**

2 **cups hot cooked rice**

Soy sauce (optional)

1 Cut chicken into bite-size strips, set aside. For sauce, in a small bowl stir together broth, lemon juice, cornstarch, and soy sauce; set aside.

2 In a large skillet cook frozen vegetables in 1 tablespoon of the hot oil over medium-high heat for 5 to 7 minutes or until crisp-tender. Remove from skillet. Add remaining 1 tablespoon oil and half of the chicken to the skillet. Cook and stir for 2 to 3 minutes or until chicken is no longer pink. Remove from skillet. Repeat with remaining chicken (add more oil, if necessary). Return all chicken to skillet. Push chicken from center of skillet.

3 Stir sauce; add to center of skillet. Cook and stir until thick and bubbly. Return vegetables to skillet; stir to coat with sauce. Cook and stir for 1 to 2 minutes more or until heated through. Serve with rice. If desired, pass additional soy sauce.

Makes 4 servings

Nutrition facts per serving: 348 cal., 9 g total fat (2 g sat. fat), 66 mg chol., 522 mg sodium, 32 g carbo., 3 g dietary fiber, 32 g protein.

Shopping list:

1 pound skinless, boneless chicken breast halves

1 14-ounce can chicken broth

1 lemon

1 16-ounce package frozen stir-fry vegetables (any blend)

Pantry list:

Cornstarch

Soy sauce

Cooking oil

Rice

Chicken with Creamy Mushrooms

(See photo on page 135.)

Start to Finish: **30 minutes**

- 1 **pound sliced fresh mushrooms, such as button or shiitake**
- 3 **tablespoons butter**
- 6 **Italian-marinated skinless, boneless chicken breast halves**
- 3 **tablespoons rice vinegar or white wine vinegar**
- 1 ½ **cups whipping cream**
- 3 **tablespoons capers, drained**
- ¼ **teaspoon freshly ground black pepper**

1 In a 12-inch skillet cook mushrooms in 1 tablespoon hot butter over medium-high heat about 5 minutes or until tender. Remove mushrooms from skillet.

2 Reduce heat to medium. Add remaining 2 tablespoons butter and chicken breast halves to skillet. Cook for 8 to 12 minutes or until no longer pink (170°F), turning once. Remove chicken from skillet and keep warm.

3 Remove skillet from heat; add vinegar, stirring to loosen browned bits on bottom of skillet. Return skillet to heat. Stir in cream, capers, and pepper. Bring to boiling; boil gently, uncovered, for 2 to 3 minutes or until sauce is slightly thick. Return mushrooms to skillet; heat through. Serve chicken with sauce.

Makes 6 servings

Nutrition facts per serving: 456 cal., 34 g total fat (19 g sat. fat), 183 mg chol., 967 mg sodium, 7 g carbo., 1 g dietary fiber, 33 g protein.

Shopping list:

2 8-ounce containers sliced fresh mushrooms

6 Italian-marinated skinless, boneless chicken breast halves

1 10-ounce bottle rice vinegar

1 8-ounce carton whipping cream

1 3.5-ounce jar capers

Pantry list:

Butter

Ground black pepper

Chicken-Pepper Kabobs

Start to Finish: 30 minutes

1   **pound skinless, boneless chicken breasts, cut into 1-inch pieces**

$2/3$ **cup bottled balsamic vinaigrette salad dressing**

1   **red sweet pepper**

1   **green sweet pepper**

8   **green onions, trimmed and cut into 2-inch pieces**

   Bottled balsamic vinaigrette salad dressing (optional)

1   Preheat broiler. Place chicken breasts in a shallow dish. Pour the $2/3$ cup dressing over chicken; stir to coat. Let marinate for 10 minutes.

2   Meanwhile, cut peppers into 1-inch pieces. Drain chicken, reserving marinade. Thread chicken, peppers, and onions on 8 metal skewers. Place on the unheated rack of a broiler pan.

3   Broil 5 to 6 inches from heat for 8 to 10 minutes or until chicken is no longer pink (170°F), brushing with reserved marinade during the first 5 minutes and turning occasionally to brown evenly. (Discard any remaining marinade.) If desired, serve with additional salad dressing.

Makes 4 to 6 servings

Nutrition facts per serving: 241 cal., 10 g total fat (2 g sat. fat), 66 mg chol., 574 mg sodium, 11 g carbo., 2 g dietary fiber, 27 g protein.

30 minutes

Shopping list:

1 pound skinless, boneless chicken breast halves

1 16-ounce bottle balsamic vinaigrette salad dressing

1 red sweet pepper

1 green sweet pepper

1 bunch green onions

Raspberry-Dijon Chicken Salad

Start to Finish: **30 minutes**

- ¼ **cup seedless raspberry preserves**
- 1 **tablespoon Dijon-style mustard**
- 1 **tablespoon bottled balsamic vinaigrette salad dressing**
- 4 **skinless, boneless chicken breast halves**
- ¼ **teaspoon salt**
- ⅛ **teaspoon ground black pepper**
- 8 **cups torn mixed salad greens**
- 1 **cup cherry tomatoes, halved**
- ¼ **cup chopped pecans, toasted**
- ⅓ **cup bottled balsamic vinaigrette salad dressing**

1 Preheat broiler. In a small bowl stir together preserves, mustard, and 1 tablespoon dressing; set aside. Season chicken with salt and pepper; place on the unheated rack of a broiler pan. Broil 4 to 5 inches from the heat for 3 minutes per side. Brush one side with preserves mixture. Broil 2 minutes more. Turn and brush with remaining mixture. Broil 2 minutes more or until no longer pink (170°F). Remove from oven; cover with foil and set aside.

2 In a very large bowl toss together greens, tomatoes, pecans, and ⅓ cup dressing. Divide among 4 serving plates. Slice chicken and place on greens.

Makes 4 servings

Nutrition facts per serving: 355 cal., 14 g total fat (2 g sat. fat), 82 mg chol., 606 mg sodium, 22 g carbo., 3 g dietary fiber, 35 g protein.

Shopping list:
- 1 12-ounce jar seedless raspberry preserves
- 1 16-ounce bottle balsamic vinaigrette salad dressing
- 4 skinless, boneless chicken breast halves
- 1 8-ounce package torn mixed salad greens
- 1 pint cherry tomatoes
- 1 4-ounce package chopped pecans

Pantry list:
Dijon-style mustard

Salt

Ground black pepper

30 minutes

20 min { **Southwestern Cobb Salad,** *page 16*

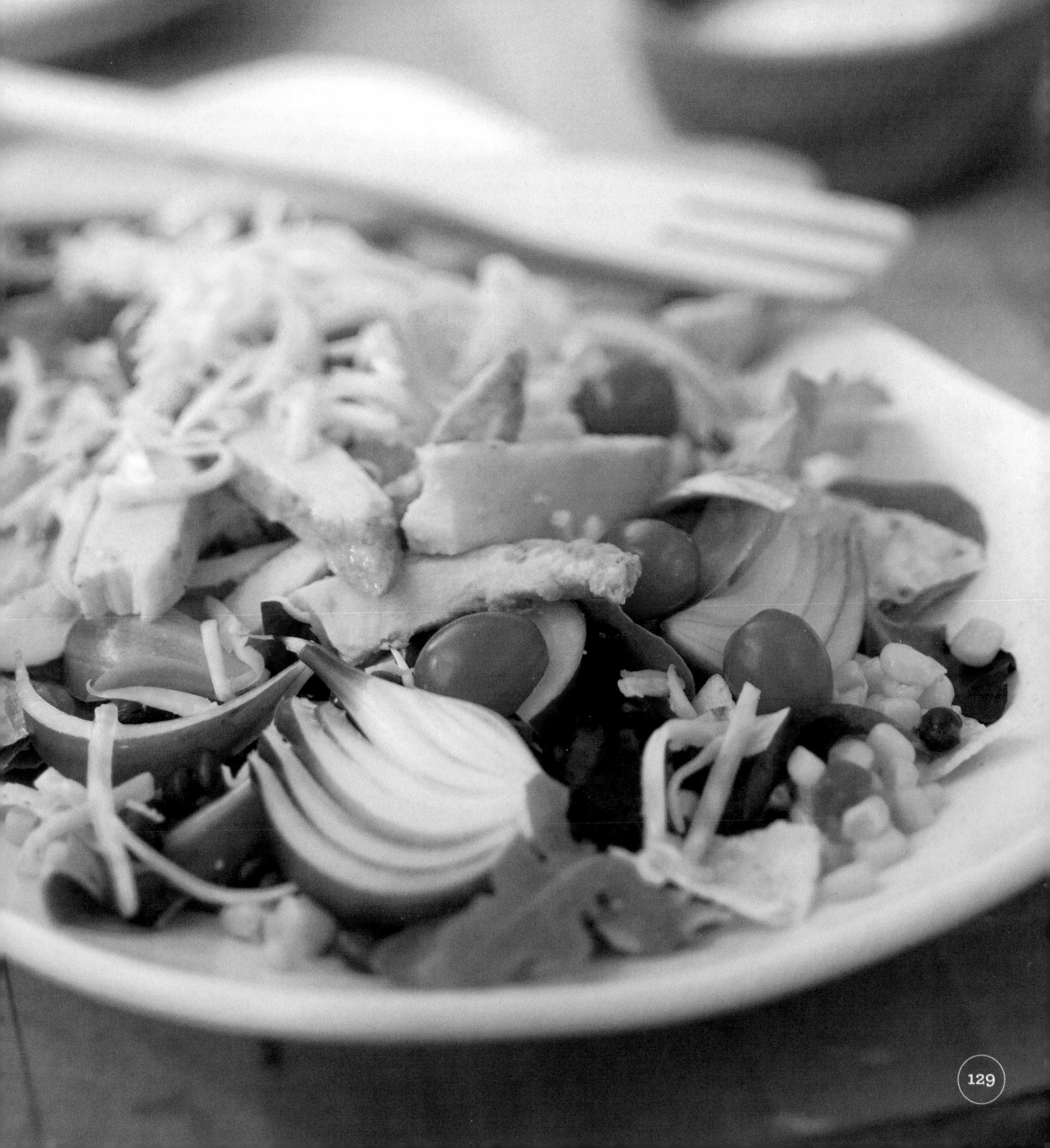

20 min { **Super Sub,** *page 73*

20 min { **Monster Meatball Sub,** *page 55*

20 min { **Thanksgiving Club Sandwich,** *page 39*

20 min { **Wasatch Mountain Chili,** *page 24*

20 min { **No-Bake Tuna and Noodles,** *page 92*

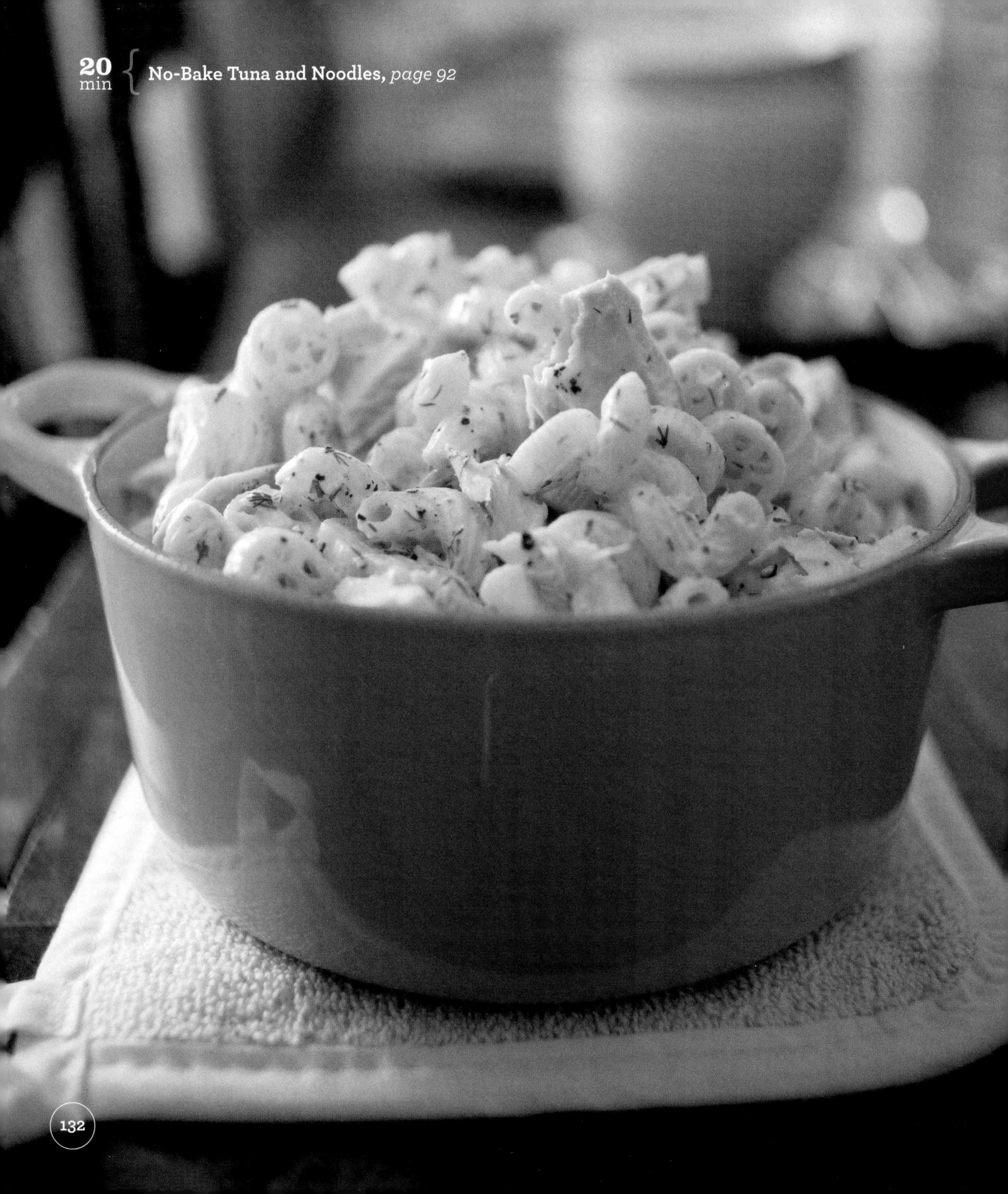

30 min { **Mediterranean Pizza Skillet,** *page 123*

20 min { **Polenta and Black Beans,** *page 105*

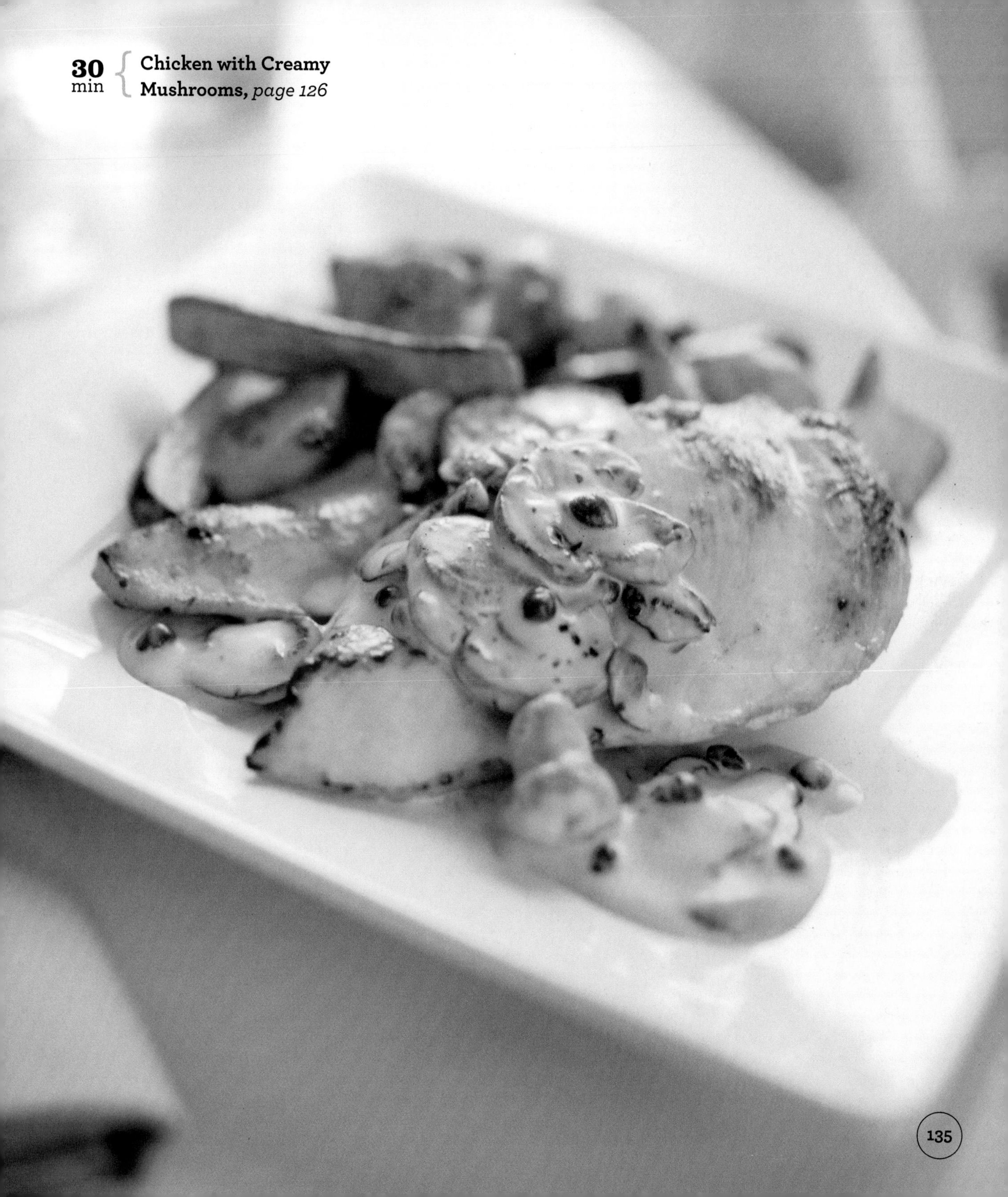

30 min **Chicken with Creamy Mushrooms,** *page 126*

30 min { **Chicken with Pretzels and Couscous,** *page 156*

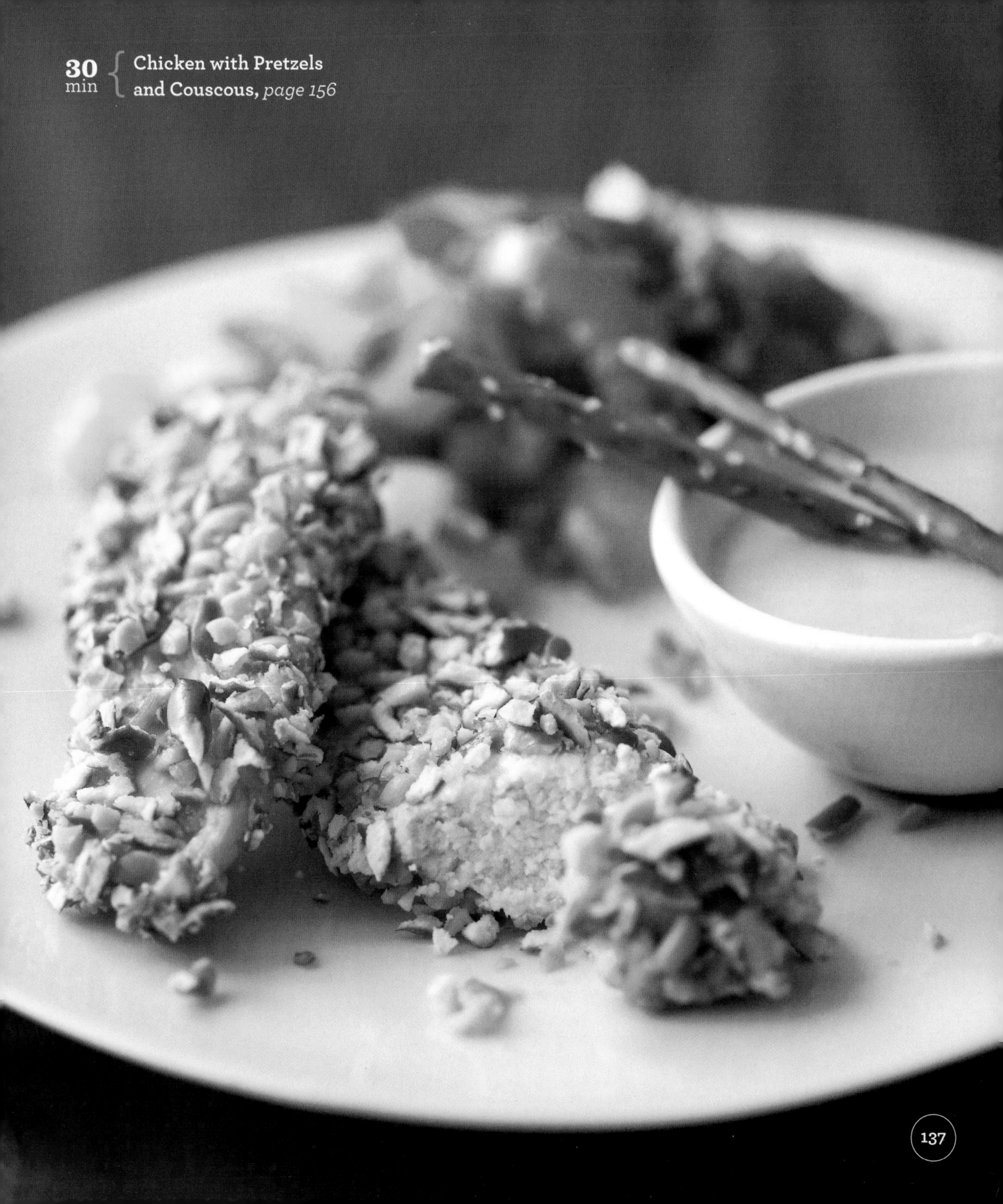

30 min { **Chicken in Phyllo Nest,** *page 152*

30 min { **Lickety-Split Lemon Chicken,** *page 154*

30 min { **Peruvian-Style Chicken Tacos,** *page 157*

30 min { **Southwest Pork Salsa Stew,** *page 191*

30 min { **Picadillo Sandwiches,** *page 197*

30 min } **Turkey Dinner Burgers,** *page 163*

30 min } Shrimp and Pea Pod Stuffed Peppers, *page 223*

30 min } **Shrimp Po' Boy,** *page 226*

Tropical Broiled Chicken

Start to Finish: 30 minutes

- 4 **skinless, boneless chicken breast halves**
- **Salt and ground black pepper**
- ⅓ **cup pineapple jam**
- 2 **tablespoons orange juice or water**
- 1 **tablespoon cooking oil**
- 1 **tablespoon snipped fresh cilantro**
- ¼ **teaspoon salt**
- ¼ **teaspoon ground black pepper**
- ½ **of a peeled, cored fresh pineapple, cut into 4 rings**

Preheat broiler. Place chicken breast halves on the unheated rack of a broiler pan. Sprinkle lightly with salt and pepper. Broil about 5 inches from the heat for 5 minutes. Meanwhile, in a small bowl combine jam, orange juice, oil, cilantro, ¼ teaspoon salt, and ¼ teaspoon pepper; brush over chicken. Turn chicken; add pineapple rings to pan. Broil 4 to 7 minutes more or until chicken is no longer pink (170°F), brushing chicken and pineapple with glaze the last 3 to 4 minutes of broiling. Spoon any remaining glaze over chicken breasts and serve.

Makes 4 servings

Nutrition facts per serving: 262 cal., 5 g total fat (1 g sat. fat), 66 mg chol., 374 mg sodium, 27 g carbo., 1 g dietary fiber, 27 g protein.

Shopping list:

4 skinless, boneless chicken breast halves

1 12-ounce jar pineapple jam

1 bunch cilantro

1 peeled, cored fresh pineapple

Pantry list:

Salt

Ground black pepper

Orange juice

Cooking oil

30 minutes

Italian Chicken Orzo Soup

Start to Finish: **25 minutes**

- **2 14-ounce cans reduced-sodium chicken broth**
- **1 pound skinless, boneless chicken breast halves or thighs, cubed**
- **1 14.5-ounce can diced tomatoes with basil, garlic, and oregano, undrained**
- **½ cup dried orzo**
- **1 cup chopped zucchini**
- **1 teaspoon finely shredded lemon peel**
- **1 tablespoon lemon juice**
- **Ground black pepper**
- **4 to 6 tablespoons purchased basil pesto**

1 In a large saucepan combine broth, chicken, undrained tomatoes, and orzo. Bring to boiling; reduce heat. Simmer, uncovered, for 6 minutes.

2 Add zucchini, lemon peel, and lemon juice. Return to boiling; reduce heat. Simmer, uncovered, for 3 to 4 minutes or until orzo and zucchini are tender and chicken is no longer pink. Season to taste with pepper. Ladle into bowls. Top with pesto.

Makes 4 to 6 servings

Nutrition facts per serving: 371 cal., 12 g total fat (0 g sat. fat), 68 mg chol., 1,180 mg sodium, 30 g carbo., 1 g dietary fiber, 35 g protein.

Shopping list:

2 14-ounce cans reduced-sodium chicken broth

1 pound skinless, boneless chicken breast halves

1 14.5-ounce can diced tomatoes with basil, garlic, and oregano

1 small zucchini

1 lemon

1 8-ounce container purchased basil pesto

Pantry list:

Dried orzo

Ground black pepper

Chicken-Hominy Chili

Start to Finish: **30 minutes**

1 **pound skinless, boneless chicken breast halves, cut into 1-inch pieces**

1 **tablespoon cooking oil**

2 **14-ounce cans reduced-sodium chicken broth**

2 **15- to 16-ounce cans navy beans, rinsed and drained**

1 **15.5-ounce can white hominy, rinsed and drained**

1 **4-ounce can diced green chile peppers**

1 **teaspoon ground cumin**

¼ **teaspoon ground black pepper**

4 **ounces Monterey Jack cheese with jalapeño peppers, shredded**

1 In a Dutch oven cook chicken, half at a time, in hot oil over medium heat until no longer pink (170°F). Return all chicken to the Dutch oven.

2 Stir in broth, navy beans, hominy, green chiles, cumin, and pepper. Bring to boiling; reduce heat. Simmer, covered, for 15 minutes.

3 Using a potato masher, gently mash the mixture to crush about half of the beans. Stir in cheese; heat just until cheese melts.

Makes 4 to 6 servings

Nutrition facts per serving: 601 cal., 15 g total fat (7 g sat. fat), 91 mg chol., 1,962 mg sodium, 62 g carbo., 14 g dietary fiber, 53 g protein.

Shopping list:

1 pound skinless, boneless chicken breast halves

2 14-ounce cans reduced-sodium chicken broth

2 15- to 16-ounce cans navy beans

1 15.5-ounce can white hominy

1 4-ounce can diced green chile peppers

1 8-ounce package shredded Monterery jack cheese with jalapeño peppers

Pantry list:

Cooking oil

Ground cumin

Ground black pepper

30 minutes

Spring Greens and **Roasted Chicken**

Start to Finish: **25 minutes**

1 purchased roasted chicken, chilled

1 5-ounce package mixed spring greens salad mix (about 8 cups)

2 cups fresh sliced strawberries or blueberries

4 ounces Gorgonzola or blue cheese, crumbled (1 cup)

½ cup honey-roasted cashews or peanuts

1 lemon, halved

3 tablespoons olive oil

¼ teaspoon salt

¼ teaspoon ground black pepper

1 Remove and discard skin from chicken. Pull meat from bones, discarding bones. Shred meat (you should have about 3 ½ cups).

2 Place greens on a platter. Top with chicken, strawberries, cheese, and nuts. Drizzle with juice from lemon and the oil; sprinkle with salt and pepper.

Makes 6 servings

Nutrition facts per serving: 426 cal., 31 g total fat (9 g sat. fat), 81 mg chol., 482 mg sodium, 12 g carbo., 2 g dietary fiber, 28 g protein.

Shopping list:

1 purchased roasted chicken

1 5-ounce package mixed spring greens salad mix

1 pint fresh strawberries

1 4-ounce package Gorgonzola cheese

1 6-ounce package honey roasted cashews

1 lemon

Pantry list:

Olive oil

Salt

Ground black pepper

30 minutes

Arroz con Pollo *(See photo on page 136.)*

Start to Finish: **25 minutes**

1 **purchased roasted chicken**

1 **14.5-ounce can diced tomatoes**

1 **4-ounce can diced green chiles**

1 **cup frozen peas**

⅓ **cup pitted green olives, sliced**

1 **8.8-ounce pouch cooked Spanish-style rice**

⅓ **cup shredded Monterey Jack cheese**

1 Remove chicken meat from bones, discarding skin and bones. Tear chicken into large pieces. Set aside 3 cups of the chicken; save remaining chicken for another use.

2 In a large skillet combine undrained tomatoes, undrained diced green chiles, peas, and olives. Bring to boiling. Stir in rice and 3 cups chicken; heat through. Top each serving with cheese.

Makes 4 servings

Nutrition facts per serving: 399 cal., 14 g total fat (4 g sat. fat), 102 mg chol., 939 mg sodium, 29 g carbo., 4 g dietary fiber, 37 g protein.

Shopping List:

1 purchased roasted chicken

1 14.5-ounce can diced tomatoes

1 4-ounce can diced green chiles

1 9-ounce package frozen peas

1 6-ounce can pitted green olives

1 8.8-ounce pouch cooked Spanish-style rice

1 8-ounce package shredded Monterey Jack cheese

Smoky Corn and **Chicken Noodle Soup**

Start to Finish: **30 minutes**

- 4 **14-ounce cans chicken broth**
- 1 **8-ounce package frozen egg noodles**
- 1 **cup frozen whole kernel corn, thawed**
- 1 **tablespoon olive oil**
- 2 **cups chopped cooked chicken**
- 1 **14.75-ounce can cream-style corn**

Ground black pepper

Shredded smoked Gouda or mozzarella cheese (optional)

1 In a Dutch oven bring chicken broth to boiling. Add noodles and cook, uncovered, for 20 minutes.

2 Meanwhile, pat whole kernel corn dry with paper towels. Line a 15x10x1-inch baking pan with foil. Spread corn in the baking pan and drizzle with olive oil; toss to coat. Broil 4 to 5 inches from the heat for 5 to 8 minutes or until light brown, stirring once; set aside.

3 Add whole kernel corn, chicken, and cream-style corn to Dutch oven. Heat through. Season to taste with pepper. Ladle into bowls. If desired, top with shredded cheese.

Makes 6 servings

Nutrition facts per serving: 307 cal., 8 g total fat (2 g sat. fat), 88 mg chol., 1,304 mg sodium, 40 g carbo., 2 g dietary fiber, 20 g protein.

Shopping list:

2 14-ounce cans chicken broth

1 8-ounce package frozen egg noodles

1 10-ounce package frozen whole kernel corn

2 cups chopped cooked chicken

1 14.75-ounce can cream-style corn

1 piece smoked Gouda cheese

Pantry list:

Olive oil

Ground black pepper

Thai Chicken in Lettuce Cups

Start to Finish: **25 minutes**

- 12 **ounces chicken breast tenderloins**
- ¼ **cup bottled Thai ginger salad dressing and marinade**
- ½ **cup thinly sliced red onion**
- 4 **Boston or Bibb lettuce cups**
- 3 **tablespoons coarsely chopped dry-roasted peanuts**

1 In a medium bowl combine chicken and marinade; toss to coat. Let stand at room temperature for 10 minutes.

2 Heat a large skillet over medium-high heat for 2 minutes; add undrained chicken mixture and onion. Cook and stir for 3 to 5 minutes or until chicken is no longer pink and onion is tender.

3 Divide chicken mixture among lettuce cups. Sprinkle with peanuts.

Makes 4 servings

Nutrition facts per serving: 156 cal., 5 g total fat (1 g sat. fat), 49 mg chol., 392 mg sodium, 6 g carbo., 0 g dietary fiber, 22 g protein.

Shopping list:

12 ounces chicken breast tenderloins

1 8-ounce bottle Thai ginger salad dressing

1 small red onion

1 head Boston lettuce

1 2.25-ounce package dry-roasted peanuts

30minutes

Chicken in Phyllo Nest *(See photo on page 138.)*

Start to Finish: 30 minutes   **Oven: 425°F**

Nonstick cooking spray

10 sheets frozen phyllo dough (14x9-inch rectangles), thawed

1 cup 2-inch pieces green onions (1 bunch)

2 tablespoons olive oil

12 ounces refrigerated grilled chicken breast strips

1 6-ounce package fresh baby spinach

¾ cup cherry tomatoes, halved or quartered (optional)

1 tablespoon snipped fresh tarragon

¼ teaspoon freshly ground black pepper

¼ cup bottled balsamic vinaigrette

1 Preheat oven to 425°F. Lightly coat a 15x10x1-inch baking pan with nonstick cooking spray; set aside. Roll the stack of phyllo sheets into a cylinder. With a sharp knife cut phyllo roll crosswise into ¼- to ½-inch slices. Place slices in the prepared baking pan. Gently separate into strips and spread into an even layer. Coat phyllo generously with additional nonstick cooking spray. Bake for 8 to 10 minutes or until phyllo is golden brown.

2 Meanwhile, in a 12-inch skillet cook green onions in oil over medium-high heat for 1 minute or until just tender. Add chicken; cook and stir until heated through. Remove skillet from heat. Add spinach, cherry tomatoes (if using), tarragon, and pepper. Toss to combine.

3 Divide phyllo among 6 serving bowls. Spoon spinach mixture over phyllo. Drizzle with balsamic vinaigrette. Serve immediately.

Makes 6 servings

Nutrition facts per serving: 197 cal., 10 g total fat (2 g sat. fat), 40 mg chol., 760 mg sodium, 14 g carbo., 1 g dietary fiber, 14 g protein.

Shopping list:
- 1 16-ounce package frozen phyllo dough
- 1 bunch green onions
- 1 12-ounce package refrigerated grilled chicken breast strips
- 1 6-ounce package fresh baby spinach leaves
- 1 pint cherry tomatoes
- 1 package fresh tarragon
- 1 8-ounce bottle balsamic vinaigrette

Pantry list:
Nonstick cooking spray

Olive oil

Ground black pepper

30 minutes

Caesar Salad **Pita Pizzas**

Start to Finish: **30 minutes** Oven: **400°F**

- 6 **pita bread rounds**
- 1 **10-ounce container refrigerated Alfredo pasta sauce**
- 1 **9-ounce package refrigerated cooked chicken breast strips**
- ¾ **cup finely shredded Parmesan cheese**
- 3 **cups packaged chopped hearts of romaine**
- ¼ **cup bottled Caesar salad dressing**

1 Preheat oven to 400°F. Line a very large baking sheet with foil; place pita rounds on baking sheet. Spread Alfredo sauce on pita rounds. Top with chicken breast strips; sprinkle with Parmesan cheese.

2 Bake for 12 to 15 minutes or until pitas are crisp and cheese softens.

3 In a medium bowl combine romaine and salad dressing. Top pizzas with salad mixture.

Makes 6 pizzas

Nutrition facts per pizza: 426 cal., 20 g total fat (9 g sat. fat), 62 mg chol., 1,321 mg sodium, 39 g carbo., 2 g dietary fiber, 21 g protein.

Shopping list:

- 6 pita bread rounds
- 1 10-ounce container refrigerated Alfredo pasta sauce
- 1 9-ounce package refrigerated cooked chicken breast strips
- 1 8-ounce package finely shredded Parmesan cheese
- 1 10-ounce package chopped hearts of romaine
- 1 8-ounce bottle Caesar salad dressing

Lickety-Split Lemon Chicken *(See photo on page 138.)*

Start to Finish: 30 minutes

- 12 **ounces chicken breast tenderloins**
- 2 **tablespoons butter**
- 1 **8-ounce package sliced mushrooms**
- 1 **medium red sweet pepper, cut into strips**
- 2 **tablespoons all-purpose flour**
- 1 **14-ounce can chicken broth**
- 1 **teaspoon finely shredded lemon peel**
- 2 **tablespoons lemon juice**
- 1 **teaspoon dried thyme, crushed**

   Salt and ground black pepper

- 1 **14.8-ounce pouch cooked long-grain white rice**

   Lemon wedges (optional)

1 In a very large skillet cook chicken in hot butter over medium heat for 6 to 8 minutes or until no longer pink (170°F). Add mushrooms and sweet pepper for the last 5 minutes of cooking time. Stir in flour. Cook and stir for 1 minute more. Add chicken broth, lemon peel, lemon juice, and thyme. Cook and stir until thick and bubbly. Cook and stir for 2 minutes more. Season to taste with salt and black pepper.

2 Meanwhile, prepare rice according to package directions. Serve chicken mixture over rice. If desired, serve with lemon wedges.

Makes 4 servings

Nutrition facts per serving: 361 cal., 10 g total fat (4 g sat. fat), 66 mg chol., 643 mg sodium, 41 g carbo., 2 g dietary fiber, 25 g protein.

Shopping List:

- 12 ounces chicken breast tenderloins
- 1 8-ounce package sliced mushrooms
- 1 medium red sweet pepper
- 1 14-ounce can chicken broth
- 1 lemon
- 1 14.8-ounce pouch cooked long-grain white rice

Pantry List:

Butter

All-purpose flour

Dried thyme

Salt

Ground black pepper

30 minutes

Coconut Chicken with Pineapple-Mango Salsa

Start to Finish: 30 minutes   Oven: **400°F**

- 1 **egg, lightly beaten**
- 1 **tablespoon cooking oil**
- ¼ **teaspoon salt**
- ⅛ **teaspoon cayenne pepper**
- 1 ¼ **cups flaked coconut**
- 14 **to 16 ounces chicken breast tenderloins**
- 1 **8-ounce can pineapple tidbits (juice pack), drained**
- 1 **cup chopped refrigerated mango slices (about 10 slices)**
- 2 **tablespoons snipped fresh cilantro (optional)**
- 1 **tablespoon lime juice**
- ¼ **teaspoon salt**

1 Preheat oven to 400°F. Line a large baking sheet with foil; lightly grease foil. Set aside. In a shallow dish whisk together egg, oil, salt, and cayenne pepper. Spread coconut in another shallow dish. Dip chicken, one piece at a time, in egg mixture, allowing excess to drip off. Coat chicken in coconut and arrange on prepared baking sheet. Bake for 10 to 12 minutes or until chicken is no longer pink (170°F).

2 Meanwhile, for salsa, in a medium bowl combine pineapple, mango, cilantro (if using), lime juice, and salt. Serve with chicken.

Makes 4 servings

Nutrition facts per serving: 401 cal., 18 g total fat (12 g sat. fat), 110 mg chol., 485 mg sodium, 33 g carbo., 3 g dietary fiber, 27 g protein.

Shopping list:
- 1 8-ounce package flaked coconut
- 14 to 16 ounces chicken breast tenderloins
- 1 8-ounce can pineapple tidbits
- 1 24-ounce jar refrigerated mango slices
- 1 lime

Pantry list:
- Egg
- Cooking oil
- Salt
- Cayenne pepper

Chicken with Pretzels and Couscous

(See photo on page 137.)

Start to Finish: 25 minutes   **Oven: 425°F**

1 **cup pretzel sticks**

²⁄₃ **cup unsalted peanuts**

¼ **to ½ teaspoon crushed red pepper (optional)**

½ **cup refrigerated or frozen egg product, thawed**

14 **to 16 ounces chicken breast tenderloins**

½ **cup reduced-sodium chicken broth**

1 **16-ounce package frozen sweet peppers and onion stir-fry vegetables**

½ **cup uncooked couscous**

2 **tablespoons seasoned rice vinegar**

1 **tablespoon cooking oil**

Honey-Mustard Dipping Sauce

1 Preheat oven to 425°F. Line a 15x10x1-inch pan with foil; coat foil with nonstick cooking spray; set pan aside. In a food processor* place pretzels, ½ cup of the peanuts, and, if desired, crushed red pepper. Cover; process until coarsely ground; transfer to resealable plastic bag.

2 Place egg product in shallow dish. Dip chicken tenderloins into egg product.; allow excess egg product to drip off. Transfer tenderloins, half at a time, to bag with crumb mixture. Seal bag; turn to coat chicken pieces. Arrange chicken in prepared pan. Bake for 10 to 15 minutes or until no longer pink (170°F).

3 Meanwhile, in a saucepan combine broth and stir-fry vegetables. Bring to boiling.

Stir in couscous; remove from heat. Cover; let stand for 5 minutes. Chop remaining peanuts. Stir peanuts, rice vinegar, and oil into couscous mixture. Serve couscous mixture with chicken and dipping sauce.

Makes 6 servings

Nutrition facts per serving: 336 cal., 12 g total fat (2 g sat. fat), 39 mg chol., 344 mg sodium, 31 g carbo., 4 g dietary fiber, 26 g protein.

*Test Kitchen Tip: If you do not have a food processor, place pretzels in a large resealable plastic bag; seal bag and finely crush pretzels using a rolling pin or meat mallet. Finely chop ½ cup of the peanuts and add to pretzel crumbs in bag.

Honey-Mustard Dipping Sauce: In a bowl combine ⅓ cup plain yogurt, 2 tablespoons yellow mustard, and 2 teaspoons honey.

30 minutes

Shopping list:

1 small bag pretzel sticks

1 2.25-ounce package unsalted peanuts

1 16-ounce carton refrigerated egg product

14 to 16 ounces chicken breast tenderloins

1 14-ounce can reduced-sodium chicken broth

1 16-ounce package frozen sweet pepper and onion stir-fry vegetables

1 12-ounce package couscous

1 10-ounce bottle seasoned rice vinegar

1 8-ounce carton plain yogurt

Pantry list:

Crushed red pepper

Cooking oil

Yellow mustard

Honey

Peruvian-Style **Chicken Tacos** *(See photo on page 138.)*

Start to Finish: **30 minutes**   Oven: **350°F**

1 **pound uncooked ground chicken**

½ **cup chopped onion (1 medium)**

2 **teaspoons ground coriander**

2 **teaspoons ground cumin**

1 **teaspoon salt**

1 **14.5-ounce can diced tomatoes, undrained**

1 **potato, peeled and finely chopped**

¼ **cup snipped pitted dried plums**

¼ **cup chopped pimiento-stuffed green olives**

12 **6- to 7-inch corn or flour tortillas**

4 **to 6 ounces Cotija or Monterey Jack cheese, shredded**

Chopped onion (optional)

Snipped fresh cilantro (optional)

1 Preheat oven to 350°F. In a large skillet cook chicken and onion until chicken is no longer pink (170°F), stirring to break up pieces. Drain off fat, if necessary. Add coriander, cumin, and salt; cook and stir for 1 to 2 minutes. Add undrained tomatoes, potato, plums, and olives. Bring to boiling; reduce heat. Simmer, covered, for 12 to 15 minutes or until potatoes are tender. Uncover; cook 5 minutes more or until most of the liquid has evaporated.

2 Wrap tortillas in foil; bake for 15 minutes or until heated. To assemble, place ⅓ cup chicken mixture in center of each tortilla; top with cheese. If desired, sprinkle with chopped onion and snipped cilantro. Fold tortillas in half.

Makes 12 tacos

Nutrition facts per taco: 194 cal., 10 g total fat (0 g sat. fat), 9 mg chol., 328 mg sodium, 18 g carbo., 3 g dietary fiber, 11 g protein.

Shopping list:

1 pound uncooked ground chicken

1 medium onion

1 small container ground coriander

1 14.5-ounce can diced tomatoes

1 medium potato

1 9-ounce package pitted dried plums

1 5-ounce jar pimiento-stuffed green olives

12 6- to 7-inch tortillas

4 to 6 ounces Cotija cheese

Pantry list:

Ground cumin

Salt

30 minutes

Easy Mexican **Chicken Chili**

Start to Finish: **30 minutes**

- 1 **pound uncooked ground chicken or turkey**
- 1 **tablespoon cooking oil**
- 1 **1.25-ounce package taco seasoning mix**
- 1 **14-ounce can chicken broth**
- 1 **cup purchased chunky salsa**
- 1 **15.25-ounce can whole kernel corn, drained**
- 1 **15-ounce can black beans, rinsed and drained**

Dairy sour cream (optional)

Shredded Monterey Jack and cheddar cheese (optional)

Corn chips (optional)

In a large saucepan cook chicken in hot oil until no longer pink (170°F), stirring occasionally to break apart. Add taco seasoning mix; cook and stir for 1 minute. Add chicken broth, salsa, corn, and beans. Heat to boiling; reduce heat. Simmer, covered, for 10 minutes. Spoon into bowls. If desired, top with sour cream, cheese, and/or corn chips.

Makes 4 servings

Nutrition facts per serving: 341 cal., 8 g total fat (1 g sat. fat), 80 mg chol., 2,082 mg sodium, 40 g carbo., 8 g dietary fiber, 33 g protein.

30 minutes

Shopping list:

1 pound uncooked ground chicken

1 1.25-ounce package taco seasoning mix

1 14-ounce can chicken broth

1 16-ounce jar chunky salsa

1 15.25-ounce can whole kernel corn

1 15-ounce can black beans

Pantry list:

Cooking oil

BBQ Chicken Burgers and Waffle Fries

(See photo on page 139.)

Start to Finish: 30 minutes   **Oven: 425°F**

⅓ cup bottled barbecue sauce

⅓ cup grape jelly or seedless raspberry jam

3 cups frozen waffle-cut or thick-cut french-fried potatoes

4 slices packaged ready-to-serve cooked bacon, chopped

2 tablespoons fine dry bread crumbs

2 tablespoons finely chopped honey-roasted walnuts or almonds

1 tablespoon bottled barbecue sauce

½ teaspoon poultry seasoning

¼ teaspoon salt

⅛ teaspoon ground black pepper

8 ounces uncooked ground chicken or turkey

½ cup shredded Italian-blend cheeses

Snipped fresh chives

8 dinner rolls or cocktail-sized hamburger buns, split

Sliced tomato and/or lettuce (optional)

1 Preheat oven to 425°F. Whisk together ⅓ cup barbecue sauce and jelly until smooth. Set aside.

2 On an ungreased baking sheet arrange potatoes in a single layer. Sprinkle with chopped bacon. Bake for 8 minutes.

3 Meanwhile, in a bowl combine bread crumbs, nuts, 1 tablespoon barbecue sauce, poultry seasoning, salt, and pepper. Add ground chicken; mix well. Shape into 8 balls; place 2 inches apart on a greased shallow baking pan. Moisten the bottom of a glass and press each ball to about ¼-inch thickness.

4 Bake fries and burgers for 5 minutes. Stir fries; turn burgers. Bake burgers and potatoes for 5 minutes more. Sprinkle cheese over fries. Brush barbecue-jelly mixture over burgers. Bake burgers and potatoes 2 minutes more or until burgers are no longer pink in center (165 °F) and cheese melts.

5 To serve, sprinkle fries with snipped chives. Place burgers in rolls; spoon remaining barbecue-jelly mixture over burgers. If desired, top with tomato slices and/or lettuce.

Makes 4 servings

Nutrition facts per serving: 537 cal., 21 g total fat (7 g sat. fat), 20 mg chol., 902 mg sodium, 66 g carbo., 4 g dietary fiber, 22 g protein.

Shopping list:

1 10-ounce jar grape jelly

1 32-ounce package frozen waffle-cut french-fried potatoes

1 2.1-ounce package ready-to-serve cooked bacon

1 small package honey-roasted walnuts

1 small container poultry seasoning

8 ounces uncooked ground chicken

1 8-ounce package shredded Italian-blend cheese

1 bunch fresh chives

8 dinner rolls

Pantry list:

Barbecue sauce

Fine dry bread crumbs

Salt

Ground black pepper

30 minutes

Creamy Turkey and Orzo

Start to Finish: **25 minutes**

²/₃ **cup dried orzo**

12 **ounces turkey breast tenderloin, cut into bite-size strips**

8 **ounces sliced fresh mushrooms**

¼ **cup sliced green onions (2)**

2 **tablespoons olive oil or cooking oil**

1 ½ **cups milk**

3 **tablespoons all-purpose flour**

½ **cup bottled blue cheese salad dressing**

1 **cup frozen peas**

Salt and ground black pepper

1 Cook orzo according to package directions; drain.

2 Meanwhile, in a large skillet cook and stir turkey, mushrooms, and green onions in hot oil over medium heat for 4 to 5 minutes or until turkey is no longer pink (170°F).

3 Combine milk, flour, and salad dressing; add all at once to skillet along with cooked orzo. Cook and stir until thickened and bubbly. Stir in peas. Cook and stir for 2 minutes more. Season to taste with salt and pepper.

Makes 4 servings

Nutrition facts per serving: 520 cal., 26 g total fat (5 g sat. fat), 65 mg chol., 515 mg sodium, 39 g carbo., 3 g dietary fiber, 33 g protein.

30 minutes

Shopping list:

12 ounces turkey breast tenderloin

1 8-ounce package sliced fresh mushrooms

1 bunch green onions

1 8-ounce bottle blue cheese salad dressing

1 10-ounce package frozen peas

Pantry list:

Dried orzo

Olive oil

Milk

All-purpose flour

Salt

Ground black pepper

Teriyaki-Glazed Turkey Tenderloin Steaks

Start to Finish: 30 minutes

- 2 **turkey breast tenderloins (1 to 1 ¼ pounds total)**
- 1 **tablespoon cooking oil**
- 1 **12-ounce package frozen broccoli, carrots, sugar snap peas, and water chestnuts in microwavable steaming bag**
- ½ **cup bottled stir-fry sauce**
- 1 **14.8-ounce pouch cooked long-grain white rice**
- ¼ **cup chopped dry roasted peanuts**

1 Split each turkey tenderloin in half horizontally to make four ½-inch-thick steaks. In a very large skillet cook turkey in hot oil over medium-high heat for 14 to 16 minutes or until no longer pink (170°F), turning once halfway through cooking. Reduce heat to medium if turkey gets too brown. Remove turkey from skillet; keep warm.

2 Meanwhile, prepare vegetables according to package directions. Transfer vegetables to the skillet used to cook the turkey. Add stir-fry sauce; heat through.

3 Heat rice according to package directions. Serve turkey and vegetable mixture over rice. Sprinkle with peanuts.

Makes 4 servings

Nutrition facts per serving: 447 cal., 11 g total fat (1 g sat. fat), 70 mg chol., 1,127 mg sodium, 48 g carbo., 4 g dietary fiber, 35 g protein.

Shopping list:
- 2 turkey breast tenderloins (1 to 1 ¼ pounds total)
- 1 12-ounce package frozen broccoli, carrots, sugar snap peas and water chestnuts in microwavable steaming bag
- 1 9 ½-ounce bottle stir-fry sauce
- 1 14.8-ounce pouch cooked long-grain rice
- 1 8-ounce jar dry roasted peanuts

Pantry list:
Cooking oil

Turkey Cranberry Fried Rice

Start to Finish: 25 minutes

1 pound uncooked ground turkey

1 stalk celery, chopped (½ cup)

1 medium onion, chopped (½ cup)

1 8.8-ounce package cooked long-grain and wild rice

½ cup apple cider

⅓ cup dried cranberries

½ teaspoon dried thyme, crushed

⅓ cup chopped pecans, toasted

Salt and ground black pepper

1 In a very large skillet cook and stir turkey, celery, and onion over medium heat until turkey is no longer pink (170°F) and vegetables are tender.

2 Meanwhile, prepare long-grain and wild rice according to package directions.

3 Stir rice, cider, cranberries, and thyme into turkey mixture in skillet. Cook and stir until liquid is absorbed. Stir in pecans. Season to taste with salt and pepper.

Makes 4 servings

Nutrition facts per serving: 385 cal., 18 g total fat (3 g sat. fat), 90 mg chol., 395 mg sodium, 34 g carbo., 2 g dietary fiber, 23 g protein.

Shopping list:

1 pound uncooked ground turkey

1 bunch celery

1 medium onion

1 8.8-ounce package cooked long-grain and wild rice

1 small bottle apple cider

1 3-ounce package dried cranberries

1 2.25-ounce package chopped pecans

Pantry list:

Dried thyme

Salt

Ground black pepper

30 minutes

Turkey Dinner **Burgers** *(See photo on page 144.)*

Start to Finish: **30 minutes**

- 1 **egg, lightly beaten**
- ½ **teaspoon salt**
- ¼ **teaspoon ground black pepper**
- 1 **pound uncooked ground turkey or ground chicken**
- ¼ **cup fine dry bread crumbs**
- ¼ **cup jalapeño pepper jelly, melted**

   Shredded red cabbage, thinly sliced red onion, and/or other desired toppings

- 4 **ciabatta rolls, potato rolls, kaiser rolls, or hamburger buns, split and toasted**

1 Preheat boiler. In a large bowl combine egg, salt, and pepper. Add turkey and bread crumbs; mix well. Shape mixture into four ¾-inch-thick patties.

2 Place patties on the unheated rack of a broiler pan. Broil 4 to 5 inches from the heat for 12 to 14 minutes (165°F), turning once halfway through cooking time. Brush patties with half of the jalapeño jelly. Broil 1 minute; turn and brush with remaining jelly. Broil 1 minute more.

3 To assemble, place cabbage, red onion, and/or other desired toppings on bottom of rolls. Top with patties and roll tops.

Makes 4 servings

Nutrition facts per serving: 354 cal., 12 g total fat (3 g sat. fat), 142 mg chol., 789 mg sodium, 37 g carbo., 2 g dietary fiber, 27 g protein.

Shopping list:

1 pound uncooked
   ground turkey

1 10-ounce jar jalapeño jelly

1 small head cabbage

1 small red onion

4 ciabatta rolls

Pantry list:

Egg

Salt

Ground black pepper

Fine dry bread crumbs

Turkey-Eggplant **Stacks**

Start to Finish: 25 minutes

1 ¼ **cups purchased tomato basil pasta sauce**

⅓ **cup seasoned fine dry bread crumbs**

1 **pound uncooked ground turkey**

¼ **teaspoon salt**

¼ **teaspoon ground black pepper**

4 ½- **to ¾-inch-thick center-cut eggplant slices**

2 **tablespoons olive oil or cooking oil**

¼ **cup finely shredded Parmesan cheese**

1 In a large mixing bowl combine ¼ cup pasta sauce, 2 tablespoons bread crumbs, turkey, salt, and pepper. Shape into four ¾-inch-thick patties. Brush eggplant slices with a small amount of pasta sauce and coat with remaining bread crumbs.

2 In a very large skillet heat oil over medium-high heat. Add burgers and eggplant slices. Reduce heat to medium. Cook, uncovered, for 12 to 14 minutes or until patties are no longer pink (165°F), turning burgers and eggplant once.

3 Meanwhile, in a small saucepan heat remaining pasta sauce. Place burgers on eggplant slices. Top with sauce; sprinkle with Parmesan cheese.

Makes 4 servings

Nutrition facts per serving: 326 cal., 19 g total fat (4 g sat. fat), 93 mg chol., 827 mg sodium, 15 g carbo., 3 g dietary fiber, 25 g protein.

Shopping list:

1 16-ounce jar tomato basil pasta sauce

1 8-ounce package fine dry bread crumbs

1 pound uncooked ground turkey

1 eggplant

1 8-ounce package finely shredded Parmesan cheese

Pantry list:

Salt

Ground black pepper

Olive oil

Turkey Pot Pies

Start to Finish: 30 minutes　　　**Oven: 425°F**

½ **of a 15-ounce package rolled refrigerated unbaked piecrust (1 crust)**

1 **2.75-ounce envelope country gravy mix**

2 **6-ounce packages refrigerated cooked turkey breast strips**

1 **10-ounce package frozen mixed vegetables**

1 **cup milk**

2 **teaspoons onion powder**

1 Preheat oven to 425°F. Let piecrust stand at room temperature while preparing filling. In a medium saucepan prepare gravy mix according to package directions. Stir in turkey, vegetables, milk, and onion powder. Cook and stir until heated through. Spoon mixture into six 10-ounce ramekins or individual baking dishes; set aside.

2 Meanwhile, unroll piecrust. Using a pizza cutter, cut piecrust into 12 wedges. Place two wedges over turkey mixture in each ramekin. Place ramekins in a shallow baking pan. Bake for 15 minutes or until crust is golden.

Makes 6 servings

Nutrition facts per serving: 333 cal., 14 g total fat (6 g sat. fat), 33 mg chol., 975 mg sodium, 34 g carbo., 3 g dietary fiber, 17 g protein.

Shopping list:

1　15-ounce package refrigerated piecrusts

1　2.75-ounce package country gravy mix

2　6-ounce packages refrigerated cooked turkey breast strips

1　10-ounce package frozen mixed vegetables

1　small container onion powder

Pantry list:

Milk

30 minutes

Turkey Panini with Basil Aioli

Start to Finish: **30 minutes**

- **2 tablespoons mayonnaise or salad dressing**
- **1 tablespoon purchased basil pesto**
- **4 ciabatta rolls, split, or 8 slices sourdough bread**
- **8 ounces thinly sliced cooked turkey breast**
- **1 3.5-ounce package thinly sliced pepperoni**
- **½ cup bottled roasted red sweet peppers, sliced**
- **4 slices provolone cheese (about 4 ounces)**
- **1 to 2 tablespoons olive oil**

1 Preheat an electric sandwich press, covered indoor grill, grill pan, or skillet. In a small bowl combine mayonnaise and pesto. Spread pesto mixture on the cut sides of the rolls. Divide turkey, pepperoni, sweet peppers, and cheese among roll bottoms. Add roll tops. Lightly brush tops and bottoms of sandwiches with olive oil.

2 Place sandwiches (half at a time, if necessary) in the sandwich press or indoor grill; cook, covered, for 7 to 9 minutes or until bread is toasted and cheese melts. (If using a grill pan or skillet, place sandwiches on grill pan. Weight sandwiches with a heavy skillet and grill about 2 minutes or until bread is lightly toasted. Turn sandwiches over, weight, and grill about 2 minutes or until second side is lightly toasted.)

Makes 4 sandwiches

Nutrition facts per sandwich: 506 cal., 30 g total fat (11 g sat. fat), 80 mg chol., 1,534 mg sodium, 30 g carbo., 2 g dietary fiber, 29 g protein.

Shopping list:
- 1 10-ounce jar basil pesto
- 1 package ciabatta rolls
- 8 ounces thinly sliced cooked turkey breast
- 1 3.5-ounce package thinly sliced pepperoni
- 1 12-ounce jar roasted red sweet peppers
- 1 6-ounce package sliced provolone cheese

Pantry list:
Mayonnaise

Olive oil

Turkey-Apple Salad Wraps

Start to Finish: **30 minutes**

- **12 ounces cooked turkey breast, shredded**
- **1 cup chopped green apple**
- **½ cup chopped celery**
- **½ cup chopped walnuts, toasted**
- **½ cup sliced green onions**
- **½ cup snipped fresh Italian (flat-leaf) parsley**
- **¼ cup dried tart cherries**
- **½ cup light dairy sour cream**
- **2 tablespoons lemon juice**
- **½ to 1 teaspoon bottled hot pepper sauce**
- **¼ teaspoon salt**
- **¼ teaspoon ground black pepper**
- **12 Bibb lettuce leaves**

1 In a large bowl combine turkey, apple, celery, walnuts, green onions, parsley, and cherries.

2 In a small bowl stir together sour cream, lemon juice, hot pepper sauce, salt, and pepper. Add sour cream mixture to turkey mixture; stir until well mixed.

3 Divide turkey mixture among lettuce leaves, spooning mixture into center of each leaf.* Fold bottom edge of each lettuce leaf up and over filling. Fold opposite sides in and over filling. Roll up from the bottom.

Makes 12 wraps

Nutrition facts per serving (3 wraps): 313 cal., 13 g total fat (3 g sat. fat), 81 mg chol., 205 mg sodium, 19 g carbo., 4 g dietary fiber, 31 g protein.

*Note: If you prefer, serve the turkey mixture over torn lettuce.

Shopping list:
12 ounces cooked turkey breast

1 large green apple

1 bunch celery

1 6-ounce package walnuts

1 bunch green onions

1 bunch fresh flat-leaf parsley

1 3-ounce package dried tart cherries

1 8-ounce carton light dairy sour cream

1 lemon

1 head Bibb lettuce

Pantry list:
Bottled hot pepper sauce

Salt

Ground black pepper

30 minutes

Turkey-Artichoke Toss

Start to Finish: **25 minutes**

1 12- to 14-ounce jar quartered marinated artichoke hearts

¼ cup bottled roasted garlic vinaigrette salad dressing or creamy Parmesan-basil salad dressing

1 tablespoon honey

1 5-ounce package baby spinach

10 ounces deli roasted turkey, cubed (2 ¼ cups)

1 cup cherry tomatoes, halved

½ cup packaged coarsely shredded fresh carrot

¼ cup sliced almonds, toasted

1 Drain artichokes, reserving ¼ cup of the marinade. For dressing, in a small bowl stir together reserved marinade, salad dressing, and honey; set aside.

2 In a large salad bowl combine artichokes, spinach, turkey, tomatoes, carrots, and almonds. Add dressing to spinach mixture; toss to mix. Serve at once.

Makes 4 servings

Nutrition facts per serving: 342 cal., 20 g total fat (2 g sat. fat), 54 mg chol., 459 mg sodium, 19 g carbo., 3 g dietary fiber, 25 g protein.

Shopping list:

1 12- to 14-ounce jar quartered marinated artichoke hearts

1 8-ounce bottle roasted garlic vinaigrette

1 5-ounce package baby spinach

10 ounces deli roasted turkey

1 pint cherry tomatoes

1 10-ounce package shredded carrot

1 2.25-ounce package sliced almonds

Pantry list:

Honey

Broccoli Beer **Cheese Soup**

Start to Finish: **30 minutes**

- **3** slices bacon, chopped
- **1** medium onion, chopped (½ cup)
- **2** tablespoons all-purpose flour
- **¼** teaspoon ground black pepper
- **2 ¾** cups chicken broth
- **2** cups bite-size broccoli florets
- **⅔** cup beer
- **12** ounces smoked turkey breast, chopped
- **6** ounces process Swiss cheese, torn
- **⅓** cup half-and-half or light cream

In a large saucepan cook bacon and onion until bacon is crisp and onion is tender, stirring occasionally. Stir in flour and pepper until well combined. Add broth, broccoli, and beer. Bring to boiling; reduce heat. Simmer, uncovered, for 3 to 5 minutes or until broccoli is nearly tender. Add turkey, cheese, and half-and-half. Cook and stir until cheese melts.

Makes 4 servings

Nutrition facts per serving: 386 cal., 22 g total fat (11 g sat. fat), 97 mg chol., 2,048 mg sodium, 13 g carbo., 2 g dietary fiber, 31 g protein.

Shopping list:
1 16-ounce package bacon

1 medium onion

1 14-ounce can chicken broth

1 head fresh broccoli

1 12-ounce can beer

12 ounces smoked turkey breast

6 ounces process Swiss cheese

1 8-ounce carton half-and-half

Pantry list:
All-purpose flour

Ground black pepper

30minutes

Steaks with Tomato Salsa

Start to Finish: 25 minutes

- ½ teaspoon salt
- ½ teaspoon ground cumin
- ½ teaspoon chili powder
- ½ teaspoon dried oregano, crushed
- ½ teaspoon packed brown sugar
- 2 8-ounce boneless beef ribeye steaks, cut ½ to ¾ inch thick
- ½ cup chopped onion (1 medium)
- 2 cloves garlic, minced
- 2 tablespoons olive oil
- 2 cups red and/or yellow cherry or pear tomatoes, halved
- 1 canned chipotle pepper in adobo sauce, drained and finely chopped
- 2 tablespoons lime juice
- ¼ cup snipped fresh cilantro

1 In a bowl stir together ¼ teaspoon salt, cumin, chili powder, oregano, and brown sugar. Rub into both sides of steaks. Lightly coat a grill pan with nonstick cooking spray. Heat pan over medium-high heat. Add steaks. Reduce heat to medium. Cook for 8 to 10 minutes or until desired doneness (145°F for medium rare or 160°F for medium), turning occasionally.

2 For salsa, in large skillet cook and stir onion and garlic in hot oil over medium heat until tender. Stir in tomatoes, chipotle, lime juice, and remaining ¼ teaspoon salt. Cook and stir for 1 minute. Transfer to a bowl; stir in cilantro. Cut each steak in half; serve with salsa.

Makes 4 servings

Nutrition facts per serving: 267 cal., 14 g total fat (4 g sat. fat), 54 mg chol., 451 mg sodium, 8 g carbo., 2 g dietary fiber, 26 g protein.

30 minutes

Shopping list:
- 2 8-ounce boneless beef ribeye steaks
- 1 medium onion
- 1 pint cherry tomatoes
- 1 7-ounce can chipotle peppers in adobo sauce
- 1 lime
- 1 bunch fresh cilantro

Pantry list:
Salt

Ground cumin

Chili powder

Dried oregano

Brown sugar

Garlic

Olive oil

Speedy Beef **Stir-Fry** *(See photo on page 140.)*

Start to Finish: 30 minutes

- 1 **8.8-ounce pouch cooked long grain rice**
- 1 **pound boneless beef top loin steak, trimmed of fat and cut into thin strips**
- 2 **tablespoons cooking oil**
- 1 **16-ounce package frozen broccoli stir-fry vegetable blend**
- ½ **cup orange juice**
- 1 **tablespoon soy sauce**
- 2 **teaspoons cornstarch**
- 1 **teaspoon ground ginger**
- ¼ **teaspoon crushed red pepper**
- ¼ **teaspoon salt**

  Toasted sliced almonds (optional)

1 Heat rice according to package directions; set aside.

2 In a large skillet cook beef strips in 1 tablespoon hot oil over medium-high heat until brown; remove from skillet. Add stir-fry vegetables and the remaining 1 tablespoon oil to skillet. Cook until tender. Drain any excess liquid.

3 In a small bowl combine orange juice, soy sauce, cornstarch, ginger, crushed red pepper, and salt.

4 Return meat to skillet. Add sauce mixture to skillet; cook and stir until thick and bubbly. Serve over rice. If desired, sprinkle with toasted almonds.

Makes 4 servings

Nutrition facts per serving: 377 cal., 14 g total fat (3 g sat. fat), 60 mg chol., 500 mg sodium, 31 g carbo., 3 g dietary fiber, 31 g protein.

Shopping List:

1 8.8-ounce pouch cooked long-grain rice

1 pound boneless beef top loin steak

1 16-ounce package frozen broccoli stir-fry vegetables

Pantry List:

Cooking oil

Orange juice

Soy sauce

Cornstarch

Ground ginger

Crushed red pepper

Salt

Pasta with Beef and Asparagus

Start to Finish: 30 minutes

- 8 **ounces boneless beef top sirloin steak**
- 1 **pound fresh asparagus**
- 8 **ounces dried bow tie pasta**
- 1 **8-ounce carton dairy sour cream**
- 2 **tablespoons all-purpose flour**
- $\frac{2}{3}$ **cup water**
- 1 **tablespoon honey**
- $\frac{1}{2}$ **teaspoon salt**
- $\frac{1}{4}$ **teaspoon ground black pepper**
- 2 **tablespoons finely chopped shallot**
- 1 **teaspoon cooking oil**
- 2 **teaspoons snipped fresh tarragon**

1 If desired, partially freeze beef before slicing. Cut off and discard woody bases from fresh asparagus. If desired, scrape off scales. Bias-slice asparagus into 1-inch pieces; set aside. Cook pasta according to package directions, adding asparagus for the last 3 minutes of cooking. Drain well; keep warm.

2 Meanwhile, trim fat from beef. Thinly slice meat across the grain into bite-size strips. In a medium bowl stir together sour cream and flour. Stir in the water, honey, salt, and pepper. Set aside.

3 In a large nonstick skillet cook and stir meat strips and shallot in hot oil over medium-high heat about 5 minutes or until brown. Drain off fat.

4 Stir sour cream mixture into meat mixture in skillet. Cook and stir until thick and bubbly. Cook and stir for 1 minute more. Stir in drained pasta, asparagus, and tarragon. Heat through.

Makes 4 servings

Nutrition facts per serving: 421 cal., 11 g total fat (4 g sat. fat), 107 mg chol., 373 mg sodium, 54 g carbo., 3 g dietary fiber, 26 g protein.

Shopping list:

8 ounces boneless beef top sirloin steak

1 pound fresh asparagus

1 16-ounce package dried bow tie pasta

1 8-ounce carton dairy sour cream

1 shallot

1 package fresh tarragon

Pantry list:

All-purpose flour

Honey

Salt

Ground black pepper

Cooking oil

Greek Beef and **Pasta Skillet**

Start to Finish: 30 minutes

- 8 ounces dried rotini
- 12 ounces boneless beef sirloin steak or top round steak
- 1 tablespoon cooking oil
- 1 26-ounce jar ripe olive and mushroom pasta sauce, ripe olive and green olive pasta sauce, or marinara pasta sauce
- ¼ teaspoon salt
- ¼ teaspoon ground cinnamon
- ½ of a 10-ounce package frozen chopped spinach, thawed and well drained
- ⅓ cup crumbled feta cheese

1 Cook pasta according to package directions; drain. Meanwhile, trim fat from beef. Thinly slice meat across the grain into bite-size strips.

2 In a large skillet cook and stir meat strips in hot oil for 2 to 3 minutes or until brown. Add pasta sauce, salt, and cinnamon. Cook and stir until sauce bubbles. Add cooked pasta and spinach. Cook and stir until heated through. Sprinkle with feta cheese.

Makes 4 servings

Nutrition facts per serving: 483 cal., 12 g total fat (3 g sat. fat), 63 mg chol., 1,063 mg sodium, 60 g carbo., 6 g dietary fiber, 32 g protein.

Shopping list:

1 16-ounce package dried rotini

12 ounces boneless beef sirloin steak

1 26-ounce jar ripe olive and mushroom pasta sauce

1 10-ounce package frozen chopped spinach

1 4-ounce container feta cheese

Pantry list:

Cooking oil

Salt

Ground cinnamon

30

minutes

Beef-Vegetable Pasta Toss

Start to Finish: 25 minutes

1　9-ounce package refrigerated fettuccine or linguine

12　ounces boneless beef sirloin steak

1　teaspoon dried Italian seasoning, crushed

1　tablespoon olive oil

1　medium onion, cut into thin wedges

2　teaspoons bottled minced garlic (4 cloves)

¼　teaspoon crushed red pepper

1　14.5-ounce can diced tomatoes with basil, garlic, and oregano, undrained

1　cup bottled roasted red sweet peppers, drained and coarsely chopped

1　tablespoon balsamic vinegar

2　cups fresh baby spinach leaves

¼　cup finely shredded Parmesan cheese (1 ounce)

1 Cook pasta according to package directions. Drain well. Return pasta to hot pan. Using kitchen shears, snip pasta in a few places to break up long pieces. Cover and keep warm. Meanwhile, trim fat from beef. Sprinkle meat evenly with Italian seasoning; rub in with your fingers. Thinly slice meat across the grain.

2 In a large skillet cook and stir beef in hot oil over medium-high heat for 3 to 4 minutes or until brown; remove from skillet using a slotted spoon. Add onion, garlic, and crushed red pepper to skillet. Cook about 5 minutes or until onion is tender, stirring occasionally.

3 Stir meat, undrained tomatoes, roasted sweet peppers, and balsamic vinegar into onion mixture in skillet. Heat through. Add meat mixture and spinach to hot pasta; toss to mix. Sprinkle with Parmesan cheese.

Makes 4 servings

Nutrition facts per serving: 413 cal., 10 g total fat (3 g sat. fat), 123 mg chol., 687 mg sodium, 50 g carbo., 3 g dietary fiber, 30 g protein.

Shopping list:

1 9-ounce package refrigerated fettuccine

12 ounces boneless beef sirloin steak

1 medium onion

1 14.5-ounce can diced tomatoes with basil, garlic, and oregano

1 7-ounce bottle roasted red sweet peppers

1 5-ounce package fresh baby spinach leaves

1 8-ounce package finely shredded Parmesan cheese

Pantry list:

Dried Italian seasoning

Olive oil

Bottled minced garlic

Crushed red pepper

Balsamic vinegar

30 minutes

Beef Stir-Fry Salad

Start to Finish: **25 minutes**

- 1   **9- to 10-ounce package chopped hearts of romaine**
- 12 **ounces beef top round steak (about ¾ inch thick)**
-    **Salt and ground black pepper**
- 1   **tablespoon cooking oil**
- 1   **medium red sweet pepper, cut into strips**
- ¾ **cup packaged coarsely shredded fresh carrots**
- ½ **cup chopped green onions**
- ½ **cup chopped dry roasted peanuts**
-    **Bottled sesame-ginger salad dressing**

1 Divide lettuce among 4 plates, set aside.

2 Thinly slice beef into bite-size strips. Season meat with salt and pepper. In a large skillet cook meat strips in hot oil over medium-high heat for 4 to 5 minutes or until brown. Add sweet pepper and carrots; cook and stir for 1 minute more. Remove skillet from heat; stir in green onions.

3 Spoon meat mixture over romaine on each plate. Sprinkle with peanuts. Drizzle with dressing. Serve immediately.

Makes 4 servings

Nutrition facts per serving: 393 cal., 25 g total fat (4 g sat. fat), 47 mg chol., 520 mg sodium, 17 g carbo., 4 g dietary fiber, 25 g protein.

Shopping list:

- 1 9- to 10-ounce package chopped hearts of romaine
- 12 ounces beef top round steak
- 1 medium red sweet pepper
- 1 10-ounce package coarsely shredded fresh carrots
- 1 bunch green onions
- 1 8-ounce jar dry roasted peanuts
- 1 16-ounce bottle sesame-ginger dressing

Pantry list:

Salt

Ground black pepper

Cooking oil

Beef and Polenta with **Red Onion Topper**

Start to Finish: **30 minutes**

1 **large red onion, cut into thin slivers**

2 **cloves garlic, minced**

2 **tablespoons olive oil**

1 **cup cherry tomatoes, halved**

½ **teaspoon dried basil or oregano, crushed**

Salt and ground black pepper

4 **beef tenderloin steaks or 2 top loin steaks, cut ¾ inch thick (about 1 pound total)**

Salt and ground black pepper

½ **of a 16-ounce tube refrigerated cooked polenta with wild mushrooms, cut into 4 slices**

¼ **cup finely shredded Parmesan cheese**

1 In a very large skillet cook and stir onion and garlic in hot oil over medium-high heat until onion is just tender. Add cherry tomatoes and basil; cook for 2 minutes more. Use a slotted spoon to remove from skillet to a bowl. Season to taste with salt and pepper. Cover and keep warm.

2 Meanwhile, sprinkle steaks with salt and pepper. If using top loin steaks, cut in half crosswise. Add steaks and polenta slices to skillet. Reduce heat to medium; cook until steak is desired doneness, turning once halfway through cooking time. For tenderloin steaks, allow 7 to 9 minutes for medium-rare (145°F) to medium doneness (160°F). For top loin steaks, allow 10 to 12 minutes for medium-rare to medium doneness.

3 Transfer steaks and polenta slices to 4 dinner plates. Spoon red onion mixture on top. Sprinkle with Parmesan cheese.

Makes 4 servings

Nutrition facts per serving: 403 cal., 20 g total fat (6 g sat. fat), 89 mg chol., 426 mg sodium, 14 g carbo., 2 g dietary fiber, 39 g protein.

Shopping list:

1 large red onion

1 pint cherry tomatoes

4 beef tenderloin steaks

1 16-ounce tube refrigerated cooked polenta with wild mushrooms

1 8-ounce package finely shredded Parmesan cheese

Pantry list:

Garlic

Olive oil

Dried basil

Salt

Ground black pepper

Southwestern Stroganoff

Start to Finish: **25 minutes**

- 1 **pound ground beef**
- 1 **small onion, cut into thin wedges**
- 1 **10-ounce can diced tomatoes and green chiles, undrained**
- 1 **15- to 16-ounce can pinto beans, rinsed and drained**
- ½ **cup dairy sour cream Southwestern ranch or Mexican-style dip**
- 1 **tablespoon all-purpose flour**
- 4 **purchased corn muffins,* split**

1 In a large skillet cook ground beef and onion until meat is brown and onion is tender; drain fat. Stir in undrained tomatoes and green chiles and pinto beans. Heat through.

2 In a small bowl whisk together dip and flour until smooth; add to mixture in skillet. Cook and stir until thickened and bubbly. Cook and stir 1 minute more. Spoon mixture over split corn muffins.

Makes 4 servings

Nutrition facts per serving: 640 cal., 35 g total fat (13 g sat. fat), 115 mg chol., 1,072 mg sodium, 50 g carbo., 7 g dietary fiber, 32 g protein.

*Note: If you can't find corn muffins at your bakery, lightly coat four 3-inch muffin cups with nonstick cooking spray. Prepare one 8.5-ounce package corn muffin mix according to package directions. Divide batter among prepared cups. Bake in a 400°F oven for 12 minutes or until golden.

Shopping list:

1 pound ground beef

1 small onion

1 10-ounce can diced tomatoes and green chiles

1 15- to 16-ounce can pinto beans

1 8-ounce container dairy sour cream Southwestern-style dip

4 corn muffins

Pantry list:

All-purpose flour

30minutes

Cheeseburger Pizza

Start to Finish: 30 minutes   Oven: **425°F**

8 ounces ground beef

1 medium onion, chopped (½ cup)

1½ cups shredded cheddar cheese (6 ounces)

2 tablespoons ketchup

1 tablespoon sweet pickle relish

1 tablespoon yellow mustard

1 12-inch thin-crust Italian bread shell (such as Boboli)

1 Preheat oven to 425°F. In a large skillet cook ground beef and onion until meat is brown and onion is tender; drain fat. Stir in ½ cup of the cheese, ketchup, pickle relish, and mustard. Cook and stir until cheese melts. Remove from heat.

2 Place Italian bread shell on a baking sheet. Spread meat mixture on bread shell. Sprinkle with remaining 1 cup cheese. Bake for 8 to 10 minutes or until heated through and cheese melts. Cut into 8 wedges.

Makes 4 servings

Nutrition facts per serving: 528 cal., 27 g total fat (14 g sat. fat), 83 mg chol., 870 mg sodium, 41 g carbo., 2 g dietary fiber, 29 g protein.

30 minutes

Shopping list:

8 ounces ground beef

1 medium onion

1 8-ounce package shredded cheddar cheese

1 8-ounce jar sweet pickle relish

1 12-inch thin-crust Italian bread shell

Pantry list:

Ketchup

Yellow mustard

Stovetop **Lasagna**

Start to Finish: **30 minutes**

1 **pound lean ground beef**

1 **large onion, chopped (1 cup)**

1 **clove garlic, minced**

3 **cups dried mini lasagna noodles or dried extra-wide noodles**

1 **24- to 26-ounce jar tomato and basil pasta sauce**

1 **cup water**

1 **cup low-fat cottage cheese or ricotta cheese**

1 **cup shredded Italian blend cheeses or mozzarella cheese**

¼ **cup grated Parmesan cheese**

1 **tablespoon snipped fresh parsley (optional)**

1 In very large skillet cook and stir ground beef, onion, and garlic over medium-high heat until meat is brown and onion is tender. Stir in noodles, pasta sauce, and the water. Bring to boiling; reduce heat. Cook, covered, for 15 minutes or until noodles are tender and liquid is absorbed.

2 Meanwhile, combine cottage cheese, Italian blend cheeses, Parmesan cheese, and, if desired, parsley. Drop by spoonfuls over meat mixture. Simmer, covered, for 5 minutes more or until cheese melts.

Makes 6 servings

Nutrition facts per serving: 532 cal., 19 g total fat (8 g sat. fat), 69 mg chol., 736 mg sodium, 54 g carbo., 4 g dietary fiber, 34 g protein.

Shopping list:

1 pound lean ground beef

1 medium onion

1 16-ounce package dried mini lasagna noodles

1 24- to 26-ounce jar tomato and basil pasta sauce

1 15-ounce carton low-fat cottage cheese

1 8-ounce package shredded Italian blend cheeses

1 8-ounce container grated Parmesan cheese

Pantry list:

Garlic

30 minutes

Tapenade Beef Burgers

Start to Finish: **30 minutes**

- ¼ **cup purchased black or green olive tapenade**
- ⅓ **cup chopped tomato**
- ½ **teaspoon ground black pepper**
- 1 **clove garlic, minced**
- 1 **pound lean ground beef**
- ⅓ **cup bottled roasted red sweet pepper strips**
- 4 **slices mozzarella cheese**
- 4 **hamburger buns, split and toasted, if desired**

1 Preheat broiler. In a medium bowl combine tapenade, tomato, black pepper, and garlic. Add beef; mix well. Shape beef mixture into four ¾-inch-thick patties.

2 Place patties on the unheated rack of a broiler pan. Broil 3 to 4 inches from the heat for 12 to 14 minutes or until done (160°F), turning once. Place roasted sweet pepper and a cheese slice on top of each patty. Broil for 1 minute more or until cheese melts. Serve patties on buns.

Makes 4 servings

Nutrition facts per serving: 542 cal., 34 g total fat (12 g sat. fat), 100 mg chol., 865 mg sodium, 24 g carbo., 2 g dietary fiber, 32 g protein.

30 minutes

Shopping list:

- 1 jar green olives or prepared tapenade
- 1 medium tomato
- 1 pound lean ground beef
- 1 7-ounce bottle roasted red sweet pepper strips
- 1 8-ounce package sliced mozzarella cheese
- 1 package hamburger buns

Pantry:

Ground black pepper

Garlic

Teriyaki **Beef and Noodles**

Start to Finish: **30 minutes**

- **1** **3-ounce package ramen noodles (any flavor)**
- **12** **ounces lean ground beef**
- **½** **cup chopped onion (1 medium)**
- **2** **14-ounce cans reduced-sodium beef broth**
- **¼** **cup teriyaki sauce**
- **1** **cup thinly sliced carrots**
- **¼** **cup sliced green onions**
- **1** **cup snow peas, trimmed and cut in half diagonally**
- **1** **tablespoon chopped fresh cilantro (optional)**

1 Break ramen noodle block into four pieces; discard seasoning packet. Set noodles aside.

2 In a 3-quart saucepan cook and stir ground beef and onion over medium-high heat until meat is brown and onion is tender. Drain fat. Stir in broth, teriyaki sauce, and carrots. Bring to boiling. Add noodles and green onions. Reduce heat to medium-low; cook for 5 minutes, stirring occasionally to separate noodles. Add snow peas and, if desired, cilantro; cook and stir for 2 minutes longer or until peas are crisp-tender. Ladle into bowls.

Makes 4 servings

Nutrition facts per serving: 335 cal., 17 g total fat (7 g sat. fat), 58 mg chol., 1,382 mg sodium, 24 g carbo., 3 g dietary fiber, 22 g protein.

Shopping list:

- 1 3-ounce package ramen noodles (any flavor)
- 12 ounces lean ground beef
- 1 small onion
- 2 14-ounce cans reduced-sodium beef broth
- 1 5-ounce bottle teriyaki sauce
- 1 1-pound bag carrots
- 1 bunch green onions
- 8 ounces snow peas

30 minutes

Beef-Vegetable Stir-Fry

Start to Finish: **25 minutes**

- 1 **16-ounce package frozen stir-fry vegetables (any blend)**
- 1 **tablespoon cooking oil**
- 1 **pound purchased beef stir-fry strips**
- ¾ **cup reduced-sodium beef broth**
- ¾ **cup purchased peanut sauce**
- 2 **3-ounce packages any flavor ramen noodles, broken**
- ¼ **cup chopped peanuts**

1 In a very large skillet cook and stir vegetables in hot oil over medium-high heat for 5 to 6 minutes or until crisp-tender. Remove from skillet.

2 Add half of the beef strips to skillet (add more oil, if necessary). Cook and stir for 2 to 3 minutes or until brown. Remove from skillet. Add remaining meat to skillet; cook and stir for 2 to 3 minutes or until brown. Return all meat and vegetables to the skillet.

3 In a small bowl stir together broth and peanut sauce. Add to skillet. Bring to boiling; add noodles (discard seasoning packets). Reduce heat. Cook, covered, for 3 to 4 minutes or until noodles are tender, stirring twice. Transfer to 4 dinner plates; sprinkle with peanuts.

Makes 4 servings

Nutrition facts per serving: 609 cal., 26 g total fat (7 g sat. fat), 54 mg chol., 1,630 mg sodium, 55 g carbo., 8 g dietary fiber, 41 g protein.

30 minutes

Shopping list:

- 1 16-ounce package frozen stir-fry vegetables
- 1 pound beef stir-fry strips
- 1 14-ounce can reduced-sodium beef broth
- 1 11.5-ounce bottle peanut sauce
- 2 3-ounce packages ramen noodles
- 1 2.25-ounce package peanuts

Pantry list:

Cooking oil

Meatball Soup with **Tiny Pasta**

Start to Finish: **25 minutes**

1 **14.5-ounce can diced tomatoes with onion and garlic, undrained**

1 **14-ounce can beef broth**

1 ½ **cups water**

½ **teaspoon dried Italian seasoning, crushed**

½ **of a 16-ounce package frozen cooked Italian-style meatballs**

1 **cup loose-pack frozen Italian blend vegetables (zucchini, carrots, cauliflower, lima beans, and Italian beans) or desired frozen mixed vegetables**

½ **cup small dried pasta (such as tripolini, farfallini, ditalini, stellini, or orzo)**

2 **tablespoons finely shredded or grated Parmesan cheese**

1 In a large saucepan stir together undrained tomatoes, beef broth, the water, and Italian seasoning; bring to boiling.

2 Add meatballs, frozen vegetables, and uncooked pasta. Return to boiling; reduce heat. Simmer, covered, about 10 minutes or until pasta and vegetables are tender. Sprinkle with Parmesan cheese.

Makes 4 servings

Nutrition facts per serving: 280 cal., 14 g total fat (6 g sat. fat), 38 mg chol., 1,335 mg sodium, 23 g carbo., 4 g dietary fiber, 15 g protein.

Shopping list:

1 14.5-ounce can diced tomatoes with onion and garlic

1 14-ounce can beef broth

1 16-ounce package frozen cooked Italian-style meatballs

1 10-ounce package frozen Italian blend vegetables

1 8-ounce package finely shredded Parmesan cheese

Pantry list:

Dried Italian seasoning

Dried pasta

30minutes

Fast French Dip **Sandwiches** *(See photo on page 141.)*

Start to Finish: **30 minutes**

1 **large sweet onion, cut into thin wedges**

1 **tablespoon olive oil**

1 **tablespoon butter**

Ground black pepper

1 **17-ounce package refrigerated cooked beef roast au jus**

¾ **cup beef broth**

4 **French rolls or hoagie buns, split and toasted**

Pimiento-stuffed green olives (optional)

1 In a large skillet cook onion in hot oil and butter for 7 to 8 minutes or until tender. Season to taste with pepper.

2 Meanwhile, reheat beef roast according to package microwave directions. Carefully drain juices from roast into a saucepan; add broth. Bring to boiling.

3 Using two forks, pull roast into shreds. Divide meat among 4 French rolls. Top with onions. If desired, garnish with olives on decorative picks. Serve sandwiches with small bowls of au jus mixture.

Makes 4 servings

Nutrition facts per serving: 643 cal., 23 g total fat (8 g sat. fat), 71 mg chol., 1,297 mg sodium, 78 g carbo., 4 g dietary fiber, 34 g protein.

Shopping List:
1 large sweet onion

1 17-ounce package refrigerated cooked beef roast au jus

1 14-ounce can beef broth

1 package French rolls

Pantry List:
Olive oil

Butter

Ground black pepper

minutes

30

Skillet Pot Roast with Mushrooms and Cherries

Start to Finish: **30 minutes**

- 1 **12-ounce package frozen unsweetened pitted dark sweet cherries**
- 1 **8-ounce package fresh button mushrooms, halved (3 cups)**
- 1 **medium red sweet pepper, cut into bite-size strips**
- 1 **large onion, chopped (1 cup)**
- 2 **teaspoons dried sage or thyme, crushed**
- 1 **tablespoon olive oil or cooking oil**
- 2 **16- to 17-ounce package refrigerated cooked beef pot roast with juices**
- 2 **tablespoons balsamic vinegar**

1 Place frozen cherries in colander. Run cold water over cherries to partially thaw. Set aside; drain well.

2 In a 12-inch skillet cook mushrooms, sweet pepper, onion, and 1 teaspoon of the sage in hot oil about 7 minutes or until tender. Add pot roast and juices, cherries, and balsamic vinegar to skillet. Bring to boiling; reduce heat. Simmer, uncovered, for 10 minutes or until heated through and juices thicken slightly, stirring occasionally. Stir in remaining sage.

Makes 4 to 6 servings

Nutrition facts per serving: 420 cal., 17 g total fat (5 g sat. fat), 104 mg chol., 1,174 mg sodium, 31 g carbo., 3 g dietary fiber, 40 g protein.

Shopping list:

1 12-ounce package frozen unsweetened pitted dark sweet cherries

1 8-ounce package fresh button mushrooms

1 medium red sweet pepper

1 large onion

1 small container dried sage

2 16- to 17-ounce packages refrigerated cooked beef pot roast with juices

Pantry list:

Olive oil

Balsamic vinegar

Barbecue Skillet Pizza

Start to Finish: **30 minutes**

- 1 **18-ounce tub refrigerated barbecue sauce with shredded beef**
- 1 **large green sweet pepper, chopped (1 cup)**
- 1 **large onion, chopped (1 cup)**
- 1 **7.5-ounce package refrigerated biscuits (10)**
- 1 **cup shredded cheddar cheese (4 ounces)**
- 1 ½ **cups shredded lettuce**
- 2 **roma tomatoes, chopped**

1 In a large microwave-safe bowl combine beef mixture, sweet pepper, and onion. Microwave on 100% power (high) for 3 minutes, stirring once. Meanwhile, lightly grease a heavy large skillet with flared sides. Press biscuits onto the bottom and halfway up the sides of the skillet, moistening edges of biscuits and pressing to seal.

2 Cook crust, covered, over medium heat for 3 minutes. Check crust and press with fork to seal any holes. Spoon meat mixture into partially cooked crust. Sprinkle with cheese. Cook, covered, for 9 to 14 minutes more or until edges of crust are light brown.

3 Loosen edges and carefully slide onto serving platter. Cut into wedges. Sprinkle with lettuce and tomato.

Makes 6 servings

Nutrition facts per serving: 313 cal., 11 g total fat (5 g sat. fat), 41 mg chol., 1,358 mg sodium, 38 g carbo., 3 g dietary fiber, 18 g protein.

Shopping list:

- 1 18-ounce tub refrigerated barbecue sauce with shredded beef
- 1 large green sweet pepper
- 1 large onion
- 1 7.5-ounce package refrigerated biscuits
- 1 8-ounce package shredded cheddar cheese
- 1 head lettuce
- 2 roma tomatoes

Roast Beef, Swiss, and **Onions on Rye**

Start to Finish: **30 minutes**

- 1 **large onion, thinly sliced**
- 3 **tablespoons olive oil**
- 8 **slices marble-rye bread**
- ¼ **cup creamy Dijon-style mustard blend**
- 8 **ounces thinly sliced deli roast beef**
- 4 **ounces thinly sliced deli Swiss cheese**

1 In a large nonstick skillet cook onion in 1 tablespoon hot oil about 8 minutes or until onion is tender and just begins to brown.

2 Spread one side of each bread slice with creamy Dijon-style mustard blend. Layer roast beef and cheese on the spread sides of 4 of the bread slices. Top with onions and remaining bread slices, spread sides down. Brush outsides of sandwiches lightly with remaining oil.

3 Cook sandwiches on a hot panini grill about 4 minutes or until heated through. Or cook sandwiches, two at a time, in a hot skillet over medium heat, weighting the sandwiches with a smaller heavy skillet. Turn after 2 to 3 minutes.

Makes 4 sandwiches

Nutrition facts per serving: 471 cal., 22 g total fat (8 g sat. fat), 52 mg chol., 1,307 mg sodium, 40 g carbo., 4 g dietary fiber, 25 g protein.

Shopping list:
- 1 large onion
- 1 loaf marble-rye bread
- 1 8-ounce bottle creamy Dijon-style mustard blend
- 8 ounces thinly sliced deli roast beef
- 8 ounces thinly sliced deli Swiss cheese

Pantry list:
- Olive oil

Maple-Glazed Pork Medallions

Start to Finish: **30 minutes**

1 1/2 cups water

3/4 cup uncooked long-grain white rice

1/4 teaspoon salt

1 1- to 1 1/4-pound pork tenderloin, cut into 3/4-inch slices

2 teaspoons cooking oil

1 large red cooking apple, cored and cut into 1/2-inch wedges

1/3 cup pure maple syrup

2 tablespoons water

1/4 teaspoon salt

1/2 teaspoon finely chopped canned chipotle peppers in adobo sauce (optional)*

1 In a large saucepan combine 1 1/2 cups water, rice, and 1/4 teaspoon salt. Bring to boiling over high heat; reduce heat to low. Cook, covered, for 15 minutes or until rice is tender and liquid is absorbed.

2 Meanwhile, in a large skillet cook pork in hot oil over medium-high heat for 6 to 8 minutes or until slightly pink (160°F). Remove meat from skillet; set aside.

3 Add apple wedges to skillet. Cook and stir for 2 minutes. Add syrup, 2 tablespoons water, 1/4 teaspoon salt, and, if using, chipotle peppers. Cook and stir until boiling; boil gently for 2 to 3 minutes or until apples are just tender. Add meat to skillet; heat through. Serve meat mixture over rice.

Makes 4 servings

Nutrition facts per serving: 394 cal., 9 g total fat (2 g sat. fat), 75 mg chol., 354 mg sodium, 52 g carbo., 2 g dietary fiber, 27 g protein.

*Note: Because hot chile peppers, such as chipotles, contain volatile oils that can burn your skin and eyes, avoid direct contact with chiles as much as possible. When working with chile peppers, wear plastic or rubber gloves. If your bare hands do touch the chile peppers, wash your hands well with soap and water.

30 minutes

Shopping list:

1 16-ounce package long-grain white rice

1 1- to 1 1/4-pound pork tenderloin

1 large red cooking apple

1 7-ounce can chipotle peppers in adobo sauce

Pantry list:

Cooking oil

Maple syrup

Salt

Pork Soft Shell **Tacos**

Start to Finish: **25 minutes**

- 8 **ounces boneless pork loin**
- 2 **teaspoons cooking oil**
- ¼ **cup dairy sour cream**
- ¼ **teaspoon ground chipotle chile pepper, crushed dried chipotle chile pepper, or chili powder**
- 4 **6-inch flour tortillas, warmed***
- ½ **cup shredded lettuce**
- ½ **cup diced tomato**
- ½ **cup shredded cheddar cheese (2 ounces)**
  Bottled salsa

1 If desired, partially freeze pork for easier slicing. Trim fat from pork. Thinly slice meat across the grain into bite-size strips. In a large skillet cook pork strips in hot oil over medium-high heat until done; set aside.

2 In a small bowl combine sour cream and ground chipotle chilé pepper; set aside.

3 Spoon one-fourth of the meat on each tortilla just below the center. Top meat with lettuce, tomato, and cheese. Fold top half of each tortilla over filling. Serve with sour cream mixture and salsa.

Makes 4 tacos

Nutrition facts per taco: 307 cal., 17 g total fat (6 g sat. fat), 53 mg chol., 329 mg sodium, 17 g carbo., 1 g dietary fiber, 20 g protein.

*Note: To warm tortillas, wrap them in foil. Place in a 350°F oven for 10 to 15 minutes or until warm.

Shopping list:

- 8 ounces boneless pork loin
- 1 8-ounce carton dairy sour cream
- 1 small container ground chipotle pepper
- 1 package 6-inch flour tortillas
- 1 head lettuce
- 1 large tomato
- 1 8-ounce package shredded cheddar cheese
  Bottled salsa

Pantry list:

Cooking oil

Peachy **Pork Chili**

Start to Finish: **30 minutes**

1 **pound lean boneless pork**

1 **tablespoon cooking oil**

2 **14.5-ounce cans diced tomatoes, undrained**

2 **15.5-ounce cans butter beans, rinsed and drained**

1 ½ **cups chopped fresh or frozen peaches**

1 **medium green sweet pepper, seeded and chopped (¾ cup)**

1 **5.25-ounce can hot-style vegetable juice**

2 **to 3 teaspoons finely chopped canned chipotles in adobo sauce**

Salt and ground black pepper

1 Trim fat from pork. Cut meat into bite-size pieces. In a 4-quart Dutch oven brown meat, half at a time, in hot oil over medium heat.

2 Add undrained tomatoes, drained beans, peaches, sweet pepper, vegetable juice, and chipotles. Bring to boiling; reduce heat. Simmer, covered, for 15 minutes. Season to taste with salt and pepper.

Makes 6 servings

Nutrition facts per serving: 279 cal., 6 g total fat (2 g sat. fat), 48 mg chol., 1,130 mg sodium, 30 g carbo., 6 g dietary fiber, 25 g protein.

Shopping list:

1 pound lean boneless pork

2 14.5-ounce cans diced tomatoes

2 15.5-ounce cans butter beans

3 medium peaches

1 medium green sweet pepper

1 5.25-ounce can hot-style vegetable juice

1 7-ounce can chipotle peppers in adobo sauce

Pantry list:

Cooking oil

Salt

Ground black pepper

Southwest Pork Salsa Stew *(See photo on page 142.)*

Start to Finish: **25 minutes**

Nonstick cooking spray

12 ounces boneless pork loin, trimmed of fat and cut into bite-size strips

1 14-ounce can reduced-sodium chicken broth

1 6-ounce can tomato paste

½ cup bottled cilantro-flavor salsa or regular salsa

½ teaspoon ground cumin

1 medium zucchini, halved lengthwise and thinly sliced (2 cups)

1 cup frozen sweet soybeans (edamame) or baby lima beans

1 small mango, pitted, peeled, and chopped (about ½ cup)*

1 Lightly coat a large saucepan with nonstick cooking spray. Heat over medium-high heat. Add pork to hot pan; cook and stir for 2 minutes or until brown.

2 Add broth, tomato paste, salsa, and cumin; stir until combined. Stir in zucchini and soybeans. Bring to boiling; reduce heat. Simmer, covered, for 10 minutes or until vegetables are tender. Top with chopped mango.

Makes 4 servings

Nutrition facts per serving: 243 cal., 7 g total fat (2 g sat. fat), 47 mg chol., 810 mg sodium, 21 g carbo., 5 g dietary fiber, 26 g protein.

*Test Kitchen Tip: Instead of fresh mango, use refrigerated mango slices, rinsed, drained, and chopped; or use frozen chopped mango, thawed.

Shopping list:

12 ounces boneless pork loin

1 14-ounce can reduced-sodium chicken broth

1 6-ounce can tomato paste

1 16-ounce jar bottled cilantro-flavor salsa

1 medium zucchini

1 12-ounce package frozen sweet soybeans

1 small mango

Pantry list:

Nonstick cooking spray

Ground cumin

Peach-Glazed Iowa Chops

Start to Finish: **25 minutes**

4 **pork loin chops,
cut 1 inch thick**

**Salt and ground
black pepper**

¾ **cup peach or
apricot preserves**

2 **tablespoons
lemon juice**

1 **tablespoon cooking oil**

2 **teaspoons Dijon-style
mustard**

Preheat broiler. Season meat with salt and pepper. Place chops on the unheated rack of a broiler pan. Broil 5 to 6 inches from the heat for 6 minutes. Meanwhile, in a small bowl combine preserves, lemon juice, oil, and mustard; brush or spoon some over chops. Turn chops. Broil about 6 minutes more or until done (155°F), spooning glaze over chops the last 3 minutes of broiling. Spoon any remaining glaze on chops before serving.

Makes 4 servings

Nutrition facts per serving: 591 cal., 16 g total fat (5 g sat. fat), 177 mg chol., 393 mg sodium, 42 g carbo., 1 g dietary fiber, 63 g protein.

Shopping list:

4 pork loin chops,
cut 1 inch thick

1 12-ounce jar peach or
apricot preserves

1 lemon

Pantry list:

Salt

Ground black pepper

Cooking oil

Dijon-style mustard

30 minutes

Pork Chops with **Plum-Grape Sauce**

Start to Finish: **25 minutes**

4 boneless pork top loin chops, cut 1 inch thick

¼ teaspoon salt

¼ teaspoon ground black pepper

2 teaspoons olive oil

⅓ cup water

¼ cup plum jam

1 tablespoon balsamic vinegar

2 teaspoons Dijon-style mustard

½ teaspoon chicken bouillon granules

1 clove garlic, minced

1 small plum, seeded and cut into thin wedges

½ cup seedless red grapes, halved

Snipped fresh chives (optional)

1 Trim fat from chops. Sprinkle both sides of chops with salt and pepper. In a large nonstick skillet cook chops in hot oil over medium heat for 8 to 12 minutes or until juices run clear (160°F), turning once. Transfer chops to a serving platter. Cover and keep warm.

2 Add the water, jam, balsamic vinegar, mustard, chicken bouillon granules, and garlic to the skillet. Whisk over medium heat until bubbly. Remove from heat. Gently stir in plum wedges and grapes. To serve, spoon plum-grape mixture over chops. If desired, sprinkle with snipped chives.

Makes 4 servings

Nutrition facts per serving: 305 cal., 10 g total fat (3 g sat. fat), 83 mg chol., 386 mg sodium, 21 g carbo., 1 g dietary fiber, 31 g protein.

Shopping list:

4 boneless pork top loin chops

1 10-ounce jar plum jam

1 2.25-ounce jar chicken bouillon granules

1 small plum

1 small bunch seedless red grapes

Pantry list:

Salt

Ground black pepper

Olive oil

Balsamic vinegar

Dijon-style mustard

Garlic

30minutes

Asian-Style Pork Burgers

Start to Finish: **30 minutes**

- ¼ **cup sliced green onions**
- 1 **tablespoon soy sauce**
- 1 ½ **teaspoons grated fresh ginger or ¾ teaspoon ground ginger**
- 1 **teaspoon toasted sesame oil**
- 1 **clove garlic, minced**
- 1 **pound ground pork**
- ⅓ **cup mayonnaise or salad dressing**
- 1 **tablespoon sliced green onions**
- 1 **small clove garlic, minced**
- ¼ **teaspoon grated fresh ginger or ⅛ teaspoon ground ginger**
- 1 ½ **cups packaged shredded cabbage with carrot (coleslaw mix)**
- 4 **burger buns, split and toasted, if desired**

1 Preheat broiler. In a large bowl combine ¼ cup green onions, soy sauce, 1 ½ teaspoons ginger, sesame oil, and 1 clove garlic; add pork and mix well. Shape mixture into four ½-inch-thick patties. Place on the unheated rack of a broiler pan. Broil 3 to 4 inches from the heat for 10 to 12 minutes or until juice runs clear (160°F).

2 Meanwhile, in a medium bowl combine mayonnaise, 1 tablespoon green onion, small clove garlic, and ¼ teaspoon ginger. Add coleslaw mix; toss to coat well.

3 Place pork patties on bun bottoms. Top with coleslaw mixture and bun tops.

Makes 4 servings

Nutrition facts per serving: 547 cal., 42 g total fat (12 g sat. fat), 88 mg chol., 630 mg sodium, 24 g carbo., 2 g dietary fiber, 24 g protein.

Shopping list:
- 1 bunch green onions
- 1 piece fresh ginger
- 1 8-ounce bottle toasted sesame oil
- 1 small piece fresh ginger
- 1 pound ground pork
- 1 16-ounce package shredded cabbage with carrot (coleslaw mix)
- 1 package hamburger buns

Pantry list:
Soy sauce

Garlic

Mayonnaise

30 minutes

Easy Skillet **Lasagna**

Start to Finish: **25 minutes**

- 1 **pound bulk Italian sausage**
- 1 **8-ounce package sliced fresh mushrooms**
- 1 **medium green sweet pepper, seeded and chopped (¾ cup)**
- 1 **medium onion, chopped (½ cup)**
- 8 **ounces dried campanelle or mafalda pasta**
- 1 **26-ounce jar mushroom pasta sauce**
- 1 **cup shredded Italian-blend cheeses**

Snipped fresh parsley (optional)

1 In a very large skillet cook sausage, mushrooms, sweet pepper, and onion over medium heat until sausage is no longer pink and vegetables are tender. Drain fat.

2 Meanwhile, cook pasta according to package directions; drain.

3 Stir pasta and pasta sauce into mixture in skillet. Return to a simmer. Sprinkle with cheeses. Cook, covered, over low heat until cheese melts. If desired, sprinkle with snipped fresh parsley.

Makes 4 to 6 servings

Nutrition facts per serving: 892 cal., 49 g total fat (19 g sat. fat), 106 mg chol., 1,881 mg sodium, 78 g carbo., 8 g dietary fiber, 36 g protein.

Shopping list:

- 1 pound bulk Italian sausage
- 1 8-ounce package sliced fresh mushrooms
- 1 medium green sweet pepper
- 1 medium onion
- 1 16-ounce package dried campanelle pasta
- 1 26-ounce jar mushroom pasta sauce
- 1 8-ounce package shredded Italian-blend cheeses

Italian Sausage and Potato Skillet

Start to Finish: **30 minutes**

1 **pound bulk sweet Italian sausage**

1 **medium onion, chopped (½ cup)**

1 **stalk celery, chopped (½ cup)**

1 **clove garlic, minced**

4 **cups frozen diced hash brown potatoes, thawed**

2 **14.5-ounce cans diced tomatoes with basil, garlic, and oregano, undrained**

1 **10-ounce package frozen chopped spinach, thawed and drained**

1 **cup finely shredded cheddar cheese (4 ounces)**

In a very large skillet cook and stir sausage, onion, celery, and garlic over medium heat until onion is tender and sausage is no longer pink. Drain fat. Stir in potatoes and undrained tomatoes; bring to boiling. Reduce heat. Simmer, covered, for 10 minutes or until potatoes are tender, stirring occasionally. Stir in spinach. Sprinkle with cheese. Cook, covered, for 2 minutes or until cheese melts.

Makes 6 servings

Nutrition facts per serving: 611 cal., 39 g total fat (15 g sat. fat), 74 mg chol., 1,382 mg sodium, 46 g carbo., 5 g dietary fiber, 24 g protein.

30 minutes

Shopping list:
1 pound bulk sweet Italian sausage

1 medium onion

1 bunch celery

1 16-ounce bag frozen diced hash brown potatoes

2 14.5-ounce cans diced tomatoes with basil, garlic, and oregano

1 10-ounce package frozen chopped spinach

1 8-ounce piece cheddar cheese

Pantry list:
Garlic

Picadillo **Sandwiches** *(See photo on page 142.)*

Start to Finish: **30 minutes**

1 **pound bulk
pork sausage**

1 **large onion,
chopped (1 cup)**

1 **14.5-ounce can
petite diced
tomatoes, undrained**

½ **cup golden raisins**

¼ **cup chopped
green olives**

2 **tablespoons tomato
paste**

1 **tablespoon balsamic
vinegar**

½ **teaspoon ground
cumin**

½ **teaspoon dried
oregano, crushed**

⅛ **teaspoon crushed red
pepper (optional)**

6 **hoagie buns, split
and toasted**

1 **cup shredded
Monterey Jack cheese
(4 ounces)**

In a 12-inch skillet cook
sausage and onion for
10 minutes or until sausage
is brown and onion is tender.
Drain off fat. Stir in undrained
tomatoes, raisins, olives, tomato
paste, vinegar, cumin, oregano,
and, if desired, crushed red
pepper. Bring to boiling; reduce
heat. Simmer, uncovered, for
10 minutes or until sauce is
thick. Serve sausage mixture on
toasted buns. Top with cheese
and bun tops.

Makes 6 sandwiches

Nutrition facts per sandwich:
750 cal., 29 g total fat (11 g sat. fat),
66 mg chol., 1,399 mg sodium, 91 g carbo.,
6 g dietary fiber, 28 g protein.

Shopping list:

1 pound bulk pork sausage

1 large onion

1 14.5-ounce can petite
diced tomatoes

1 12-ounce package
golden raisins

1 5-ounce jar green olives

1 6-ounce can tomato paste

1 package hoagie buns

1 8-ounce package shredded
Monterey Jack cheese

Pantry list:

Balsamic vinegar

Ground cumin

Dried oregano

Pasta with Ham, Dried Tomatoes, and Cheese

Start to Finish: **30 minutes**

1   **16-ounce package dried bow tie pasta**

1 ¼   **cups half-and-half or light cream**

2   **egg yolks**

½   **teaspoon garlic salt**

6   **ounces cooked ham, cut into bite-size strips**

1   **cup shredded Italian blend cheeses**

½   **cup oil-packed dried tomatoes, well drained and chopped**

2   **green onions, thinly sliced (¼ cup)**

1   In a 4-quart Dutch oven cook pasta according to package directions. Drain pasta and return to pan; cover to keep warm.

2   Meanwhile, in a medium saucepan whisk together half-and-half, egg yolks, and garlic salt. Cook and stir over medium heat until just bubbly. Pour sauce over hot cooked pasta. Add ham, cheese, and tomatoes. Stir to combine. Cook over medium-low heat until heated through. Stir before serving. Sprinkle each serving with green onions.

Makes 6 servings

Nutrition facts per serving: 473 cal., 15 g total fat (7 g sat. fat), 114 mg chol., 719 mg sodium, 61 g carbo., 3 g dietary fiber, 23 g protein.

30 minutes

Shopping list:

1 16-ounce package bow tie pasta

1 pint half-and-half

1 8-ounce cooked ham slice

1 8-ounce package shredded Italian blend cheeses

1 8-ounce jar oil-packed dried tomatoes

1 bunch green onions

Pantry list:

Eggs

Garlic salt

Ham-Basil-Broccoli **Wraps**

Start to Finish: **25 minutes**

1 ¼ **cups packaged shredded broccoli (broccoli slaw mix)**

8 **ounces cooked ham or smoked turkey, cut into bite-size strips**

6 **tablespoons bottled peppercorn ranch salad dressing or ranch salad dressing**

¼ **cup chopped walnuts, toasted**

¼ **cup oil-packed dried tomatoes, well drained and cut into thin strips**

4 **8- or 9-inch tomato or spinach flour tortillas**

12 **large fresh basil or spinach leaves**

In a medium bowl combine broccoli, ham, 4 tablespoons of the salad dressing, walnuts, and tomatoes. Spread tortillas with the remaining 2 tablespoons salad dressing. Top with basil leaves and ham mixture. Roll up tortillas. Halve rolls and secure with wooden picks, if necessary.

Makes 4 wraps

Nutrition facts per wrap: 481 cal., 27 g total fat (5 g sat. fat), 36 mg chol., 1,321 mg sodium, 42 g carbo., 5 g dietary fiber, 18 g protein.

Shopping list:

1 16-ounce package shredded broccoli (broccoli slaw mix)

8 ounces cooked ham

1 8-ounce bottle peppercorn ranch salad dressing

1 2.25-ounce package chopped walnuts

1 7-ounce jar oil-packed dried tomatoes

1 10-ounce package tomato flour tortillas

1 package fresh basil leaves

Double Pork Cuban **Sandwiches**

Start to Finish: **30 minutes**

- 2 **tablespoons Dijon-style mustard**
- 2 **tablespoons mayonnaise or salad dressing**
- 1 **teaspoon lime juice**
- ⅛ **teaspoon ground cumin**
- 4 **English muffins or ciabatta rolls, split**
- 8 **ounces thinly sliced smoked ham**
- 8 **slices packaged ready-to-serve cooked bacon**
- 8 **lengthwise sandwich pickle slices**
- 4 **slices provolone or Swiss cheese (about 4 ounces)**
- 1 **tablespoon butter, softened**

1 Preheat an electric sandwich press, covered indoor grill, grill pan, or skillet. In a small bowl combine mustard, mayonnaise, lime juice, and cumin. Spread evenly on the cut sides of the English muffins. Layer ham, bacon, pickle slices, and cheese on spread sides of muffin bottoms. Top with muffin tops, spread sides down. Spread butter on tops and bottoms of sandwiches.

2 Place sandwiches (two at a time, if necessary) in the sandwich press or indoor grill; cover and cook for 7 to 9 minutes or until bread is toasted and cheese melts. (If using a grill pan or skillet, place sandwiches on grill pan. Weight sandwiches with a heavy skillet and cook about 2 minutes or until bread is lightly toasted. Turn sandwiches over, weight, and cook until remaining side is lightly toasted.)

Makes 4 servings

Nutrition facts per serving: 426 cal., 22 g total fat (10 g sat. fat), 65 mg chol., 1,755 mg sodium, 29 g carbo., 2 g dietary fiber, 24 g protein.

Shopping list:
1 lime

1 package English muffins

8 ounces thinly sliced smoked ham

1 2.1-ounce package ready-to-serve cooked bacon

1 16-ounce jar lengthwise sandwich pickle slices

1 6-ounce package sliced provolone or Swiss cheese

Pantry list:
Dijon-style mustard

Mayonnaise

Ground cumin

Butter

30 minutes

Lamb Chops with Cinnamon Apples

Start to Finish: **25 minutes**

8 **lamb loin chops, cut 1 inch thick**

1 **tablespoon butter**

1 **tablespoon water**

3 **medium red cooking apples, cored and sliced (3 cups)**

1 **tablespoon packed brown sugar**

¼ **teaspoon salt**

¼ **teaspoon ground cinnamon**

1 Trim fat from chops. In a large skillet cook chops in hot butter over medium heat for 9 to 11 minutes for medium doneness (160°F), turning once. Transfer chops to a serving platter; keep warm.

2 Add water to skillet. Cook and stir until bubbly to loosen any browned bits on bottom of skillet. Add apple slices. Cook about 5 minutes or until apples are tender, stirring occasionally. Add brown sugar, salt, and cinnamon. Cook and stir about 2 minutes or until sugar dissolves. Spoon apple mixture over chops.

Makes 4 servings

Nutrition facts per serving: 394 cal., 14 g total fat (6 g sat. fat), 153 mg chol., 287 mg sodium, 19 g carbo., 4 g dietary fiber, 47 g protein.

Shopping list:

8 lamb loin chops

3 medium red cooking apples

Pantry list:

Butter

Brown sugar

Salt

Ground cinnamon

30minutes

Crispy Almond **Fish**

Start to Finish: **30 minutes**

- 1 **pound fresh or frozen skinless white fish fillets, such as tilapia, cod, or flounder**
- ⅓ **cup all-purpose flour**
- 1 **egg, lightly beaten**
- 2 **tablespoons milk**
- ⅓ **cup fine dry bread crumbs**
- ⅓ **cup finely chopped almonds**
- ½ **teaspoon dried thyme, crushed**
- 2 **to 3 tablespoons cooking oil**

1 Thaw fish, if frozen. Rinse fish; pat dry with paper towels. If necessary, cut into 4 serving-size pieces. Measure thickness of fish.

2 Place flour in a shallow dish. In a second shallow dish whisk together egg and milk. In a third shallow dish combine bread crumbs, almonds, and thyme. Coat both sides of fillets with flour. Dip fillets in the egg mixture then dip in bread crumb mixture to coat.

3 In a large skillet heat 2 tablespoons oil over medium heat. Add fish fillets (if necessary, cook fish half at a time). Cook until golden and fish flakes when tested with a fork, turning once (allow 4 to 6 minutes per ½-inch thickness of fish).

Makes 4 servings

Nutrition facts per serving: 308 cal., 15 g total fat (3 g sat. fat), 110 mg chol., 145 mg sodium, 16 g carbo., 2 g dietary fiber, 28 g protein.

Shopping list:

1 pound fresh or frozen skinless whitefish fillets

1 2.25-ounce package almonds

Pantry list:

All-purpose flour

Egg

Milk

Dried bread crumbs

Dried thyme

Cooking oil

Fish à l'Orange

Start to Finish: **30 minutes**

4   4- to 5-ounce fresh or frozen skinless catfish or other white fish fillets

2   cups water

1   cup long-grain white rice

½   teaspoon salt

½   teaspoon ground black pepper

¼   cup golden raisins

¼   cup pecan pieces, toasted

1   tablespoon butter

½   cup orange marmalade

1   Thaw fish, if frozen. Rinse fish; pat dry with paper towels; set aside. In a large saucepan combine the water, rice, ¼ teaspoon of the salt, and ¼ teaspoon of the pepper. Bring to boiling over high heat; reduce heat. Simmer, covered, about 15 minutes or until rice is tender and liquid is absorbed. Remove from heat; stir in raisins and pecans. Let stand, covered, for 5 minutes.

2   Meanwhile, sprinkle fish with remaining ¼ teaspoon salt and ¼ teaspoon pepper. Measure thickness of fish. In very large skillet cook fish in hot butter over medium heat until fish flakes when tested with a fork, turning once (allow 4 to 6 minutes per ½-inch thickness).

3   Transfer fish to a serving platter; keep warm. Add orange marmalade to skillet. Cook and stir until heated through. Spoon over fish. Serve with rice.

Makes 4 servings

Nutrition facts per serving: 526 cal., 17 g total fat (4 g sat. fat), 61 mg chol., 402 mg sodium, 72 g carbo., 2 g dietary fiber, 22 g protein.

Shopping list:

4 4- to 5-ounce fresh or frozen skinless catfish fillets

1 16-ounce package long-grain white rice

1 6-ounce package golden raisins

1 4-ounce package pecan pieces

1 12-ounce jar orange marmalade

Pantry list:

Salt

Ground black pepper

Butter

30
minutes

Fish Fillets with Roasted Red Pepper Sauce

Start to Finish: **30 minutes**

- 1 **12-ounce jar roasted red sweet peppers, drained**
- 2 **cloves garlic, minced**
- 1 ¼ **cups water**
- 2 **tablespoons tomato paste**
- 1 **tablespoon red wine vinegar**
- 1 **teaspoon sugar**
- 1 **teaspoon dried basil, crushed**
- ⅛ **teaspoon salt**
  Dash cayenne pepper
- 4 **4-ounce fresh cod or haddock fillets, about ¾ to 1 inch thick**
- 1 **lemon, sliced**
- ¼ **teaspoon salt**
- ¼ **teaspoon lemon-pepper seasoning**

1 For sauce, in a blender or food processor combine roasted peppers and garlic. Cover and process until nearly smooth. Add ½ cup of the water, tomato paste, vinegar, sugar, basil, ⅛ teaspoon salt, and cayenne pepper. Cover; blend or process with several on-off turns until mixture is nearly smooth. Transfer to a small saucepan; cook over medium heat, stirring frequently, until heated through.

2 Meanwhile, rinse fish; pat dry with paper towels. Measure thickness of fish. Bring the remaining ¾ cup water and half of the lemon slices just to boiling in a large skillet. Carefully add fish. Return just to boiling; reduce heat. Simmer, covered, until fish flakes when tested with a fork (allow 4 to 6 minutes per ½-inch thickness of fish). Remove fish from skillet. Gently pat tops of fish dry with paper towels. Sprinkle fish lightly with the ¼ teaspoon salt and the lemon-pepper seasoning.

3 To serve, spoon some of the sauce onto 4 plates. Place a fillet on top of sauce. Garnish with remaining lemon slices.

Makes 4 servings

Nutrition facts per serving: 128 cal., 1 g total fat (0 g sat. fat), 49 mg chol., 357 mg sodium, 10 g carbo., 3 g dietary fiber, 22 g protein.

Shopping list:
- 1 12-ounce jar roasted red sweet peppers
- 1 6-ounce can tomato paste
- 1 12-ounce bottle red wine vinegar
- 4 fresh cod fillets
- 1 lemon
- 1 small container lemon-pepper seasoning

Pantry list:
Garlic

Sugar

Dried basil

Salt

Cayenne pepper

Panfried Tilapia with Balsamic Butter Sauce

Start to Finish: 30 minutes

8 ounces dried fettuccine or bucatini

¼ cup butter

3 tablespoons snipped fresh parsley (optional)

4 5-ounce fresh tilapia fillets

½ teaspoon garlic salt

¼ teaspoon coarsely ground black pepper

2 tablespoons balsamic vinegar

1 In a large saucepan cook fettuccine according to package directions. Drain; return pasta to pan. Toss pasta with 2 tablespoons of the butter and, if desired, 2 tablespoons of the parsley. Keep warm.

2 Meanwhile, rinse fish; pat dry with paper towels. Season tilapia with garlic salt and pepper. In large skillet cook tilapia in 1 tablespoon hot butter over medium heat for 8 to 10 minutes or until fish flakes when tested with a fork, turning once. Remove tilapia to serving platter. Quickly add balsamic vinegar to skillet. Whisk in remaining 1 tablespoon butter until smooth and combined. If desired, stir in remaining 1 tablespoon parsley. Pour over fish. Serve fish with hot pasta.

Makes 4 servings

Nutrition facts per serving: 455 cal., 15 g total fat (8 g sat. fat), 101 mg chol., 277 mg sodium, 43 g carbo., 1 g dietary fiber, 36 g protein.

Shopping list:

1 16-ounce package dried fettuccine

4 5-ounce tilapia fillets

Pantry list:

Butter

Garlic salt

Ground black pepper

Balsamic vinegar

30 minutes

Salmon with Feta and Pasta

Start to Finish: 25 minutes

- 12 **ounces fresh or frozen skinless salmon fillet**
- 8 **ounces dried rotini**
  Nonstick cooking spray
- 2 **cloves garlic, minced**
  Salt
- 4 **large roma tomatoes, chopped (2 cups)**
- 1 **cup sliced green onions (8)**
- ⅓ **cup sliced pitted ripe olives**
- 3 **tablespoons snipped fresh basil**
- ½ **teaspoon coarsely ground black pepper**
- 2 **teaspoons olive oil**
- 1 **4-ounce package crumbled feta cheese**
  Fresh basil sprigs (optional)

1 Thaw fish, if frozen. Rinse fish; pat dry with paper towels. Cut fish into 1-inch pieces. Cook pasta according to pasta directions. Drain. Keep warm.

2 Meanwhile, lightly coat a large nonstick skillet with cooking spray. Heat skillet over medium-high heat. Add garlic; cook and stir for 15 seconds. Lightly season fish pieces with salt. Add fish to skillet. Cook fish for 4 to 6 minutes or until fish flakes when tested with a fork, turning fish pieces occasionally. Stir in tomatoes, green onions, olives, basil, and pepper. Heat through.

3 In a large bowl toss together hot pasta, oil, salmon mixture, and cheese. If desired, garnish with basil sprigs.

Makes 5 servings

Nutrition facts per serving: 373 cal., 13 g total fat (5 g sat. fat), 56 mg chol., 443 mg sodium, 41 g carbo., 3 g dietary fiber, 24 g protein.

30 minutes

Shopping list:
12 ounces fresh or frozen skinless salmon fillet

1 16-ounce package dried rotini

4 large roma tomatoes

1 bunch green onions

1 2.25-ounce can sliced pitted ripe olives

1 package fresh basil

1 4-ounce package crumbled feta cheese

Pantry list:
Nonstick cooking spray

Garlic

Salt

Ground black pepper

Olive oil

Tilapia with **Pimiento Sauce**

Start to Finish: **25 minutes**

- 1 **small onion, cut into thin wedges**
- 1 **clove garlic, minced**
- 1 **tablespoon olive oil**
- 1 **14.5-ounce can diced tomatoes, undrained**
- 1 **cup sliced cremini or button mushrooms**
- ¾ **cup pimiento-stuffed olives, coarsely chopped**
- 1 **tablespoon snipped fresh oregano or ½ teaspoon dried oregano, crushed**
- ¼ **teaspoon salt**
- ⅛ **teaspoon freshly ground black pepper**
- 4 **6- to 8-ounce fresh tilapia fillets**

1 In a large skillet cook onion and garlic in hot oil over medium heat for 2 to 3 minutes or until onion is tender. Add tomatoes, mushrooms, olives, oregano, salt, and pepper. Bring sauce to boiling.

2 Meanwhile, rinse fish; pat dry with paper towels. Gently place fish in sauce in skillet, spooning sauce over fish. Return to boiling; reduce heat. Simmer, covered, for 8 to 10 minutes or until fish flakes when tested with a fork. With a wide spatula, lift fish from skillet to a serving dish. Spoon sauce over fish.

Makes 4 servings

Nutrition facts per serving: 367 cal., 12 g total fat (1 g sat. fat), 0 mg chol., 767 mg sodium, 33 g carbo., 2 g dietary fiber, 32 g protein.

Shopping list:
- 1 small onion
- 1 14.5-ounce can diced tomatoes
- 1 8-ounce package fresh cremini mushrooms
- 1 5-ounce jar pimiento-stuffed green olives
- 1 package fresh oregano
- 4 6- to 8-ounce tilapia fillets

Pantry list:
Olive oil

Garlic

Salt

Ground black pepper

Prosciutto-Wrapped Roughy

Start to Finish: **30 minutes**

2 **fresh or frozen orange roughy or cod fillets, ½ inch thick, or 4 skinless flounder, catfish, or trout fillets, about ¼ inch thick**

4 **2-inch sprigs fresh rosemary or 2 teaspoons dried rosemary, crushed**

4 **slices thinly sliced prosciutto or thinly sliced cooked ham**

3 **tablespoons lemon juice**

Freshly ground black pepper

2 **medium roma tomatoes, halved**

Olive oil

1 **19-ounce can cannellini beans, rinsed and drained**

1 **tablespoon olive oil**

1 **clove garlic, minced**

2 **teaspoons snipped fresh rosemary or ½ teaspoon dried rosemary, crushed**

⅛ **teaspoon salt**

1 Thaw fish, if frozen. Rinse fish; pat dry with paper towels. Cut each fillet in half crosswise. If using roughy or cod, place a rosemary sprig on top of each fillet half or sprinkle with the 2 teaspoons dried rosemary. If using thinner fish fillets, place rosemary sprigs or dried rosemary on half of the pieces and top with remaining fish pieces to make four stacks. Wrap one slice of prosciutto around fish and rosemary. Sprinkle fish with 1 tablespoon of the lemon juice and pepper. Set aside.

2 Heat a nonstick or well-seasoned grill pan on stovetop over medium heat until hot. Meanwhile, cut tomatoes in half lengthwise. Brush tomatoes lightly with olive oil. Add tomato halves to grill pan, cut side down. Cook for 6 to 8 minutes or until tomatoes are very tender, turning once.

Remove tomatoes from grill; set aside to cool slightly.

3 Place fish fillets on grill pan,* rosemary sprig side up (if fillets are not stacked). Cook for 4 to 6 minutes or until fish flakes when tested with a fork, turning once halfway through cooking.

4 Coarsely chop grilled tomatoes. In a medium bowl gently toss together tomatoes, remaining 2 tablespoons lemon juice, beans, 1 tablespoon olive oil, garlic, 2 teaspoons snipped rosemary, and salt. Place fish on bean mixture. Remove rosemary sprigs.

Makes 4 servings

Nutrition facts per serving: 276 cal., 7 g total fat (1 g sat. fat), 49 mg chol., 989 mg sodium, 21 g carbo., 7 g dietary fiber, 39 g protein.

*Test Kitchen Tip: If the grill pan is large enough, grill the tomatoes and fish at the same time.

Shopping list:
- 2 orange roughy fillets
- 1 package fresh rosemary
- 4 slices prosciutto
- 1 lemon
- 2 medium roma tomatoes
- 1 19-ounce can cannellini beans

Pantry list:
- Ground black pepper
- Olive oil
- Garlic
- Salt

30 minutes

Spring Salmon Chowder *(See photo on page 143.)*

Start to Finish: **30 minutes**

- 12 ounces fresh or frozen skinless salmon fillets, cut into 1-inch pieces
- 6 tiny new potatoes, skin on, cut into quarters
- 2 14-ounce cans vegetable broth
- ½ cup frozen whole kernel corn, thawed
- 6 2-inch sprigs fresh thyme or ½ teaspoon dried thyme, crushed
- 1 cup packed baby spinach leaves
- ¼ cup sliced green onion

  Salt and ground black pepper

1 Thaw fish, if frozen. Rinse fish; pat dry with paper towels. Cut fish into 1-inch pieces; set aside. In a large saucepan cook potatoes, covered, in boiling vegetable broth about 5 minutes or until potatoes are tender but not cooked through. Add corn and thyme. Return to boiling; reduce heat. Cook, covered, about 4 minutes or until vegetables are tender. Reduce heat.

2 Carefully add salmon to saucepan. Simmer, uncovered, for 3 to 5 minutes or until salmon flakes when tested with a fork. Remove thyme sprigs, if using. Stir in spinach and green onions; cook for 1 minute or until spinach begins to wilt. Season to taste with salt and pepper.

Makes 6 servings

Nutrition facts per serving: 169 cal., 7 g total fat (1 g sat. fat), 37 mg chol., 639 mg sodium, 14 g carbo., 2 g dietary fiber, 14 g protein.

Shopping list:

- 12 ounces fresh or frozen skinless salmon
- 6 tiny new potatoes
- 2 14-ounce cans vegetable broth
- 1 10-ounce package frozen whole kernel corn
- 1 package fresh thyme
- 1 6-ounce package fresh baby spinach leaves
- 1 bunch green onions

Pantry list:

Salt

Ground black pepper

Broiled Halibut with Pineapple-Cherry Chutney

Start to Finish: **25 minutes**

4   **4- to 5-ounce fresh boneless halibut fillets**

4   **teaspoons olive oil**

     Salt and ground black pepper

1   **8-ounce can pineapple tidbits (juice pack)**

¼   **cup dried tart cherries**

3   **tablespoons lemon juice**

1 ½ **teaspoons cornstarch**

¼   **teaspoon salt**

⅛   **teaspoon ground ginger**

1 Preheat broiler. Rinse fish; pat dry with paper towels. Brush halibut with oil and season with salt and pepper. Place on the unheated rack of a broiler pan. Broil 5 inches from the heat for 6 minutes. Turn and broil for 3 to 4 minutes more or until halibut flakes when tested with a fork.

2 Meanwhile, in a small saucepan combine undrained pineapple, cherries, lemon juice, cornstarch, salt, and ginger. Cook and stir over medium-high heat until slightly thick and bubbly; cook and stir 2 minutes more. Serve over halibut.

Makes 4 servings

Nutrition facts per serving: 231 cal., 7 g total fat (1 g sat. fat), 36 mg chol., 359 mg sodium, 16 g carbo., 1 g dietary fiber, 24 g protein.

Shopping list:

4 4- to 5-ounce boneless halibut fillets

1 8-ounce can pineapple tidbits (juice pack)

1 6-ounce package dried tart cherries

1 lemon

1 small container ground ginger

Pantry list:

Olive oil

Salt

Ground black pepper

Cornstarch

30 minutes

Broiled Lemon-Tarragon Tilapia

Start to Finish: **30 minutes**

Nonstick cooking spray

1 ½ pounds fresh tilapia fillets

1 tablespoon canola oil or cooking oil

2 teaspoons finely shredded lemon peel

1 tablespoon lemon juice

1 teaspoon dried tarragon, crushed

½ teaspoon salt

¼ teaspoon ground black pepper

2 cups chicken broth

1 10-ounce package couscous

⅓ cup sliced almonds, toasted

1 Preheat broiler. Rinse fish; pat dry with paper towels. Lightly coat the unheated rack of a broiler pan with cooking spray. Place fish on rack. In a small bowl combine oil, 1 teaspoon lemon peel, lemon juice, tarragon, salt, and pepper. Brush mixture on tilapia. Broil about 5 inches from the heat for 8 to 10 minutes or until fish flakes when tested with a fork.

2 Meanwhile, in a medium saucepan bring broth to boiling. Stir in couscous. Remove from heat; let stand 5 minutes. Fluff with a fork. Stir in remaining 1 teaspoon lemon peel and the almonds. Serve fish with couscous.

Makes 4 to 5 servings

Nutrition facts per serving: 513 cal., 11 g total fat (2 g sat. fat), 86 mg chol., 867 mg sodium, 57 g carbo., 5 g dietary fiber, 45 g protein.

Shopping list:
1 ½ pounds fresh tilapia fillets

1 bottle canola oil

1 lemon

1 small container dried tarragon

1 32-ounce package chicken broth

1 10-ounce package couscous

1 2.25-ounce package sliced almonds

Pantry list:
Nonstick cooking spray

Salt

Ground black pepper

30minutes

Buttery Almond Salmon with Apricot Sauce

Start to Finish: 30 minutes

1 **24-ounce package refrigerated mashed sweet potatoes or mashed potatoes**

6 **6- to 8-ounce fresh skinless salmon fillets**

½ **teaspoon salt**

¼ **teaspoon garlic-pepper seasoning**

½ **cup sliced almonds**

3 **tablespoons butter, melted**

⅓ **cup apricot preserves**

1 Heat mashed potatoes according to package directions. Keep warm.

2 Preheat broiler. Rinse salmon; pat dry with paper towels. Place salmon on the unheated rack of a broiler pan; sprinkle with salt and garlic-pepper seasoning. Broil 4 to 5 inches from the heat for 7 to 8 minutes or until nearly done, turning once. Meanwhile, in a small bowl, combine almonds and melted butter. Spoon nuts on top of each piece of salmon. Broil about 1 ½ minutes more or until nuts are toasted and fish flakes when tested with a fork.

3 Place preserves in a small bowl or glass measure. Microwave on 100% power (high) for 20 to 30 seconds or until hot. If necessary, add a little water to thin. Spoon over salmon. Serve with potatoes.

Makes 6 servings

Nutrition facts per serving: 542 cal., 28 g total fat (8 g sat. fat), 116 mg chol., 383 mg sodium, 34 g carbo., 4 g dietary fiber, 37 g protein.

minutes
30

Shopping list:

1 24-ounce package refrigerated mashed sweet potatoes

6 6- to 8-ounce skinless, boneless salmon fillets

1 small container garlic-pepper seasoning

1 2.25-ounce package sliced almonds

1 12-ounce jar apricot preserves

Pantry list:

Salt

Butter

Citrus-Glazed Salmon *(See photo on page 273.)*

Start to Finish: **30 minutes**   Oven: **450°F**

- 1 **2-pound fresh or frozen skinless salmon fillet**
- **Salt and ground black pepper**
- ¾ **cup orange marmalade**
- 2 **green onions, sliced (¼ cup)**
- 1 **clove garlic, minced**
- 2 **teaspoons dry white wine**
- 1 **teaspoon grated fresh ginger**
- 1 **teaspoon Dijon-style mustard**
- ¼ **teaspoon cayenne pepper**
- ⅛ **teaspoon five-spice powder**
- 3 **tablespoons sliced almonds, toasted**

1 Thaw fish, if frozen. Preheat oven to 450°F. Rinse fish; pat dry with paper towels. Measure the thickest portion of the fillet; season with salt and pepper. Place in a shallow baking pan; set aside.

2 In a small bowl stir together orange marmalade, green onions, garlic, wine, ginger, mustard, cayenne pepper, and five-spice powder. Spoon mixture over salmon.

3 Bake, uncovered, for 4 to 6 minutes per ½-inch thickness or until salmon flakes when tested with a fork. Transfer fish and glaze to a serving dish with a lip. Sprinkle with almonds.

Makes 8 servings

Nutrition facts per serving: 227 cal., 6 g total fat (1 g sat. fat), 59 mg chol., 170 mg sodium, 21 g carbo., 1 g dietary fiber, 24 g protein.

Shopping list:

1 2-pound fresh or frozen salmon fillet

1 10-ounce jar orange marmalade

1 bunch green onions

1 bottle dry white wine

1 piece fresh ginger

1 small container five-spice powder

1 2.25-ounce package sliced almonds

Pantry list:

Salt

Ground black pepper

Garlic

Dijon-style mustard

Cayenne pepper

30 minutes

Island Salmon

Start to Finish: **30 minutes**   Oven: **450°F**

6 **5-ounce fresh salmon fillets**

½ **cup pineapple juice**

¼ **cup lemon juice**

1 **tablespoon finely shredded lemon peel**

3 **tablespoons packed brown sugar**

1 **tablespoon chili powder**

1 **teaspoon ground cumin**

¾ **teaspoon salt**

¼ **teaspoon ground cinnamon**

1 Preheat oven to 450°F. Rinse salmon; pat dry with paper towels. Place salmon in a large resealable plastic bag set in a shallow dish. Pour pineapple and lemon juice over salmon. Seal bag and marinate in the refrigerator for 15 minutes.

2 Meanwhile, in a small bowl combine lemon peel, brown sugar, chili powder, cumin, salt, and cinnamon; set aside.

3 Remove salmon from marinade, discarding marinade. Place salmon, skin side down, on a greased shallow baking pan. Rub lemon peel mixture over salmon. Bake, uncovered, for 4 to 6 minutes per ½-inch thickness of fish or until fish flakes when tested with a fork.

Makes 6 servings

Nutrition facts per serving: 306 cal., 16 g total fat (3 g sat. fat), 84 mg chol., 392 mg sodium, 11 g carbo., 1 g dietary fiber, 29 g protein.

30 minutes

Shopping list:
6 5-ounce fresh salmon fillets
1 8-ounce can pineapple juice
1 lemon

Pantry list:
Brown sugar
Chili powder
Ground cumin
Salt
Ground cinnamon

Nut-Crusted Salmon with Slaw

Start to Finish: 30 minutes   Oven: **450°F**

- **4** **4- to 5-ounce fresh or frozen skinless salmon fillets**
- **Nonstick cooking spray**
- **3** **tablespoons orange marmalade**
- **½** **cup finely chopped walnuts**
- **¼** **teaspoon salt**
- **¼** **teaspoon ground black pepper**
- **3** **cups packaged shredded cabbage with carrot (coleslaw mix)**
- **⅓** **cup bottled ranch salad dressing**
- **1** **tablespoon honey mustard**

1 Thaw salmon, if frozen. Preheat oven to 450°F. Rinse salmon; pat dry with paper towels. Measure thickness of fish. Lightly coat a 2-quart square baking dish with nonstick cooking spray. Place fish in baking dish. Spread tops and sides of fish with marmalade. Sprinkle evenly with nuts, salt, and ⅛ teaspoon of the pepper.

2 Bake until fish flakes when tested with a fork (allow 4 to 6 minutes per ½-inch thickness of fish).

3 Meanwhile, in a large bowl stir together coleslaw mix, dressing, honey mustard, and remaining ⅛ teaspoon pepper; toss to coat. Serve salmon with slaw.

Makes 4 servings

Nutrition facts per serving: 403 cal., 26 g total fat (3 g sat. fat), 69 mg chol., 372 mg sodium, 17 g carbo., 2 g dietary fiber, 25 g protein.

Shopping list:

4 4- to 5-ounce fresh or frozen skinless salmon fillets

1 10-ounce jar orange marmalade

1 2.25-ounce package chopped walnuts

1 16-ounce package shredded cabbage with carrot (coleslaw mix)

1 6-ounce bottle honey mustard

Pantry list:

Nonstick cooking spray

Salt

Ground black pepper

Bottled ranch salad dressing

30minutes

Tuna with Chipotle-Raspberry Sauce

Start to Finish: **25 minutes**

- 4 **5- to 6-ounce fresh or frozen tuna steaks, cut 1 inch thick**
- 1 **tablespoon olive oil**
- ¼ **teaspoon salt**
- ¼ **teaspoon ground black pepper**
- ½ **cup raspberry preserves**
- 1 **tablespoon chopped chipotle pepper in adobo sauce***
- 2 **tablespoons orange juice**

1 Thaw tuna, if frozen. Preheat broiler. Rinse tuna; pat dry with paper towels. Brush tuna with oil; season with salt and pepper. Place tuna on the rack of an unheated broiler pan or a foil-lined baking sheet. Broil 4 to 5 inches from the heat for 8 to 12 minutes or until fish flakes when tested with a fork, turning once.

2 Meanwhile, in small bowl combine raspberry preserves, chipotle pepper, and orange juice. About 1 minute before fish is done, spoon a small amount of the preserves on each steak. Serve with additional sauce.

Makes 4 servings

Nutrition facts per serving: 300 cal., 5 g total fat (1 g sat. fat), 64 mg chol., 228 mg sodium, 29 g carbo., 1 g dietary fiber, 33 g protein.

*Note: Because hot chile peppers, such as chipotles, contain volatile oils that can burn your skin and eyes, avoid direct contact with chiles as much as possible. When working with chile peppers, wear plastic or rubber gloves. If your bare hands do touch the chile peppers, wash your hands well with soap and water.

30 minutes

Shopping list:

4 5- to 6-ounce fresh or frozen tuna steaks

1 12-ounce jar raspberry preserves

1 7-ounce can chipotle peppers in adobo sauce

Pantry list:

Olive oil

Salt

Ground black pepper

Orange juice

Garden Greens with Swordfish

Start to Finish: **30 minutes**

1 pound fresh or frozen swordfish or tuna steaks, cut 1 inch thick

1 tablespoon lemon juice

1 teaspoon dried Italian seasoning, crushed

¼ teaspoon garlic salt

⅛ teaspoon ground black pepper

6 cups torn mixed salad greens

12 red and/or yellow tiny pear-shape tomatoes or cherry tomatoes, halved

Roasted Pepper Dressing

1 Thaw fish, if frozen. Preheat broiler. Rinse fish; pat dry with paper towels. Brush fish with lemon juice. In a small bowl stir together Italian seasoning, garlic salt, and pepper; rub over fish. Place fish on the greased rack of an unheated broiler pan.

2 Broil 4 inches from the heat for 5 minutes. Using a wide spatula, carefully turn fish over. Broil 3 to 7 minutes more or until fish flakes when tested with a fork. Cool; cut fish into bite-size strips.

3 Divide salad greens among 4 plates. Top with fish and tomatoes. Drizzle Roasted Pepper Dressing over salads.

Makes 4 servings

Nutrition facts per serving: 282 cal., 18 g total fat (3 g sat. fat), 45 mg chol., 374 mg sodium, 6 g carbo., 2 g dietary fiber, 24 g protein.

Roasted Pepper Dressing:

In a blender or food processor combine ½ of a 7-ounce jar roasted red sweet peppers, drained (½ cup); ¼ cup salad oil; 3 tablespoons vinegar; ¼ teaspoon salt; and dash cayenne pepper. Cover and blend or process until nearly smooth. Cover and chill for up 24 hours.

Shopping list:

1 pound fresh or frozen swordfish steaks

1 lemon

1 10-ounce package cups torn mixed salad greens

1 pint tiny pear-shaped tomatoes

1 7-ounce jar roasted red sweet peppers

Pantry list:

Dried Italian seasoning

Garlic salt

Ground black pepper

Salad oil

Balsamic vinegar

Cayenne pepper

30
minutes

Broiled Swordfish with Rosemary Butter Sauce

Start to Finish: **30 minutes**

4 **4- to 5-ounce fresh swordfish steaks, about 1 inch thick**

¼ **teaspoon salt**

⅛ **teaspoon ground black pepper**

2 **tablespoons butter, melted**

1 **tablespoon honey**

1 **teaspoon lemon juice**

1 **teaspoon dried rosemary, crushed**

Preheat broiler. Rinse fish; pat dry with paper towels. Measure thickness of fish. Season fish with salt and pepper; place on the greased unheated rack of a broiler pan. In a small bowl combine butter, honey, lemon juice, and rosemary; divide mixture in half. Brush half of the mixture on both sides of the swordfish. Broil 4 inches from the heat for 4 to 6 minutes per ½-inch thickness or until fish flakes when tested with a fork, turning once halfway through broiling. Drizzle reserved sauce over fish.

Makes 4 servings

Nutrition facts per serving: 204 cal., 10 g total fat (5 g sat. fat), 59 mg chol., 289 mg sodium, 4 g carbo., 0 g dietary fiber, 23 g protein.

Shopping list:

4 4- to 5-ounce fresh swordfish steaks

1 lemon

1 small container dried rosemary

Pantry list:

Salt

Ground black pepper

Butter

Honey

30 minutes

Salmon, Rice, and Pesto Salad

Start to Finish: **25 minutes**

1 ½ cups sugar snap peas or 1-inch pieces fresh asparagus

1 8.8-ounce pouch cooked long-grain and wild rice

¼ cup purchased basil or dried tomato pesto

¼ cup light mayonnaise or salad dressing

1 8-ounce piece smoked salmon, flaked, and skin and bones removed

1 cup cherry tomatoes, halved

⅓ cup thinly sliced radishes

Lettuce leaves

1 In a medium saucepan cook sugar snap peas in a small amount of boiling lightly salted water for 2 minutes; drain. Place in a bowl of ice water to chill; drain.

2 In a large bowl combine rice, pesto, and mayonnaise. Gently stir in peas, salmon, tomatoes, and radishes. Spoon salad onto lettuce-lined plates.

Makes 4 servings

Nutrition facts per serving: 312 cal., 14 g total fat (3 g sat. fat), 23 mg chol., 892 mg sodium, 28 g carbo., 3 g dietary fiber, 16 g protein.

Shopping list:

6 ounces fresh sugar snap peas

1 8.8-ounce pouch cooked long-grain and wild rice

1 8-ounce container basil pesto

1 8-ounce piece smoked salmon

1 pint cherry tomatoes

1 bunch radishes

1 head lettuce

Pantry list:

Light mayonnaise

30minutes

Tuna Salad with Capers

Start to Finish: 25 minutes

- ½ **cup mayonnaise or salad dressing**
- 2 **tablespoons capers, drained**
- 2 **tablespoons lemon juice**
- 1 **tablespoon snipped fresh tarragon**
- 1 **teaspoon Cajun seasoning**
- 1 **12-ounce can solid white tuna**
- 2 **tablespoons milk**
- 1 **10-ounce package torn mixed greens (romaine blend) or 8 cups torn romaine**
- 2 **cups shredded cabbage with carrot (coleslaw mix)**
- 2 **small tomatoes, cut into wedges**

1 In a small bowl combine mayonnaise, capers, lemon juice, tarragon, and Cajun seasoning. Set aside. In a large bowl flake tuna into large chunks; toss with 3 tablespoons of the mayonnaise mixture. Stir milk into remaining mayonnaise mixture.

2 Divide greens among 6 plates; top with coleslaw mix, tuna, and tomato wedges. Serve with remaining mayonnaise mixture.

Makes 6 servings

Nutrition facts per serving: 228 cal., 17 g total fat (3 g sat. fat), 38 mg chol., 455 mg sodium, 5 g carbo., 2 g dietary fiber, 15 g protein.

Shopping list:

- 1 3.5-ounce jar capers
- 1 lemon
- 1 package fresh tarragon
- 1 small container Cajun seasoning
- 1 12-ounce can solid white tuna
- 1 10-ounce package torn mixed greens
- 1 16-ounce package shredded cabbage with carrot (coleslaw mix)
- 2 small tomatoes

Pantry list:

Mayonnaise

Milk

30 minutes

Salad Niçoise on **Flatbread**

Start to Finish: **25 minutes**

- 4 ounces fresh green beans, trimmed, (if desired), and cut into 1-inch pieces (about 1 cup)
- 1 12-ounce can chunk white or light tuna (water pack), drained and flaked
- 1 cup halved cherry tomatoes
- ⅓ cup chopped pitted niçoise or kalamata olives
- ¼ cup finely chopped sweet onion (such as Vidalia, Walla Walla, or Maui)
- 2 tablespoons snipped fresh mint
- 1 tablespoon lemon juice
- 2 teaspoons olive oil
- ⅛ teaspoon ground black pepper
- 3 cups packaged mesclun (mixed salad greens)
- 3 Greek pita flatbreads

1 In a medium saucepan cook green beans, covered, in boiling water about 4 minutes or until crisp-tender. Drain. Rinse under cold water; drain again.

2 Place green beans in a large bowl. Stir in tuna, cherry tomatoes, olives, onion, and mint. Add lemon juice, oil, and pepper; toss to combine. Stir in mesclun.

3 To serve, cut pita flatbreads in half crosswise. Split each pita half to form a pocket. Fill each pita pocket with about ½ cup of the tuna mixture.

Makes 6 servings

Nutrition facts per serving: 210 cal., 5 g total fat (1 g sat. fat), 24 mg chol., 527 mg sodium, 23 g carbo., 3 g dietary fiber, 17 g protein.

Shopping list:

- 4 ounces fresh green beans
- 1 12-ounce can chunk white tuna (water-pack)
- 1 pint cherry tomatoes
- 1 5-ounce jar niçoise olives
- 1 small sweet onion
- 1 package fresh mint
- 1 lemon
- 1 8-ounce package mesclun
- 1 package Greek pita flatbreads

Pantry list:

Olive oil

Ground black pepper

30 minutes

Shrimp Quesadillas

Start to Finish: **30 minutes**

- 12 ounces fresh or frozen shrimp
- ¼ cup purchased basil pesto
- 8 6- to 7-inch flour tortillas
- 2 cloves garlic, minced
- 1 tablespoon olive oil
- ½ cup sliced onion, separated into rings
- ½ cup green sweet pepper strips
- ½ cup red sweet pepper strips
- 1 ½ cups shredded Mexican-style four-cheese blend (6 ounces)

  Dairy sour cream

  Salsa or habanero pepper sauce

1 Thaw shrimp, if frozen. Peel and devein shrimp. Rinse shrimp; pat dry with paper towels. Set aside. Spread a scant 2 teaspoons pesto on one side of each tortilla. Cover; set aside.

2 In a large skillet cook shrimp and garlic in hot oil over medium heat for 1 to 3 minutes or until shrimp are opaque. Remove from skillet and keep warm. In the same skillet cook onion and sweet peppers for 3 to 4 minutes or until vegetables are crisp-tender (add additional oil, if necessary). Remove from skillet; keep warm.

3 To assemble quesadillas, layer shrimp mixture, vegetables, and cheese onto the pesto side of half of the tortillas. Top with the remaining tortillas, pesto sides down.

4 In a large skillet cook one quesadilla over medium heat for 2 to 3 minutes or until light brown, turning once. Remove quesadilla from skillet; place on a baking sheet. Keep warm in a 300°F oven. Repeat with remaining quesadillas. To serve, cut quesadillas into wedges. Serve with sour cream and salsa.

Makes 4 servings

Nutrition facts per serving: 600 cal., 33 g total fat (12 g sat. fat), 132 mg chol., 986 mg sodium, 47 g carbo., 4 g dietary fiber, 29 g protein.

30 minutes

Shopping list:

- 12 ounces fresh or frozen shrimp
- 1 8-ounce container basil pesto
- 1 15-ounce package flour tortillas
- 1 medium onion
- 1 medium green sweet pepper
- 1 medium red sweet pepper
- 1 8-ounce package shredded Mexican-style four-cheese blend
- 1 8-ounce carton dairy sour cream
- 1 8-ounce jar salsa

Pantry list:

Garlic

Olive oil

Shrimp and Pea Pod **Stuffed Peppers**

(See photo on page 144.)

Start to Finish: 30 minutes

- 4 **small or 2 large sweet peppers**
- 1 **3-ounce package shrimp- or mushroom-flavor ramen noodles**
- 8 **ounces frozen peeled and deveined cooked shrimp**
- ⅓ **cup bottled hoisin or stir-fry sauce**
- 1½ **cups chopped bok choy**
- ¾ **cup pea pods, strings and tips removed and halved or ½ of a 6-ounce package frozen pea pods, thawed and halved**
- 4 **green onions, thinly sliced**
- ¼ **teaspoon crushed red pepper (optional)**
- 2 **teaspoons toasted sesame seeds**

1 Cut tops off small peppers or halve large peppers lengthwise. Remove membranes and seeds. In a 4-quart Dutch oven cook sweet peppers in boiling water for 3 minutes. Remove; drain peppers, cut sides down, on paper towels.

2 For filling, break noodles. In a saucepan cook noodles and seasoning according to package directions. Add shrimp and cook for 30 seconds. Drain noodle mixture, discarding liquid. Return noodle mixture to pot. Add hoisin sauce, bok choy, pea pods, green onions, and, if desired, crushed red pepper; heat through.

3 Arrange peppers, cut sides up, on a serving platter. Spoon filling into peppers. Spoon any remaining filling around peppers. Sprinkle with toasted sesame seeds. Serve warm or refrigerate and serve cold.

Makes 4 servings

Nutrition facts per serving: 256 cal., 6 g total fat (2 g sat. fat), 111 mg chol., 1,050 mg sodium, 33 g carbo., 4 g dietary fiber, 19 g protein.

Shopping list:

1 4 small sweet peppers

1 3-ounce package shrimp-flavor ramen noodles

8 ounces frozen peeled and deveined cooked shrimp

1 8-ounce bottle hoisin sauce

1 bunch bok choy

2 ounces fresh pea pods

1 bunch green onions

1 small container sesame seeds

30minutes

Shanghai **Pasta** *(See photo on page 275.)*

Start to Finish: 30 minutes

- 8 ounces dried fusilli, linguine, or spaghetti
- 3 tablespoons soy sauce
- 1 tablespoon bottled plum sauce
- 1 teaspoon toasted sesame oil
- ½ teaspoon red chili paste (optional)
- 1 tablespoon cooking oil
- 1 medium red and/or green sweet pepper, cut into bite-size pieces
- 1 cup fresh green beans, cut into 1-inch pieces, or 1 cup pea pods, trimmed
- 12 ounces frozen peeled and deveined large shrimp without tails, thawed (26 to 30 shrimp per pound count)
- 2 cloves garlic, minced
- 1 teaspoon grated fresh ginger
- ¼ teaspoon ground black pepper
- 2 green onions, bias-sliced into 1-inch pieces
- 2 teaspoons sesame seeds, toasted

1 Cook pasta according to package directions. Drain. Set aside. Keep warm. For sauce, stir together soy sauce, plum sauce, sesame oil, and if desired, chili paste. Set aside.

2 Pour cooking oil into a wok or large skillet. (If necessary, add more oil during cooking.) Cook and stir sweet pepper and beans in hot oil for 5 minutes. Push from center of wok. Add shrimp, garlic, ginger, and black pepper to center of wok. Cook and stir for 2 to 3 minutes or until shrimp are opaque. Stir in sauce and pea pods. Stir in pasta; heat through. To serve, top with green onions and sesame seeds.

Makes 4 servings

Nutrition facts per serving: 387 cal., 8 g total fat (1 g sat. fat), 129 mg chol., 850 mg sodium, 51 g carbo., 3 g dietary fiber, 27 g protein.

Shopping list:
- 1 16-ounce package dried fusilli
- 1 5.5-ounce bottle plum sauce
- 1 8-ounce bottle toasted sesame oil
- 1 medium red sweet pepper
- 6 ounces fresh green beans
- 12 ounces frozen peeled and deveined large shrimp without tails
- 1 piece fresh ginger
- 1 bunch green onions
- 1 small container sesame seeds

Pantry list:
Soy sauce

Cooking oil

Garlic

Ground black pepper

30 minutes

Southwestern Shrimp

Start to Finish: **30 minutes**

1 ½ **pounds fresh or frozen peeled and deveined medium shrimp***

2 **cloves garlic, minced**

1 **teaspoon ground chipotle chile pepper**

½ **teaspoon ground cumin**

¼ **teaspoon salt**

1 **tablespoon cooking oil**

½ **teaspoon finely shredded lime peel**

2 **tablespoons lime juice**

1 **teaspoon honey**

3 **tablespoons snipped fresh cilantro**

1 **14.8-ounce pouch cooked long-grain white rice**

1 **15-ounce can black beans, rinsed and drained**

1 If frozen, place shrimp in a bowl of cool water; let stand for 10 minutes. Drain well. In a large bowl combine shrimp, garlic, chile pepper, cumin, and salt. In a large skillet cook and stir shrimp mixture in hot oil over medium-high heat for 2 to 3 minutes or until shrimp are opaque. Remove from heat. Stir in lime peel, 1 tablespoon of the lime juice, honey, and 1 tablespoon of the cilantro.

2 Meanwhile, heat rice according to package directions. In a medium bowl combine rice, black beans, remaining 2 tablespoons cilantro, and remaining 1 tablespoon lime juice. Serve rice mixture with shrimp mixture.

Makes 6 servings

Nutrition facts per serving: 303 cal., 6 g total fat (1 g sat. fat), 172 mg chol., 534 mg sodium, 35 g carbo., 4 g dietary fiber, 28 g protein.

*Note: If shrimp have intact tails, allow about 5 minutes to remove tails.

Shopping list:

1 ½ pounds fresh or frozen peeled and deveined medium shrimp

1 small container ground chipotle chile pepper

1 lime

1 bunch fresh cilantro

1 14.8-ounce pouch cooked long-grain white rice

1 15-ounce can black beans

Pantry list:

Garlic

Ground cumin

Salt

Cooking oil

Honey

30 minutes

Shrimp Po' Boy *(See photo on page 144.)*

Start to Finish: **30 minutes**

- 1 **12-ounce package frozen medium shrimp**
- 2 **teaspoons Old Bay seasoning**
- ¼ **teaspoon ground black pepper**
- 1 **tablespoon cooking oil**
- 1 **cup purchased deli coleslaw**
- 2 **teaspoons prepared horseradish**
- ½ **teaspoon bottled hot pepper sauce**
- 4 **French or hoagie rolls, split and toasted**

  Potato chips or corn chips (optional)

1 Place shrimp in a medium bowl half-filled with cool water. Let stand for 5 minutes; drain. Remove tails, if present. In the same bowl toss shrimp with Old Bay seasoning and pepper.

2 In a large skillet cook shrimp in hot oil over medium-high heat for 3 minutes or until opaque.

3 In a small mixing bowl combine coleslaw, horseradish, and hot pepper sauce. To serve, divide shrimp among roll bottoms. Top with coleslaw mixture. Add roll tops. If desired, serve with chips.

Makes 4 servings

Nutrition facts per serving: 545 cal., 14 g total fat (3 g sat. fat), 132 mg chol., 1,158 mg sodium, 77 g carbo., 4 g dietary fiber, 29 g protein.

Shopping list:
- 1 12-ounce package frozen medium uncooked shrimp
- 1 6-ounce container Old Bay seasoning
- ½ pint deli coleslaw
- 1 8-ounce jar prepared horseradish
- 1 package French rolls

Pantry list:
Ground black pepper

Cooking oil

Bottled hot pepper sauce

Mediterranean Scallops and Pasta

Start to Finish: **30 minutes**

1 **pound fresh or frozen sea scallops**

2 **tablespoons olive oil**

2 **tablespoons lemon juice**

2 **teaspoons dried Mediterranean seasoning, crushed**

8 **ounces dried fettuccine**

1 **6-ounce jar quartered marinated artichoke hearts, drained**

¼ **cup oil-packed dried tomatoes, well drained and sliced**

¼ **cup purchased basil pesto**

1 Thaw scallops, if frozen. Rinse scallops; drain well. Halve any large scallops. In a medium bowl combine olive oil, lemon juice, and Mediterranean seasoning; add scallops and toss to coat. Cover and chill for 15 minutes.

2 Meanwhile, in a 4-quart Dutch oven or saucepan cook pasta according to package directions. Drain well; return to pot. Add artichokes, tomatoes, and pesto. Toss to coat. Keep warm.

3 In a large skillet bring scallop mixture to boiling over medium-high heat. Boil gently, uncovered, for 3 to 4 minutes or until scallops are opaque, turning scallops occasionally. Add scallop mixture to pasta mixture. Toss to coat. Heat through. Serve immediately.

Makes 4 servings

Nutrition facts per serving: 537 cal., 22 g total fat (1 g sat. fat), 40 mg chol., 592 mg sodium, 54 g carbo., 2 g dietary fiber, 29 g protein.

Shopping list:

1 pound fresh or frozen sea scallops

1 lemon

1 small container Mediterranean seasoning

1 16-ounce package dried fettuccine

1 6-ounce jar marinated quartered artichoke hearts

1 8-ounce jar oil-packed dried tomatoes

1 7-ounce container basil pesto

Pantry list:

Olive oil

30 minutes

Fettuccine and Vegetables **Alfredo**

Start to Finish: **20 minutes**

- 1 16-ounce package frozen sugar snap stir-fry vegetable blend (carrot, snap peas, onion, and mushrooms)
- 1 cup frozen sweet soybeans (edamame)
- 1 9-ounce package refrigerated fettuccine
- 1 16-ounce jar **Alfredo pasta sauce**
- ½ cup finely shredded Parmesan cheese
- ¼ cup milk
- 2 tablespoons purchased basil pesto

1 In a 4-quart Dutch oven bring a large amount of water to boiling. Add stir-fry vegetable blend and soybeans. Cook for 3 minutes. Add fettuccine; cook 3 minutes more or according to package directions. Drain mixture and return to Dutch oven.

2 Meanwhile, for sauce, in a medium saucepan heat pasta sauce, ¼ cup of the Parmesan cheese, milk, and pesto until heated through.

3 Add sauce to pasta mixture; toss to coat. Top with remaining ¼ cup Parmesan cheese.

Makes 4 servings

Nutrition facts per serving: 691 cal., 37 g total fat (16 g sat. fat), 117 mg chol., 1,107 mg sodium, 61 g carbo., 7 g dietary fiber, 28 g protein.

Shopping list:

- 1 16-ounce package frozen sugar snap stir-fry vegetable blend
- 1 12-ounce package frozen sweet soybeans
- 1 9-ounce package refrigerated fettuccine
- 1 16-ounce jar Alfredo pasta sauce
- 1 8-ounce package finely shredded Parmesan cheese
- 1 8-ounce container basil pesto

Pantry list:

Milk

Cheese Ravioli with Roasted Pepper Sauce

Start to Finish: **25 minutes**

1 **16-ounce package refrigerated 3-cheese ravioli or two 9-ounce packages refrigerated 4-cheese ravioli**

1 **25- to 32-ounce jar roasted red pepper marinara sauce**

1 **2.25-ounce can sliced pitted ripe olives, drained**

1 **4-ounce can mushroom stems and pieces, drained**

½ **cup finely chopped green sweet pepper**

¾ **cup whipping cream**

¼ **cup shredded fresh basil (optional)**

1 In a large saucepan cook ravioli according to package directions. Drain well.

2 Meanwhile, in a medium saucepan combine marinara sauce, drained olives, drained mushrooms, sweet pepper, and whipping cream. Heat over medium heat until bubbly, stirring frequently. If desired, stir in basil. Divide ravioli among 6 plates. Pour sauce over ravioli; serve immediately.

Makes 6 servings

Nutrition facts per serving: 467 cal., 26 g total fat (15 g sat. fat), 98 mg chol., 1,018 mg sodium, 44 g carbo., 6 g dietary fiber, 13 g protein.

Shopping list:

1 16-ounce package refrigerated 3-cheese ravioli

1 25- to 32-ounce jar roasted red pepper marinara sauce

1 2.25-ounce can sliced pitted ripe olives

1 4-ounce can mushroom stems and pieces

1 green sweet pepper

1½- pint carton whipping cream

Bow Tie Pasta with **Fresh Mozzarella**

Start to Finish: **30 minutes**

1 **16-ounce package dried bow tie pasta**

3 **tablespoons olive oil**

4 **large roma tomatoes, seeded and chopped, or 2 cups cherry tomatoes, halved**

1 **15-ounce can cannellini beans (white kidney beans), rinsed and drained**

8 **ounces fresh mozzarella cheese, cubed**

¼ **cup finely shredded Parmesan cheese**

¼ **cup snipped fresh basil or 1 teaspoon dried basil, crushed**

2 **cloves garlic, minced**

¼ **teaspoon salt**

In a 5- to 6-quart Dutch oven cook pasta according to package directions; drain and return to pan. Add olive oil and toss with pasta to coat. Add tomatoes, cannellini beans, mozzarella and Parmesan cheeses, basil, garlic, and salt; toss gently to coat.

Makes 6 servings

Nutrition facts per serving: 513 cal., 17 g total fat (7 g sat. fat), 29 mg chol., 385 mg sodium, 69 g carbo., 6 g dietary fiber, 24 g protein.

minutes

30

Shopping list:

1 16-ounce package dried bow tie pasta

4 large roma tomatoes

1 15-ounce can cannellini beans (white kidney beans)

8 ounces fresh mozzarella cheese

1 8-ounce package finely shredded Parmesan cheese

1 bunch fresh basil

Pantry list:

Olive oil

Garlic

Salt

Italian Pasta Primavera

Start to Finish: **30 minutes**

- 1 **16-ounce package dried fusilli**
- 8 **ounces broccoli, rinsed, trimmed, and cut into florets (about 2 cups)**
- 8 **ounces cauliflower, rinsed, trimmed, and cut into florets (about 2 cups)**
- 1 ½ **cups milk**
- 3 **tablespoons all-purpose flour**
- 1 **teaspoon salt**
- ¼ **teaspoon ground black pepper**
- 1 **cup grated Parmesan cheese**
- ¼ **cup oil-packed dried tomatoes, well drained and chopped**

1 In a 4- to 6-quart Dutch oven cook pasta according to package directions, adding broccoli and cauliflower the last 4 to 5 minutes of cooking time. Drain and return to Dutch oven.

2 Meanwhile, in a medium microwave-safe mixing bowl whisk together milk, flour, salt, and pepper. Microwave on 100% power (high) for 3 to 4 minutes, stirring every 30 seconds until thickened. Add milk mixture, Parmesan cheese, and dried tomatoes to cooked pasta in Dutch oven. Stir gently to combine.

Makes 6 servings

Nutrition facts per serving: 415 cal., 7 g total fat (3 g sat. fat), 17 mg chol., 657 mg sodium, 68 g carbo., 5 g dietary fiber, 19 g protein.

Shopping list:
1 16-ounce package fusilli

8 ounces broccoli

8 ounces cauliflower

1 4-ounce package grated Parmesan cheese

1 8-ounce jar oil-packed dried tomatoes

Pantry list:
Milk

All-purpose flour

Salt

Ground black pepper

30 minutes

Rotini with Broccoli in Alfredo Sauce

Start to Finish: **30 minutes**

1 **16-ounce package dried rotini**

12 **ounces broccoli, cut into bite-size pieces**

1 **small red sweet pepper, cut into bite-size strips**

1 **cup whipping cream**

1 **egg yolk**

½ **cup butter, melted**

1½ **cups finely shredded Parmesan cheese**

1 In a Dutch oven cook rotini according to package directions, adding the broccoli and sweet pepper for the last 4 minutes of cooking time. Meanwhile, in a small bowl whisk together cream and egg yolk; set aside.

2 Drain pasta; return to pan. Add cream mixture, butter, and Parmesan cheese. Cook and stir over low heat for 2 to 3 minutes or until heated through (165°F).

Makes 6 servings

Nutrition facts per serving: 662 cal., 38 g total fat (23 g sat. fat), 145 mg chol., 481 mg sodium, 61 g carbo., 4 g dietary fiber, 20 g protein.

Shopping list:

1 16-ounce package dried rotini

12 ounces fresh broccoli

1 small red sweet pepper

1 8-ounce carton whipping cream

1 8-ounce package finely shredded Parmesan cheese

Pantry list:

Egg

Butter

30 minutes

Tex-Mex **Lasagna**

Start to Finish: **30 minutes**   Oven: **400°F**

Nonstick cooking
spray

6 10-inch flour tortillas

1 15-ounce can
   tomato sauce

1 15-ounce can
   black beans, rinsed
   and drained

1 cup frozen whole
   kernel corn

½ cup chopped
   green onions

1 8-ounce package
   sliced Colby-Jack or
   shredded Mexican-
   style four-cheese blend

Dairy sour cream
(optional)

Salsa (optional)

Preheat oven to 400°F. Lightly coat a 3-quart rectangular baking dish with nonstick cooking spray; set aside. Cut tortillas in half; cover bottom of dish with 4 of the tortilla halves, cut side facing edge of dish. Layer with ⅓ each of the tomato sauce, beans, corn, green onions, and cheese. Repeat layers twice. Cover with foil; bake for 20 minutes or until heated through. If desired, serve with sour cream and salsa.

Makes 6 servings

Nutrition facts per serving: 465 cal., 18 g total fat (9 g sat. fat), 34 mg chol., 1,242 mg sodium, 60 g carbo., 8 g dietary fiber, 19 g protein.

Shopping list:

1 package 10-inch flour tortillas

1 15-ounce can tomato sauce

1 15-ounce can black beans

1 9-ounce package frozen
   whole kernel corn

1 bunch green onions

1 8-ounce package sliced
   Colby-Monterey Jack cheese

Pantry list:

Nonstick cooking spray

30minutes

White Bean and Sweet Potato Chili

Start to Finish: **30 minutes**

1 large onion, chopped (1 cup)

3 cloves garlic, minced

1 tablespoon cooking oil

2 15- to 19-ounce cans cannellini beans (white kidney beans), rinsed and drained

2 14.5-ounce cans Mexican-style stewed tomatoes, cut up, undrained

1 14-ounce can chicken broth

1 4-ounce can diced green chile peppers

1 15-ounce can cut sweet potatoes, drained and cut in bite-size pieces

In a 4-quart Dutch oven cook onion and garlic in hot oil over medium heat until tender. Stir in beans, undrained tomatoes, broth, and green chiles. Bring to boiling, reduce heat. Stir in sweet potatoes. Simmer, uncovered, for 15 minutes.

Makes 6 servings

Nutrition facts per serving: 162 cal., 3 g total fat (0 g sat. fat), 1 mg chol., 1,007 mg sodium, 33 g carbo., 7 g dietary fiber, 10 g protein.

Shopping list:

1 large onion

2 15- to 19-ounce cans cannellini beans

2 14.5-ounce cans Mexican-style stewed tomatoes

1 14-ounce can chicken broth

1 4-ounce can diced green chile peppers

1 15-ounce can cut sweet potatoes

Pantry list:

Garlic

Cooking oil

30 minutes

Spanish-Style **Rice**

Start to Finish: **30 minutes**

1 **14.5-ounce can Mexican-style stewed tomatoes, cut up, undrained**

½ **cup water**

1 **teaspoon chili powder**

½ **cup uncooked long-grain rice**

¼ **teaspoon salt**

⅛ **teaspoon ground black pepper**

Several dashes bottled hot pepper sauce (optional)

¼ **cup chopped pimiento-stuffed olives or chopped pitted ripe olives**

½ **cup shredded cheddar cheese**

In a medium saucepan combine tomatoes, the water, chili powder, rice, salt, pepper, and, if desired, hot pepper sauce. Bring to boiling; reduce heat. Simmer, covered, about 20 minutes or until rice is tender and most of the liquid is absorbed. Stir in olives. Sprinkle with cheese.

Makes 4 or 5 servings

Nutrition facts per serving: 185 cal., 6 g total fat (3 g sat. fat), 15 mg chol., 590 mg sodium, 25 g carbo., 2 g dietary fiber, 6 g protein.

Shopping list:
1 14.5-ounce can Mexican-style stewed tomatoes

1 7-ounce package long-grain rice

1 5-ounce jar pimiento-stuffed green olives

1 8-ounce package shredded cheddar cheese

Pantry list:
Chili powder

Salt

Ground black pepper

Quick Rice and Black Beans

Start to Finish: **25 minutes**

1 ¼ cups uncooked instant brown rice

1 14-ounce can reduced-sodium chicken broth

1 15-ounce can black beans, rinsed and drained

1 ½ cups frozen whole kernel corn

1 cup salsa

2 tablespoons snipped fresh cilantro

1 cup shredded Monterey Jack or cheddar cheese (4 ounces)

In a large saucepan combine rice, broth, beans, corn, and salsa. Bring to boiling; reduce heat. Simmer, covered, for 10 minutes. Remove from heat. Stir in cilantro and half of the cheese. Let stand, covered, for 5 minutes. Top with remaining cheese.

Makes 4 servings

Nutrition facts per serving: 411 cal., 12 g total fat (6 g sat. fat), 25 mg chol., 1,188 mg sodium, 62 g carbo., 10 g dietary fiber, 22 g protein.

30 minutes

Shopping list:
1 8-ounce package instant brown rice

1 14-ounce can reduced-sodium chicken broth

1 15-ounce can black beans

1 10-ounce package frozen whole kernel corn

1 8-ounce jar salsa

1 small bunch fresh cilantro

1 8-ounce package shredded cheddar cheese

Italian Bean and **Pasta Soup**

Start to Finish: **30 minutes**

1 large onion, chopped (1 cup)

1 teaspoon bottled minced garlic

1 tablespoon olive oil

2 14-ounce cans vegetable broth

1 medium green sweet pepper, seeded and chopped

½ cup dried orzo

2 14.5-ounce cans diced tomatoes with basil, garlic, and oregano, undrained

1 19-ounce can fava beans, rinsed and drained

1 15-ounce can navy beans, rinsed and drained

¼ cup snipped fresh Italian (flat-leaf) parsley

1 In 4-to 5-quart Dutch oven cook onion and garlic in hot oil over medium heat for 5 minutes or until tender, stirring occasionally. Add broth; bring to boiling.

2 Add sweet pepper and orzo. Return to boiling; reduce heat. Simmer, uncovered, for 8 to 10 minutes or until orzo is tender. Stir in undrained tomatoes, fava beans, and navy beans. Cover and simmer for 5 minutes. Stir in parsley.

Makes 6 servings

Nutrition facts per serving: 295 cal., 3 g total fat (0 g sat. fat), 0 mg chol., 1,953 mg sodium, 54 g carbo., 9 g dietary fiber, 15 g protein.

Shopping list:

1 large onion

2 14-ounce cans vegetable broth

1 medium green sweet pepper

2 14.5-ounce cans diced tomatoes with basil, garlic, and oregano

1 19-ounce can fava beans

1 15-ounce can navy beans

1 bunch fresh Italian (flat-leaf) parsley

Pantry list:

Bottled minced garlic

Olive oil

Dried orzo

Hearty Black Bean **Soup**

Start to Finish: 30 minutes

2 **14-ounce cans vegetable broth**

2 **15-ounce cans black beans, rinsed and drained**

1 **14.5-ounce can diced tomatoes and green chilies, undrained**

1 **11-ounce can whole kernel corn with sweet peppers, drained**

1 **teaspoon ground cumin**

Dairy sour cream (optional)

Shredded cheddar cheese (optional)

In a large saucepan combine broth, beans, tomatoes, corn, and cumin. Bring to boiling; reduce heat. Simmer, covered, for 10 minutes. Ladle soup into bowls. If desired, garnish each serving with sour cream and shredded cheese.

Makes 6 servings

Nutrition facts per serving: 155 cal., 1 g total fat (0 g sat. fat), 0 mg chol., 1,348 mg sodium, 33 g carbo., 9 g dietary fiber, 11 g protein.

Shopping list:

2 14-ounce cans vegetable broth

2 15-ounce cans black beans

1 14.5-ounce can diced tomatoes and green chilies

1 11-ounce can whole kernel corn with sweet peppers

Pantry list:

Ground cumin

Cheesy Corn and Potato Chowder

Start to Finish: **30 minutes**

- 4 **cups vegetable broth**
- ½ **of a 32-ounce package frozen diced hash brown potatoes (3 ½ cups)**
- 2 **cups frozen whole kernel corn**
- 1 **large onion, chopped (1 cup)**
- 1 **stalk celery, chopped (½ cup)**
- 1 ½ **cups milk**
- 3 **tablespoons all-purpose flour**
- ¼ **teaspoon salt**
- ¼ **teaspoon ground black pepper**
- 1 **8-ounce package shredded cheddar cheese**

1 In 4-quart Dutch oven combine vegetable broth, hash browns, corn, onion, and celery. Bring mixture to boiling; reduce heat. Simmer, covered, for 12 to 15 minutes or until potatoes are tender, stirring occasionally.

2 Meanwhile, in a 2-cup glass measure whisk together milk, flour, salt, and pepper. Add to potato mixture. Cook and stir over medium heat until thick and bubbly. Gradually stir in cheese until melted.

Makes 6 servings

Nutrition facts per serving: 432 cal., 23 g total fat (12 g sat. fat), 45 mg chol., 1,019 mg sodium, 44 g carbo., 4 g dietary fiber, 16 g protein.

*Test Kitchen Tip: Heat the broth, hash browns, and corn while chopping the onion and celery. Cover the Dutch oven while bringing the mixture to boiling.

Shopping list:

- 3 14-ounce cans vegetable broth
- 1 32-ounce package frozen diced hash brown potatoes
- 1 16-ounce package frozen whole kernel corn
- 1 large onion
- 1 bunch celery
- 1 8-ounce package shredded cheddar cheese

Pantry list:

Milk

All-purpose flour

Salt

Ground black pepper

30 minutes

Mediterranean Pizza with Bruschetta Topping

Start to Finish: **30 minutes**   Oven: **400°F**

1   26-ounce 4-cheese (mozzarella, cheddar, provolone, and Parmesan) frozen pizza

1   2.25-ounce can sliced pitted ripe olives, drained

1   6-ounce jar marinated artichoke hearts, drained and cut up

1 ½   cups chopped roma tomatoes (about 6 small)

1   teaspoon dried basil, crushed

½   teaspoon bottled minced garlic

¼   teaspoon salt

1 Preheat oven to 400°F. Place frozen pizza on pizza pan or baking sheet. Evenly sprinkle olives and chopped artichoke hearts over pizza. Bake for 19 to 23 minutes or until crust is light golden brown.

2 Meanwhile, for bruschetta topping, in a small bowl, combine tomatoes, basil, garlic, and salt. Spoon topping over hot pizza and serve.

Makes 4 servings

Nutrition facts per serving: 557 cal., 28 g total fat (8 g sat. fat), 26 mg chol., 1,233 mg sodium, 61 g carbo., 7 g dietary fiber, 22 g protein.

30 minutes

Shopping list:
1 26-ounce 4-cheese pizza

1 2.25-ounce can sliced pitted ripé olives

1 6-ounce jar marinated artichoke hearts

6 small roma tomatoes

Pantry list:
Dried basil

Bottled minced garlic

Salt

Dinnertime Scrambled Egg **Quesadillas**

Start to Finish: **30 minutes**

1 medium red or green sweet pepper, chopped (¾ cup)

¼ cup finely chopped onion

1 tablespoon butter

6 eggs

1 3-ounce package cream cheese, cut into ½-inch cubes

¼ teaspoon salt

⅛ teaspoon ground black pepper

4 10-inch flour tortillas

Nonstick cooking spray

Salsa

1 In a large skillet cook and stir sweet pepper and onion in hot butter over medium heat for 3 minutes. Meanwhile, in a large mixing bowl, beat eggs using a whisk. Add cream cheese, salt, and pepper; pour over pepper and onion in skillet. Cook over medium heat, without stirring, until mixture begins to set on the bottom and around edge. With a spatula or a large spoon, lift and fold the partially cooked egg mixture so that the uncooked portion flows underneath. Continue cooking over medium heat for 2 to 3 minutes or until egg mixture is cooked through, but is still glossy and moist. Remove from heat.

2 Lightly coat one side of a tortilla with cooking spray. Place tortilla, coated side down on a work surface. Spoon one-fourth of the egg mixture over one side of tortilla; fold opposite side over filling. Place filled tortilla in a large skillet or on a griddle. Cook over medium low heat for 3 to 4 minutes, turning once, until tortilla is light brown and crisp. Repeat with remaining tortillas and egg mixture. Serve with salsa.

Makes 4 servings

Nutrition facts per serving: 462 cal., 23 g total fat (10 g sat. fat), 348 mg chol., 872 mg sodium, 46 g carbo., 4 g dietary fiber, 18 g protein.

Shopping list:

1 medium red or green sweet pepper

1 small onion

1 3-ounce package cream cheese

1 package 10-inch flour tortillas

1 8-ounce jar salsa

Pantry list:

Butter

Eggs

Salt

Ground black pepper

Nonstick cooking spray

30 minutes

Mediterranean Frittata

Start to Finish: 25 minutes

- 1 **cup chopped onion (1 large)**
- 2 **cloves garlic, minced**
- 3 **tablespoons olive oil**
- 8 **eggs, beaten**
- ¼ **cup half-and-half, light cream, or milk**
- ½ **cup crumbled feta cheese (2 ounces)**
- ½ **cup chopped bottled roasted red sweet peppers**
- ½ **cup sliced kalamata or pitted ripe olives (optional)**
- ¼ **cup slivered fresh basil**
- ⅛ **teaspoon ground black pepper**
- ½ **cup onion-and-garlic croutons, coarsely crushed**
- 2 **tablespoons finely shredded Parmesan cheese**

  Fresh basil leaves (optional)

1 Preheat broiler. In a large broilerproof skillet cook onion and garlic in 2 tablespoons hot oil until onion is just tender.

2 Meanwhile, in a medium bowl beat together eggs and half-and-half. Stir in feta cheese, roasted sweet pepper, olives (if desired), basil, and black pepper. Pour egg mixture over onion mixture in skillet. Cook over medium heat. As mixture sets, run a spatula around the edge of the skillet, lifting egg mixture so uncooked portion flows underneath. Continue cooking and lifting edges until egg mixture is almost set (surface will be moist). Reduce heat as necessary to prevent overcooking.

3 In a small bowl combine crushed croutons, Parmesan cheese, and the remaining 1 tablespoon oil; sprinkle mixture over frittata.

4 Broil 4 to 5 inches from heat for 1 to 2 minutes or until top is set and crumbs are golden. Cut frittata in wedges to serve. If desired, garnish with fresh basil leaves.

Makes 6 servings

Nutrition facts per serving: 246 cal., 19 g total fat (5 g sat. fat), 295 mg chol., 383 mg sodium, 8 g carbo., 1 g dietary fiber, 11 g protein.

Shopping list:
- 1 large onion
- 1 8-ounce carton half-and-half
- 1 4-ounce package crumbled feta cheese
- 1 7-ounce jar roasted red sweet peppers
- 1 8-ounce jar kalamata olives
- 1 package fresh basil
- 1 package onion-and-garlic croutons
- 1 8-ounce package finely shredded Parmesan cheese

Pantry list:
- Garlic
- Olive oil
- Eggs
- Black pepper

30 minutes

40 minute meals

Chicken with Pan Sauce

Start to Finish: **35 minutes**

- 4 **skinless, boneless chicken breast halves**
- ¼ **teaspoon salt**
- ¼ **teaspoon freshly ground black pepper**
- 5 **tablespoons cold butter**
- ⅔ **cup dry white wine**
- ½ **cup chicken broth**
- ¼ **cup finely chopped shallot or onion**
- 2 **tablespoons whipping cream**

1 Place 1 chicken breast half between two pieces of plastic wrap. Using the flat side of a meat mallet, pound the chicken lightly to about ¼ inch thick. Remove plastic wrap. Repeat with remaining chicken. Sprinkle chicken with salt and pepper.

2 In a large skillet cook chicken in 1 tablespoon hot butter over medium heat for 6 to 8 minutes or until no longer pink (170°F), turning once. Transfer chicken to a platter; cover with foil to keep warm.

3 Add wine, broth, and shallot to hot skillet. Cook and stir to scrape up browned bits from the bottom of the pan. Bring to boiling. Boil gently for 10 to 15 minutes or until liquid is reduced to ¼ cup. Reduce heat to medium-low.

4 Stir cream into skillet. Add remaining 4 tablespoons butter, 1 tablespoon at a time, stirring after each addition until butter melts. Sauce should be slightly thick. Season to taste with additional salt and pepper. Serve sauce over chicken.

Makes 4 servings

Nutrition facts per breast half + 2 tablespoons sauce: 325 cal., 20 g total fat (10 g sat. fat), 117 mg chol., 444 mg sodium, 2 g carbo., 0 g dietary fiber, 27 g protein.

40 minutes

Shopping list:
- 4 skinless, boneless chicken breast halves
- 1 bottle dry white wine
- 1 14-ounce can chicken broth
- 2 shallots
- 1 8-ounce carton whipping cream

Pantry list:
- Salt
- Black pepper
- Butter

Greek-Style Chicken Skillet

Start to Finish: 40 minutes

4 skinless, boneless chicken breast halves

Salt and ground black pepper

1 tablespoon olive oil or cooking oil

1 medium zucchini, sliced (about 1 ½ cups)

1 medium green sweet pepper, chopped (¾ cup)

1 medium onion, sliced and separated into rings

2 cloves garlic, minced

⅛ teaspoon ground black pepper

¼ cup water

1 10.75-ounce can condensed tomato soup

2 cups hot cooked couscous*

½ cup crumbled feta cheese (2 ounces)

Lemon wedges

1 Season chicken with salt and black pepper. In a large skillet cook chicken in hot oil over medium heat for 12 to 15 minutes or until no longer pink (170°F), turning once. Remove chicken from skillet; keep warm.

2 Add zucchini, sweet pepper, onion, garlic, and ⅛ teaspoon black pepper to skillet. Add the water; reduce heat. Cover and cook for 5 minutes, stirring once or twice. Stir in tomato soup. Bring to boiling; reduce heat. Simmer, covered, for 5 minutes, stirring once.

3 To serve, divide couscous among 4 dinner plates. Place chicken on couscous. Spoon vegetable mixture over chicken and couscous. Sprinkle with feta cheese. Serve with lemon wedges.

Makes 4 servings

Nutrition facts per serving: 401 cal., 10 g total fat (4 g sat. fat), 99 mg chol., 827 mg sodium, 36 g carbo., 4 g dietary fiber, 41 g protein.

*Note: For 2 cups cooked couscous, in a small saucepan bring 1 cup water and dash salt to boiling. Stir in ⅔ cup quick-cooking couscous. Remove from heat. Cover and let stand for 5 minutes. Fluff with a fork before serving.

Shopping list:
4 skinless, boneless chicken breast halves

1 medium zucchini

1 medium green sweet pepper

1 medium onion

1 10.75-ounce can condensed tomato soup

1 8-ounce package couscous

1 4-ounce package feta cheese

1 lemon

Pantry list:
Salt

Ground black pepper

Olive oil

Garlic

40 minutes

Chicken with Onions, Tomato, and Pasta

Start to Finish: **35 minutes**

1 ½ teaspoons coarsely ground pepper blend

¾ teaspoon salt

1 clove garlic, minced

4 skinless, boneless chicken breast halves

2 large onions, sliced

2 tablespoons olive oil

3 medium tomatoes, chopped (1 pound)

1 tablespoon tomato paste

2 to 3 teaspoons minced fresh ginger

8 ounces dried spaghetti

¼ cup purchased or fresh basil pesto

1 Combine 1 teaspoon of the pepper blend, ½ teaspoon of the salt, and garlic. Rub over chicken. In a large skillet cook chicken and onions in hot oil over medium heat about 16 minutes or until chicken is no longer pink (170°F) and onions are tender, turning chicken once and stirring onions occasionally. Remove chicken from pan, cut into strips. Return chicken to pan. Add tomatoes, tomato paste, ginger, remaining ½ teaspoon pepper blend, and ¼ teaspoon salt. Cook and stir just until heated through.

2 Meanwhile, cook spaghetti according to package directions. Drain. Return to cooking pot. Stir in pesto. Serve chicken and sauce with spaghetti.

Makes 4 servings

Nutrition facts per serving: 560 cal., 17 g total fat (3 g sat. fat), 85 mg chol., 665 mg sodium, 57 g carbo., 4 g dietary fiber, 44 g protein.

40 minutes

Shopping list:

1 small container ground pepper blend

4 skinless, boneless chicken breast halves

2 large onions

3 medium tomatoes

1 6-ounce can tomato paste

1 piece fresh ginger

1 4-ounce container basil pesto

Pantry list:

Salt

Garlic

Olive oil

Spaghetti

Garlic Chicken and Noodles

Start to Finish: **40 minutes**

- 4 **skinless, boneless chicken breast halves**
- ¼ **teaspoon salt**
- ¼ **teaspoon ground black pepper**
- 1 **tablespoon olive oil**
- 6 **cloves garlic, thickly sliced**
- ½ **cup chicken broth**
- 1 **12-ounce package frozen home-style egg noodles**
- ¾ **cup whipping cream**
- 2 **tablespoons white wine vinegar or cider vinegar**
- **Snipped fresh parsley**

1 Sprinkle both sides of chicken with salt and pepper. In a large skillet cook chicken in hot oil over medium-high heat for 5 minutes or until brown, turning once. Remove chicken from skillet. Add garlic to skillet; cook and stir for 30 seconds. Add broth; bring to boiling, stirring to loosen any browned bits from bottom of skillet. Return chicken to skillet. Reduce heat to medium-low; cover and cook about 15 minutes or until chicken is no longer pink (170°F).

2 Meanwhile, cook noodles according to package directions and drain.

3 Remove chicken from skillet; cover to keep warm. Increase heat to medium-high. Add cream and vinegar to skillet. Bring to boiling; boil gently about 5 minutes or until thick, stirring occasionally.

4 Serve chicken with noodles. Spoon cream sauce over chicken and noodles and top with snipped fresh parsley.

Makes 4 servings

Nutrition facts per serving: 594 cal., 25 g total fat (12 g sat. fat), 243 mg chol., 391 mg sodium, 48 g carbo., 2 g dietary fiber, 41 g protein.

Shopping list:
- 4 skinless, boneless chicken breast halves
- 1 14-ounce can chicken broth
- 1 12-ounce package frozen home-style egg noodles
- 1 8-ounce carton whipping cream
- 1 bottle white wine vinegar
- 1 bunch fresh parsley

Pantry list:
- Salt
- Ground black pepper
- Olive oil
- Garlic

40 minutes

Pecan-Crust Chicken

Start to Finish: **35 minutes**

- 2 tablespoons orange marmalade
- 2 tablespoons pure maple syrup
- 1 cup finely chopped pecans
- 3 tablespoons all-purpose flour
- ¼ teaspoon salt
- 4 skinless, boneless chicken breast halves
- 2 tablespoons cooking oil
- 1 tablespoon butter

1 In a small bowl stir together orange marmalade and maple syrup; set aside. In a shallow dish combine pecans, flour, and salt. Brush both sides of chicken breast halves with marmalade mixture. Dip chicken into pecan mixture to coat, pressing pecan mixture onto chicken, if necessary.

2 In a 12-inch skillet heat cooking oil and butter over medium heat until butter melts and mixture begins to bubble. Add chicken and cook for 6 minutes. Turn chicken. Cook for 6 to 9 minutes more or until golden brown and no longer pink (170°F). Watch closely and reduce heat if chicken browns too quickly.

Makes 4 servings

Nutrition facts per serving: 506 cal., 32 g total fat (5 g sat. fat), 90 mg chol., 279 mg sodium, 21 g carbo., 3 g dietary fiber, 36 g protein.

40 minutes

Shopping list:
- 1 8-ounce jar orange marmalade
- 1 8-ounce package pecans
- 4 skinless, boneless chicken breast halves

Pantry list:
Maple syrup

All-purpose flour

Salt

Cooking oil

Butter

Pronto **Pasta**

Start to Finish: **40 minutes**

8 ounces dried
   fettuccine, linguine,
   or spaghetti

2 teaspoons dried
   thyme, crushed

1 ½ teaspoons lemon-
   pepper seasoning

½ teaspoon bottled
   minced garlic

4 skinless, boneless
   chicken breast halves

1 tablespoon olive oil

2 medium yellow
   summer squash and/
   or zucchini, sliced
   (2 ½ cups)

1 medium green or red
   sweet pepper, cut into
   thin strips

1 cup chicken broth

4 teaspoons all-purpose
   flour

1 medium tomato,
   seeded and cut into
   chunks (optional)

1 Cook pasta according to package directions. Meanwhile, in a small bowl combine thyme, lemon-pepper seasoning, and garlic. Set aside half of the mixture. Rub remaining herb mixture into chicken.

2 In a large skillet heat oil over medium-high heat. Add chicken; reduce heat to medium. Cook for 8 to 12 minutes or until no longer pink (170°F), turning once.

3 Remove chicken from skillet; cover and keep warm. Add squash, sweet pepper, and reserved herb mixture to skillet. Cook and stir over medium heat for 3 to 4 minutes or until vegetables are crisp-tender. In a small bowl combine broth and flour. Add to skillet. Cook and stir until thick and bubbly. Cook and stir for 1 minute more.

4 Drain pasta and return to pan; add vegetable mixture and toss gently to combine. Arrange pasta mixture on dinner plates. Slice chicken and arrange on top of pasta mixture. If desired, sprinkle with tomato.

Makes 4 servings

Nutrition facts per serving: 396 cal., 6 g total fat (1 g sat. fat), 66 mg chol., 727 mg sodium, 48 g carbo., 3 g dietary fiber, 35 g protein.

Shopping list:

1 16-ounce package dried fettuccine

1 small container lemon-pepper seasoning

4 skinless, boneless chicken breast halves

2 medium yellow summer squash

1 medium green sweet pepper

1 14-ounce can chicken broth

Pantry list:

Dried thyme

Bottled minced garlic

Olive oil

All-purpose flour

40 minutes

Quick **Chicken Stew**

Start to Finish: **35 minutes**

3 tablespoons all-purpose flour

⅛ teaspoon salt

⅛ teaspoon ground black pepper

4 skinless, boneless chicken breast halves, halved crosswise

2 tablespoons olive oil

2 cups fresh mushrooms, quartered

2 tablespoons finely chopped onion

1 teaspoon minced garlic

6 ounces baby carrots with tops

2 cups fresh green beans, cut into 2-inch lengths

¾ cup chicken broth

¾ cup dry white wine

2 teaspoons lemon juice

1 tablespoon snipped fresh dillweed or ½ teaspoon dried dillweed

1 In a shallow bowl combine flour, salt, and pepper. Coat chicken breasts with flour mixture, shaking off excess and reserving remaining flour. In a large skillet cook chicken in hot oil for 4 minutes or until golden brown, turning once. Remove chicken; set aside.

2 Add mushrooms, onion, and garlic to skillet. Cook and stir about 3 minutes or until vegetables are tender. Meanwhile, remove all but 1 inch of carrot tops; halve carrots lengthwise and discard greens. Add carrots and beans to skillet. Sprinkle vegetables with remaining flour mixture; stir well.

3 Remove skillet from heat; stir in broth and wine. Return skillet to heat; return chicken breasts to pan. Bring mixture to boiling; reduce heat. Simmer, covered, about 5 minutes or until chicken is no longer pink (170°F). Stir in lemon juice and dillweed.

Makes 4 servings

Nutrition facts per serving: 293 cal., 10 g total fat (2 g sat. fat), 66 mg chol., 356 mg sodium, 15 g carbo., 4 g dietary fiber, 30 g protein.

Shopping list:

4 skinless, boneless chicken breast halves

1 8-ounce package fresh mushrooms

1 small onion

6 ounces fresh baby carrots

8 ounces fresh green beans

1 14-ounce can chicken broth

1 bottle dry white wine

1 lemon

1 package fresh dillweed

Pantry list:

All-purpose flour

Salt

Ground black pepper

Olive oil

Garlic

40 minutes

Skillet **Cacciatore** *(See photo on page 274.)*

Start to Finish: 40 minutes

- 8 ounces dried bow tie pasta (3 cups)
- 4 skinless, boneless chicken breast halves
- 1 tablespoon olive oil
- 1 8-ounce package sliced mushrooms
- 1 ½ cups red, green and/or orange sweet pepper cut into bite-size strips
- 1 medium onion, cut into thin wedges
- 1 14-ounce can diced tomatoes with basil, garlic, and oregano, undrained
- 1 teaspoon dried Italian seasoning, crushed
- ¼ teaspoon crushed red pepper
- Finely shredded Parmesan cheese

1 Prepare pasta according to package directions; drain.

2 Meanwhile, in a large skillet cook chicken in hot oil about 5 minutes or until brown, turning once; remove from skillet. Add mushrooms, sweet peppers, and onion to skillet. Cook over medium-high heat for 5 minutes or until tender. Stir in undrained tomatoes, Italian seasoning, and crushed red pepper. Bring to boiling. Return chicken to skillet; reduce heat. Simmer, covered, for 15 minutes or until chicken is no longer pink (170°F). Serve chicken and sauce over pasta; sprinkle with Parmesan cheese.

Makes 4 servings

Nutrition facts per serving: 476 cal., 8 g total fat (2 g sat. fat), 87 mg chol., 374 mg sodium, 55 g carbo., 5 g dietary fiber, 45 g protein.

Shopping list:

1 16-ounce package dried bow tie pasta

4 skinless, boneless chicken breast halves

1 8-ounce package sliced mushrooms

2 medium red sweet peppers

1 medium onion

1 14-ounce can diced tomatoes with basil, garlic, and oregano

1 5-ounce package finely shredded Parmesan cheese

Pantry list:

Olive oil

Dried Italian seasoning

Crushed red pepper

Oven-Fried Barbecue **Chicken** (See photo on page 275.)

Start to Finish: **40 minutes**   Oven: **375°F**

4 **skinless, boneless chicken breast halves**

1 **tablespoon barbecue spice**

¼ **cup butter, melted**

¾ **cup finely crushed cornflakes**

1 **15-ounce can black beans, rinsed and drained**

1 **11-ounce can whole kernel corn with sweet peppers, drained**

1 **medium tomato, chopped**

1 **jalapeño pepper, finely chopped* (optional)**

1 **tablespoon lime juice**

1 **teaspoon ground cumin**

2 **jalapeño peppers, halved lengthwise and broiled (optional)**

1 Preheat oven to 375°F. Lightly grease a baking sheet; set aside. Sprinkle both sides of chicken with barbecue spice. Place butter in a shallow dish; dip chicken in butter to coat. Place cornflakes in a resealable plastic bag. Add chicken breast halves to the bag one at a time; seal bag and shake to coat. Place chicken on prepared baking sheet. Sprinkle chicken with any remaining crushed cornflakes.

2 Bake for 20 to 25 minutes or until chicken is no longer pink (170°F). Meanwhile, in a medium bowl combine black beans, corn, tomato, chopped jalapeño pepper (if desired), lime juice, and cumin. Serve salsa with chicken and, if desired, broiled jalapeños.

Makes 4 servings

Nutrition facts per serving: 448 cal., 14 g total fat (8 g sat. fat), 113 mg chol., 1,658 mg sodium, 45 g carbo., 8 g dietary fiber, 41 g protein.

*Note: Because hot chile peppers, such as jalapeños, contain volatile oils that can burn your skin and eyes, avoid direct contact with chiles as much as possible. When working with chile peppers, wear plastic or rubber gloves. If your bare hands do touch the chile peppers, wash your hands well with soap and water.

40 minutes

Shopping list:

4 skinless, boneless chicken breast halves

1 small container barbecue spice

1 18-ounce box cornflakes

1 15-ounce can black beans

1 11-ounce can whole kernel corn with sweet peppers

1 medium tomato

1 lime

Pantry list:

Butter

Ground cumin

Spicy Stuffed Chicken Breasts

Start to Finish: **40 minutes**   Oven: **425°F**

- 4 **skinless, boneless chicken breast halves**
- ½ **cup semisoft cheese with garlic and herb**
- ¼ **cup chopped, drained pepperoncini salad peppers**
- **Salt and ground black pepper**
- 1 **tablespoon olive oil**

1 Preheat oven to 425°F. Using a small sharp knife, cut a horizontal slit in the side of each chicken breast half, cutting to, but not through the opposite side; set aside. In a small bowl combine cheese and salad peppers. Stuff chicken pockets with cheese mixture. Secure openings with wooden toothpicks. Sprinkle chicken lightly with salt and pepper.

2 In a large ovenproof skillet cook chicken in hot oil over medium-high heat until brown, turning once. Transfer skillet to oven. Bake for 15 to 20 minutes or until chicken is no longer pink (170°F). Remove chicken from skillet and remove toothpicks. Stir dripping in skillet until smooth; spoon over chicken.

Makes 4 servings

Nutrition facts per serving: 288 cal., 14 g total fat (7 g sat. fat), 107 mg chol., 458 mg sodium, 2 g carbo., 0 g dietary fiber, 35 g protein.

Shopping list:

- 4 skinless, boneless chicken breast halves
- 1 4-ounce container semisoft cheese with garlic and herb
- 1 12-ounce jar pepperoncini salad peppers

Pantry list:

- Salt
- Ground black pepper
- Olive oil

40
minutes

Buffalo Chicken Sandwich

Start to Finish: **40 minutes**

- 4 **skinless, boneless chicken breast halves**
- **Salt and ground black pepper**
- 1 **egg, lightly beaten**
- 1 **tablespoon bottled hot pepper sauce**
- ½ **cup fine dry bread crumbs**
- 2 **tablespoons cooking oil**
- 4 **kaiser rolls, split and toasted**
- ¼ **cup bottled blue cheese salad dressing**
- 2 **medium carrots, cut into bite-size sticks**
- 2 **stalks celery, cut into bite-size sticks**
- **Bottled blue cheese salad dressing**
- **Bottled hot pepper sauce**

1 Place each chicken breast half between two pieces of plastic wrap. Using the flat side of a meat mallet, pound the boned side of chicken lightly until it is an even ½-inch thickness. Sprinkle chicken lightly with salt and pepper.

2 In a shallow dish stir together egg and 1 tablespoon hot pepper sauce. In another dish place bread crumbs. Dip chicken in egg mixture then in crumbs to coat.

3 In a large skillet cook chicken in hot oil over medium heat for 10 to 12 minutes or until chicken is no longer pink (170°F), turning once. (Reduce heat to medium-low if chicken browns too quickly.)

4 Place a chicken piece on the bottom of each bun. Drizzle each with 1 tablespoon dressing. Add bun tops. Serve with carrots, celery, additional dressing, and pepper sauce.

Makes 4 servings

Nutrition facts per serving: 698 cal., 37 g total fat (7 g sat. fat), 143 mg chol., 1,249 mg sodium, 47 g carbo., 3 g dietary fiber, 45 g protein.

Shopping list:
- 4 skinless, boneless chicken breast halves
- 1 package kaiser rolls
- 1 16-ounce bottle blue cheese salad dressing
- 1 1-pound bag carrots
- 1 bunch celery

Pantry list:
- Salt
- Ground black pepper
- Egg
- Fine dry bread crumbs
- Bottled hot pepper sauce
- Cooking oil

40 minutes

Curried Chicken

Start to Finish: **40 minutes**

1 ¼ to 1 ½ **pounds skinless, boneless chicken breast halves**

2 **teaspoons curry powder**

¼ **teaspoon ground black pepper**

2 **tablespoons butter**

1 **small red sweet pepper, seeded and chopped**

¾ **cup sliced green onions (6)**

1 **10.75-ounce can reduced-fat cream of chicken soup**

1 ¾ **cups chicken broth**

¾ **cup long-grain white rice**

Salt (optional)

1 Cut chicken into 1-inch pieces; place in a medium bowl. Add curry powder and black pepper; toss to coat. Let stand for 10 minutes.

2 In a large skillet cook and stir chicken in hot butter over medium heat for 4 to 5 minutes or until brown. Using a slotted spoon, remove chicken from skillet. Add sweet pepper and ½ cup of the green onions; cook and stir about 5 minutes or until tender. Stir in soup and ¼ cup of the broth. Stir in chicken. Bring to boiling; reduce heat and simmer, covered, for 15 minutes or until chicken is no longer pink.

3 Meanwhile, in a medium saucepan bring remaining 1 ½ cups chicken broth to boiling; add rice. Cover and simmer for 15 minutes. Stir in remaining ¼ cup green onions. Let stand, covered, for 5 minutes. Serve chicken mixture over rice. If desired, season to taste with salt.

Makes 4 servings

Nutrition facts per serving: 398 cal., 9 g total fat (5 g sat. fat), 105 mg chol., 737 mg sodium, 38 g carbo., 2 g dietary fiber, 38 g protein.

Shopping list:

1 ¼ to 1 ½ pounds skinless, boneless chicken breast halves

1 small container curry powder

1 small red sweet pepper

1 bunch green onions

1 10.75-ounce can reduced-fat cream of chicken soup

1 14-ounce can chicken broth

1 16-ounce package long-grain white rice

Pantry list:

Ground black pepper

Butter

Chicken Fajita **Pasta**

Start to Finish: **35 minutes**

- 12 ounces dried pappardelle or egg noodles
- 1 8-ounce carton dairy sour cream
- ½ cup chipotle liquid meat marinade
- 2 tablespoons lime juice
- 1 teaspoon chili powder
- 1 teaspoon ground cumin
- ½ teaspoon crushed red pepper
- 1 medium onion, halved and thinly sliced
- 1 medium red sweet pepper, seeded and cut into thin bite-size strips
- 1 fresh Anaheim chile pepper, seeded and cut into thin bite-size strips* (⅓ cup)
- 2 tablespoons olive oil
- 1 to 1 ¼ pounds skinless, boneless chicken breast halves, cut into thin bite-size strips
- 1 tablespoon snipped fresh cilantro (optional)

  Lime wedges (optional)

1 In a 4- to 5-quart Dutch oven cook pasta in lightly salted boiling water according to package directions. Drain and return pasta to pan; keep warm. Meanwhile, in a medium bowl combine sour cream, marinade, lime juice, chili powder, cumin, and crushed red pepper. Set aside.

2 In a large skillet cook onion, sweet pepper, and Anaheim pepper in 1 tablespoon oil over medium heat for 4 to 5 minutes or until crisp-tender. Remove vegetables from skillet; set aside. Add remaining 1 tablespoon oil to skillet. Add half of the chicken; cook and stir over medium-high heat for 2 to 3 minutes or until chicken is no longer pink. Remove from skillet. Repeat with remaining chicken, adding additional oil if necessary.

3 Add chicken, vegetables, and sour cream mixture to pasta. Toss to coat. Cook over low heat until heated through. If desired, sprinkle with cilantro and serve with lime wedges.

Makes 6 to 8 servings

Nutrition facts per serving: 453 cal., 15 g total fat (6 g sat. fat), 60 mg chol., 589 mg sodium, 53 g carbo., 3 g dietary fiber, 27 g protein.

*Note: Because hot chile peppers contain volatile oils that can burn your skin and eyes, avoid direct contact with chiles as much as possible. When working with chile peppers, wear plastic or rubber gloves. If your bare hands do touch the chile peppers, wash your hands well with soap and water.

Shopping list:
- 1 16-ounce package pappardelle
- 1 8-ounce carton dairy sour cream
- 1 12-ounce bottle chipotle meat marinade
- 1 lime
- 1 medium onion
- 1 medium red sweet pepper
- 1 fresh Anaheim chile pepper
- 3 skinless, boneless chicken breast halves

Pantry list:
Chili powder

Ground cumin

Crushed red pepper

Olive oil

40 minutes

Ozark Mountain Succotash

Start to Finish: 40 minutes

- 12 ounces skinless, boneless chicken breast halves
- 1/3 cup all-purpose flour
- 1/3 cup yellow cornmeal
- 1/4 teaspoon salt
- 1/8 teaspoon ground black pepper
- 1 egg, lightly beaten
- 1 tablespoon milk
- 8 ounces whole okra, cut into 1/2-inch pieces (2 cups)
- 1 medium green sweet pepper, chopped (3/4 cup)
- 1 medium onion, chopped (1/2 cup)
- 2 cloves garlic, minced
- 1/3 cup cooking oil
- 1 small yellow summer squash, cut into thin bite-size strips (1 cup)
- 1 cup frozen whole kernel corn, thawed

1 Cut chicken into bite-size strips. Set side.

2 In a plastic bag combine flour, cornmeal, salt, and black pepper. In a small bowl combine egg and milk. Toss okra pieces in egg mixture. Add okra to the plastic bag, one-fourth at a time; close bag and shake to coat okra well. Set aside.

3 In a large skillet cook and stir sweet pepper, onion, and garlic in 1 tablespoon hot oil over medium-high heat for 3 to 4 minutes or until onion is tender. Add squash and corn. Cook and stir for 2 to 3 minutes more or until corn is tender. Remove from skillet. Drain vegetables on paper towels. Set aside.

4 Carefully add another 1 tablespoon oil to skillet. Add chicken. Cook and stir over medium-high heat for 2 to 3 minutes or until no longer pink. Add to vegetables. Set aside.

5 In the same skillet heat remaining oil. Fry okra, half at a time, over medium-high heat for 3 to 4 minutes or until golden, turning once. Using a slotted spoon, remove okra from skillet, reserving 2 tablespoons oil in skillet (add more oil if necessary during cooking). Return all okra to skillet.

6 Return chicken and vegetables to skillet. Heat and stir gently until heated through. Season to taste. Serve immediately.

Makes 4 servings

Nutrition facts per serving: 427 cal., 21 g total fat (4 g sat. fat), 103 mg chol., 231 mg sodium, 34 g carbo., 5 g dietary fiber, 27 g protein.

Shopping list:
- 1 12-ounce package skinless, boneless chicken breast halves
- 1 24-ounce package yellow cornmeal
- 8 ounces okra
- 1 medium green sweet pepper
- 1 medium onion
- 1 small yellow summer squash
- 1 10-ounce package frozen whole kernel corn

Pantry list:
- All-purpose flour
- Salt
- Ground black pepper
- Egg
- Milk
- Garlic
- Cooking oil

40 minutes

Tortilla Chicken Soup

Start to Finish: **40 minutes**

- 2 14-ounce cans reduced-sodium chicken broth
- 1 10.75-ounce can condensed tomato soup
- 1 medium onion, chopped (½ cup)
- ½ cup chopped green sweet pepper
- 4 skinless, boneless chicken breast halves, cut into bite-size pieces
- 1 cup loose-pack frozen whole kernel corn
- 1 ½ teaspoons chili powder
- ½ teaspoon ground cumin
- ⅛ teaspoon ground black pepper
- 3 cups tortilla chips, coarsely crushed
- 1 cup shredded Monterey Jack cheese (4 ounces)
- 1 avocado, pitted, peeled, and cut up (optional)

  Snipped fresh cilantro (optional)

1 In a 4-quart Dutch oven combine chicken broth, tomato soup, onion, and green pepper. Bring to boiling. Add chicken. Return to boiling; reduce heat. Simmer, covered, for 10 minutes.

2 Add corn, chili powder, cumin, and black pepper. Return to boiling; reduce heat. Simmer, covered, for 10 minutes more.

3 To serve, top with tortilla chips and cheese. If desired, serve with avocado and cilantro.

Makes 6 servings

Nutrition facts per serving: 318 cal., 11 g total fat (5 g sat. fat), 71 mg chol., 905 mg sodium, 24 g carbo., 3 g dietary fiber, 31 g protein.

Shopping list:
- 2 14-ounce cans reduced-sodium chicken broth
- 1 10.75-ounce can condensed tomato soup
- 1 medium onion
- 1 medium green sweet pepper
- 4 skinless, boneless chicken breast halves
- 1 10-ounce package frozen whole kernel corn
- 1 16-ounce package tortilla chips
- 1 8-ounce package shredded Monterey Jack cheese

Pantry list:
Chili powder

Ground cumin

Ground black pepper

40 minutes

Chicken with Black-Eyed Peas and Yellow Rice

Start to Finish: **35 minutes**

- 1 **cup chopped red onion**
- 1 **tablespoon olive oil**
- 1 ½ **pounds chicken breast tenderloins**
- 2 **cloves garlic, minced**
- 1 **14-ounce can reduced-sodium chicken broth**
- ½ **teaspoon poultry seasoning**
- ¼ **to ½ teaspoon ground black pepper**
- ¼ **teaspoon crushed red pepper**
- ¾ **cup saffron-flavor yellow rice mix***
- 1 **15-ounce can black-eyed peas, rinsed and drained**
- 1 **tablespoon snipped fresh thyme**

1 In a 12-inch skillet cook onion in hot oil over medium heat about 4 minutes or until tender. Add chicken and garlic; cook about 4 minutes more or until chicken is brown, turning once.

2 Stir in broth, poultry seasoning, black pepper, and crushed red pepper. Bring mixture to boiling. Stir in uncooked rice. Reduce heat. Cook, covered, about 10 minutes or until rice is almost tender.

3 Stir in black-eyed peas and thyme. Cook, covered, about 10 minutes or until heated through and liquid is absorbed.

Makes 6 servings

Nutrition facts per serving: 280 cal., 4 g total fat (1 g sat. fat), 66 mg chol., 641 mg sodium, 28 g carbo., 4 g dietary fiber, 32 g protein.

*Note: You can find saffron-flavored yellow rice mix with other rice mixes in the supermarket. Look for a brand that combines the seasonings and the rice. If the brand comes with a separate seasoning packet, mix the seasonings with the rice in a separate bowl and measure out ¾ cup.

Shopping list:
- 1 large red onion
- 1½ pounds chicken breast tenderloins
- 1 14-ounce can reduced-sodium chicken broth
- 1 small container poultry seasoning
- 1 8-ounce package saffron-flavor yellow rice mix
- 1 15-ounce can black-eyed peas
- 1 package fresh thyme

Pantry list:
Olive oil

Garlic

Ground black pepper

Crushed red pepper

40 minutes

Chicken Soup with **Ham and Orzo**

Start to Finish: **35 minutes**

2 chicken breast halves

4 14-ounce cans reduced-sodium chicken broth

1 cup dried orzo

12 ounces asparagus spears, bias-cut into 1 ½-inch pieces

4 cups lightly packed, thinly sliced Swiss chard leaves

4 roma tomatoes, seeded and chopped

2 ounces cooked ham, cubed

Salt and freshly ground black pepper

Snipped fresh chives and/or flat-leaf parsley (optional)

1 In a 4-quart Dutch oven combine chicken and chicken broth. Bring to boiling; reduce heat. Simmer, covered, for 20 minutes or until chicken is no longer pink (170°F). Remove chicken from broth; cool slightly. Discard skin and bones; shred chicken into bite-size pieces.

2 Return broth to boiling; add orzo. Cook, uncovered, for 7 minutes. Add asparagus; cook 3 minutes more. Add chard, tomatoes, ham, and shredded chicken; heat through. Season to taste with salt and pepper. If desired, sprinkle with chives.

Makes 6 servings

Nutrition facts per serving: 286 cal., 8 g total fat (2 g sat. fat), 44 mg chol., 1,115 mg sodium, 26 g carbo., 2 g dietary fiber, 25 g protein.

40 minutes

Shopping list:

2 chicken breast halves

4 14-ounce cans reduced-sodium chicken broth

1 8-ounce package dried orzo

12 ounces fresh asparagus spears

5 ounces Swiss chard leaves

4 roma tomatoes

2 ounces cooked ham

Pantry list:

Salt

Black pepper

Chicken **Gremolata**

Start to Finish: **40 minutes**   Oven: **425°F**

Nonstick cooking spray

¼ cup snipped fresh Italian (flat-leaf) parsley

2 tablespoons finely shredded lemon peel

1 teaspoon bottled minced garlic

8 chicken drumsticks

¼ teaspoon salt

¼ teaspoon ground black pepper

Lemon wedges (optional)

1 Preheat oven to 425°F. Line a 15x10x1-inch baking pan with foil; coat foil with nonstick spray. In a small bowl stir together parsley, lemon peel, and garlic. Use your fingers to gently separate the skin from the meat on the drumsticks. Spread parsley mixture under skin and all around each drumstick. Place drumsticks in prepared pan. Sprinkle with salt and pepper.

2 Bake for 25 minutes or until chicken is no longer pink (180°F). If desired, serve with lemon wedges.

Makes 4 servings

Nutrition facts per serving: 240 cal., 13 g total fat (4 g sat. fat), 118 mg chol., 269 mg sodium, 1 g carbo., 1 g dietary fiber, 28 g protein.

Shopping list:
1 bunch fresh parsley

2 lemons

8 chicken drumsticks

Pantry list:
Nonstick cooking spray

Bottled minced garlic

Salt

Ground black pepper

40 minutes

Sesame-Honey Baked Chicken

Start to Finish: 40 minutes   Oven: **400°F**

Nonstick cooking spray

12 **chicken drumsticks and/or thighs**

¼ **teaspoon salt**

¼ **teaspoon ground black pepper**

¼ **cup honey**

1 **tablespoon soy sauce**

1 **teaspoon toasted sesame oil**

¼ **to ½ teaspoon crushed red pepper**

2 **tablespoons sesame seeds**

1 Preheat oven to 400°F. Lightly coat a 15x10x1-inch baking pan with cooking spray; set aside. Season drumsticks with salt and black pepper.

2 In a small bowl stir together honey, soy sauce, sesame oil, and crushed red pepper. Brush both sides of chicken pieces with honey mixture. Arrange in prepared pan. Sprinkle chicken with sesame seeds.

3 Bake chicken, uncovered, for 30 to 35 minutes or until chicken is no longer pink (180°F). Drizzle with pan juices.

Makes 6 servings

Nutrition facts per serving: 304 cal., 15 g total fat (4 g sat. fat), 118 mg chol., 388 mg sodium, 13 g carbo., 1 g dietary fiber, 29 g protein.

40 minutes

Shopping list:
12 chicken drumsticks or thighs

1 8-ounce bottle toasted sesame oil

1 small container sesame seeds

Pantry list:
Nonstick cooking spray

Salt

Ground black pepper

Honey

Soy sauce

Crushed red pepper

Kalamata **Lemon Chicken** *(See photo on page 275.)*

Start to Finish: 40 minutes   Oven: **400°F**

1 to 1 ¼ **pounds skinless, boneless chicken thighs**

1 **tablespoon olive oil**

⅔ **cup dried orzo**

½ **cup pitted kalamata olives**

1 **14-ounce can chicken broth**

½ **of a lemon, cut into wedges**

1 **tablespoon lemon juice**

1 **teaspoon dried Greek seasoning**

¼ **teaspoon salt**

¼ **teaspoon freshly ground black pepper**

Hot chicken broth (optional)

Fresh snipped oregano (optional)

1 Preheat oven to 400°F. In a 4-quart Dutch oven cook chicken in hot oil over medium-high heat for 5 minutes, turning once. Stir in orzo, olives, broth, lemon wedges, lemon juice, Greek seasoning, salt, and pepper.

2 Bake, covered, for 35 minutes or until chicken is no longer pink (180°F). If desired, serve in shallow bowls with additional broth and snipped oregano.

Makes 4 servings

Nutrition facts per serving: 309 cal., 11 g total fat (2 g sat. fat), 91 mg chol., 837 mg sodium, 24 g carbo., 2 g dietary fiber, 27 g protein.

Shopping list:

1 pound skinless, boneless chicken thighs

1 6-ounce jar pitted kalamata olives

1 14-ounce can chicken broth

1 lemon

1 small container Greek seasoning

Pantry list:

Olive oil

Dried orzo

Salt

Black pepper

Coconut Chicken Thighs

Start to Finish: **40 minutes**

1 ½ cups chicken broth

2 tablespoons lime juice

1 tablespoon packed brown sugar

1 teaspoon grated fresh ginger

1 cup uncooked basmati rice or long-grain white rice

1 medium red sweet pepper, cut into bite-size strips

1 small onion, cut into wedges

2 tablespoons cooking oil

1 ½ pounds skinless, boneless chicken thighs

¾ cup unsweetened coconut milk

½ teaspoon salt

⅛ teaspoon crushed red pepper

¼ cup snipped fresh cilantro

1 In a medium saucepan stir together broth, lime juice, brown sugar, and ginger. Bring to boiling. Stir in rice. Reduce heat. Simmer, covered, for 20 minutes or until rice is tender and liquid is absorbed.

2 Meanwhile, in a large skillet cook sweet pepper and onion in 1 tablespoon hot oil for 3 minutes. Remove from skillet. Add remaining 1 tablespoon oil to skillet. Add chicken. Cook for 5 to 6 minutes or until chicken is brown, turning once. Return vegetables to skillet.

Add coconut milk, salt, and crushed red pepper. Bring to boiling; reduce heat. Simmer, covered, for 5 to 10 minutes or until chicken is no longer pink (180°F). Sprinkle with cilantro.

3 To serve, remove chicken and vegetables to a serving dish with rice. Drizzle with some of the cooking liquid. Pass remaining cooking liquid.

Makes 6 servings

Nutrition facts per serving: 377 cal., 16 g total fat (8 g sat. fat), 95 mg chol., 539 mg sodium, 31 g carbo., 2 g dietary fiber, 26 g protein.

Shopping list:

1 14-ounce can chicken broth

1 lime

1 piece fresh ginger

1 16-ounce package basmati or long grain rice

1 red sweet pepper

1 small onion

1 ½ pounds skinless, boneless chicken thighs

1 13- to 14-ounce can unsweetened coconut milk

1 bunch fresh cilantro

Pantry list:

Brown sugar

Cooking oil

Salt

Crushed red pepper

40 minutes

Chicken and **Biscuits**

Start to Finish: **40 minutes**   Oven: **400°F**

- 1 **cup packaged biscuit mix**
- ¼ **cup shredded cheddar cheese**
- 1 **tablespoon chopped fresh parsley**
- ⅓ **cup milk**
- 1 **purchased roasted chicken**
- 1 **medium onion, chopped**
- 2 **tablespoons butter**
- 2 **tablespoons all-purpose flour**
- ½ **teaspoon dried thyme, crushed**
- ¼ **teaspoon ground black pepper**
- 1 **14-ounce can chicken broth**
- 1 **15-ounce can large-cut mixed vegetables, drained**
- ½ **cup milk**

1 Preheat oven to 400°F. Grease a large baking sheet; set aside. In a medium bowl combine biscuit mix, cheese, parsley, and ⅓ cup milk. Spoon into 4 mounds on prepared baking sheet. Bake for 10 to 12 minutes or until bottoms are light brown.

2 Meanwhile, remove 3 cups meat from chicken and coarsely chop. Reserve remaining chicken for another use.

3 In a large skillet cook onion in hot butter over medium heat for 5 minutes or until tender. Stir in flour, thyme, and pepper. Add broth all at once. Cook and stir until thick and bubbly. Stir in chicken, vegetables, and ½ cup milk.

4 Divide chicken mixture among 4 shallow bowls. Serve with warm biscuits.

Makes 4 servings

Nutrition facts per serving: 495 cal., 22 g total fat (9 g sat. fat), 122 mg chol., 1,220 mg sodium, 33 g carbo., 5 g dietary fiber, 39 g protein.

Shopping list:
- 1 20-ounce box biscuit mix
- 1 8-ounce package shredded cheddar cheese
- 1 bunch fresh parsley
- 1 purchased roasted chicken
- 1 medium onion
- 1 14-ounce can chicken broth
- 1 15-ounce can large-cut mixed vegetables

Pantry list:
Milk

Butter

All-purpose flour

Dried thyme

Ground black pepper

40
minutes

Spring Chicken Salad

Start to Finish: **35 minutes**

1 **purchased roasted chicken**

4 **cups coarsely chopped, peeled, cored pineapple; peeled, seeded mango; and/or peeled kiwifruit**

2 **cups coarsely chopped peeled jicama**

2 **tablespoons thinly sliced green onions**

$\frac{1}{2}$ **cup mayonnaise or salad dressing**

$\frac{1}{2}$ **teaspoon finely shredded lime peel**

2 **tablespoons lime juice**

1 **clove garlic, minced**

2 **teaspoons Jamaican jerk, Mediterranean, or Greek seasoning**

$\frac{1}{4}$ **teaspoon salt**

Bibb lettuce or radicchio leaves

1 Remove meat from roasted chicken. Coarsely chop (you should have about 3 cups). Discard skin and bones.

2 In a very large bowl combine chicken, pineapple, jicama, and green onions; set aside.

3 For dressing, in a small bowl combine mayonnaise, lime peel, lime juice, garlic, jerk seasoning, and salt. Pour about half the dressing over chicken mixture; toss to coat.

4 Line 6 to 8 plates with Bibb lettuce and radicchio leaves. Arrange chicken mixture on lettuce. Drizzle with remaining dressing.

Makes 6 to 8 servings

Nutrition facts per serving: 401 cal., 25 g total fat (5 g sat. fat), 73 mg chol., 366 mg sodium, 21 g carbo., 2 g dietary fiber, 22 g protein.

40 minutes

Shopping list:

1 purchased roasted chicken

1 pineapple

1 large jicama

1 bunch green onions

1 lime

1 small container Jamaican jerk seasoning

1 head Bibb lettuce

Pantry list:

Mayonnaise

Garlic

Salt

Chicken-Corn **Chowder**

Start to Finish: **40 minutes**

1 medium onion, chopped (½ cup)

1 tablespoon butter

1 ½ cups reduced-sodium chicken broth

1 large potato, peeled and chopped (1 ½ cups)

2 cups fresh or frozen whole kernel corn (4 ears)

1 4-ounce can diced green chile peppers, drained

¼ teaspoon coarsely ground black pepper

2 cups milk

2 tablespoons all-purpose flour

5 ounces cooked chicken, cut into thin strips

2 tablespoons snipped fresh cilantro or 2 teaspoons snipped fresh oregano

1 In a large saucepan cook onion in hot butter for 3 to 4 minutes or until tender. Add broth, potato, corn, chile peppers, and black pepper. Bring to boiling; reduce heat. Simmer, covered, about 15 minutes or until potato is tender, stirring occasionally.

2 In a screw-top jar combine milk and flour; cover and shake well. Add to potato mixture. Cook and stir until thick and bubbly. Add chicken and cilantro. Heat through.

Makes 4 servings

Nutrition facts per serving: 300 cal., 8 g total fat (4 g sat. fat), 44 mg chol., 486 mg sodium, 39 g carbo., 4 g dietary fiber, 20 g protein.

Shopping list:

1 medium onion

2 14-ounce cans reduced-sodium chicken broth

1 large potato

4 ears fresh sweet corn

1 4-ounce can diced green chile peppers

1 purchased roasted chicken

1 small bunch fresh cilantro

Pantry list:

Butter

Ground black pepper

Milk

All-purpose flour

40minutes

Chicken Caesar Calzones

Start to Finish: 40 minutes   **Oven: 400°F**

- 1   13.8-ounce can refrigerated pizza dough
- 1 ½ cups shredded roast chicken
- ⅓   cup bottled creamy Caesar salad dressing
- ½   of a 10-ounce package frozen chopped spinach, thawed and well-drained*
- 1   large roma tomato, chopped
- 1   clove garlic, minced
- 1 ½ cups shredded Italian blend cheese (6 ounces)

1 Preheat oven to 400°F. Grease a large baking sheet; set aside. Unroll pizza dough onto a lightly floured surface; roll into a 12x12-inch square. Cut into six 6x4-inch rectangles.

2 In a medium bowl stir together shredded chicken, dressing, spinach, tomato, and garlic. Stir in cheese. Spoon about ½ cup chicken mixture onto half of each dough rectangle. Fold unfilled side over filling; press edges to seal. Place on prepared baking sheet. Bake about 18 minutes or until crust is golden.

Makes 6 servings

Nutrition facts per serving: 345 cal., 16 g total fat (6 g sat. fat), 56 mg chol., 566 mg sodium, 28 g carbo., 2 g dietary fiber, 23 g protein.

*Thawing spinach: Thaw spinach overnight in the refrigerator or place in a microwave-safe bowl and microwave on 30% power for 8 to 10 minutes or until thawed, breaking up spinach after 5 minutes.

40 minutes

Shopping list:
- 1 13.8-ounce can refrigerated pizza dough
- 1 purchased roasted chicken
- 1 16-ounce bottle creamy Caesar salad dressing
- 1 10-ounce package frozen chopped spinach
- 1 large roma tomato
- 1 8-ounce bag shredded Italian blend cheese

Pantry list:
Garlic

Cobb Salad Hoagies

Start to Finish: **35 minutes**

- 2 **eggs**
- 3 **tablespoons olive oil**
- 1 **tablespoon white wine vinegar**
- 1 **teaspoon Dijon-style mustard**
- ½ **teaspoon salt**
- ½ **teaspoon ground black pepper**
- 1 **avocado, halved, seeded, peeled, and finely chopped**
- 1 ⅓ **cups chopped cooked chicken**
- 2 **roma tomatoes, chopped**
- 4 **slices bacon, crisp-cooked, drained, and crumbled**
- ½ **cup crumbled blue cheese (4 ounces)**
- 4 **Boston lettuce leaves**
- 4 **hoagie buns, split, hollowed, and toasted**

1 Place eggs in a small saucepan. Add enough cold water to cover eggs by at least 1 inch. Bring to a rapid boil over high heat. Remove from heat, and let stand, covered, for 15 minutes; drain. Run cold water over eggs or place in ice water until cool enough to handle. Drain eggs and peel. Chop eggs; set aside.

2 Meanwhile, for dressing, in a small bowl whisk together olive oil, vinegar, mustard, salt, and pepper. Stir in avocado; set aside.

3 In a medium bowl combine chicken, tomatoes, bacon, and blue cheese. Pour dressing mixture over chicken mixture and toss to coat. Place lettuce leaves on bottom halves of the buns. Spoon chicken mixture on top of lettuce. Sprinkle with chopped eggs. Add bun tops.

Makes 4 sandwiches

Nutrition facts per sandwich: 659 cal., 35 g total fat (9 g sat. fat), 165 mg chol., 1,214 mg sodium, 55 g carbo., 5 g dietary fiber, 32 g protein.

Shopping list:
- 1 8-ounce bottle white wine vinegar
- 1 avocado
- 1 9-ounce package frozen chopped cooked chicken breast
- 2 roma tomatoes
- 1 12-ounce package bacon
- 1 4-ounce package blue cheese
- 1 head Boston lettuce
- 1 package hoagie buns

Pantry list:
Eggs

Olive oil

Dijon-style mustard

Salt

Ground black pepper

40 minutes

Herbed Chicken **Pasta Primavera**

Start to Finish: **40 minutes**

8 ounces dried
mostaccioli pasta

Nonstick cooking
spray

8 ounces packaged
peeled baby carrots,
cut in half lengthwise

1 ½ cups fresh green
beans bias-sliced into
2-inch pieces

2 green onions, sliced

1 clove garlic, minced

1 small zucchini, sliced

2 tablespoons water

2 cups chopped cooked
chicken (about 10
ounces)

1 10.75-ounce can
condensed cream of
chicken soup

½ cup milk

1 teaspoon dried basil,
crushed

1 teaspoon dried
oregano, crushed

¼ cup pine nuts, toasted

Cracked black pepper

1 Cook mostaccioli according to package directions; drain and return pasta to saucepan.

2 Meanwhile, lightly coat a large skillet with nonstick cooking spray. Heat skillet over medium-high heat. Add carrots; cook and stir for 5 minutes. Add green beans, green onions, and garlic. Cook and stir for 2 minutes more. Stir in zucchini and water. Reduce heat. Cook, covered, for 4 to 5 minutes or until vegetables are crisp-tender.

3 Stir chicken, cream of chicken soup, milk, basil, oregano, and vegetables into pasta. Heat through. Sprinkle with pine nuts and cracked pepper. Serve immediately.

Makes 8 servings

Nutrition facts per serving: 269 cal., 9 g total fat (2 g sat. fat), 36 mg chol., 333 mg sodium, 31 g carbo., 3 g dietary fiber, 17 g protein.

Shopping list:

1 16-ounce package mostaccioli

1 16-ounce package baby carrots

8 ounces fresh green beans

1 bunch green onions

1 small zucchini

1 purchased roasted chicken

1 10.75-ounce can condensed cream of chicken soup

1 2-ounce package pine nuts

Pantry list:

Nonstick cooking spray

Garlic

Milk

Dried basil

Dried oregano

Cracked black pepper

40 minutes

Thai Chicken and Nectarine Salad

Start to Finish: **40 minutes**

¼ cup reduced-sodium chicken broth

3 tablespoons reduced-sodium soy sauce

2 tablespoons bottled hoisin sauce

1 tablespoon sugar

1 tablespoon salad oil or olive oil

2 teaspoons toasted sesame oil

3 cloves garlic, minced

1 ½ teaspoons grated fresh ginger

1 teaspoon crushed red pepper

4 ounces dried angel hair pasta

2 cups chopped cooked chicken

3 medium nectarines or peeled peaches, pitted and sliced

2 cups torn mixed greens

2 green onions, thinly sliced

1 For dressing, in a screw-top jar combine broth, soy sauce, hoisin sauce, sugar, salad oil, sesame oil, garlic, ginger, and crushed red pepper. Cover; shake well. Set aside.

2 Cook pasta according to package directions; drain.

3 In a large bowl toss pasta with 3 tablespoons of the dressing. Divide pasta mixture among 4 dinner plates. Top with chicken, nectarines, mixed greens, and green onions. Drizzle with remaining dressing.

Makes 4 servings

Nutrition facts per serving: 382 cal., 12 g total fat (2 g sat. fat), 63 mg chol., 662 mg sodium, 42 g carbo., 4 g dietary fiber, 27 g protein.

Shopping list:

1 14-ounce can reduced-sodium chicken broth

1 5-ounce bottle reduced-sodium soy sauce

1 8-ounce bottle hoisin sauce

1 8-ounce bottle toasted sesame oil

1 piece fresh ginger

1 16-ounce package angel hair pasta

2 6-ounce packages refrigerated chopped cooked chicken breast

3 medium nectarines

1 5-ounce package mixed greens

1 bunch green onions

Pantry list:

Sugar

Salad oil

Garlic

Crushed red pepper

40 minutes

Turkey and **Sweet Potatoes**

Start to Finish: **40 minutes**

1 pound sweet potatoes

2 turkey breast tenderloins (1 to 1 ¼ pounds)

½ teaspoon salt

¼ teaspoon ground black pepper

1 tablespoon cooking oil

1 cup purchased chunky salsa

¼ cup orange juice

Snipped fresh cilantro or parsley (optional)

1 Peel potatoes; cut into 1-inch pieces. In a saucepan cook sweet potatoes, covered, in enough boiling water to cover for 10 to 12 minutes or until potatoes are just tender; drain.

2 Meanwhile, cut turkey crosswise into ½-inch slices. Sprinkle with salt and pepper. In a large nonstick skillet cook turkey in hot oil over medium-high heat for 3 to 4 minutes per side or until turkey is no longer pink (170°F).

3 Add salsa and orange juice to skillet; add sweet potatoes. Cook until heated through, stirring gently. If desired, sprinkle with snipped fresh cilantro.

Makes 4 servings

Nutrition facts per serving: 251 cal., 4 g total fat (1 g sat. fat), 70 mg chol., 775 mg sodium, 22 g carbo., 7 g dietary fiber, 30 g protein.

minutes

40

Shopping list:

1 pound sweet potatoes

2 turkey breast tenderloins

1 16-ounce jar chunky salsa

Pantry list:

Salt

Ground black pepper

Cooking oil

Orange juice

40 min { **Skillet Cacciatore,** *page 251*

30 min { **Shanghai Pasta,** *page 224*

40 min { Sirloin Stroganoff, *page 298*

40 min { Kalamata Lemon Chicken, *page 263*

40 min { Oven-Fried Barbecue Chicken, *page 252*

40 min { **Steak and Potato Pizza,** *page 295*

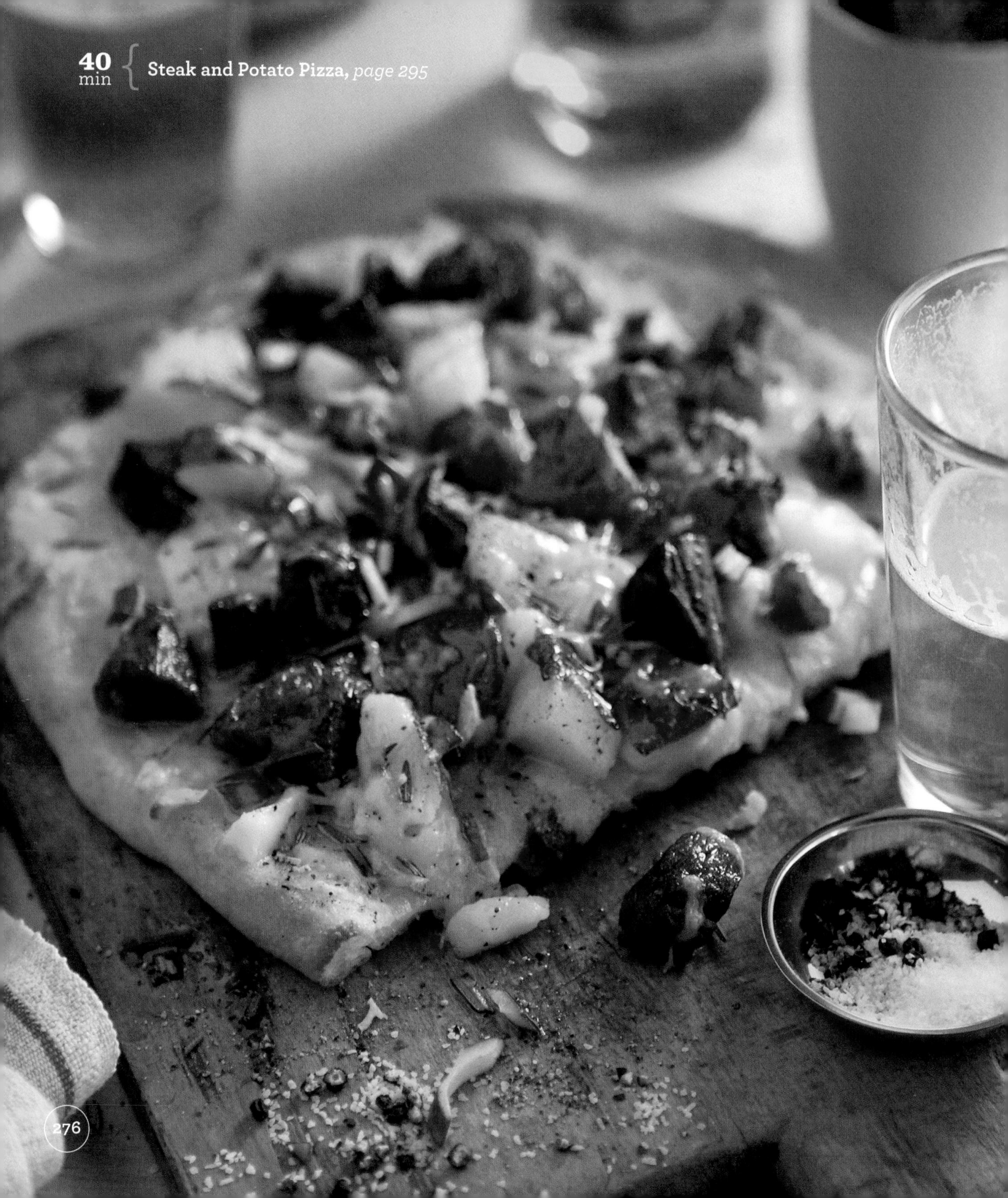

40 min { **Pasta with Baby Salisbury Steaks,** *page 302*

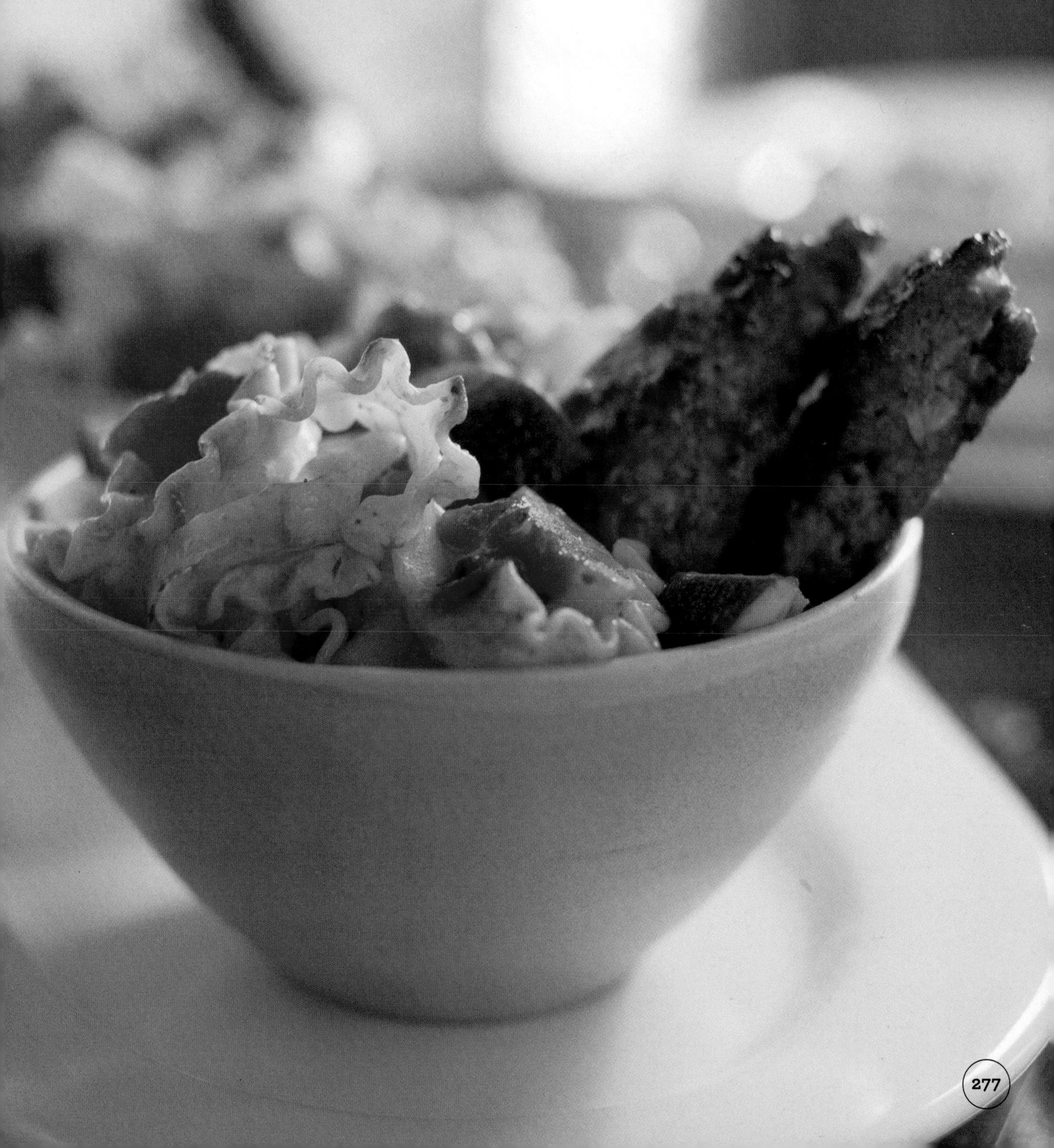

40 min { **Pork with Spaetzle and Braised Cabbage,** *page 319*

40 min { **Asian Salmon Burgers,** *page 345*

15 min { **BLT Coleslaw,** *page 380*

15 min { **Festive Fall Salad,** *page 379*

40 min { **Rice Noodles with Shrimp,** *page 349*

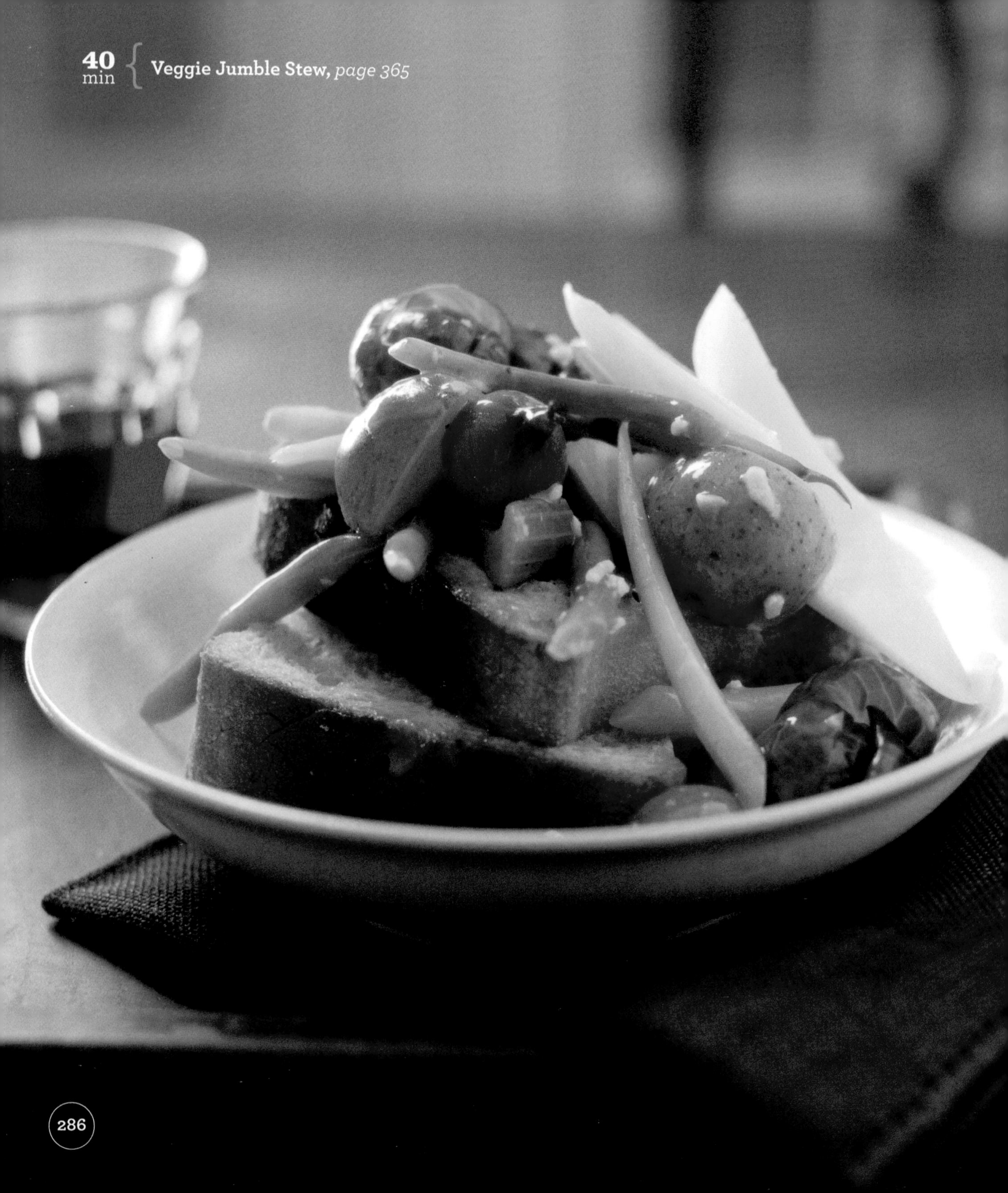

40 min { **Veggie Jumble Stew,** *page 365*

15 min { **Cinnamon Toasted Pound Cake and Strawberries,** *page 397*

Tasty Turkey **Chili**

Start to Finish: **40 minutes**

1 ¼ **pounds uncooked ground turkey**

2 **large onions, chopped (2 cups)**

¼ **cup water**

2 **cloves garlic, minced**

1 **15-ounce can tomato sauce**

1 **14.5-ounce can tomatoes, cut up, undrained**

1 **cup water**

1 **tablespoon chili powder**

1 **teaspoon ground cumin**

½ **teaspoon sugar**

1 **15-ounce can pinto beans, rinsed and drained**

1 **cup frozen whole kernel corn**

1 **cup shredded cheddar cheese (4 ounces)**

1 In a large saucepan cook ground turkey until no longer pink; drain. Stir in onions, the ¼ cup water, and garlic. Cook about 5 minutes more or until onion is tender, stirring often. Stir in tomato sauce, undrained tomatoes, the 1 cup water, chili powder, cumin, and sugar. Bring to boiling; reduce heat. Cover and simmer for 20 minutes, stirring occasionally.

2 Stir in beans and corn. Return to boiling; reduce heat. Cover and simmer for 10 minutes more, stirring occasionally. Ladle into bowls; sprinkle with cheese.

Makes 6 servings

Nutrition facts per serving: 342 cal., 12 g total fat (4 g sat. fat), 88 mg chol., 822 mg sodium, 30 g carbo., 7 g dietary fiber, 30 g protein.

Shopping list:

1 ¼ pounds uncooked ground turkey

2 large onions

1 15-ounce can tomato sauce

1 14.5-ounce can tomatoes

1 15-ounce can pinto beans

1 10-ounce package frozen whole kernel corn

1 8-ounce package shredded cheddar cheese

Pantry list:

Garlic

Chili powder

Ground cumin

Sugar

Smoky Mac and Cheese **Skillet**

Start to Finish: **40 minutes**

8 ounces dried bow tie or penne pasta

½ cup panko (Japanese-style bread crumbs) or coarse soft bread crumbs

1 medium onion, chopped (½ cup)

½ cup chopped red sweet pepper

2 tablespoons butter

2 tablespoons all-purpose flour

2 cups milk

6 ounces smoked cheddar or smoked gouda cheese, shredded (1 ½ cups)

6 ounces American cheese, shredded (1 ½ cups)

8 ounces chopped smoked boneless turkey breast (1 ½ cups)

1 Cook pasta according to package directions; drain.

2 Meanwhile, in a large dry skillet toast bread crumbs over medium heat until golden, stirring frequently. Remove from skillet.

3 In the same skillet cook onion and sweet pepper in hot butter over medium heat until tender. Stir in flour. Add milk all at once. Cook and stir until slightly thick and bubbly. Add cheese, one-fourth at a time, stirring until melted. Stir in turkey and heat through. Stir in pasta to coat. Top with toasted bread crumbs.

Makes 4 servings

Nutrition facts per serving: 767 cal., 38 g total fat (23 g sat. fat), 113 mg chol., 1,536 mg sodium, 62 g carbo., 3 g dietary fiber, 43 g protein.

Shopping list:

1 16-ounce package dried bow tie pasta

1 8-ounce package panko (Japanese-style bread crumbs)

1 medium onion

1 medium red sweet pepper

6 ounces smoked cheddar cheese

6 ounces American cheese

8 ounces smoked boneless turkey breast

Pantry list:

Butter

All-purpose flour

Milk

minutes

40

Cranberry-Sauced
Hot Turkey Sandwiches

Start to Finish: **30 minutes**

4   ¾-inch diagonally cut slices Italian bread or Texas toast, toasted

1   24-ounce package refrigerated garlic mashed potatoes or 2 ⅔ cups leftover mashed potatoes, reheated

2   tablespoons butter

12 ounces cooked turkey breast, sliced

3   tablespoons packed brown sugar

1   tablespoon cornstarch

1   16-ounce can whole cranberry sauce

¼   teaspoon finely shredded orange peel

⅓   cup dry red wine or orange juice

¼   cup orange juice

¼   teaspoon salt

⅛   teaspoon ground black pepper

1 Place one slice of toast on each of 4 plates. Prepare refrigerated mashed potatoes according to package microwave directions. Set aside.

2 Meanwhile, in a large skillet melt butter over medium heat. Add turkey slices; cover and cook for 5 minutes or until heated through. Place turkey on toast slices. Place a scoop of mashed potatoes next to the toast. Cover and keep warm.

3 For sauce, carefully stir brown sugar and cornstarch into drippings in skillet; stir in cranberry sauce, orange peel, wine, orange juice, salt, and pepper. Cook and stir over medium-high heat until thick and bubbly. Cook and stir for 1 minute more. Spoon sauce over turkey and potatoes.

Makes 4 servings

Nutrition facts per serving: 629 cal., 10 g total fat (4 g sat. fat), 86 mg chol., 682 mg sodium, 96 g carbo., 4 g dietary fiber, 32 g protein.

Shopping list:
1 loaf Italian bread
1 24-ounce package refrigerated garlic mashed potatoes
12 ounces cooked turkey breast
1 16-ounce can whole cranberry sauce
1 orange
1 bottle dry red wine

Pantry list:
Butter
Brown sugar
Cornstarch
Orange juice
Salt
Ground black pepper

40 minutes

Sausage and Vegetables with Polenta

Start to Finish: **35 minutes**

1 tablespoon olive oil

1 16-ounce tube refrigerated cooked polenta, cut into 12 slices and quartered

8 ounces light smoked turkey sausage, halved lengthwise and cut into ½-inch slices

2 medium red, green, and/or yellow sweet peppers, cut into bite-size pieces

1 medium onion, cut into bite-size pieces

1 cup sliced fresh mushrooms

½ cup purchased pasta sauce

1 In a 12-inch nonstick skillet heat oil over medium heat. Add polenta in a single layer; cook for 10 to 12 minutes or until light brown, stirring occasionally. Remove from skillet; keep warm.

2 Add sausage, sweet peppers, onion, and mushrooms to skillet. Cook and stir until sausage is brown and vegetables are crisp-tender. Stir in pasta sauce. Add polenta; gently toss to combine ingredients. Heat through.

Makes 4 servings

Nutrition facts per serving: 260 cal., 9 g total fat (2 g sat. fat), 38 mg chol., 1,088 mg sodium, 32 g carbo., 5 g dietary fiber, 14 g protein.

40 minutes

Shopping list:

1 16-ounce tube refrigerated cooked polenta

8 ounces light smoked turkey sausage

2 medium red sweet peppers

1 medium onion

1 8-ounce package sliced fresh mushrooms

1 8-ounce jar pasta sauce

Pantry list:

Olive oil

Sausage-Pepper Medley

Start to Finish: **40 minutes**

- **6**   **uncooked turkey Italian sausage links (about 1 ½ pounds)**
- **2**   **cloves garlic, minced**
- **1**   **tablespoon olive oil**
- **4**   **medium red, green, and/or yellow sweet peppers, seeded and cut into thin strips**
- **1**   **large onion, thinly sliced and separated into rings**
- **1**   **14.5-ounce can diced tomatoes, undrained**
- **1 ½**   **teaspoons dried Italian seasoning, crushed**
- **¼**   **teaspoon crushed red pepper (optional)**
- **⅓**   **cup shredded Parmesan cheese**

1   In a 12-inch nonstick skillet cook sausage over medium heat for 5 to 8 minutes or until brown, turning frequently. Reduce heat to medium-low. Cook, covered, about 10 minutes more or until juices run clear. Remove sausage links from skillet; thinly bias slice. Set aside.

2   In same skillet cook garlic in hot olive oil over medium heat for 30 seconds. Add sweet peppers and onion; cook about 5 minutes or until crisp-tender, stirring occasionally.

3   Add sausage, undrained tomatoes, Italian seasoning, and, if desired, crushed red pepper to skillet. Bring to boiling; reduce heat. Simmer, uncovered, for 5 minutes. Sprinkle with Parmesan cheese.

Makes 6 servings

Nutrition facts per serving: 269 cal., 15 g total fat (4 g sat. fat), 74 mg chol., 1,123 mg sodium, 11 g carbo., 3 g dietary fiber, 23 g protein.

Shopping list:

6 uncooked turkey Italian sausage links

4 medium red sweet peppers

1 large onion

1 14.5-ounce can diced tomatoes

1 8-ounce package shredded Parmesan cheese

Pantry list:

Garlic

Olive oil

Dried Italian seasoning

Crushed red pepper

40 minutes

Seared Beef with **Orange Salsa**

Start to Finish: **35 minutes**

- 4 **large oranges**
- 2 **teaspoons fennel seeds, crushed**
- 2 **teaspoons black peppercorns, crushed**
- ¼ **teaspoon salt**
- 12 **ounces beef tenderloin, cut into 4 steaks**
- 1 **tablespoon olive oil**
- ½ **cup finely chopped red onion**
- ¼ **cup pitted kalamata olives, quartered**
- ¼ **cup snipped fresh Italian (flat-leaf) parsley**
- 2 **tablespoons lemon juice**
- 2 **tablespoons olive oil**
- 1 **clove garlic, minced**
- ½ **teaspoon paprika**
- 4 **cups torn arugula**

1 Finely shred enough of the orange peel to make 2 teaspoons. In a small bowl combine orange peel, fennel seeds, peppercorns, and salt. Sprinkle mixture evenly over beef.

2 In a large skillet cook steaks in 1 tablespoon hot oil over medium heat for 7 to 9 minutes or until desired doneness (145°F for medium-rare or 160°F for medium), turning once. Thinly slice meat across the grain.

3 Meanwhile, peel oranges, removing white pith. Section oranges. In a large bowl combine orange sections, red onion, olives, parsley, lemon juice, 2 tablespoons olive oil, garlic, and paprika. Stir gently to combine.

4 Add arugula to orange mixture; toss to combine. Divide arugula mixture among 4 dinner plates. Serve with sliced meat.

Makes 4 servings

Nutrition facts per serving: 318 cal., 18 g total fat (4 g sat. fat), 52 mg chol., 263 mg sodium, 21 g carbo., 5 g dietary fiber, 20 g protein.

Shopping list:

- 4 large oranges
- 1 small container fennel seeds
- 1 small container whole black peppercorns
- 12 ounces beef tenderloin
- 1 medium red onion
- 1 6-ounce jar pitted kalamata olives
- 1 bunch fresh Italian (flat-leaf) parsley
- 1 lemon
- 1 small container paprika
- 1 8-ounce package arugula

Pantry list:

Salt

Olive oil

Garlic

40 minutes

Steak and Potato **Pizza** *(See photo on page 276.)*

Start to Finish: 40 minutes   **Oven: 425°F**

- 2 medium potatoes, scrubbed and cut into 1-inch pieces
- 1 cup water
- 12 ounces beef ribeye steak, trimmed of fat and cut into 1-inch pieces
- 4 to 6 cloves garlic, minced
- 1 tablespoon olive oil
- 1 13.8-ounce package refrigerated pizza dough
- 1 8-ounce package shredded pizza cheese
- 2 to 3 teaspoons snipped fresh rosemary or 1 teaspoon dried rosemary, crushed
- ⅓ cup thin slivers red onion

  Cracked black pepper

1 Preheat oven to 425°F. In a skillet combine potatoes and water. Bring to boiling; reduce heat. Simmer, covered, for 10 minutes or until tender; drain. Set aside. Wipe skillet. In same skillet, cook steak and garlic in hot oil over medium-high heat for 4 to 5 minutes or until steak is brown, stirring occasionally. Remove from heat; set aside.

2 Unroll pizza dough onto a greased large baking sheet; press into a 16x11-inch oval. Build up edges. Bake for 8 to 10 minutes or until golden. Sprinkle with 1½ cups cheese. Add potatoes and meat. Top with remaining cheese and rosemary.

3 Bake for 10 to 12 minutes more or until cheese melts. Sprinkle with onion and pepper.

Makes 4 servings

Nutrition facts per serving: 648 cal., 25 g total fat (12 g sat. fat), 81 mg chol., 982 mg sodium, 60 g carbo., 3 g dietary fiber, 43 g protein.

Shopping list:
- 2 medium potatoes
- 12 ounces beef ribeye steak
- 1 13.8-ounce package refrigerated pizza dough
- 1 8-ounce package shredded pizza cheese
- 1 package fresh rosemary
- 1 small red onion

Pantry list:
- Garlic
- Olive oil
- Cracked black pepper

Peppercorn Steaks

Start to Finish: **35 minutes**

- **2** **6-ounce boneless beef ribeye steaks or beef top sirloin steaks, cut about 1 inch thick**
- **1** **tablespoon multicolor peppercorns, crushed**
- **½** **teaspoon salt**
- **2** **tablespoons butter, softened**
- **2** **teaspoons mild-flavor molasses**
- **¼** **teaspoon finely shredded lemon peel**
- **1** **teaspoon lemon juice**
- **2** **cups sugar snap peas**
- **½** **cup carrot cut into thin bite-size strips**

1 Preheat broiler. Trim fat from steaks. Using your fingers, press crushed peppercorns and salt onto both sides of each steak.

2 Place steaks on the unheated rack of a broiler pan. Broil 3 to 4 inches from the heat until desired doneness, turning once halfway through broiling time. For ribeye steaks, allow 12 to 14 minutes for medium-rare (145°F) or 15 to 18 minutes for medium (160°F). For sirloin steaks, allow 15 to 17 minutes for medium-rare (145°F) or 20 to 22 minutes for medium (160°F).

3 Meanwhile, in a small bowl combine butter, molasses, lemon peel, and lemon juice (mixture will appear curdled). Set aside.

4 Remove strings and tips from peas. In a medium saucepan cook sugar snap peas and carrots, covered, in a small amount of boiling salted water for 2 to 4 minutes or until crisp-tender. Drain well. Stir in 1 tablespoon of the molasses mixture.

5 To serve, dot remaining molasses mixture evenly over steaks. Slice steaks and toss with vegetable mixture.

Makes 4 servings

Nutrition facts per serving: 247 cal., 12 g total fat (6 g sat. fat), 66 mg chol., 418 mg sodium, 13 g carbo., 3 g dietary fiber, 20 g protein.

40 minutes

Shopping list:
- 2 6-ounce boneless beef ribeye steaks
- 1 small container multicolor peppercorns
- 1 12-ounce bottle mild-flavor molasses
- 1 lemon
- 6 ounces fresh sugar snap peas
- 1 carrot

Pantry list:
Salt

Butter

Steak 'n' Bake

Start to Finish: **35 minutes**

4   **medium baking potatoes**

12 **to 16 ounces boneless beef sirloin steak, cut 1 inch thick**

2   **cups fresh baby spinach**

¾   **cup bottled blue cheese salad dressing**

1   **small red onion, cut into thin wedges**

1 Wash potatoes; pierce with fork. Arrange potatoes on a microwave-safe plate in spoke formation, leaving 1 inch between potatoes. Microwave, uncovered, on 100% power (high) for 14 to 18 minutes or until tender. (Or bake potatoes in a 425°F oven for 40 to 60 minutes.) Let stand 5 minutes.

2 Meanwhile, preheat broiler. Trim fat from steak. Place meat on the unheated rack of a broiler pan. Broil 3 to 4 inches from the heat for 16 to 18 minutes for medium-rare (145°F) or 19 to 21 minutes for medium (160°F), turning once halfway through broiling. Transfer meat to cutting board; let stand 5 minutes.

3 To serve, roll each potato gently under your hand. Cut an X in top of potato. Press in and up on ends of potato. Cut steak into bite-size strips. Top potatoes with meat and spinach; drizzle with dressing. Top with onion wedges.

Makes 4 servings

Nutrition facts per serving: 580 cal., 35 g total fat (9 g sat. fat), 65 mg chol., 577 mg sodium, 35 g carbo., 4 g dietary fiber, 32 g protein.

Shopping list:

4 medium baking potatoes

12 to 16 ounces boneless beef sirloin steak

1 15-ounce package fresh baby spinach

1 8-ounce bottle blue cheese salad dressing

1 small red onion

40minutes

Sirloin **Stroganoff** *(See photo on page 275.)*

Start to Finish: **40 minutes**

- 1 **20-ounce package refrigerated red potato wedges**
- 1 **large onion, chopped (1 cup)**
- 3 **cloves garlic, minced**
- 2 **tablespoons butter**
- 12 **to 16 ounces boneless beef sirloin steak, thinly sliced into bite-size strips**
- 4 **small apples, halved and cored, or 2 large apples, quartered**
- 1 **cup apple cider**
- 1 **8-ounce carton dairy sour cream**
- ¼ **teaspoon salt**
- ¼ **teaspoon ground black pepper**

1 In an extra-large skillet cook potatoes, onion, and garlic in hot butter over medium-high heat for 8 minutes or until nearly tender. Stir in beef strips. Cook and stir for 3 minutes more or until meat is desired doneness; remove meat and potatoes to plate. Cover; keep warm.

2 In same skillet cook apples, cut side down, in drippings for 2 minutes or until brown. Stir in apple cider. Bring to boiling; reduce heat. Simmer, covered, for 6 to 8 minutes or until tender. Use a slotted spoon to transfer apples from skillet to plate. Cover; keep warm.

3 Remove skillet from heat. For sauce, whisk sour cream, salt, and pepper into juices in skillet until smooth. Spoon sauce over meat, potatoes, and apples.

Makes 4 servings

Nutrition facts per serving: 538 cal., 25 g total fat (14 g sat. fat), 82 mg chol., 359 mg sodium, 51 g carbo., 5 g dietary fiber, 22 g protein.

Shopping list:

- 1 20-ounce package refrigerated red potato wedges
- 1 large onion
- 12 to 16 ounces boneless beef sirloin steak
- 4 small apples
- 1 32-ounce bottle apple cider
- 1 8-ounce carton dairy sour cream

Pantry list:

Garlic

Butter

Salt

Ground black pepper

40 minutes

Jalapeño Beef Tips

Start to Finish: **40 minutes**

- 1 **pound boneless beef sirloin steak**
- 1 **tablespoon olive oil**
- 1 **medium onion, halved and thinly sliced**
- 1 **16-ounce jar salsa**
- 1 **4.5-ounce can diced tomatoes, drained**
- 2 **tablespoons Worcestershire sauce**
- 2 **tablespoons canned diced jalapeño peppers**
- **Warm flour tortillas or hot cooked rice**
- ¼ **to ½ cup dairy sour cream**
- ¼ **cup snipped fresh cilantro**

1 Trim fat from steak. Cut meat into 1-inch cubes. In a large skillet cook meat in hot oil over medium-high heat for 5 minutes or until brown, stirring occasionally. Use a slotted spoon to remove meat from skillet; set aside.

2 Add onion to the skillet. Cook about 5 minutes or until tender, stirring occasionally. Stir in salsa, tomatoes, Worcestershire sauce, and jalapeño peppers. Bring to boiling; reduce heat. Simmer, covered, for 10 minutes. Stir in meat. Heat through.

3 Serve meat mixture with flour tortillas or over cooked rice. Dollop with sour cream; sprinkle with cilantro.

Makes 4 servings

Nutrition facts per serving: 509 cal., 16 g total fat (5 g sat. fat), 66 mg chol., 1,460 mg sodium, 57 g carbo., 7 g dietary fiber, 35 g protein.

Shopping list:

1 pound boneless beef sirloin steak

1 medium onion

1 16-ounce jar salsa

1 14.5-ounce can diced tomatoes

1 4-ounce can diced jalapeño peppers

1 package flour tortillas

1 8-ounce carton dairy sour cream

1 bunch fresh cilantro

Pantry list:

Olive oil

Worcestershire sauce

Beef and Vegetables with **Spaghetti**

Start to Finish: **35 minutes**

- 4 ounces dried whole grain or whole wheat spaghetti, broken in half
- 12 ounces boneless beef sirloin steak
- 1 teaspoon salt
- ½ teaspoon freshly ground black pepper
- 1 tablespoon olive oil
- 1 medium onion, cut into thin wedges
- 4 cloves garlic, minced
- ¼ teaspoon crushed red pepper
- 1 14.5-ounce can diced tomatoes with basil, garlic, and oregano, undrained
- 1 cup bottled roasted red sweet peppers, drained and coarsely chopped
- 1 tablespoon balsamic vinegar
- 2 cups fresh baby arugula or spinach leaves
- 1 tablespoon snipped fresh Italian (flat-leaf) parsley
- 1 ounce Romano cheese, shaved

1 Cook pasta according to package directions. Drain; return pasta to hot pan. Cover and keep warm. Meanwhile, trim fat from steak. Thinly slice meat across the grain. Toss meat slices with salt and pepper.

2 In a large skillet cook meat in hot oil over medium-high heat for 3 to 4 minutes or until desired doneness. Using a slotted spoon, remove meat from skillet; set aside. Add onion, garlic, and crushed red pepper to skillet. Cook about 5 minutes or until onion is tender, stirring occasionally.

3 Stir meat, undrained tomatoes, roasted red peppers, and balsamic vinegar into onion mixture in skillet. Heat through. Add meat mixture, arugula, and parsley to hot pasta; toss to combine.

4 To serve, divide pasta mixture among 4 shallow bowls. Top with Romano cheese.

Makes 4 servings

Nutrition facts per serving: 324 cal., 8 g total fat (2 g sat. fat), 57 mg chol., 1,122 mg sodium, 38 g carbo., 2 g dietary fiber, 26 g protein.

Shopping list:

- 1 16-ounce package dried whole grain spaghetti
- 12 ounces boneless beef sirloin steak
- 1 medium onion
- 1 14.5-ounce can diced tomatoes with basil, garlic, and oregano
- 1 7-ounce jar roasted red sweet peppers
- 1 8-ounce package baby arugula
- 1 bunch fresh Italian (flat-leaf) parsley
- 1 piece Romano cheese

Pantry list:

Salt

Ground black pepper

Olive oil

Garlic

Crushed red pepper

Balsamic vinegar

40 minutes

Balsamic-Glazed Sirloin Kabobs

Start to Finish: **40 minutes**

- ½ cup balsamic vinegar
- 1 clove garlic, minced
- 1 pound boneless beef sirloin steak, trimmed and cut into 1-inch pieces
- 2 small red sweet peppers, seeded and cut into 1-inch pieces
- ½ of a large sweet onion, cut into 1-inch pieces
- 1 teaspoon dried Italian seasoning, crushed
- ½ teaspoon salt
- ¼ teaspoon ground black pepper
- 1 14.8-ounce pouch cooked long grain white rice
- ¼ cup sliced green onions
- Salt and ground black pepper

1 Preheat broiler. In a small saucepan bring vinegar and garlic to boiling. Reduce heat; boil gently, uncovered, for 8 to 10 minutes or until mixture is reduced to 3 tablespoons. Remove from heat. Set aside.

2 In a large bowl combine beef, sweet pepper, and sweet onion pieces. Add Italian seasoning, salt, and black pepper; toss to coat. Thread beef, sweet pepper, and sweet onion pieces on 12-inch skewers.*

3 Place kabobs on the unheated rack of a broiler pan. Broil 3 to 4 inches from the heat for 8 to 10 minutes or until beef is desired doneness and vegetables are crisp-tender, turning kabobs once during broiling. Brush vinegar mixture over kabobs just before serving.

4 Meanwhile, heat rice according to package directions. Stir in green onions; season to taste with salt and pepper. Serve with kabobs.

Makes 4 servings

Nutrition facts per serving: 371 cal., 7 g total fat (2 g sat. fat), 48 mg chol., 510 mg sodium, 43 g carbo., 2 g dietary fiber, 29 g protein.

*Test Kitchen Tip: If using wooden or bamboo skewers, soak them in water for 30 minutes before using.

Shopping list:

- 1 pound boneless beef sirloin steak
- 2 small red sweet peppers
- 1 large sweet onion
- 1 14.8-ounce pouch cooked long grain rice
- 1 bunch green onions

Pantry list:

- Balsamic vinegar
- Garlic
- Dried Italian seasoning
- Salt
- Ground black pepper

40 minutes

Pasta with **Baby Salisbury Steaks**

(See photo on page 277.)

Start to Finish: **40 minutes**

- **Nonstick cooking spray**
- 8 **ounces mafalda or tagliatelle**
- 2 **slices raisin bread or cinnamon-raisin bread, torn into small pieces**
- ¼ **cup milk**
- 1 **pound lean ground beef**
- ½ **cup finely chopped onion**
- 1 **egg, lightly beaten**
- ½ **teaspoon dried oregano, crushed**
- ¼ **teaspoon salt**
- 2 **cups sliced zucchini and/or summer squash**
- 1 **tablespoon olive oil**
- 1 **26-ounce jar pasta sauce**
- **Finely shredded Parmesan cheese (optional)**

1 Preheat broiler. Lightly coat the unheated rack of a broiler pan with nonstick cooking spray; set aside. In a large saucepan cook pasta according to package directions. Drain pasta; set aside.

2 Meanwhile, in a large bowl stir together bread and milk; let stand for 5 minutes. Add ground beef, onion, egg, oregano, and salt. Mix well. Place a piece of waxed paper on a large cutting board. Pat meat mixture into a 8x6-inch rectangle on the waxed paper. Invert cutting board onto prepared rack of broiler pan. Discard waxed paper.

3 Broil meat mixture 4 to 5 inches from the heat about 20 minutes, turning once, or until meat is no longer pink (160°F). Using a long sharp knife, cut into four 4x3-inch rectangles. Cut each rectangle diagonally forming two triangles.

4 In the pasta pan, cook squash in hot oil for 2 to 3 minutes or until crisp-tender. Stir in pasta sauce and pasta and heat through. Serve steaks with pasta mixture. If desired, sprinkle each serving with Parmesan cheese.

Makes 4 servings

Nutrition facts per serving: 618 cal., 20 g total fat (7 g sat. fat), 131 mg chol., 1,254 mg sodium, 76 g carbo., 8 g dietary fiber, 37 g protein.

Shopping list:
- 1 16-ounce package mafalda
- 2 slices raisin bread
- 1 pound lean ground beef
- 1 medium onion
- 2 medium zucchini
- 1 26-ounce jar pasta sauce

Pantry list:
- Nonstick cooking spray
- Milk
- Egg
- Dried oregano
- Salt
- Olive oil

40 minutes

Tastes-Like-a-Taco **Pasta Sauce**

Start to Finish: **35 minutes**

8 ounces lean ground beef

1 large onion, chopped (1 cup)

1 medium green, red, or yellow sweet pepper, seeded and chopped ($^{3}/_{4}$ cup)

2 cloves garlic, minced

1 15-ounce can tomato sauce

1 14.5-ounce can diced tomatoes, undrained

1 $^{1}/_{2}$ teaspoons chili powder

$^{1}/_{4}$ teaspoon ground cumin

Salt and ground black pepper

10 ounces dried pasta

2 tablespoons snipped fresh cilantro

$^{1}/_{2}$ cup shredded Monterey Jack or cheddar cheese

1 In a large saucepan cook beef, onion, sweet pepper, and garlic over medium heat until beef is brown. Drain off fat. Stir in tomato sauce, undrained tomatoes, chili powder, and cumin. Bring to boiling; reduce heat. Simmer, uncovered, for 10 to 15 minutes or until desired consistency, stirring occasionally. Season to taste with salt and black pepper.

2 Meanwhile, cook pasta according to package directions; drain. Just before serving, stir cilantro into sauce. Serve sauce over hot cooked pasta. Sprinkle with cheese.

Makes 6 servings

Nutrition facts per serving: 325 cal., 7 g total fat (3 g sat. fat), 32 mg chol., 562 mg sodium, 47 g carbo., 3 g dietary fiber, 17 g protein.

Shopping list:
8 ounces lean ground beef

1 large onion

1 medium green sweet pepper

1 15-ounce can tomato sauce

1 14.5-ounce can diced tomatoes

1 16-ounce package dried pasta

1 bunch fresh cilantro

1 8-ounce package shredded Monterey Jack cheese

Pantry list:
Garlic

Chili powder

Ground cumin

Salt

Ground black pepper

40 minutes

Fire-and-Spice Beef Burgers

Start to Finish: **35 minutes**

- 1 egg, lightly beaten
- ¾ cup soft bread crumbs (1 slice)
- ⅓ cup finely chopped onion
- 2 tablespoons plain yogurt
- ½ teaspoon salt
- ½ teaspoon ground cinnamon or ground cardamom
- ½ teaspoon ground coriander or mace
- ¼ teaspoon cayenne pepper
- 1 pound ground beef, lamb, or pork
- ¼ cup jalapeño or hot pepper jelly
- 4 lettuce leaves
- 2 large pita bread rounds, halved crosswise

1 Preheat broiler. In a large bowl combine egg and bread crumbs. Stir in onion, yogurt, salt, cinnamon, coriander, and cayenne pepper. Add ground meat; mix well. Shape mixture into four oval patties about 5 inches long and ½ inch thick.

2 Place patties on the unheated rack of a broiler pan. Broil 3 to 4 inches from the heat for 11 to 13 minutes or until done (160°F), turning halfway through broiling time, and brushing once with 2 tablespoons of the jelly. Spoon remaining jelly over patties before serving. Serve burgers in lettuce-lined pita halves.

Makes 4 servings

Nutrition facts per serving: 410 cal., 16 g total fat (6 g sat. fat), 125 mg chol., 585 mg sodium, 37 g carbo., 2 g dietary fiber, 28 g protein.

Shopping list:

1 loaf bread

1 small onion

1 8-ounce container plain yogurt

1 small container coriander

1 pound ground beef

1 10-ounce jar jalapeño jelly

1 head lettuce

1 package large pita bread rounds

Pantry list:

Egg

Salt

Ground cinnamon

Cayenne pepper

40 minutes

Smoky Double **Cheeseburger** *(See photo on page 279.)*

Start to Finish: **40 minutes**

- 1 **egg, lightly beaten**
- ½ **cup soft bread crumbs**
- 3 **ounces smoked cheddar cheese or cheddar cheese, finely shredded (¾ cup)**
- 3 **green onions, chopped**
- 2 **tablespoons Worcestershire sauce**
- 1 **tablespoon Dijon-style mustard**
- ¼ **teaspoon ground black pepper**
- 1¼ **pounds ground beef round or ground sirloin**
- 4 **onion slices (optional)**
- 4 **hamburger buns, split and toasted**
- ¼ **cup mango chutney or cranberry relish**
- ½ **cup arugula leaves or watercress**
- 1 **to 2 ounces Asiago or Parmesan cheese, shaved**

1 In a large bowl combine egg, bread crumbs, smoked cheddar, green onions, Worcestershire sauce, mustard, and pepper. Add ground beef; mix gently. Firmly shape into four 12-inch-thick patties; set aside.

2 Heat a nonstick or well-seasoned grill pan over medium-high heat until hot. Reduce heat to medium; add onion slices, if using, to grill pan. Grill for 6 to 8 minutes or until tender and light brown, turning once. Remove from pan. Add patties to pan. Cook for 9 to 12 minutes or until meat is done (160°F), turning once.

3 Spread bottoms of hamburger buns with chutney; top with arugula, patties, onion slices, if using, and shaved cheese. Add bun top.

Makes 4 servings

Nutrition facts per serving: 586 cal., 31 g total fat (14 g sat. fat), 172 mg chol., 777 mg sodium, 35 g carbo., 2 g dietary fiber, 41 g protein.

Shopping list:

- 1 loaf bread
- 1 8-ounce package smoked cheddar cheese
- 1 bunch green onions
- 1¼ pounds ground beef round
- 1 large onion
- 1 package hamburger buns
- 1 12-ounce jar mango chutney
- 1 8-ounce package arugula leaves
- 1 piece Asiago cheese

Pantry list:

Egg

Worcestershire sauce

Dijon-style mustard

Ground black pepper

40
minutes

Individual Mexican **Meat Loaves**

Start to Finish: **40 minutes**   Oven: **375°F**

- 1 **medium onion, finely chopped (½ cup)**
- 1 **small green sweet pepper, seeded and chopped (½ cup)**
- 3 **cloves garlic, minced**
- 1 **tablespoon cooking oil**
- 1 **egg, lightly beaten**
- 4 **corn tortillas (5 to 6 inches in diameter), finely chopped**
- ¾ **cup shredded cheddar cheese (3 ounces)**
- ¼ **cup milk**
- 1½ **teaspoons Mexican seasoning**
- ½ **teaspoon salt**
- 1 **pound lean ground beef**

  Dairy sour cream and/or purchased salsa (optional)

1 Preheat oven to 375°F. In a large skillet cook onion, sweet pepper, and garlic in hot oil over medium heat for 5 to 7 minutes or until tender, stirring occasionally. Meanwhile, in a large bowl combine egg, tortillas, ½ cup of the cheese, milk, Mexican seasoning, and salt. Add ground meat and onion mixture; mix well.

2 Form beef mixture into four 5x3x1-inch loaves. Place loaves in a 13x9x2-inch baking pan. Bake for 20 to 25 minutes or until done (160°F). Sprinkle remaining ¼ cup cheese evenly over loaves before serving. If desired, serve meat loaves with sour cream and/or salsa.

Makes 4 servings

Nutrition facts per serving: 460 cal., 30 g total fat (12 g sat. fat), 154 mg chol., 610 mg sodium, 17 g carbo., 2 g dietary fiber, 31 g protein.

Shopping list:

1 medium onion

1 small green sweet pepper

1 package corn tortillas (5 to 6 inches in diameter)

1 4-ounce package shredded cheddar cheese

1 small container Mexican seasoning

1 pound lean ground beef

Pantry list:

Garlic

Cooking oil

Egg

Milk

Salt

40 minutes

Polenta with Italian Beef Stew

Start to Finish: **40 minutes**

- 1 **pound lean ground beef**
- 1 **14.5-ounce can diced tomatoes with basil, garlic, and oregano, undrained**
- 3 **medium carrots, cut into ½-inch slices**
- 2 **medium onions, cut into thin wedges**
- 1 **large red sweet pepper, cut into 1-inch pieces**
- ½ **cup beef broth**
- 3 **tablespoons tomato paste**
- ¼ **teaspoon salt**
- ¼ **teaspoon ground black pepper**
- 1 **teaspoon bottled minced garlic**
- 1 **medium zucchini, halved lengthwise and cut into ¼-inch slices**
- ⅓ **cup purchased basil pesto**
- 1 **16-ounce tube refrigerated cooked polenta**

1 In a large skillet cook ground beef over medium heat until brown. Drain off fat. Stir in undrained tomatoes, carrots, onions, sweet pepper, beef broth, tomato paste, salt, black pepper, and garlic. Bring to boiling; reduce heat. Cover and simmer for 10 to 15 minutes or until carrots are tender. Stir in zucchini and pesto. Cover and simmer for 5 minutes more.

2 Meanwhile, prepare polenta according to package directions. Serve meat mixture with polenta.

Makes 6 servings

Nutrition facts per serving: 362 cal., 16 g total fat (3 g sat. fat), 50 mg chol., 978 mg sodium, 34 g carbo., 5 g dietary fiber, 20 g protein.

Shopping list:
- 1 pound lean ground beef
- 1 14.5-ounce can diced tomatoes with basil, garlic, and oregano
- 1 package carrots
- 2 medium onions
- 1 large red sweet pepper
- 1 14-ounce can beef broth
- 1 6-ounce can tomato paste
- 1 medium zucchini
- 1 4-ounce jar basil pesto
- 1 16-ounce tube refrigerated cooked polenta

Pantry list:
Salt

Ground black pepper

Bottled minced garlic

40
minutes

Soft-Shell **Burritos**

Start to Finish: **35 minutes**   Oven: **350°F**

- 6 8-inch flour tortillas
- 12 ounces ground beef
- ½ cup chopped onion (1 medium)
- 2 cloves garlic, minced
- ½ cup chopped green sweet pepper (1 small)
- ½ cup bottled salsa or picante sauce
- 2 teaspoons Mexican seasoning
- 1½ cups shredded lettuce
- 1 cup chopped tomatoes (2 medium)
- ½ cup shredded cheddar or Monterey Jack cheese (2 ounces)
- Shredded cheddar or Monterey Jack cheese (optional)
- Bottled salsa or picante sauce (optional)

1 Preheat oven to 350°F. Wrap tortillas in foil; bake in a 350°F oven about 10 minutes or until warm.

2 Meanwhile, in a large skillet cook ground beef, onion, and garlic over medium-high heat until meat is brown and onion is tender. Drain off fat. Stir in sweet pepper, ½ cup salsa, and Mexican seasoning. Bring to boiling; reduce heat. Simmer, covered, for 10 minutes.

3 Place tortillas on work surface. Top each tortilla with about ½ cup of the meat mixture and some of the lettuce and tomatoes. Sprinkle with the ½ cup cheese. Fold in sides; roll up. Cut in half to serve. If desired, sprinkle with additional cheese and pass additional salsa.

Makes 6 servings

Nutrition facts per serving: 252 cal., 7 g total fat (3 g sat. fat), 42 mg chol., 532 mg sodium, 29 g carbo., 2 g dietary fiber, 16 g protein.

40 minutes

Shopping list:
- 1 package 8-inch flour tortillas
- 12 ounces ground beef
- 1 medium onion
- 1 small green sweet pepper
- 1 8-ounce bottle salsa
- 1 small container Mexican seasoning
- 1 head lettuce
- 2 medium tomatoes
- 1 8-ounce package shredded cheddar cheese

Pantry list:
Garlic

Taco Shepherd's Pie *(See photo on page 280.)*

Start to Finish: **40 minutes**   Oven: **400°F**

1 **18-ounce package taco sauce with seasoned ground beef**

1 **24-ounce package refrigerated country-style mashed potatoes**

1 **15-ounce can black beans, rinsed and drained**

1 **11-ounce can whole kernel corn with sweet peppers, drained**

1 **14.5-ounce can Mexican-style stewed tomatoes, drained**

1 **4-ounce can diced green chilies**

1 **cup shredded Mexican-style four-cheese blend**

Dairy sour cream (optional)

1 Preheat oven to 400°F. Heat taco meat and mashed potatoes according to package directions. Stir beans and corn into taco meat. Stir drained tomatoes and green chilies into mashed potatoes.

2 Spoon meat mixture into a 2-quart square baking dish. Spoon mashed potato mixture in mounds over meat mixture. Sprinkle cheese over potatoes. Bake, uncovered, for 20 minutes or until mixture is bubbly. If desired, top each serving with sour cream.

Makes 6 servings

Nutrition facts per serving: 401 cal., 15 g total fat (7 g sat. fat), 39 mg chol., 1,624 mg sodium, 47 g carbo., 7 g dietary fiber, 20 g protein.

Shopping List:

1 18-ounce package taco sauce with seasoned ground beef

1 24-ounce package refrigerated country-style mashed potatoes

1 15-ounce can black beans

1 14.5-ounce can Mexican-style stewed tomatoes

1 11-ounce can whole kernel corn with sweet peppers

1 4-ounce can diced green chilies

1 8-ounce package shredded Mexican-style four-cheese blend

Pork with **Mushrooms**

Start to Finish: **40 minutes**

- 1 **pound fresh mushrooms (such as stemmed shiitake, cremini, and/or button), sliced**
- 2 **tablespoons olive oil**
- ½ **cup finely chopped onion (1 medium)**
- 6 **cloves garlic, minced**
- 1 **tablespoon snipped fresh thyme**
- ½ **cup dry white wine**
- 1 **tablespoon grated Parmesan cheese**
- 1 **tablespoon snipped fresh Italian (flat-leaf) parsley**
- ¼ **teaspoon salt**
- ⅛ **teaspoon freshly ground black pepper**
- 4 **boneless pork loin chops**

  Salt and freshly ground black pepper
- 1 **cup chicken broth**

1 In a large skillet cook mushrooms in 1 tablespoon hot oil over medium-high heat about 5 minutes or until tender and starting to brown, stirring occasionally. Add onion; cook and stir about 4 minutes or until onion is tender. Add garlic and thyme; cook and stir for 1 minute. Carefully add wine to skillet. Bring to boiling; reduce heat. Boil gently, uncovered, for 2 to 3 minutes or until most of the liquid evaporates. Remove from heat; transfer to a medium bowl. Stir in Parmesan cheese, parsley, ¼ teaspoon salt, and ⅛ teaspoon pepper.

2 Season chops lightly with additional salt and pepper. In the same skillet cook chops in remaining 1 tablespoon oil over medium-high heat for 6 minutes, turning once. Add mushroom mixture and broth to skillet around chops. Bring to boiling; reduce heat. Cover and simmer for 7 to 10 minutes or until chops are done (160°F). Transfer chops to a serving platter; cover and keep warm.

3 Bring mixture in skillet to boiling; reduce heat. Boil gently, uncovered, for 5 minutes. Spoon some of mushroom mixture over chops; pass remaining mushroom mixture.

Makes 4 servings

Nutrition facts per serving: 334 cal., 11 g total fat (2 g sat. fat), 80 mg chol., 769 mg sodium, 21 g carbo., 3 g dietary fiber, 35 g protein.

40 minutes

Shopping list:

- 2 8-ounce containers fresh mushrooms
- 1 medium onion
- 1 package fresh thyme
- 1 bottle dry white wine
- 1 7-ounce container grated Parmesan cheese
- 1 bunch fresh Italian (flat-leaf) parsley
- 4 boneless pork loin chops
- 1 14-ounce can chicken broth

Pantry list:

Olive oil

Garlic

Salt

Black pepper

Spicy Skillet Pork Chops

Start to Finish: **40 minutes**

1 ½ **cups frozen whole kernel corn**

1 **10-ounce can chopped tomatoes and green chile peppers, undrained**

½ **teaspoon ground cumin**

¼ **teaspoon bottled hot pepper sauce**

2 **cloves garlic, minced**

4 **boneless pork loin chops, cut ¾ inch thick**

½ **teaspoon chili powder**

2 **teaspoons cooking oil**

1 **medium onion, cut into thin wedges**

1 **tablespoon snipped fresh cilantro**

1 In a medium bowl combine corn, undrained tomatoes, cumin, hot pepper sauce, and garlic; set aside.

2 Trim fat from chops. Sprinkle both sides of each chop with chili powder. In a 12-inch nonstick skillet cook chops in hot oil over medium-high heat about 4 minutes or until brown, turning once. Remove chops from skillet, reserving drippings. Reduce heat to medium. Add onion to skillet; cook and stir for 3 minutes. Stir corn mixture into onion mixture in skillet. Place chops on corn mixture. Bring to boiling; reduce heat. Simmer, covered, for 10 to 12 minutes or until pork juices run clear (160°F).

3 To serve, remove chops from skillet. Stir snipped cilantro into corn mixture in skillet; serve corn mixture with chops.

Makes 4 servings

Nutrition facts per serving: 330 cal., 11 g total fat (3 g sat. fat), 93 mg chol., 360 mg sodium, 18 g carbo., 2 g dietary fiber, 40 g protein.

Shopping list:

1 10-ounce package frozen whole kernel corn

1 10-ounce can chopped tomatoes and green chile peppers

4 boneless pork loin chops

1 medium onion

1 bunch fresh cilantro

Pantry list:

Ground cumin

Bottled hot pepper sauce

Garlic

Chili powder

Cooking oil

40 minutes

Pork and Chorizo Stew

Start to Finish: **40 minutes**

1 **1-pound pork tenderloin, cut into 1-inch cubes**

8 **ounces cooked smoked chorizo sausage, cut into ¼-inch slices**

1 **tablespoon cooking oil**

1 **cup coarsely chopped onion (1 large)**

2 **cloves garlic, minced**

2 **tablespoons all-purpose flour**

½ **teaspoon dried thyme, crushed**

2 ½ **cups reduced-sodium beef broth**

1 **cup frozen peas and carrots**

Salt and ground black pepper

2 **cups dried egg noodles**

1 In a 4-quart Dutch oven cook pork cubes and chorizo in hot oil over medium-high heat for 10 minutes or until brown. Using a slotted spoon, transfer meat to a plate; set aside.

2 Add onion and garlic to pan. Cook and stir for 4 to 5 minutes or until tender. Return meat and any accumulated juices to pan. Add flour and thyme. Cook and stir for 1 minute.

3 Gradually add broth, stirring to loosen any browned bits from bottom of pan. Add frozen peas and carrots. Bring to boiling; reduce heat. Simmer, uncovered, for 15 to 20 minutes. Season to taste with salt and pepper.

4 Meanwhile, in a large pan cook egg noodles according to package directions. Drain well. Serve stew with noodles.

Makes 4 servings

Nutrition facts per serving: 555 cal., 30 g total fat (10 g sat. fat), 140 mg chol., 1,211 mg sodium, 26 g carbo., 3 g dietary fiber, 43 g protein.

Shopping list:

1 1-pound pork tenderloin

8 ounces cooked smoked chorizo sausage

1 large onion

2 14-ounce cans reduced-sodium beef broth

1 16-ounce package frozen peas and carrots

1 16-ounce package dried package egg noodles

Pantry list:

Cooking oil

Garlic

All-purpose flour

Dried thyme

Salt

Ground black pepper

40 minutes

Asian Pork Tenderloin with Ramen Noodle Salad

Start to Finish: **35 minutes**

1 12- to 16-ounce pork tenderloin

   Salt and ground black pepper

1 3-ounce package ramen noodles (any flavor)

2 tablespoons cooking oil

¼ cup plum sauce

1 tablespoon soy sauce

½ cup thinly sliced bok choy

½ cup packaged coarsely shredded fresh carrot

⅓ cup bias-sliced green onion

½ of a small red sweet pepper, cut into thin strips

¼ cup lightly packed cilantro leaves

⅓ cup bottled light ginger vinaigrette salad dressing

1 Cut tenderloin into ½-inch slices. Place each slice between two sheets of plastic wrap; with the flat side of a meat mallet pound to ¼ inch thick. Sprinkle lightly with salt and black pepper. Set aside.

2 Discard seasoning packet from noodles. Cook noodles according to package directions. Drain noodles. Rinse with cold water until cool; drain again. Snip through noodles a few times with clean kitchen scissors to make shorter lengths.

3 Meanwhile, in a very large skillet heat oil over medium-high heat. Add half of the tenderloin slices; reduce heat to medium. Cook about 2 minutes per side or until barely pink in center. Remove; cook remaining pork. Return all pork to skillet. Add plum sauce and soy sauce, turning meat to coat. Remove from skillet.

4 For salad, in a serving bowl combine ramen noodles, bok choy, carrot, green onions, sweet pepper, and cilantro. Add salad dressing and toss to combine. Serve salad with pork.

Makes 4 servings

Nutrition facts per serving: 352 cal., 17 g total fat (4 g sat. fat), 55 mg chol., 1,182 mg sodium, 29 g carbo., 2 g dietary fiber, 21 g protein.

Shopping list:
- 1 12- to 16-ounce pork tenderloin
- 1 3-ounce package ramen noodles (any flavor)
- 1 5.5-ounce jar plum sauce
- 1 bunch bok choy
- 1 16-ounce bag shredded carrots
- 1 bunch green onions
- 1 small red sweet pepper
- 1 bunch fresh cilantro
- 1 16-ounce bottle light ginger vinaigrette salad dressing

Pantry list:
- Salt
- Ground black pepper
- Cooking oil
- Soy sauce

40 minutes

Maple-Shallot Pork Tenderloin

Start to Finish: **40 minutes**   Oven: **425°F**

- 1 **1-pound pork tenderloin, trimmed**
- ¼ **teaspoon garlic salt**
- ¼ **teaspoon ground black pepper**
- ½ **cup thinly sliced shallot or onion**
- 1 **tablespoon butter**
- ¾ **cup pure maple syrup or maple-flavor syrup**
- 1 **tablespoon rice vinegar**
- 1 **24-ounce package refrigerated mashed sweet potatoes***
- ½ **cup pecan pieces, toasted**

  Additional maple syrup or maple-flavor syrup

1 Preheat oven to 425°F. Place tenderloin on a rack in a shallow roasting pan. Sprinkle tenderloin with garlic salt and pepper. Roast for 25 to 30 minutes or until no longer pink (155°F).

2 Meanwhile, in a small saucepan cook shallot in hot butter until tender and light brown. Stir in ¾ cup maple syrup and vinegar. Bring just to boiling; reduce heat. Simmer, uncovered, about 15 minutes or until reduced to about ⅔ cup. Remove from heat and set aside.

3 Prepare sweet potatoes according to package directions. Stir in pecans and, if desired, drizzle with additional maple syrup.

4 Remove tenderloin from oven and spoon about 2 tablespoons of the maple syrup mixture over the meat. Cover and let stand for 5 minutes before slicing.

5 Serve with sweet potatoes; pass remaining maple syrup mixture.

Makes 4 servings

Nutrition facts per serving: 628 cal., 19 g total fat (5 g sat. fat), 82 mg chol., 192 mg sodium, 89 g carbo., 6 g dietary fiber, 27 g protein.

*Note: If you can't locate refrigerated sweet potatoes, use refrigerated mashed potatoes, but do not drizzle with additional maple syrup.

Shopping list:

1 1-pound pork tenderloin
4 medium shallots
1 12-ounce bottle rice vinegar
1 24-ounce package refrigerated mashed sweet potatoes
1 4-ounce package pecan pieces

Pantry list:

Garlic salt
Ground black pepper
Butter
Maple syrup

40 minutes

Pork and Vegetable Supper

Start to Finish: **35 minutes**

- 2 **tablespoons snipped fresh thyme**
- 1 ¼ **teaspoons lemon-pepper seasoning**
- ½ **teaspoon bottled minced garlic**
- 12 **ounces pork tenderloin**
- 1 **tablespoon olive oil**
- 1 **medium yellow summer squash, sliced (1¼ cups)**
- 1 **medium red or green sweet pepper, seeded and cut into thin strips**
- 1 **cup chicken broth**
- 4 **teaspoons all-purpose flour**
- 8 **ounces dried fettuccine or linguine, cooked and drained**
- 1 **medium tomato, seeded and cut up (optional)**

1 In a small bowl combine thyme, lemon-pepper seasoning, and garlic. Set aside half of the mixture. Rub remaining herb mixture into pork.

2 In a large skillet brown pork on all sides in hot oil over medium-high heat. Reduce heat to medium-low; cook, covered, for 15 to 20 minutes or until done (160°F), turning once.

3 Remove meat from skillet; set aside and keep warm. Add squash, sweet pepper, and reserved thyme mixture to skillet. Cook and stir over medium heat for 2 to 3 minutes or until crisp-tender. Use a slotted spoon to transfer vegetables to the serving dish; keep warm.

4 In a small bowl combine broth and flour. Add to skillet. Cook and stir over medium heat until thick and bubbly. Cook and stir 1 minute more. Add sauce and pasta to vegetables in serving dish. Toss to combine. Slice pork and arrange slices on top of pasta mixture. If desired, sprinkle with tomato.

Makes 4 servings

Nutrition facts per serving: 401 cal., 6 g total fat (1 g sat. fat), 66 mg chol., 652 mg sodium, 49 g carbo., 3 g dietary fiber, 35 g protein.

Shopping list:

- 1 package fresh thyme
- 1 small container lemon-pepper seasoning
- 12 ounces pork tenderloin
- 1 medium yellow summer squash
- 1 medium red sweet pepper
- 1 14-ounce can chicken broth
- 1 16-ounce package dried fettuccine

Pantry list:

Bottled minced garlic

Olive oil

All-purpose flour

40 minutes

Pork Tenderloin with Creamy Mustard Sauce

Start to Finish: **40 minutes**   Oven: **425°F**

1   1-pound pork tenderloin, trimmed

Nonstick cooking spray

Salt and ground black pepper

¼   cup finely chopped shallot or onion

1   clove garlic, minced

1   tablespoon olive oil

¼   cup beef broth

1   to 2 tablespoons Dijon-style mustard

¼   teaspoon dried thyme, crushed

1   cup whipping cream

1   Preheat oven to 425°F. Place tenderloin in an ungreased 13x9x2-inch baking pan. Lightly coat tenderloin with cooking spray and sprinkle with salt and pepper. Roast, uncovered for 25 to 30 minutes or until juices run clear (155°F). Cover with foil; let stand for 10 minutes. (The temperature of the meat after standing should be 160°F.)

2   Meanwhile, in a medium skillet cook shallot and garlic in hot oil for 3 to 4 minutes or until tender. Add broth; simmer, uncovered, until most of the liquid evaporates. Stir in mustard and thyme. Stir in cream; simmer, uncovered, for 4 to 5 minutes or until thickened to desired consistency. Serve sauce over pork.

Makes 4 servings

Nutrition facts per serving: 386 cal., 30 g total fat (16 g sat. fat), 156 mg chol., 372 mg sodium, 4 g carbo., 0 g dietary fiber, 25 g protein.

Shopping list:

1   1-pound pork tenderloin

2   medium shallots

1   14-ounce can beef broth

1   8-ounce container whipping cream

Pantry list:

Nonstick cooking spray

Salt

Ground black pepper

Garlic

Olive oil

Dijon-style mustard

Dried thyme

Tex-Mex Pork and Corn Soup

Start to Finish: **35 minutes**

- 12 ounces pork tenderloin or lean boneless pork, cut into bite-size strips
- 1 tablespoon olive oil
- 1 cup chopped red onion
- 4 cloves garlic, minced
- 1 10-ounce package frozen whole kernel corn
- 2 14-ounce cans reduced-sodium chicken broth
- 1 cup bottled chipotle-style salsa or regular salsa
- 1 cup chopped red and/or yellow sweet pepper
- ¼ cup snipped fresh cilantro
- ½ cup chopped tomato
- Dairy sour cream (optional)

1 In a large saucepan cook and stir pork strips in hot oil over medium-high heat for 4 to 5 minutes or until no pink remains. Remove pork strips from saucepan; set aside. Add onion and garlic to saucepan. Cook and stir for 3 to 4 minutes or until onion is tender.

2 Add corn to saucepan. Cook and stir for 4 minutes. Stir in broth, salsa, and sweet pepper. Bring to boiling; reduce heat. Simmer, uncovered, for 10 minutes. Return meat to saucepan; heat through. Remove saucepan from heat; stir in cilantro. Top each serving with tomato, and, if desired, sour cream.

Makes 5 servings

Nutrition facts per serving: 199 cal., 6 g total fat (1 g sat. fat), 44 mg chol., 561 mg sodium, 20 g carbo., 3 g dietary fiber, 19 g protein.

Shopping list:
- 12 ounces pork tenderloin
- 1 large red onion
- 1 10-ounce package frozen whole kernel corn
- 2 14-ounce cans reduced-sodium chicken broth
- 1 16-ounce jar chipotle-style salsa
- 1 red sweet pepper
- 1 bunch fresh cilantro
- 1 medium tomato

Pantry list:
- Olive oil
- Garlic

40 minutes

Mexi-Pork Wraps

Start to Finish: **35 minutes**

- 8 ounces lean boneless pork, cut into thin bite-size strips
- 1 clove garlic, minced
- 1 tablespoon olive oil
- ¾ cup frozen whole kernel corn, thawed
- ½ cup chopped roasted red sweet peppers
- ¼ cup sliced green onions (2)
- 3 tablespoons lime juice
- ½ teaspoon ground cumin
- ⅛ teaspoon cayenne pepper (optional)
- ½ cup refried black beans*
- 4 9- or 10-inch whole grain tortillas
- ½ cup shredded romaine
- ½ cup chopped tomatoes

  Light dairy sour cream (optional)

1 In a large skillet cook and stir pork strips and garlic in hot oil over medium-high heat for 4 to 5 minutes or until no pink remains; set aside.

2 In a medium bowl stir together corn, roasted sweet peppers, green onions, 2 tablespoons of the lime juice, cumin, and, if desired, cayenne pepper. In a small bowl stir together refried beans and remaining 1 tablespoon lime juice.

3 Spread 2 tablespoons of black bean mixture in a 2-inch-wide strip on center of each tortilla. Top with pork strips, corn mixture, romaine, and tomato. Fold bottom edge of each tortilla over the filling. Roll up tortillas around filling. If desired, serve with sour cream.

Makes 4 wraps

Nutrition facts per wrap: 316 cal., 11 g total fat (3 g sat. fat), 36 mg chol., 484 mg sodium, 39 g carbo., 5 g dietary fiber, 17 g protein.

*Note: If you can't find refried black beans, rinse and drain ½ of a 15-ounce can black beans. In a small bowl mash beans; stir in 1 tablespoon lime juice.

Mexi-Chicken Wraps:
Prepare as above, except substitute skinless, boneless chicken breast halves, cut into bite-size strips, for the pork.

Shopping list:
- 8 ounces boneless pork
- 1 10-ounce package frozen whole kernel corn
- 1 7-ounce jar roasted red sweet peppers
- 1 bunch green onions
- 1 8-ounce bottle lime juice
- 1 16-ounce can refried black beans
- 1 package whole grain tortillas
- 1 head romaine
- 1 large fresh tomato

Pantry list:
Garlic

Olive oil

Ground cumin

Cayenne pepper

40 minutes

Pork with Spaetzle and Braised Cabbage

(See photo on page 278.)

Start to Finish: **40 minutes**

1 **10.5-ounce package dried spaetzle**

3 **tablespoons butter**

1 **tablespoon chopped fresh parsley**

Salt and ground black pepper

2 **tablespoons packed brown sugar**

2 **tablespoons cider vinegar**

2 **tablespoons water**

3 **cups shredded red or green cabbage**

1 **17-ounce package refrigerated cooked pork roast au jus**

1 Cook spaetzle according to package directions; drain. In a large skillet cook spaetzle in 2 tablespoons of the butter over medium heat for 8 to 10 minutes, gently stirring occasionally. Stir in parsley and season to taste with salt and pepper. Remove from skillet and keep warm.

2 In the same skillet combine brown sugar, vinegar, the water, and remaining 1 tablespoon butter. Bring to boiling over medium heat, stirring to dissolve brown sugar. Add cabbage. Return to boiling; reduce heat. Cook, covered, for 5 minutes or until cabbage is crisp-tender. Season to taste with salt and pepper.

3 Meanwhile, reheat pork roast according to package directions. Serve pork roast with spaetzle and cabbage.

Makes 4 servings

Nutrition facts per serving: 565 cal., 17 g total fat (8 g sat. fat), 152 mg chol., 1,453 mg sodium, 64 g carbo., 4 g dietary fiber, 37 g protein.

Shopping list:

1 10.5-ounce package dried spaetzle

1 bunch fresh parsley

1 head red cabbage

1 17-ounce package refrigerated cooked pork roast au jus

Pantry list:

Butter

Salt

Ground black pepper

Brown sugar

Cider vinegar

40 minutes

German Sausage **Chowder**

Start to Finish: **35 minutes**

1 medium onion, chopped (½ cup)

1 stalk celery, chopped (½ cup)

2 tablespoons butter

2 tablespoons all-purpose flour

1 32-ounce box chicken broth

2 cups packaged shredded cabbage with carrot (coleslaw mix)

2 cups packaged refrigerated diced potatoes with onions

8 ounces cooked, smoked Polish sausage (kielbasa), cut into ½-inch slices

1 teaspoon dried thyme, crushed

Salt and ground black pepper

1 cup shredded Swiss cheese (4 ounces)

1 In a large saucepan cook onion and celery in butter over medium heat until tender. Stir in flour; cook for 1 minute more. Stir in broth. Bring to boiling; cook until slightly thick.

2 Stir coleslaw mix, potatoes, kielbasa, and thyme into broth mixture. Cook until cabbage is wilted and potatoes are heated through. Season to taste with salt and pepper. Top individual servings with Swiss cheese.

Makes 6 to 8 servings

Nutrition facts per serving: 317 cal., 22 g total fat (12 g sat. fat), 45 mg chol., 1,149 mg sodium, 17 g carbo., 2 g dietary fiber, 13 g protein.

Shopping list:

1 medium onion

1 bunch celery

1 32-ounce box chicken broth

1 16-ounce package shredded cabbage with carrot (coleslaw mix)

1 20-ounce package refrigerated diced potatoes with onions

8 ounces cooked, smoked Polish sausage (kielbasa)

1 8-ounce package shredded Swiss cheese

Pantry list:

Butter

All-purpose flour

Dried thyme

Salt

Ground black pepper

40 minutes

Sausage Pasta Skillet

Start to Finish: **35 minutes**

8 ounces dried campanelle, cellentani, or penne

8 ounces bulk hot or sweet Italian sausage

1 medium onion, cut into thin wedges

1 26-ounce jar garlic pasta sauce

$\frac{2}{3}$ cup roasted red sweet peppers, cut into bite-size strips

$\frac{1}{4}$ cup pitted kalamata olives, quartered

1 cup shredded Italian blend cheeses

1 Cook pasta according to package directions; drain.

2 In a large skillet cook sausage and onion until sausage is brown and onion is tender; drain fat. Stir in pasta sauce, roasted sweet peppers, and olives. Bring to boiling. Stir in pasta to coat. Top with shredded cheese.

Makes 4 servings

Nutrition facts per serving: 616 cal., 28 g total fat (11 g sat. fat), 63 mg chol., 1,037 mg sodium, 65 g carbo., 6 g dietary fiber, 26 g protein.

Shopping list:

1 1-pound package dried campanelle

8 ounce bulk hot Italian sausage

1 medium onion

1 26-ounce jar garlic pasta sauce

1 7-ounce jar roasted red sweet peppers

1 8-ounce jar pitted kalamata olives

1 8-ounce package shredded Italian blend cheeses

40minutes

Fruited Lamb Chops with Couscous

Start to Finish: **30 minutes**

- 1 **teaspoon dried thyme, crushed**
- ½ **teaspoon coarsely ground black pepper**
- ¼ **teaspoon salt**
- 8 **lamb rib or loin chops, cut ¾ to 1 inch thick**
- 1 **tablespoon cooking oil**
- 2 **tablespoons finely chopped shallot or onion**
- 2 **tablespoons balsamic vinegar**
- 2 **tablespoons honey**
- 2 **small pears or apples, cored and thickly sliced**
- 2 **to 3 tablespoons dried cranberries, golden raisins, or raisins**

  Nutty Couscous

1 In a small bowl combine thyme, pepper, and salt. Trim fat from chops. Rub thyme mixture over both sides of chops.

2 In a large skillet heat oil over medium-high heat until very hot. Add lamb chops; reduce heat to medium and cook for 7 to 9 minutes or until done (160°F), turning once. Remove from skillet; set aside. Add shallot to drippings in skillet; cook and stir until tender.

3 Meanwhile, in a small bowl combine vinegar and honey. Add to skillet. Bring to boiling; add pears and cranberries to skillet. Return to boiling; reduce heat. Simmer, covered, for 3 minutes, stirring once. Return lamb to skillet. Cook, covered, 3 minutes more or until fruit is tender and lamb is heated through. To serve, spoon apples and sauce over lamb. Serve with Nutty Couscous.

Makes 4 servings

Nutrition facts per serving: 739 cal., 25 g total fat (7 g sat. fat), 113 mg chol., 676 mg sodium, 82 g carbo., 7 g dietary fiber, 46 g protein.

Nutty Couscous: In a medium saucepan bring one 14-ounce can chicken broth or 1 ¾ cups apple juice to boiling. Stir in 1 ½ cups couscous. Cover and remove from heat. Let stand 5 minutes. Fluff couscous lightly with a fork. Stir in ⅓ cup chopped pistachios or hazelnuts; season to taste with salt and ground black pepper.

40 minutes

Shopping list:
8 lamb rib chops
1 shallot
2 small pears
1 3-ounce package dried cranberries

1 14-ounce can chicken broth
1 8-ounce package couscous
1 4-ounce package pistachio nuts

Pantry list:
Dried thyme

Ground black pepper
Salt
Cooking oil
Balsamic vinegar
Honey

Lamb Chops with Ginger-Dijon Sauce

Start to Finish: **40 minutes**

- 6 ounces fingerling and/ or tiny Yukon Gold potatoes
- 1 teaspoon grated fresh ginger
- 1 teaspoon snipped fresh tarragon
- 1/8 teaspoon coarsely ground black pepper
- 4 lamb rib chops, cut 1 inch thick

  Salt and ground black pepper
- 2 teaspoons cooking oil
- 1/3 cup dry white wine or chicken broth
- 1 to 2 teaspoons Dijon-style mustard

1 Halve any large potatoes. Cook potatoes in a small amount of lightly salted boiling water for 10 to 13 minutes or until just tender. Drain well and set aside. Meanwhile, in a small bowl combine ginger, tarragon, and 1/8 teaspoon pepper; set aside.

2 Trim fat from chops; sprinkle chops lightly with salt and pepper. In a large skillet cook chops and potatoes in hot oil over medium heat for 9 to 11 minutes for medium doneness (160°F), turning once. Turn potatoes occasionally to brown evenly. Remove chops and potatoes from skillet; keep warm.

3 Remove skillet from heat. Drain off fat. Carefully pour wine into skillet; return to heat. Stir to loosen any browned bits from bottom of pan. Add ginger mixture. Simmer and stir for 2 minutes or until liquid is reduced by half. Stir in mustard. Return to a simmer. Place chops and potatoes on 2 warm serving plates; top with sauce.

Makes 2 servings

Nutrition facts per serving: 293 cal., 11 g total fat (3 g sat. fat), 88 mg chol., 174 mg sodium, 15 g carbo., 1 g dietary fiber, 26 g protein.

Shopping list:
6 ounces fingerling potatoes

1 piece fresh ginger

1 package fresh tarragon

4 lamb rib chops

1 bottle dry white wine

Pantry list:
Ground black pepper

Salt

Cooking oil

Dijon-style mustard

40 minutes

Quick Lamb **Gyros**

Start to Finish: **40 minutes**   Oven: **350°F**

- 4 **Greek pita flatbreads or pita bread rounds**
- 12 **ounces lean boneless lamb, cut into thin strips**
- 1 **medium onion, cut into thin wedges**
- 2 **teaspoons Greek seasoning**
- 1 **tablespoon olive oil**
- 1 **6-ounce carton plain low-fat yogurt**
- ⅓ **cup finely chopped cucumber**
- 1 **teaspoon snipped fresh mint**
- 1 **clove garlic, minced**
- 1 **medium tomato, coarsely chopped**

1 Preheat oven to 350°F. Wrap pita flatbreads in foil. Heat in oven for 10 minutes.

2 Meanwhile, in a large skillet cook lamb, onion, and Greek seasoning in hot oil over medium-high heat until onion is tender and lamb is desired doneness.

3 In a small bowl combine yogurt, cucumber, mint, and garlic. Serve lamb mixture on top of pita flatbreads with yogurt sauce and chopped tomato. Fold in half to serve.

Makes 4 servings

Nutrition facts per serving: 365 cal., 10 g total fat (3 g sat. fat), 57 mg chol., 458 mg sodium, 41 g carbo., 2 g dietary fiber, 27 g protein.

Shopping list:

1 package Greek pita flatbread

12 ounces lean boneless lamb

1 medium onion

1 small container Greek seasoning

1 6-ounce carton plain low-fat yogurt

1 cucumber

1 bunch fresh mint

1 medium tomato

Pantry list:

Olive oil

Garlic

40 minutes

Curried Lamb Pilaf

Start to Finish: **40 minutes**

- 12 ounces lamb stew meat
- 1 tablespoon olive oil
- 1 medium onion, chopped
- 2 cloves garlic, minced, or 1 teaspoon bottled minced garlic
- 2 teaspoons curry powder
- ¼ teaspoon ground cinnamon
- 1 cup basmati rice
- 1 14-ounce can beef broth
- ¼ cup water
- ⅓ cup dried cherries or raisins
- ⅓ cup pine nuts, toasted

1 In a 4-quart Dutch oven cook lamb in hot oil over medium-high heat for 5 minutes or until brown. Drain off fat. Add onion; cook and stir about 5 minutes or until tender (add additional oil if needed). Stir in garlic, curry powder, and cinnamon.

2 Stir in rice until coated. Add broth and water; bring to boiling. Reduce heat; cover and simmer for 15 minutes or until rice is tender. Stir in cherries and pine nuts.

Makes 4 servings

Nutrition facts per serving: 439 cal., 16 g total fat (3 g sat. fat), 55 mg chol., 428 mg sodium, 50 g carbo., 2 g dietary fiber, 23 g protein.

Shopping list:

12 ounces lamb stew meat

1 medium onion

1 small container curry powder

1 12-ounce package basmati rice

1 14-ounce can beef broth

1 3-ounce package dried tart cherries

1 2-ounce package pine nuts

Pantry list:

Olive oil

Garlic

Ground cinnamon

40 minutes

Lamb and Eggplant Pitas

Start to Finish: **40 minutes**

- 1 **small eggplant**
- 2 **tablespoons olive oil**
  Salt and ground black pepper
- 1 **pound ground lamb**
- 8 **ounces lean ground beef**
- ¼ **cup snipped fresh Italian (flat-leaf) parsley**
- 1 **tablespoon dried Greek seasoning**
- ½ **teaspoon salt**
- 1 **medium tomato, chopped**
- ⅓ **cup plain yogurt**
- ¼ **cup chopped cucumber**
- 1 **clove garlic, minced**
- 3 **large pita bread rounds, halved**

1 Preheat broiler. Peel eggplant, if desired. Cut eggplant into 1-inch cubes (should have about 4 cups). Place in a 15 x 10 x 1-inch baking pan. Drizzle with oil and sprinkle lightly with salt and pepper; toss to coat. Broil eggplant 4 to 5 inches from the heat for 5 to 8 minutes or until brown and tender, stirring once. Remove from oven and set aside.

2 Meanwhile, in a large bowl combine lamb, ground beef, parsley, Greek seasoning, and ½ teaspoon salt; mix well. Form mixture into 6 oval patties about ½ inch thick. Arrange patties on the unheated rack of a broiler pan. Broil patties 4 to 5 inches from heat for 12 to 15 minutes or until done (160°F), turning once.

3 In a medium bowl stir together eggplant, tomato, yogurt, cucumber, and garlic. Serve patties in pita bread halves with eggplant mixture.

Makes 6 servings

Nutrition facts per serving: 446 cal., 29 g total fat (11 g sat. fat), 82 mg chol., 575 mg sodium, 22 g carbo., 3 g dietary fiber, 24 g protein.

minutes
40

Shopping list:

- 1 small eggplant
- 1 pound ground lamb
- 8 ounces lean ground beef
- 1 bunch fresh Italian (flat-leaf) parsley
- 1 small container Greek seasoning
- 1 medium tomato
- 1 6-ounce carton plain yogurt
- 1 small cucumber
- 1 package large pita bread rounds

Pantry list:

Olive oil

Salt

Ground black pepper

Garlic

Salmon Packets with **Mushrooms**

Start to Finish: 40 minutes   **Oven: 450°F**

- 4 5- to 6-ounce fresh or frozen skinless salmon fillets, 1 inch thick
- 2 large onions, halved and thinly sliced (2 cups)
- ⅛ teaspoon salt
- 1 cup sliced fresh shiitake mushroom caps or sliced button mushrooms
- ½ cup hoisin sauce
- 1 clove garlic, minced
- ¼ teaspoon crushed red pepper
- 1 medium red sweet pepper, finely chopped (¾ cup)

1 Thaw fish, if frozen. Preheat oven to 450°F. Rinse fish; pat dry with paper towels. Set aside. Cut four 12x12-inch sheets of heavy foil. Arrange ½ cup onion in center of each sheet. Top each with a salmon fillet. Sprinkle salmon with salt. Set aside.

2 In a medium bowl stir together mushrooms, hoisin sauce, garlic, and crushed red pepper. Spread mushroom mixture over fillets. Sprinkle sweet pepper over each.

3 Bring together two opposite foil edges and seal with a double fold. Fold remaining edges together to completely enclose the food, allowing space for steam to build. Place foil packets in a single layer in a 15x10x1-inch baking pan.

4 Bake about 20 minutes or until fish flakes when tested with a fork. Open packets carefully to allow steam to escape. Transfer packets to plates.

Makes 4 servings

Nutrition facts per serving: 389 cal., 17 g total fat (3 g sat. fat), 85 mg chol., 679 mg sodium, 28 g carbo., 4 g dietary fiber, 31 g protein.

Shopping list:
- 4 5- to 6-ounce fresh or frozen skinless salmon fillets, 1 inch thick
- 2 large onions
- 1 8-ounce package shiitake mushrooms
- 1 8-ounce jar hoisin sauce
- 1 medium red sweet pepper

Pantry list:
- Salt
- Garlic
- Crushed red pepper

40 minutes

Herb-Crusted Salmon with Roasted Pepper Cream

Start to Finish: 40 minutes   **Oven: 400°F**

4   **6-ounce fresh or frozen skinless salmon fillets**

3   **tablespoons honey Dijon-style mustard**

3   **tablespoons seasoned fine dry bread crumbs**

½   **cup drained chopped roasted red sweet peppers**

1   **cup whipping cream**

1 Thaw fish, if frozen. Preheat oven to 400°F. Rinse fish; pat dry with paper towels. Brush one side of each piece with 2 tablespoons of the mustard. Sprinkle with bread crumbs. Place fish, crumb sides up, in a 3-quart rectangular baking dish. Bake, uncovered, for 20 to 25 minutes or until crumbs are golden and fish flakes when tested with a fork.

2 Meanwhile, in a medium saucepan combine remaining 1 tablespoon mustard, roasted sweet peppers, and cream. Bring to boiling; reduce heat. Boil gently, uncovered, for 15 minutes or until reduced to 1 cup. Serve sauce over fish.

Makes 4 servings

Nutrition facts per serving: 576 cal., 32 g total fat (15 g sat. fat), 227 mg chol., 359 mg sodium, 11 g carbo., 0 g dietary fiber, 57 g protein.

40 minutes

Shopping list:

1   8-ounce package seasoned fine dry bread crumbs

4   6-ounce fresh or frozen skinless salmon fillets

1   8-ounce jar honey Dijon-style mustard

1   7-ounce jar roasted red sweet peppers

1   8-ounce carton whipping cream

Cajun Baked **Salmon**

Start to Finish: **40 minutes**   Oven: **375°F**

- 1   medium onion, thinly sliced and separated into rings
- 1   small green sweet pepper, seeded and cut into thin strips
- 1   1 ¼-pound fresh skinless salmon fillet
- 1   tablespoon olive oil
- 1 ½   to 2 teaspoons Cajun seasoning
- ¾   cup mayonnaise
- 1   tablespoon thinly sliced green onions
- 1   tablespoon Creole mustard or spicy brown mustard
- 1   tablespoon lime juice
    Few drops bottled hot pepper sauce (optional)

1   Preheat oven to 375°F. Line a 15x10x1-inch baking pan with foil; lightly grease foil. Arrange onion slices and sweet pepper in the center of the prepared pan. Rinse fish, pat dry with paper towels. Drizzle salmon with some of the oil; drizzle remaining oil over vegetables. Place fish on top of vegetables; sprinkle with Cajun seasoning. Bake, uncovered, about 30 minutes or until fish flakes when tested with a fork.

2   Meanwhile, in a small bowl combine mayonnaise, green onions, mustard, lime juice, and, if desired, hot pepper sauce. Serve with fish and vegetables.

Makes 4 servings

Nutrition facts per serving: 610 cal., 52 g total fat (10 g sat. fat), 98 mg chol., 440 mg sodium, 4 g carbo., 1 g dietary fiber, 29 g protein.

Shopping list:
1 medium onion
1 small green sweet pepper
1 1 ¼-pound skinless salmon fillet
1 small container Cajun seasoning
1 bunch green onions
1 4-ounce jar Creole mustard
1 lime

Pantry list:
Olive oil
Mayonnaise

40minutes

Grouper with **Tropical Salsa** *(See photo on page 283.)*

Start to Finish: **35 minutes**   Oven: **450°F**

4   **6- to 8-ounce fresh or frozen grouper or catfish fillets**

½   **cup all-purpose flour**

½   **cup finely chopped pistachio nuts or almonds**

1   **teaspoon ground black pepper**

½   **teaspoon salt**

½   **teaspoon dried tarragon, crushed**

½   **teaspoon dried basil, crushed**

¼   **cup milk**

¼   **cup lemon-flavor olive oil or olive oil**

1   **15.25-ounce can tropical fruit salad, drained and coarsely chopped**

1   **tablespoon white balsamic vinegar**

1   **tablespoon lime juice**

1   **tablespoon snipped fresh cilantro**

1 Thaw fish, if frozen. Preheat oven to 450°F. Grease a 15x10x1-inch baking pan; set aside. Rinse fish; pat dry with paper towels.

2 In a shallow dish combine flour, pistachios, pepper, salt, tarragon, and basil. Place milk in another shallow dish. Dip fish in milk then coat with flour mixture, patting flour mixture onto fish, if necessary. Place in a single layer in prepared pan. Drizzle fish with oil. Bake for 12 to 15 minutes or until fish flakes when tested with a fork.

3 Meanwhile, for salsa, in a small bowl combine tropical fruit salad, vinegar, lime juice, and cilantro. Serve salsa with fish.

Makes 4 servings

Nutrition facts per serving: 490 cal., 23 g total fat (3 g sat. fat), 64 mg chol., 405 mg sodium, 33 g carbo., 3 g dietary fiber, 39 g protein.

Shopping list:

4 6- to 8-ounce fresh or frozen grouper fillets

1 2.25-ounce package pistachio nuts

1 small container dried tarragon

1 small bottle lemon-flavor olive oil

1 15.25-ounce can tropical fruit salad

1 8-ounce bottle white balsamic vinegar

1 lime

1 bunch fresh cilantro

Pantry list:

All-purpose flour

Ground black pepper

Salt

Dried basil

Milk

40 minutes

Fish Enchilada Stacks

Start to Finish: **40 minutes**   Oven: **450°F/350°F**

- **12** ounces fresh or frozen skinless fish fillets, ½ inch thick
- **1** tablespoon olive oil
- **1** tablespoon lime juice
- **¼** teaspoon ground cumin
- **⅛** teaspoon garlic powder
- **2** 10-ounce cans or one 19-ounce can enchilada sauce
- **1** 15-ounce can refried black beans
- **12** 5- to 6-inch corn tortillas
- **2** cups shredded cheddar cheese (8 ounces)
- **¼** cup chopped green onions
- **¼** cup chopped pitted ripe olives

1 Thaw fish, if frozen. Preheat oven to 425°F. Rinse fish; pat dry with paper towels. Cut fish crosswise into ¾-inch slices. Place fish in a single layer in a greased shallow baking pan. In a small bowl stir together oil, lime juice, cumin, and garlic powder. Brush over fish. Bake for 4 to 6 minutes or until fish flakes when tested with a fork. Flake fish and set aside. Reduce oven temperature to 350°F.

2 Meanwhile, in a medium skillet warm enchilada sauce over low heat; keep warm. In a small saucepan warm beans over low heat, stirring until smooth; remove from heat.

3 Dip a tortilla in warm sauce. Place tortilla in a greased 15x10x1-inch baking pan. Repeat with 3 more tortillas, spacing tortillas evenly in pan. Top tortillas with half of the beans, half of the fish, and ⅔ cup of the cheese. Top with 4 more dipped tortillas, remaining beans and fish, and ⅔ cup of the cheese. Dip remaining tortillas and top stacks. Sprinkle with remaining ⅔ cup cheese.

4 Bake, uncovered, for 8 to 10 minutes or until cheese melts and stacks are heated through. Transfer stacks to serving plates. Spoon any remaining warm sauce over stacks. Sprinkle with green onions and olives.

Makes 4 servings

Nutrition facts per serving: 640 cal., 29 g total fat (13 g sat. fat), 96 mg chol., 1,841 mg sodium, 58 g carbo., 11 g dietary fiber, 39 g protein.

40minutes

Shopping list:

- 12 ounces fresh or frozen skinless fish fillets
- 1 lime
- 2 10-ounce cans enchilada sauce
- 1 15-ounce can refried black beans
- 1 package 5- to 6-inch corn tortillas
- 1 8-ounce package shredded cheddar cheese
- 1 bunch green onions
- 1 2.25-ounce can chopped pitted ripe olives

Pantry list:

Olive oil

Ground cumin

Garlic powder

Crab-Stuffed Tilapia Fillets

Start to Finish: **40 minutes**   Oven: **375°F**

- 4 **4- to 5-ounce fresh or frozen tilapia fillets**
- 3 **tablespoons chopped green onions**
- 1 **cup chopped mushrooms**
- 2 **tablespoons butter**
- 1 **6-ounce can crabmeat, drained, flaked, and cartilage removed**
- 3 **tablespoons mayonnaise**
- 1 **tablespoon lemon juice**
- ½ **teaspoon dry mustard**
- ¼ **teaspoon salt**
  Ground black pepper

1 Thaw fish, if frozen. Preheat oven to 375°F. Rinse fish; pat dry with paper towels. Set aside.

2 In a medium skillet cook and stir green onions and mushrooms in 1 tablespoon hot butter over medium heat for 4 to 5 minutes or until tender. Remove from heat. Add crabmeat, mayonnaise, lemon juice, dry mustard, and salt; gently stir to combine.

3 Spread crab mixture evenly over fillets. Roll fillets to enclose filling. Secure rolls with wooden toothpicks; place in a greased 2-quart square baking dish. Melt remaining 1 tablespoon butter and drizzle over fish. Sprinkle fish with pepper.

4 Bake for 15 to 20 minutes or until fish flakes when tested with a fork. Remove toothpicks before serving.

Makes 4 servings

Nutrition facts per serving: 285 cal., 16 g total fat (6 g sat. fat), 114 mg chol., 448 mg sodium, 2 g carbo., 0 g dietary fiber, 33 g protein.

Shopping list:

- 4 4- to 5-ounce fresh or frozen tilapia fillets
- 1 bunch green onions
- 1 8-ounce package mushrooms
- 1 6-ounce can crabmeat
- 1 lemon
- 1 small container dry mustard

Pantry list:

Butter

Mayonnaise

Salt

Ground black pepper

40 minutes

Lemony Orange Roughy Bake

Start to Finish: **40 minutes**   Oven: **400°F**

- 1 **pound fresh or frozen orange roughy, cod, or catfish fillets**
- 1 **cup chopped onion (1 large)**
- 1 **cup chopped red and/or green sweet pepper**
- 4 **cloves garlic, minced**
- 1 **tablespoon cooking oil**
- 1 **10.75-ounce can condensed cream of shrimp or cream of mushroom soup**
- ¾ **cup half-and-half or light cream**
- 1 **teaspoon lemon juice**
- ½ **teaspoon lemon-pepper seasoning**
- ¼ **cup fine dry bread crumbs**
- ¼ **cup freshly grated Parmesan cheese (1 ounce)**

1 Thaw fish, if frozen. Preheat oven to 400°F. Rinse fish; pat dry. Cut fish fillets into 4 serving-size pieces, if necessary. Set aside.

2 In a large skillet cook onion, sweet pepper, and garlic in hot oil over medium heat until vegetables are tender. Transfer vegetables to a greased 2-quart baking dish. Arrange fish on top of vegetables. Bake, uncovered, for 10 minutes.

3 Meanwhile, in the same skillet combine soup, half-and-half, lemon juice, and lemon-pepper seasoning. Bring to boiling; reduce heat. Simmer, uncovered, for 5 minutes. Pour soup mixture over fish. In a small bowl combine bread crumbs and Parmesan cheese. Sprinkle over soup mixture. Bake, uncovered, for 5 to 10 minutes more or until bread crumbs are brown.

Makes 4 servings

Nutrition facts per serving: 300 cal., 16 g total fat (6 g sat. fat), 55 mg chol., 1,001 mg sodium, 18 g carbo., 2 g dietary fiber, 23 g protein.

Shopping list:

- 1 pound fresh or frozen orange roughy fillets
- 1 large onion
- 1 large red sweet pepper
- 1 10.75-ounce can condensed cream of shrimp soup
- 1 8-ounce carton half-and-half
- 1 lemon
- 1 small container lemon-pepper seasoning
- 1 8-ounce package fine dry bread crumbs
- 1 4-ounce package grated Parmesan cheese

Pantry list:

Garlic

Cooking oil

40 minutes

Snapper Veracruz

Start to Finish: 40 minutes   Oven: **300°F**

1 ¼ to 1 ½ pounds skinless fresh or frozen red snapper fillets or firm-textured whitefish fillets, ½ to ¾ inch thick

1   14.5-ounce can Mexican-style stewed tomatoes, undrained

1   cup pitted ripe olives

2   tablespoons olive oil

1   10-ounce package seasoned yellow rice

1 Thaw fish, if frozen. Preheat oven to 300°F. Rinse fish; pat dry with paper towels. Cut into 4 serving-size pieces. In a large ovenproof skillet combine undrained tomatoes and olives. Top with fish fillets; drizzle with oil. Bake, uncovered, for 15 minutes. Spoon some of the tomato mixture over fish and bake 15 minutes more or until fish flakes when tested with a fork.

2 Meanwhile, prepare rice according to package directions. Serve fish and sauce with rice.

Makes 4 servings

Nutrition facts per serving: 566 cal., 19 g total fat (3 g sat. fat), 52 mg chol., 1,466 mg sodium, 63 g carbo., 3 g dietary fiber, 36 g protein.

40 minutes

Shopping list:

1 ¼ to 1 ½ pounds skinless fresh or frozen red snapper fillets

1 14.5-ounce can Mexican-style stewed tomatoes

1 6-ounce can pitted ripe olives

1 10-ounce packaged seasoned yellow rice

Pantry list:

Olive oil

Whitefish with **Roasted Asparagus**

Start to Finish: **35 minutes** Oven: **450°F**

- 1 **pound fresh or frozen skinless whitefish fillets or other white-fleshed fish fillets, about ½ inch thick**
- ½ **cup chopped onion (1 medium)**
- ½ **cup chopped carrot (1 medium)**
- ¼ **cup reduced-sodium chicken broth**
- 2 **cloves garlic, minced**
- ¼ **teaspoon salt**
- ¼ **teaspoon smoked paprika or paprika**
- ¼ **teaspoon ground black pepper**
- 12 **ounces fresh asparagus spears, trimmed and bias-sliced into 1-inch pieces (1 ½ cups)**

1 Thaw fish, if frozen. Preheat oven to 450°F. Rinse fish; pat dry. Cut fish into 4 serving-size portions; set aside. In a 2-quart rectangular baking dish stir together onion, carrot, broth, and garlic. Top with fish fillets, tucking under any thin edges. Sprinkle with salt, paprika, and pepper. Top with asparagus.

2 Bake, covered, for 15 to 20 minutes or until fish flakes when tested with a fork. Serve fish with vegetables.

Makes 4 servings

Nutrition facts per serving: 176 cal., 6 g total fat (1 g sat. fat), 65 mg chol., 249 mg sodium, 6 g carbo., 2 g dietary fiber, 23 g protein.

Shopping list:
- 1 pound fresh or frozen skinless whitefish fillets
- 1 medium onion
- 1 package carrots
- 1 14-ounce can reduced-sodium chicken broth
- 1 small container smoked paprika
- 12 ounces fresh asparagus spears

Pantry list:
Garlic

Salt

Ground black pepper

40 minutes

Spicy Salmon **Stir-Fry**

Start to Finish: **40 minutes**

- 2 **tablespoons soy sauce**
- 2 **tablespoons seasoned rice vinegar**
- 2 **tablespoons honey**
- 2 **tablespoons grated fresh ginger**
- 1 **clove garlic, minced**
- ¼ **teaspoon salt**
- 1 **12-ounce salmon fillet, about 1 inch thick**
- 1 **tablespoon toasted sesame oil**
- 2 **cups sugar snap peas**
- 2 **red and/or yellow sweet peppers, cut into bite-size strips**
- 1 ½ **cups broccoli florets**
- ¼ **teaspoon crushed red pepper**
- 3 **cups hot cooked Texmati rice**

1 In a small bowl whisk together soy sauce, vinegar, honey, ginger, and garlic; set aside.

2 Sprinkle salt over salmon. Cut salmon into 4 serving-size pieces. In a large nonstick skillet cook salmon in hot oil over medium heat for 3 to 5 minutes on each side or until fish flakes when tested with a fork. Remove from skillet; keep warm.

3 Add sugar snap peas, sweet peppers, broccoli, crushed red pepper, and ginger mixture to hot skillet. Cook and stir for 3 to 5 minutes or until vegetables are crisp-tender. Serve vegetables and salmon over rice.

Makes 4 servings

Nutrition facts per serving: 451 cal., 14 g total fat (3 g sat. fat), 50 mg chol., 729 mg sodium, 56 g carbo., 4 g dietary fiber, 25 g protein.

Shopping list:

- 1 10-ounce bottle seasoned rice vinegar
- 1 piece fresh ginger
- 1 12-ounce salmon fillet
- 1 8-ounce bottle toasted sesame oil
- 6 ounces fresh sugar snap peas
- 2 medium red sweet peppers
- 1 head broccoli
- 1 package Texmati rice

Pantry list:

Soy sauce

Honey

Garlic

Salt

Crushed red pepper

40 minutes

Salmon with Asparagus and Mushrooms

Start to Finish: 40 minutes

4 **fresh or frozen skinless salmon fillets, about 1 inch thick (about 1 pound total)**

Salt and ground black pepper

2 **cups sliced fresh mushrooms**

2 **tablespoons olive oil**

1 **cup chopped onion (1 large)**

6 **cloves garlic, minced**

1 **tablespoon snipped fresh thyme**

1 **cup dry white wine or chicken broth**

1 **cup clam juice or chicken broth**

2 **cups asparagus cut into 1 ½-inch pieces**

1 **cup cherry tomatoes, halved**

1 **tablespoon snipped fresh Italian (flat-leaf) parsley**

1 **teaspoon lemon juice**

1 Thaw fish, if frozen. Rinse fish; pat dry with paper towels. Measure thickness of fish fillets. Season fish with salt and pepper. Set aside.

2 In a large skillet cook mushrooms in 1 tablespoon hot oil over medium heat about 5 minutes or until golden brown. Add onion, garlic, and thyme; cook until mushrooms are tender, stirring occasionally. Add wine. Bring to boiling; reduce heat. Simmer, uncovered, about 15 minutes or until liquid is reduced to ¼ cup.

3 Add clam juice. Return to boiling; reduce heat. Simmer, uncovered, about 15 minutes more or until liquid is reduced

to ¾ cup. Add asparagus. Cook, covered, about 3 minutes or until asparagus is crisp-tender. Stir in tomatoes, parsley, and lemon juice. Season to taste with salt and pepper. Transfer to a serving platter and keep warm.

4 In the same skillet cook salmon in remaining 1 tablespoon hot oil over medium heat for 4 to 6 minutes per ½-inch thickness of salmon or until salmon flakes when tested with a fork, turning once. Serve salmon over vegetable mixture.

Makes 4 servings

Nutrition facts per serving: 371 cal., 20 g total fat (4 g sat. fat), 67 mg chol., 289 mg sodium, 12 g carbo., 3 g dietary fiber, 28 g protein.

Shopping list:

4 fresh or frozen skinless salmon fillets

1 8-ounce package sliced fresh mushrooms

1 large onion

1 package fresh thyme

1 bottle dry white wine

1 8-ounce bottle clam juice

1 pound fresh asparagus

1 pint cherry tomatoes

1 bunch fresh parsley

1 lemon

Pantry list:

Salt

Ground black pepper

Olive oil

Garlic

Italian **Fish Fingers** *(See photo on page 281.)*

Start to Finish: **40 minutes**

1 pound fresh or frozen firm white fish fillets, ¹/₂ to ³/₄ inch thick

Salt and ground black pepper

¹/₂ cup all-purpose flour

3 eggs, lightly beaten

²/₃ cup Italian seasoned fine dry bread crumbs

¹/₃ cup grated Parmesan cheese

¹/₃ cup olive oil

1 cup purchased marinara sauce

1 Thaw fish, if frozen. Rinse fish; pat dry with paper towels. Cut fish into 3x1-inch pieces. Sprinkle with salt and pepper.

2 Place flour in a shallow dish. Place eggs in a second shallow dish. In a third shallow dish combine bread crumbs and Parmesan cheese. Dip fish pieces in flour; shake off excess. Dip in egg, then dip in crumb mixture to coat.

3 In a large skillet cook fish pieces, one-fourth at a time, in hot oil over medium heat for 5 minutes or until golden brown and fish flakes when tested with a fork, turning to brown on all sides. Drain on paper towels. Keep cooked fish warm in a 200°F oven while cooking remaining fish.

4 Meanwhile, in a small saucepan cook marinara sauce over medium heat until heated through. Serve fish fingers with marinara sauce for dipping.

Makes 4 servings

Nutrition facts per serving: 505 cal., 26 g total fat (4 g sat. fat), 213 mg chol., 1,159 mg sodium, 33 g carbo., 2 g dietary fiber, 32 g protein.

*Baking Option: Preheat oven to 450°F. Line a baking sheet with foil. Lightly coat the foil with olive oil cooking spray. Place the coated fish fingers on the prepared baking sheet. Coat fish pieces well with olive oil cooking spray. Bake for 13 to 15 minutes or until golden brown and fish flakes easily when tested with a fork, turning once halfway through baking.

40 minutes

Shopping list:

1 pound fresh or frozen firm white fish fillets, ¹/₂ to ³/₄ inch thick

1 9-ounce package Italian seasoned fine dry bread crumbs

1 8-ounce package grated Parmesan cheese

1 14-ounce jar marinara sauce

Pantry list:

Salt

Ground black pepper

All-purpose flour

Eggs

Olive oil

Jumbo Fish Pot Stickers

Start to Finish: **40 minutes**

1 ½ **pounds lean white fish fillets (such as tilapia, sole, or bass)**

¼ **cup canned sliced water chestnuts**

2 **green onions, cut into 1-inch pieces**

½ **teaspoon five-spice powder**

¼ **teaspoon salt**

12 **egg roll wrappers**

1 **egg, beaten**

1 **cup water or vegetable broth**

2 **tablespoons cooking oil**

Bottled teriyaki sauce

1 Rinse fish; pat dry with paper towels. Cut fish into 1-inch pieces; set aside. In a food processor combine water chestnuts and green onions; cover and process until finely chopped. Add fish, five-spice powder, and salt; cover and process with several on/off turns until finely chopped. Set aside.

2 Cut egg roll wrappers into 6-inch circles. (Use an inverted bowl as a template.) Keep egg roll circles covered with plastic wrap to prevent drying. Place about ¼ cup fish mixture on half of one circle. Brush edges of wrapper lightly with beaten egg. Fold wrap over to enclose filling; press edges firmly with fingers to seal. Set sealed edge of pot sticker upright and press gently to slightly flatten the bottom. Set pot sticker aside; keep covered with plastic wrap. Repeat with remaining egg roll circles and filling.

3 In a very large nonstick skillet with a tight-fitting lid bring water and cooking oil to boiling. Add pot stickers, seam side up. Reduce heat to medium-low. Cook, covered, for 10 minutes. Uncover skillet; cook for 4 to 6 minutes more or until water evaporates and bottoms of pot stickers are golden brown. Serve with teriyaki sauce for dipping.

Makes 12 pot stickers

Nutrition facts per serving: 192 cal., 4 g total fat (1 g sat. fat), 49 mg chol., 958 mg sodium, 22 g carbo., 1 g dietary fiber, 16 g protein.

Shopping list:

1½ pounds lean white fish fillets

1 8-ounce can water chestnuts

1 bunch green onions

1 small container five-spice powder

1 16-ounce package egg roll wrappers

1 12-ounce bottle teriyaki sauce

Pantry list:

Salt

Egg

Cooking oil

40 minutes

Basil-Lime Salmon

Start to Finish: **40 minutes**

4 5- to 6-ounce fresh or frozen salmon or halibut steaks, cut 1 inch thick

Salt and ground black pepper

⅓ cup finely chopped fresh basil

3 tablespoons olive oil

1 tablespoon fresh lime juice

1 clove garlic, minced

¼ teaspoon salt

⅛ teaspoon cayenne pepper

Nonstick cooking spray

Lime wedges

1 Thaw fish, if frozen. Preheat broiler. Rinse fish; pat dry with paper towels. Sprinkle lightly with salt and pepper. Set aside.

2 In a small bowl whisk together basil, oil, lime juice, garlic, salt, and cayenne pepper until well combined. Place fish in a shallow dish. Pour basil mixture over fish, turning to coat. Cover and refrigerate for 20 minutes.

3 Lightly coat the unheated rack of a broiler pan with cooking spray. Place fish on the broiler pan. Broil 4 to 5 inches from the heat for 8 to 12 minutes or until fish flakes when tested with a fork, turning once halfway through broiling. Serve fish with lime wedges.

Makes 4 servings

Nutrition facts per serving: 355 cal., 26 g total fat (5 g sat. fat), 84 mg chol., 375 mg sodium, 2 g carbo., 0 g dietary fiber, 28 g protein.

40 minutes

Shopping list:
4 5- to 6-ounce fresh or frozen salmon steaks, 1 inch thick

1 bunch fresh basil

2 limes

Pantry list:
Salt

Black pepper

Olive oil

Garlic

Cayenne pepper

Nonstick cooking spray

Hot 'n' Spicy **Fish Soup**

Start to Finish: **35 minutes**

- 2 **6-ounce fresh or frozen halibut steaks, cut 1 inch thick**
- ¼ **teaspoon cumin seeds**
- 2 **teaspoons cooking oil**
- 1 **small onion, chopped (⅓ cup)**
- 2 **to 3 teaspoons grated fresh ginger**
- 1 **fresh serrano pepper, seeded and finely chopped***
- 2 **small roma tomatoes, chopped (½ cup)**
- ¾ **cup water**
- ½ **teaspoon ground coriander**
- ¼ **teaspoon ground turmeric**
- ¼ **teaspoon salt**

1 Thaw fish, if frozen. Rinse fish; pat dry with paper towels. Remove skin and bones. Cut fish into 1-inch pieces; set aside.

2 In a medium saucepan cook and stir cumin seeds in hot oil over medium heat about 1 minute or until toasted. Add onion; cook and stir for 4 to 5 minutes or until tender. Add ginger and serrano pepper; cook and stir for 1 minute more. Add tomatoes; cook and stir for 2 to 3 minutes more or until tomatoes are soft. Stir in the water, coriander, turmeric, and salt. Bring just to boiling; reduce heat. Stir in fish. Cook, covered, about 5 minutes or until fish flakes when tested with a fork. Serve immediately.

Makes 2 servings

Nutrition facts per serving: 252 cal., 9 g total fat (1 g sat. fat), 54 mg chol., 392 mg sodium, 5 g carbo., 1 g dietary fiber, 36 g protein.

*Note: Because chile peppers contain volatile oils that can burn your skin and eyes, avoid direct contact as much as possible. When working with chile peppers, wear plastic or rubber gloves. If your bare hands do touch the peppers, wash your hands and nails well with soap and warm water.

Shopping list:

2 6-ounce fresh or frozen halibut steaks

1 small container cumin seeds

1 small onion

1 piece fresh ginger

1 fresh serrano pepper

2 small roma tomatoes

1 small container ground coriander

1 small container ground turmeric

Pantry list:

Cooking oil

Salt

40 minutes

Fish and **Clam Chowder**

Start to Finish: **40 minutes**

1 pound fresh or frozen skinless halibut

½ cup chopped onion (1 medium)

½ cup sliced celery (1 stalk)

1 tablespoon butter

1 14-ounce can chicken broth

12 ounces round red potatoes, cut into ½- to 1-inch cubes

½ teaspoon dried dillweed

¼ teaspoon salt

¼ teaspoon ground black pepper

4 cups milk

⅓ cup all-purpose flour

1 6.5-ounce can minced clams, undrained

4 slices packaged ready-to-serve cooked bacon, chopped

1 Thaw fish, if frozen; set aside. In a 4- to 6-quart Dutch oven cook onion and celery in hot butter over medium heat about 5 minutes or until crisp-tender. Add broth, potatoes, dillweed, salt, and pepper. Bring to boiling; reduce heat. Simmer, covered, about 10 minutes or until potatoes are just tender.

2 Meanwhile, rinse fish; pat dry with paper towels. Cut fish into 1-inch pieces. In a small bowl whisk together 1 cup of the milk and flour until smooth. Add flour mixture and remaining 3 cups milk to potato mixture. Cook and stir until bubbly.

3 Add fish pieces; return to simmer. Simmer, uncovered, for 2 to 3 minutes or until fish is opaque and just begins to flake. Stir in undrained clams and bacon.

Makes 6 servings

Nutrition facts per serving: 279 cal., 8 g total fat (4 g sat. fat), 49 mg chol., 751 mg sodium, 25 g carbo., 2 g dietary fiber, 24 g protein.

Shopping list:

1 pound fresh or frozen skinless halibut

1 medium onion

1 bunch celery

1 14-ounce can chicken broth

12 ounces round red potatoes

1 small container dried dillweed

1 6.5-ounce can minced clams

1 2- to 3-ounce package ready-to-serve cooked bacon

Pantry list:

Butter

Salt

Ground black pepper

Milk

All-purpose flour

40 minutes

Baked Rosemary Trout with Parmesan Polenta

Start to Finish: **40 minutes**   Oven: **450°F**

4 **8- to 10-ounce fresh or frozen pan-dressed, boned rainbow trout**

¼ **cup lemon juice**

3 **tablespoons olive oil**

½ **teaspoon salt**

½ **teaspoon ground black pepper**

1 **teaspoon dried rosemary, crushed**

1 **lemon, thinly sliced**

1 **16-ounce tube refrigerated cooked polenta**

2 **tablespoons olive oil**

¼ **cup finely shredded Parmesan cheese**

Snipped fresh parsley (optional)

1 Thaw fish, if frozen. Preheat oven to 450°F. Remove heads and tails, if present. Rinse fish; pat dry with paper towels. Using a sharp knife, score the sides of the fish in a crisscross pattern spacing cuts about 1 inch apart. Place fish on a 15x10x1-inch baking pan. Drizzle with lemon juice and 3 tablespoons olive oil. Turn fish to coat. Let fish marinate for 10 minutes, turning fish over once.

2 Sprinkle fish inside and out with salt and pepper. Sprinkle ¼ teaspoon rosemary in the cavity of each fish. Arrange lemon slices in the cavity of each fish; fold fish closed. Bake fish in marinade about 15 minutes or until fish flakes when tested with a fork.

3 Meanwhile, cut polenta into 16 slices. In a very large skillet heat 2 tablespoons olive oil over medium heat. Place polenta slices in pan; cook about 5 minutes or until light golden brown, turning once. Sprinkle polenta with Parmesan cheese and, if desired, parsley. Serve with trout.

Makes 4 servings

Nutrition facts per serving: 357 cal., 25 g total fat (6 g sat. fat), 58 mg chol., 587 mg sodium, 13 g carbo., 2 g dietary fiber, 21 g protein.

Shopping list:
4 8- to 10-ounce fresh or frozen dressed, boned rainbow trout

2 lemons

1 small container dried rosemary

1 16-ounce tube refrigerated cooked polenta

1 6-ounce package shredded Parmesan cheese

Pantry list:
Olive oil

Salt

Ground black pepper

40minutes

Tuna, Fennel, and Rotini Casserole

Start to Finish: **40 minutes**   Oven: **375°F**

- 1 ½ **cups dried rotini**
- 2 **tablespoons butter**
- ¾ **cup seasoned croutons, slightly crushed**
- 2 **cups sliced fennel (about 2 small fennel bulbs)**
- 1 **10-ounce container refrigerated light Alfredo sauce**
- 2 **tablespoons capers, drained (optional)**
- 2 **6-ounce cans chunk tuna (packed in oil), drained and broken up**

1 Preheat oven to 375°F. Cook rotini according to package directions; drain.

2 Meanwhile, in a medium saucepan melt butter. In a bowl combine croutons with 1 tablespoon of the melted butter; toss to coat.

3 Add fennel to remaining butter in saucepan. Cook, covered, for 6 to 8 minutes or until fennel is just tender, stirring occasionally. Stir in Alfredo sauce, rotini, and capers, if using. Stir in drained tuna.

4 Transfer tuna mixture to a 1 ½-quart casserole. Top with croutons. Bake, uncovered, for 20 minutes or until heated through.

Makes 6 servings

Nutrition facts per serving: 306 cal., 11 g total fat (6 g sat. fat), 44 mg chol., 527 mg sodium, 29 g carbo., 9 g dietary fiber, 20 g protein.

40 minutes

Shopping list:
1 6-ounce package dried rotini

1 6-ounce package seasoned croutons

2 small fennel bulbs

1 10-ounce container refrigerated light Alfredo sauce

1 3.5-ounce jar capers

2 6-ounce cans chunk white tuna packed in oil

Pantry list:
Butter

Asian **Salmon Burgers** *(See photo on page 282.)*

Start to Finish: **40 minutes**

1 egg, lightly beaten

¼ cup milk

½ cup sliced green onions (4)

1 teaspoon five-spice powder

1 14.75-ounce can salmon, drained, flaked, and skin and bones removed

¼ cup panko (Japanese-style bread crumbs)

1 tablespoon cooking oil

3 cups packaged shredded cabbage and carrot (coleslaw mix)

1 medium red sweet pepper, cut into bite-size strips

2 tablespoons chopped fresh cilantro

⅓ cup bottled Asian toasted sesame salad dressing

4 hamburger buns, split and toasted

1 In a medium bowl combine egg, milk, half of the green onions, and five-spice powder. Add salmon and panko; mix well. Form mixture into four ¾-inch-thick patties. In a large skillet cook patties in hot oil over medium heat about 6 minutes or until golden brown and heated through (160°F), turning once.

2 In a medium bowl combine cabbage, sweet pepper, remaining green onions, and cilantro. Add salad dressing; toss to mix. Place salmon patties in buns; top patties with some of the coleslaw mix. Serve remaining coleslaw mix on the side.

Makes 4 servings

Nutrition facts per serving: 435 cal., 19 g total fat (4 g sat. fat), 112 mg chol., 1,036 mg sodium, 35 g carbo., 3 g dietary fiber, 28 g protein.

Shopping list:
1 bunch green onions

1 small jar five-spice powder

1 14.75-ounce can salmon

1 8-ounce package panko (Japanese-style bread crumbs)

1 16-ounce package shredded cabbage and carrot (coleslaw mix)

1 medium red sweet pepper

1 bunch cilantro

1 16-ounce bottle Asian toasted sesame salad dressing

1 package hamburger buns

Pantry list:
Egg

Milk

Cooking oil

40minutes

Shrimp Tacos

Start to Finish: **35 minutes**   Oven: **350°F**

- 8 **6-inch corn tortillas**
- 1 ½ **cups chopped, seeded tomato**
- 1 **cup chopped, seeded cucumber**
- ⅓ **cup thinly sliced green onions**
- ¼ **cup snipped fresh cilantro**
- 3 **tablespoons lime juice**
- ¼ **teaspoon salt**
- 8 **ounces fresh green beans, trimmed and halved crosswise**
- 1 **teaspoon Jamaican jerk seasoning**
- 1 **pound medium to large shrimp in shells, peeled and deveined**
- 1 **tablespoon olive oil**

1 Preheat oven to 350°F. Wrap tortillas in heavy foil. Heat tortillas in oven for 10 minutes. Meanwhile, for salsa, in a medium bowl combine tomato, cucumber, green onions, cilantro, lime juice, and salt; set aside.

2 In a bowl toss beans with ½ teaspoon of the seasoning. In another bowl toss shrimp with remaining ½ teaspoon seasoning. In a large skillet cook and stir green beans in hot oil over medium-high heat for 3 minutes. Add shrimp to skillet; cook and stir for 2 to 3 minutes more or until shrimp are opaque.

3 Fill each warm tortilla with about ⅓ cup of the shrimp mixture. Serve with salsa.

Makes 4 servings

Nutrition facts per serving: 274 cal., 7 g total fat (1 g sat. fat), 129 mg chol., 381 mg sodium, 33 g carbo., 7 g dietary fiber, 22 g protein.

Shopping list:

- 1 package 6-inch corn tortillas
- 2 medium tomatoes
- 1 medium cucumber
- 1 bunch green onions
- 1 bunch fresh cilantro
- 1 lime
- 8 ounces fresh green beans
- 1 small container Jamaican jerk seasoning
- 1 pound medium shrimp in shells

Pantry list:

Salt

Olive oil

40 minutes

Sesame Shrimp Stir-Fry

Start to Finish: **40 minutes**

6 ounces fresh or frozen large shrimp in shells

¼ cup unsweetened apple juice

1 teaspoon dry Chinese-style hot mustard

1 teaspoon reduced-sodium soy sauce

1 teaspoon grated fresh ginger

Nonstick cooking spray

1 small red sweet pepper, seeded and cut into ½-inch pieces

2 ounces small fresh mushrooms, halved

2 green onions, chopped

½ cup fresh sugar snap peas, trimmed and cut in half crosswise

1 medium carrot, cut into thin bite-size strips

¼ cup thinly sliced celery

1 clove garlic, minced

1 teaspoon sesame seeds, toasted*

1 Thaw shrimp, if frozen. Peel and devein shrimp. Rinse shrimp; pat dry with paper towels. Cut shrimp in half lengthwise; set aside. In a small bowl combine apple juice, mustard, soy sauce, and ginger; set aside.

2 Coat a large nonstick skillet with cooking spray. Heat skillet over medium-high heat. Cook sweet pepper, mushrooms, and green onions in skillet for 2 to 4 minutes or until mushrooms are tender, stirring frequently. Stir in sugar snap peas, carrot, celery, and garlic. Cook and stir for 2 to 4 minutes more or until the peas are crisp-tender. Remove vegetables from skillet.

3 Add shrimp to skillet; cook and stir for 1 to 2 minutes or until the shrimp are opaque. Return vegetables to skillet. Stir to combine. Add apple juice mixture to skillet. Cook and stir until heated through.

Makes 2 servings

Nutrition facts per serving: 164 cal., 3 g total fat (0 g sat. fat), 129 mg chol., 261 mg sodium, 15 g carbo., 3 g dietary fiber, 21 g protein.

＊Note: To toast sesame seeds, spread seeds in a shallow baking pan. Bake in a 350°F oven for 5 to 10 minutes or until light golden brown, stirring once.

Shopping list:

6 ounces fresh or frozen large shrimp in shells

1 5-ounce can unsweetened apple juice

1 small container dry Chinese-style hot mustard

1 5-ounce bottle reduced-sodium soy sauce

1 piece fresh ginger

1 small red sweet pepper

1 8-ounce package fresh mushrooms

1 bunch green onions

2 ounces fresh sugar snap peas

1 package carrots

1 bunch celery

1 small container sesame seeds

Pantry list:

Nonstick cooking spray

Garlic

40 minutes

Rice with Shrimp and **Andouille Sausage**

Start to Finish: **40 minutes**

- 1 **pound fresh or frozen medium shrimp**
- 1 **tablespoon cooking oil**
- 1 **cup uncooked long-grain white rice**
- 1 ½ **cups chicken broth**
- 1 **15-ounce can diced tomatoes with garlic and onion, undrained**
- 4 **ounces cooked andouille sausage or kielbasa, chopped**
- 1 **to 2 teaspoons Cajun seasoning**
- ½ **cup sliced green onions (4)**

1 Thaw shrimp, if frozen.

2 In a large saucepan heat oil over medium heat. Add rice; cook and stir for 3 to 5 minutes or until rice is golden. Add broth, undrained tomatoes, sausage, and Cajun seasoning. Bring to boiling; reduce heat. Simmer, covered, for 20 to 25 minutes or until rice is tender and liquid is nearly absorbed.

3 Meanwhile peel and devein shrimp. Rinse shrimp; pat dry with paper towels. Add shrimp and green onions to rice mixture. Cook, covered, for 2 to 4 minutes or until shrimp are opaque.

Makes 4 servings

Nutrition facts per serving: 401 cal., 8 g total fat (1 g sat. fat), 197 mg chol., 1,300 mg sodium, 47 g carbo., 1 g dietary fiber, 34 g protein.

40 minutes

Shopping list:
- 1 pound fresh or frozen medium shrimp
- 1 16-ounce package long grain white rice
- 1 14 ounce can chicken broth
- 1 15-ounce can diced tomatoes with garlic and onion
- 1 12-ounce package andouille sausage or kielbasa
- 1 small container Cajun seasoning
- 1 bunch green onions

Pantry list:
Cooking oil

Rice Noodles with Shrimp *(See photo on page 284.)*

Start to Finish: **35 minutes**

- 1 **tablespoon green curry paste**
- 2 **tablespoons olive oil**
- 1 **14-ounce can unsweetened coconut milk**
- 1 **14-ounce can chicken broth**
- ¼ **cup lemon juice**
- 2 **tablespoons fish sauce**
- 1 **14-ounce package wide rice stick noodles**
- 1 **pound large shrimp, peeled, deveined, and halved lengthwise**
- 1 **large red sweet pepper, cut into thin strips**
- 1 **cup fresh snow pea pods, trimmed**
- ¼ **cup chopped fresh cilantro**
- 2 **hard-cooked eggs, quartered**

1 In a saucepan cook curry paste in hot oil until fragrant and beginning to stick to pan. Add coconut milk, broth, lemon juice, and fish sauce. Bring to boiling; reduce heat. Simmer, uncovered, for 8 to 10 minutes or until reduced to 3 ½ cups.

2 Cook noodles in boiling salted water for 4 to 6 minutes or until tender; drain. Rinse under cold water; drain. Divide noodles among 4 bowls. Add shrimp, sweet pepper, and snow peas to sauce. Return to boiling; reduce heat. Simmer, uncovered, for 1 to 3 minutes or until shrimp are opaque and vegetables are crisp-tender. Stir in cilantro. Spoon over noodles. Top with eggs.

Makes 4 servings

Nutrition facts per serving: 781 cal., 32 g total fat (19 g sat. fat), 236 mg chol., 1,402 mg sodium, 96 g carbo., 3 g dietary fiber, 24 g protein.

Shopping list:
- 1 4-ounce jar green curry paste
- 1 14-ounce can unsweetened coconut milk
- 1 14-ounce can chicken broth
- 1 lemon
- 1 7-ounce bottle fish sauce
- 1 14-ounce package wide rice stick noodles
- 1 pound large shrimp
- 1 large red sweet pepper
- 3 ounces fresh snow pea pods
- 1 bunch fresh cilantro

Pantry list:
Olive oil

Eggs

40 minutes

Italian-Style **Shrimp**

Start to Finish: 40 minutes

1 pound fresh or frozen medium shrimp, peeled and deveined

2 cups sliced fresh mushrooms

½ cup chopped onion (1 medium)

½ cup chopped green sweet pepper

2 cloves garlic, minced

2 tablespoons butter

1 10.75-ounce can condensed tomato bisque soup

⅔ cup water

½ teaspoon dried Italian seasoning, crushed

Hot cooked penne or rotini

Shredded or grated Parmesan cheese (optional)

1 Thaw shrimp, if frozen. Rinse shrimp; pat dry with paper towels. Set aside.

2 In a large skillet cook mushrooms, onion, sweet pepper, and garlic in hot butter over medium heat about 5 minutes or until tender. Stir in tomato bisque soup, the water, and Italian seasoning. Bring to boiling; reduce heat. Simmer, covered, for 10 minutes.

3 Add shrimp to skillet; cook for 3 to 4 minutes or until shrimp are opaque. Serve with hot cooked pasta. If desired, top with Parmesan cheese.

Makes 6 servings

Nutrition facts per serving: 269 cal., 7 g total fat (4 g sat. fat), 98 mg chol., 510 mg sodium, 34 g carbo., 2 g dietary fiber, 17 g protein.

Shopping list:

1 pound fresh or frozen medium shrimp

1 8-ounce package sliced fresh mushrooms

1 medium onion

1 medium green sweet pepper

1 10.75-ounce can condensed tomato bisque soup

1 16-ounce package penne

Pantry list:

Garlic

Butter

Dried Italian seasoning

Easy **Paella**

Start to Finish: **35 minutes**

- 2 **cloves garlic, minced**
- 2 **teaspoons mustard seed**
- 2 **tablespoons cooking oil**
- 1 **8- to 10-ounce package yellow rice mix**
- 1/4 **teaspoon saffron threads, crushed, or 1/8 teaspoon ground saffron (optional)**
- 2 2/3 **cups water**
- 1 **16-ounce jar mild or medium thick and chunky salsa**
- 12 **ounces frozen peeled and deveined shrimp, thawed and tails removed, if present**
- 1 **8- to 9-ounce package frozen sugar snap peas**

In a 12-inch skillet cook and stir garlic and mustard seeds in hot oil for 2 minutes. Stir in rice mix, saffron (if desired), the water, and salsa. Bring to boiling; reduce heat. Simmer, covered, for 20 minutes, stirring once halfway through cooking. Add shrimp and sugar snap peas. Cook, covered, for 5 minutes more until shrimp are opaque. Remove from heat and let stand 5 minutes before serving.

Makes 4 servings

Nutrition facts per serving: 430 cal., 9 g total fat (1 g sat. fat), 129 mg chol., 1,900 mg sodium, 63 g carbo., 2 g dietary fiber, 23 g protein.

Shopping list:
1 small container mustard seeds

1 8- to 10-ounce package yellow rice mix

1 16-ounce jar thick and chunky salsa

12 ounces frozen peeled and deveined shrimp

1 8- to 9-ounce package frozen sugar snap peas

Pantry list:
Garlic

Cooking oil

Linguine and Scallops

Start to Finish: **35 minutes**

- **8 ounces fresh or frozen sea scallops**
- **8 ounces dried linguine**
- **2 tablespoons butter**
- **1 tablespoon olive oil**
- **2 cloves garlic, minced**
- **12 ounces fresh asparagus, trimmed and cut into 3-inch pieces**
- **1½ cups sliced fresh mushrooms**
- **1½ cups seeded and coarsely chopped roma tomatoes**
- **Salt and ground black pepper**
- **¼ cup pine nuts, toasted**

1 Thaw scallops, if frozen. Cut any large scallops in half. Rinse scallops; pat dry with paper towels. Set aside.

2 Cook linguine according to package directions. Drain; keep warm.

3 Meanwhile, in a very large skillet heat butter and oil over medium heat. Add garlic; cook and stir for 15 seconds. Add asparagus, mushrooms, tomatoes, and scallops. Cook, covered, over medium-high heat for 4 to 5 minutes or until asparagus is crisp-tender and scallops are opaque, stirring once. Remove from heat. Season to taste with salt and pepper. Add scallop mixture to cooked linguine; toss gently to combine. Top with pine nuts.

Makes 4 servings

Nutrition facts per serving: 429 cal., 17 g total fat (5 g sat. fat), 35 mg chol., 215 mg sodium, 51 g carbo., 3 g dietary fiber, 22 g protein.

Shopping list:

- 8 ounces fresh or frozen sea scallops
- 1 16-ounce package dried linguine
- 12 ounces fresh asparagus spears
- 1 8-ounce package sliced fresh mushrooms
- 3 large roma tomatoes
- 1 2.2-ounce package pine nuts

Pantry list:

Butter

Olive oil

Garlic

Salt

Ground black pepper

40 minutes

Scallops with Chipotle Cream

Start to Finish: 40 minutes

- 1 **8.5-ounce package corn muffin mix***
- ¼ **cup sliced green onions**
- ½ **cup shredded cheddar cheese (2 ounces)**
- 1 **pound fresh or frozen sea scallops**
- ¼ **teaspoon salt**
- ¼ **teaspoon ground black pepper**
- 1 **tablespoon olive oil**
- 1 **14.5-ounce can diced tomatoes, undrained**
- 2 **to 3 teaspoons finely chopped canned chipotle chile peppers in adobo sauce****
- ½ **cup whipping cream**
  Sliced green onions (optional)

1 Prepare corn muffin mix according to package directions, using an 8x8x2-inch baking pan, except stir ¼ cup green onions into the batter. After removing from the oven, sprinkle with cheese. Set aside to cool in pan on a wire rack.

2 Meanwhile, thaw scallops, if frozen. Rinse scallops; pat dry with paper towels. Sprinkle with salt and pepper. In a large skillet heat oil over medium-high heat for 1 to 2 minutes. Add scallops. Cook for 4 to 6 minutes or until scallops are opaque and brown, turning once. Remove scallops from skillet. Set aside.

3 Add undrained tomatoes to skillet. Bring to boiling. Boil gently, uncovered, for 3 minutes or until liquid is almost gone, stirring occasionally. Stir in chipotle chiles and cream; bring to boiling. Boil gently, uncovered, for 1 minute or until slightly thick. Stir in scallops. If desired, sprinkle with additional green onions. Serve mixture with warm corn bread.

Makes 4 servings

Nutrition facts per serving: 411 cal., 21 g total fat (10 g sat. fat), 87 mg chol., 934 mg sodium, 30 g carbo., 4 g dietary fiber, 24 g protein.

*Note: Store leftover corn bread in sealed storage containers in the refrigerator for up to 2 days or in the freezer for up to 3 months. Wrap in foil and reheat in a 350°F oven for 5 to 10 minutes.

**Note: Because hot chile peppers, such as chipotles, contain volatile oils that can burn your skin and eyes, avoid direct contact with chiles. When working with chile peppers, wear plastic or rubber gloves. If your bare hands do touch the chile peppers, wash your hands well with soap and water.

Shopping list:

- 1 8.5-ounce package corn muffin mix
- 1 bunch green onions
- 1 4-ounce package shredded cheddar cheese
- 1 pound fresh or frozen sea scallops
- 1 14.5-ounce can diced tomatoes
- 1 7-ounce can chipotle chile peppers in adobo sauce
- 1 8-ounce carton whipping cream

Pantry list:

Salt

Ground black pepper

Olive oil

40 minutes

Veggie-Stuffed Pasta Shells

Start to Finish: 40 minutes

- 12 **dried jumbo shell macaroni**
- 1 ½ **cups purchased coarsely shredded fresh carrots**
- 1 **medium zucchini, shredded (1 ⅓ cups)**
- 1 **small onion, finely chopped (½ cup)**
- 2 **tablespoons olive oil**
- 1 **10-ounce package frozen chopped spinach, thawed and squeezed dry**
- ½ **of a 15-ounce carton ricotta cheese**
- 1 ½ **cups shredded Italian blend cheeses (6 ounces)**
- ¼ **teaspoon salt**
- ⅛ **teaspoon cayenne pepper**
- 1 **14- to 16-ounce jar pasta sauce**

1 Cook pasta according to package directions; drain. Rinse pasta with cold water; drain again.

2 Meanwhile, in a large skillet cook carrots, zucchini, and onion in hot oil over medium-high heat for 3 to 5 minutes or until tender. Stir in spinach; cook and stir for 1 minute. Transfer spinach mixture to a large bowl.

3 Stir ricotta cheese, 1 cup of the Italian blend cheese, salt, and cayenne pepper into vegetable mixture. Spoon a rounded 2 tablespoons cheese mixture into each pasta shell. Place pasta sauce in skillet; place filled shells in sauce.

4 Heat shells and sauce, covered, over medium heat for 10 minutes or until heated through. Sprinkle with remaining ½ cup cheese before serving.

Makes 4 servings

Nutrition facts per serving: 497 cal., 27 g total fat (12 g sat. fat), 57 mg chol., 997 mg sodium, 43 g carbo., 7 g dietary fiber, 25 g protein.

Shopping list:

- 1 16-ounce package dried jumbo shell macaroni
- 1 10-ounce package coarsely shredded fresh carrots
- 1 medium zucchini
- 1 small onion
- 1 10-ounce package frozen chopped spinach
- 1 15-ounce carton ricotta cheese
- 1 8-ounce package shredded Italian blend cheeses
- 1 14- to 16-ounce jar pasta sauce

Pantry list:

Olive oil

Salt

Cayenne pepper

40 minutes

Tortellini and Veggies

Start to Finish: **40 minutes**

- 1 **large onion, coarsely chopped (1 cup)**
- 1 **8-ounce package fresh mushrooms, halved**
- 1 **medium red sweet pepper, cut into ¾-inch pieces**
- 2 **cloves garlic, minced**
- 2 **tablespoons olive oil**
- 1 **14.5-ounce can diced tomatoes, undrained**
- 1 **9-ounce package refrigerated cheese-filled tortellini**
- ½ **cup water**
- ¼ **cup dry red wine or vegetable broth**
- 2 **teaspoons dried Italian seasoning, crushed**
- ¼ **teaspoon ground black pepper**
- 4 **small zucchini, halved lengthwise and cut into ½-inch slices**
- ½ **cup shredded Asiago or Parmesan cheese (2 ounces)**

In a very large skillet cook onion, mushrooms, sweet pepper, and garlic in hot oil over medium heat about 5 minutes or until onion is tender. Stir in undrained tomatoes, tortellini, the water, wine, Italian seasoning, and black pepper. Bring to boiling; reduce heat. Simmer, covered, for 10 minutes. Stir in zucchini. Cook, uncovered, 5 minutes more or until zucchini is crisp-tender. Remove from heat. Sprinkle with Asiago cheese.

Makes 4 to 6 servings

Nutrition facts per serving: 414 cal., 18 g total fat (6 g sat. fat), 45 mg chol., 566 mg sodium, 46 g carbo., 4 g dietary fiber, 18 g protein.

Shopping list:
- 1 large onion
- 1 8-ounce package fresh mushrooms
- 1 medium red sweet pepper
- 1 14.5-ounce can diced tomatoes
- 1 9-ounce package refrigerated cheese-filled tortellini
- 1 bottle dry red wine
- 4 small zucchini
- 1 8-ounce package shredded Asiago cheese

Pantry list:
- Garlic
- Olive oil
- Dried Italian seasoning
- Ground black pepper

40
minutes

Pasta with Mushrooms and Aged Jack Cheese *(See photo on page 285.)*

Start to Finish: **35 minutes**

8 ounces dried penne or campanelle

1 tablespoon butter

1 large sweet onion, cut into thin wedges

4 cloves garlic, minced

2 tablespoons butter

3 cups sliced fresh mushrooms

½ cup whipping cream

¼ cup chicken broth

4 ounces aged (dry) Jack cheese, finely shredded (1 cup firmly packed)

Salt and freshly ground black pepper

Fresh thyme (optional)

1 In a large saucepan cook pasta according to package directions. Drain; return to saucepan. Stir in 1 tablespoon butter. Cover and keep warm.

2 In a large skillet cook and stir onion and garlic in 2 tablespoons hot butter over medium heat for 4 to 5 minutes or until tender. Stir in mushrooms; cook 3 minutes more or until tender.

3 Meanwhile, in a small saucepan heat whipping cream and broth over medium heat just to boiling. Reduce heat to low; stir in cheese. Continue stirring until cheese nearly melts. Add mushroom mixture and cream mixture to pasta. Toss to combine; heat through. Season to taste with salt and pepper. If desired, sprinkle with thyme.

Makes 4 servings

Nutrition facts per serving: 586 cal., 36 g total fat (18 g sat. fat), 76 mg chol., 352 mg sodium, 50 g carbo., 4 g dietary fiber, 19 g protein.

40 minutes

Shopping list:

1 16-ounce package dried penne

1 large sweet onion

2 8-ounce packages sliced fresh mushrooms

1 8-ounce carton whipping cream

1 14-ounce can chicken broth

4 ounces aged Jack cheese

Pantry list:

Butter

Garlic

Salt

Black pepper

Spicy Tortellini **Stew**

Start to Finish: **40 minutes**

8   ounces fresh
    mushrooms, sliced
    (3 cups)

1   medium onion,
    chopped (½ cup)

2   tablespoons olive oil

2   14.5-ounce cans diced
    tomatoes, undrained

1   14-ounce can
    vegetable broth

1   8-ounce can tomato
    sauce

½   cup bottled salsa

2   teaspoons dried
    Italian seasoning,
    crushed

1   7-ounce package dried
    cheese tortellini

1 In a Dutch oven cook mushrooms and onion in hot oil over medium heat for 5 to 8 minutes or until mushrooms are tender, stirring occasionally.

2 Stir in undrained tomatoes, broth, tomato sauce, salsa, and Italian seasoning. Add tortellini. Bring to boiling; reduce heat. Simmer, covered, about 20 minutes or until tortellini is tender, stirring occasionally.

Makes 6 servings

Nutrition facts per serving: 237 cal., 8 g total fat (1 g sat. fat), 0 mg chol., 1,153 mg sodium, 33 g carbo., 4 g dietary fiber, 10 g protein.

Shopping list:

1 8-ounce package fresh
  mushrooms

1 medium onion

2 14.5-ounce cans diced
  tomatoes

1 14-ounce can vegetable broth

1 8-ounce can tomato sauce

1 16-ounce jar salsa

1 7-ounce package dried
  cheese tortellini

Pantry list:

Olive oil

Dried Italian seasoning

Peanut Butter Mac 'n' Cheese

Start to Finish: **40 minutes**   Oven: **350°F**

- 8 **ounces dried elbow macaroni (2 cups)**
- 1/3 **cup chopped onion (1 small)**
- 2 **tablespoons butter**
- 2 **tablespoons all-purpose flour**
- 2 **cups milk**
- 1/4 **teaspoon salt**
- 1/4 **teaspoon dry mustard**
- 1 1/2 **cups shredded cheddar cheese (6 ounces)**
- 1/4 **cup creamy peanut butter**
- 4 **slices bacon, crisp-cooked, drained, and crumbled**

1 Preheat oven to 350°F. Cook macaroni according to package directions. Drain; return pasta to pan.

2 Meanwhile, in a 2-quart saucepan cook and stir onion in hot butter over medium heat for 4 to 5 minutes or until tender. Stir in flour. Add milk all at once. Cook and stir until mixture is slightly thick and bubbly. Remove pan from heat; stir in salt and mustard. Stir in cheese and peanut butter until melted. Add sauce to macaroni and stir until macaroni is well coated.

3 Transfer macaroni mixture to a 2-quart square baking dish. Sprinkle bacon over top of macaroni. Bake, uncovered, about 20 minutes or until heated through.

Makes 6 servings

Nutrition facts per serving: 456 cal., 24 g total fat (9 g sat. fat), 36 mg chol., 623 mg sodium, 38 g carbo., 2 g dietary fiber, 22 g protein.

40 minutes

Shopping list:

1 16-ounce package dried elbow macaroni

1 small onion

1 small container dry mustard

1 8-ounce package shredded cheddar cheese

1 12-ounce package bacon

Pantry list:

Butter

All-purpose flour

Milk

Salt

Peanut butter

Two-Bean Chili with **Avocado**

Start to Finish: **40 minutes**

1 **large onion, chopped (1 cup)**

2 **teaspoons dried oregano, crushed**

2 **teaspoons olive oil**

2 **14.5-ounce cans diced tomatoes, undrained**

1 **15-ounce can black or kidney beans, rinsed and drained**

1 **15-ounce can pinto beans, rinsed and drained**

½ **cup bottled salsa**

½ **cup water**

1 **medium ripe avocado, peeled, seeded, and diced**

¼ **cup snipped fresh cilantro**

In a large saucepan cook onion and oregano in hot oil over medium-high heat for 3 to 5 minutes or until onion is tender, stirring occasionally. Stir in undrained tomatoes, beans, salsa, and the water. Bring to boiling; reduce heat. Simmer, covered, for 25 minutes. To serve, top with avocado and snipped cilantro.

Makes 4 servings

Nutrition facts per serving: 325 cal., 10 g total fat (1 g sat. fat), 0 mg chol., 985 mg sodium, 50 g carbo., 15 g dietary fiber, 14 g protein.

Shopping list:
1 large onion

2 14.5-ounce cans diced tomatoes

1 15-ounce can black beans

1 15-ounce can pinto beans

1 8-ounce bottle salsa

1 medium avocado

1 bunch fresh cilantro

Pantry list:
Dried oregano

Olive oil

40 minutes

Pumpkin-Bean Burritos

Start to Finish: **40 minutes**   Oven: **350°F**

6 10-inch flour tortillas

1 15-ounce can pumpkin

1 15-ounce can black beans, rinsed and drained

1 8.8-ounce package cooked Spanish-style rice

¼ cup sliced green onions (2)

1 tablespoon Mexican seasoning

¼ teaspoon salt

1½ cups shredded Mexican-style four-cheese blend

Purchased salsa (optional)

1 Preheat oven to 350°F. Stack tortillas; wrap in foil. Bake for 10 minutes or until warm. (Or wrap in microwave-safe paper towels; microwave on 100% power (high), for 1 minute or until warm). Meanwhile, in a large bowl stir together pumpkin, beans, rice, green onions, Mexican seasoning, and salt.

2 Spoon about ½ cup pumpkin mixture onto each tortilla just below the center. Top with cheese. Fold bottom edge of each tortilla up and over filling. Fold opposite sides in and over filling. Roll up from the bottom.

3 Arrange burritos, seam sides down, on a baking sheet. Bake about 20 minutes or until light brown and heated through. If desired, serve burritos with salsa.

Makes 6 servings

Nutrition facts per serving: 474 cal., 15 g total fat (7 g sat. fat), 25 mg chol., 1,149 mg sodium, 68 g carbo., 8 g dietary fiber, 17 g protein.

40 minutes

Shopping list:

1 package 10-inch flour tortillas

1 15-ounce can pumpkin

1 15-ounce can black beans

1 8.8-ounce package cooked Spanish-style rice

1 bunch green onions

1 small container Mexican seasoning

1 8-ounce package shredded Mexican-style four-cheese blend

Pantry list:

Salt

Roasted Squash with **Linguine**

Start to Finish: 40 minutes   Oven: **425°F**

- 4 **cups ½-inch cubes peeled butternut squash**
- ¾ **cup coarsely chopped sweet onion**
- 2 **tablespoons olive oil**
- 2 **cloves garlic, minced, or 1 teaspoon bottled minced garlic**
- 1 **teaspoon dried thyme**
- ¼ **teaspoon salt**
- ¼ **teaspoon ground black pepper**
- 1 **15-ounce can cannellini beans (white kidney beans), rinsed and drained**
- 8 **ounces dried linguine**
- 2 **tablespoons butter**

1 Preheat oven to 425°F. In a large bowl combine squash, onion, oil, garlic, thyme, salt, and pepper. Spread mixture in a 15x10x1-inch baking pan. Roast for 20 to 25 minutes or until squash is tender and begins to brown, stirring once. Remove from oven; stir in drained cannellini beans. Return to oven; roast for 3 to 4 minutes or until cannellini beans are heated through.

2 Meanwhile, cook linguine according to package directions. Drain well. Return linguine to pan; add butter and toss until melted. Transfer to serving dish; top with squash mixture.

Makes 4 servings

Nutrition facts per serving: 480 cal., 14 g total fat (5 g sat. fat), 15 mg chol., 617 mg sodium, 78 g carbo., 9 g dietary fiber, 15 g protein.

Shopping list:
1 medium butternut squash

1 medium sweet onion

1 15-ounce can cannellini beans

1 16-ounce package dried linguine

Pantry list:
Olive oil

Garlic

Dried thyme

Salt

Ground black pepper

Butter

40minutes

Portobello Pizzas

Start to Finish: **40 minutes**

- 4   **8-inch Italian bread shell (such as Boboli)**
- 2   **large portobello mushrooms**
- 1   **medium red sweet pepper, seeded and cut into bite-size strips**
- 1   **tablespoon olive oil**
- ½   **cup mayonnaise**
- 1   **clove garlic, minced, or ½ teaspoon bottled minced garlic**
- ½   **teaspoon crushed red pepper**
- 2   **cups mixed salad greens**
- ¼   **cup shredded Parmesan cheese**

1 On a very large baking sheet arrange bread shells. Bake according to package directions.

2 Cut off mushroom stems even with caps; discard stems. Cut caps into ¼-inch strips. In a large skillet cook mushrooms and sweet pepper in hot oil over medium heat for 5 to 8 minutes or until tender. In a small bowl combine mayonnaise, garlic, and crushed red pepper; set aside.

3 Spread mayonnaise mixture evenly over bread shells. Top with greens. Arrange mushroom mixture over greens. Sprinkle with Parmesan cheese. Serve immediately.

Makes 4 servings

Nutrition facts per serving: 976 cal., 50 g total fat (7 g sat. fat), 31 mg chol., 1,630 mg sodium, 105 g carbo., 2 g dietary fiber, 32 g protein.

Shopping list:

4 8-inch Italian bread shells

2 large portobello mushrooms

1 medium red sweet pepper

1 10-ounce package mixed salad greens

1 4-ounce package shredded Parmesan cheese

Pantry list:

Olive oil

Mayonnaise

Garlic

Crushed red pepper

40 minutes

Stuffed **Spinach Pizza**

Start to Finish: **40 minutes**   Oven: **450°F**

1   **6-ounce package fresh spinach leaves, coarsely chopped (6 cups)**

2   **cups shredded mozzarella cheese (8 ounces)**

1   **16-ounce jar pizza sauce**

1   **teaspoon bottled hot pepper sauce (optional)**

2   **13.8-ounce cans refrigerated pizza dough**

6   **ounces sliced provolone cheese**

¼   **cup shredded Parmesan cheese**

1   Preheat oven to 450°F. In a very large bowl combine spinach, mozzarella, 1 cup pizza sauce, and, if desired, hot pepper sauce. Set aside.

2   Grease a 13x9x2-inch baking pan. On a lightly floured surface, roll one pizza crust into a 17x13-inch rectangle. Place in pan, pressing crust over the bottom and up the sides. Line bottom of crust with provolone cheese slices. Spread spinach mixture over provolone. On the lightly floured surface, roll second crust into a 13x9-inch rectangle. Place over spinach mixture. Pinch edges of crusts together to seal. Prick top of crust all over with a fork.

3   Bake for 20 minutes or until crust is deep golden brown. Remove pizza from oven. Sprinkle with Parmesan cheese. Let stand a few minutes to melt cheese. Heat remaining pizza sauce and pass with pizza.

Makes 6 to 8 servings

Nutrition facts per serving: 539 cal., 23 g total fat (11 g sat. fat), 44 mg chol., 1,139 mg sodium, 58 g carbo., 4 g dietary fiber, 27 g protein.

Shopping list:

1 6-ounce package baby spinach

1 8-ounce package shredded mozzarella cheese

1 16-ounce jar pizza sauce

2 13.8-ounce packages refrigerated pizza dough

1 6-ounce package sliced provolone cheese

1 4-ounce package shredded Parmesan cheese

Pantry list:

Bottled hot pepper sauce

40minutes

Curried Lentils and Potatoes

Start to Finish: **35 minutes**

3 ½ cups water

1 ½ cups lentils, rinsed and drained

1 ½ cups red potatoes, cut into ½-inch cubes

1 tablespoon grated fresh ginger or 1 teaspoon ground ginger

2 teaspoons curry powder

1 clove garlic, minced, or 1 teaspoon bottled minced garlic

¾ teaspoon salt

4 cups shredded fresh spinach

1 6-ounce carton plain low-fat yogurt

1 cup chopped tomato

1 In a large saucepan combine the water, lentils, potatoes, ginger, curry powder, garlic, and salt. Bring to boiling; reduce heat. Simmer, covered, for 25 to 30 minutes or until lentils are tender and liquid is absorbed. Stir in spinach until wilted.

2 In a small bowl stir together yogurt and tomato. Serve with lentil mixture.

Makes 4 servings

Nutrition facts per serving: 345 cal., 2 g total fat (1 g sat. fat), 3 mg chol., 507 mg sodium, 60 g carbo., 25 g dietary fiber, 24 g protein.

Shopping list:

1 16-ounce package dried lentils

8 ounces round red potatoes

1 piece fresh ginger

1 small container curry powder

1 9-ounce package fresh spinach

1 6-ounce carton plain low-fat yogurt

1 large tomato

Pantry list:

Garlic

Salt

40 minutes

Veggie Jumble Stew *(See photo on page 286.)*

Start to Finish: **40 minutes**

- 2 tablespoons olive oil
- 3 tablespoons all-purpose flour
- ¼ teaspoon salt
- ¼ teaspoon ground black pepper
- 1 pound tiny new potatoes, halved
- 1 8- to 10-ounce package frozen Brussels sprouts
- 1½ cups packaged peeled baby carrots
- 1 cup frozen small whole onions
- 2 stalks celery, cut into ½-inch pieces
- 1½ teaspoons bottled minced garlic
- 1 14-ounce can reduced-sodium chicken broth or vegetable broth
- 1½ cups apple cider
- 1 9-ounce package frozen cut green beans
- 1 1-pound loaf white or wheat bread, cut into 12 slices and toasted
- 3 ounces thinly sliced white cheddar cheese or Swiss cheese

1 In a 4-quart Dutch oven or large pot heat oil over medium heat. Stir in flour, salt, and pepper; cook and stir for 2 minutes. Add potatoes, Brussels sprouts, carrots, onions, celery, and garlic. Cook and stir for 5 minutes more.

2 Stir in broth and cider. Bring to boiling; reduce heat. Simmer, uncovered, for 10 minutes. Add green beans. Simmer about 10 minutes more or until vegetables are tender.

3 To serve, place toasted bread in 6 bowls. Ladle stew over bread. Top with cheese.

Makes 6 servings

Nutrition facts per serving: 461 cal., 12 g total fat (4 g sat. fat), 16 mg chol., 818 mg sodium, 72 g carbo., 7 g dietary fiber, 15 g protein.

Shopping list:

1 pound tiny new potatoes

1 8- to 10-ounce package frozen Brussels sprouts

1 16-ounce package fresh baby carrots

1 16-ounce package frozen small whole onions

1 bunch celery

1 14-ounce can reduced-sodium chicken broth

1 32-ounce bottle apple cider

1 9-ounce package frozen cut green beans

3 ounces thinly sliced white cheddar cheese

Pantry list:

Olive oil

All-purpose flour

Salt

Ground black pepper

Bottled minced garlic

White bread

Stuffed Portobello Mushrooms

Start to Finish: **35 minutes**   Oven: **350°F**

- 4   **4-inch portobello mushrooms**
- 4   **teaspoons Worcestershire sauce**
- ¼   **cup finely chopped onion**
- 1   **clove garlic, minced**
- 1   **tablespoon olive oil**
- 1   **15-ounce can cannellini beans (white kidney beans), rinsed and drained**
- ½   **cup shredded Swiss cheese (2 ounces)**
- 1   **tablespoon Dijon-style mustard**
- ½   **teaspoon dried thyme, crushed**
- ¼   **cup fine dry bread crumbs**
- 1   **tablespoon butter, melted**

1 Preheat oven to 350°F. Remove mushroom stems, if present. Remove gills from mushrooms, if desired. Brush both sides of mushrooms with Worcestershire sauce. Place mushroom caps, stem sides up, in an ungreased shallow baking pan.

2 In a large skillet cook onion and garlic in hot oil over medium heat for 3 to 4 minutes or until tender. Remove from heat. Stir in beans, cheese, mustard, and thyme. With a potato masher or the back of a spoon, slightly mash bean mixture. Spoon bean mixture evenly into mushrooms caps.

3 In a small bowl stir together bread crumbs and melted butter. Sprinkle over bean mixture. Bake about 15 minutes or until topping is golden and mushrooms are tender.

Makes 4 servings

Nutrition facts per serving: 233 cal., 11 g total fat (5 g sat. fat), 21 mg chol., 554 mg sodium, 26 g carbo., 6 g dietary fiber, 14 g protein.

40 minutes

Shopping list:

- 4 4-inch portobello mushrooms
- 1 small onion
- 1 15-ounce can cannellini beans
- 1 8-ounce package shredded Swiss cheese
- 1 10-ounce container fine dry bread crumbs

Pantry list:

Worcestershire sauce

Garlic

Olive oil

Dijon-style mustard

Dried thyme

Butter

Spinach-Parmesan **Polenta**

Start to Finish: **40 minutes**

- 4 **cups vegetable broth**
- 1 **cup yellow cornmeal**
- 1 **clove garlic, minced**
- 1 **tablespoon olive oil**
- 8 **ounces fresh mushrooms, sliced (3 cups)**
- 4 **cups torn fresh spinach**
- ¾ **cup chopped walnuts, toasted**
- ¾ **cup shredded Parmesan cheese (3 ounces)**
- ½ **teaspoon ground black pepper**

1 In a medium saucepan heat 3 cups of the broth to boiling. Meanwhile stir together cornmeal and remaining broth. Gradually add cornmeal mixture to boiling broth, stirring constantly. Cook and stir until mixture returns to boiling; reduce heat to low. Cook for 15 to 20 minutes or until very thick, stirring frequently.

2 Meanwhile, in a medium skillet cook garlic in hot oil over medium heat for 30 seconds. Add mushrooms; cook until tender. Add spinach; cook about 1 minute more or until wilted. Drain spinach, pressing to remove excess liquid.

3 Stir spinach mixture, walnuts, ½ cup of the Parmesan cheese, and pepper into cooked polenta. Sprinkle with remaining ¼ cup Parmesan cheese.

Makes 4 servings

Nutrition facts per serving: 405 cal., 22 g total fat (4 g sat. fat), 11 mg chol., 1,222 mg sodium, 47 g carbo., 3 g dietary fiber, 14 g protein.

Shopping list:

3 14-ounce cans vegetable broth

1 1-pound box yellow cornmeal

1 8-ounce package fresh mushrooms

1 9-ounce package fresh spinach

1 6-ounce package walnuts

1 4-ounce package shredded Parmesan cheese

Pantry list:

Garlic

Olive oil

Ground black pepper

Artichoke Risotto

Start to Finish: **40 minutes**

- 1 **medium onion, chopped (¹⁄₂ cup)**
- 1 **tablespoon olive oil**
- 1 **cup arborio rice**
- 2 **cloves garlic, minced, or 1 teaspoon bottled minced garlic**
- 3 **cups vegetable broth**
- ³⁄₄ **cup purchased finely shredded Parmesan cheese (3 ounces)**
- ¹⁄₄ **teaspoon ground black pepper**
- 2 **6-ounce jars quartered marinated artichoke hearts, drained and coarsely chopped**
- 1 **cup grape tomatoes, halved**
- ¹⁄₂ **cup frozen peas**

1 In a large saucepan cook onion in hot oil over medium heat for 5 minutes or until onion is just tender, stirring occasionally. Add rice and garlic. Cook and stir over medium heat about 2 minutes or until rice begins to brown.

2 Meanwhile, in another saucepan bring broth to boiling; reduce heat. Cover and simmer. Slowly add 1 cup broth to the rice mixture, stirring constantly. Continue to cook and stir over medium heat until liquid is absorbed. Add another ¹⁄₂ cup broth to rice mixture, stirring frequently. Continue to cook and stir until liquid is absorbed. Add remaining broth, ¹⁄₂ cup at a time, stirring frequently until broth is absorbed before adding more. (This should take 20 to 25 minutes total.) Rice should be creamy and just tender.

3 Add cheese and pepper to rice. Stir until cheese melts. Stir in artichoke hearts, tomatoes, and peas. Heat through. Serve immediately.

Makes 4 servings

Nutrition facts per serving: 458 cal., 21 g total fat (6 g sat. fat), 11 mg chol., 1,276 mg sodium, 51 g carbo., 2 g dietary fiber, 12 g protein.

Shopping list:

- 1 medium onion
- 1 12-ounce package arborio rice
- 2 14-ounce cans vegetable broth
- 1 8-ounce package finely shredded Parmesan cheese
- 2 6-ounce jars quartered marinated artichoke hearts
- 1 pint grape tomatoes
- 1 10-ounce package frozen peas

Pantry list:

Olive oil

Garlic

Ground black pepper

40 minutes

15 minute

minute

sides and desserts

Snow Peas and Tomatoes

Start to Finish: **15 minutes**

1 large shallot, sliced, or ½ cup thinly sliced red onion or green onion

2 teaspoons cooking oil

¼ teaspoon toasted sesame oil (optional)

2 teaspoons sesame seeds

2 6-ounce packages frozen snow peas

2 tablespoons bottled teriyaki sauce

½ cup grape, cherry, and/or pear-shaped red and/or yellow tomatoes, halved

1 In a large skillet cook shallot in hot cooking and sesame oil (if using) over medium heat until tender. Add sesame seeds. Cook and stir for 1 minute more or until seeds are lightly toasted.

2 Add snow peas and teriyaki sauce. Cook and stir for 2 to 3 minutes or until snow peas are crisp-tender. Stir in tomatoes; cook for 1 minute more.

Makes 6 servings

Nutrition facts per serving: 59 cal., 2 g total fat (0 g sat. fat), 0 mg chol., 211 mg sodium, 9 g carbo., 2 g dietary fiber, 3 g protein.

Shopping list:

1 large shallot

1 small container sesame seeds

2 6-ounce packages frozen snow peas

1 8-ounce bottle teriyaki sauce

1 pint grape tomatoes

Pantry list:

Cooking oil

15 minutes

Skillet Scalloped Corn

Start to Finish: **15 minutes**

2   **teaspoons butter**

½   **cup crushed rich round, wheat, or rye crackers**

1   **11-ounce can whole kernel corn with sweet peppers, drained**

1   **7- to 8.75-ounce can whole kernel corn with sweet peppers, whole kernel corn, or white corn, drained**

2   **1-ounce slices process Swiss cheese, torn**

⅓   **cup milk**

⅛   **teaspoon onion powder**

    Dash ground black pepper

1 For topping, in a large skillet melt butter over medium heat. Add 2 tablespoons of the crushed crackers. Cook and stir until light brown; remove and set aside.

2 In the same skillet combine remaining crushed crackers, both kinds of corn, cheese, milk, onion powder, and pepper. Cook, stirring frequently, until cheese melts. Transfer to a serving dish; sprinkle with reserved topping.

Makes 4 servings

Nutrition facts per serving: 183 cal., 9 g total fat (4 g sat. fat), 18 mg chol., 704 mg sodium, 19 g carbo., 2 g dietary fiber, 6 g protein.

Shopping list:

1 8-ounce package rich round crackers

1 11-ounce can whole kernel corn with sweet peppers

1 7- to 8.75-ounce can whole kernel corn with sweet peppers

1 8-ounce packaged sliced process Swiss cheese

1 small container onion powder

Pantry list:

Butter

Milk

Ground black pepper

Orange-Glazed Baby Carrots

Start to Finish: 15 minutes

2 **cups packaged peeled fresh baby carrots**

2 **tablespoons orange marmalade**

1 **tablespoon butter**

1 In a medium saucepan cook carrots, covered, in lightly salted boiling water for 5 minutes. Drain; set aside.

2 In the same saucepan cook and stir drained carrots and marmalade in hot butter over medium heat for 2 to 3 minutes or until carrots are tender and glazed.

Makes 4 servings

Nutrition facts per serving: 77 cal., 3 g total fat (2 g sat. fat), 8 mg chol., 57 mg sodium, 13 g carbo., 2 g dietary fiber, 1 g protein.

15 minutes

Shopping list:

1 16-ounce package fresh baby carrots

1 10-ounce jar orange marmalade

Pantry list:

Butter

Asparagus with **Almond Sauce**

Start to Finish: **15 minutes**

1 **pound fresh asparagus, trimmed**

2 **tablespoons sliced almonds**

1 **tablespoon butter**

½ **cup chicken broth**

1 **teaspoon cornstarch**

2 **teaspoons lemon juice**

Dash ground black pepper

1 In a large saucepan cook asparagus, covered, in boiling lightly salted water for 3 to 5 minutes or until crisp-tender. Drain well; transfer to a serving platter. Keep warm.

2 Meanwhile, for sauce, in a large skillet cook and stir almonds in hot butter over medium heat for 2 to 3 minutes or until golden. In a small bowl stir together broth, cornstarch, lemon juice, and pepper; add to skillet. Cook and stir until thick and bubbly. Cook and stir 1 minute more. Spoon sauce over asparagus.

Makes 4 servings

Nutrition facts per serving: 76 cal., 5 g total fat (2 g sat. fat), 8 mg chol., 143 mg sodium, 6 g carbo., 3 g dietary fiber, 3 g protein.

Shopping list:
1 pound fresh asparagus

1 2.25-ounce package sliced almonds

1 14-ounce can chicken broth

1 lemon

Pantry list:
Butter

Cornstarch

Ground black pepper

Potatoes with the Works

Start to Finish: **10 minutes**

1 **24-ounce package refrigerated mashed potatoes**

½ **cup dairy sour cream**

2 **tablespoons snipped fresh chives**

4 **slices packaged ready-to-serve cooked bacon, torn into bite-size pieces**

½ **cup shredded cheddar cheese**

Heat potatoes according to package directions. (If using microwave directions, transfer potatoes to a medium bowl.) Stir in sour cream, chives, and bacon. Top each serving with cheese.

Makes 4 servings

Nutrition facts per serving: 284 cal., 15 g total fat (7 g sat. fat), 34 mg chol., 547 mg sodium, 24 g carbo., 1 g dietary fiber, 11 g protein.

15 minutes

Shopping list:

1 24-ounce package refrigerated mashed potatoes

1 8-ounce carton dairy sour cream

1 bunch fresh chives

1 2.1-ounce package ready-to-serve cooked bacon

1 8-ounce package shredded cheddar cheese

Zesty **Mashed Potatoes**

Start to Finish: **15 minutes**

½ **cup chopped red onion and/or sliced green onions**

1 **tablespoon butter**

1 ½ **teaspoons Jamaican jerk seasoning**

¼ **teaspoon ground black pepper**

2 **20-ounce packages refrigerated mashed potatoes**

1 **8-ounce carton dairy sour cream**

In a large saucepan cook onion in hot butter over medium heat for 3 to 4 minutes or until tender. Stir in jerk seasoning and pepper. Stir in mashed potatoes and sour cream. Cook until heated through, stirring frequently.

Makes 8 servings

Nutrition facts per serving: 189 cal., 10 g total fat (5 g sat. fat), 17 mg chol., 300 mg sodium, 21 g carbo., 1 g dietary fiber, 4 g protein.

Shopping list:

1 medium red onion

1 small container Jamaican jerk seasoning

2 20-ounce packages refrigerated mashed potatoes

1 8-ounce carton dairy sour cream

Pantry list:

Butter

Ground black pepper

Mixed Greens Salad **with Pears**

Start to Finish: **15 minutes**

1 **5-ounce bag spring mixed salad greens**

2 **medium fresh pears, cored and sliced**

2 **ounces Gruyère cheese, cubed**

White Wine Vinaigrette or $\frac{1}{4}$ cup bottled red wine vinaigrette plus 2 teaspoons honey

Thin fresh pear slices (optional)

In a large bowl combine greens, pears, and cheese. Drizzle vinaigrette over greens mixture and toss to coat. If desired, garnish with pear slices.

Makes 6 servings

Nutrition facts per serving: 148 cal., 10 g total fat (3 g sat. fat), 10 mg chol., 85 mg sodium, 12 g carbo., 2 g dietary fiber, 3 g protein.

White Wine Vinaigrette: In a screw-top jar combine 3 tablespoons salad oil; 2 tablespoons white wine vinegar; 1 tablespoon honey; $\frac{1}{4}$ teaspoon dried basil or oregano, crushed; $\frac{1}{8}$ teaspoon salt; $\frac{1}{8}$ teaspoon dry mustard; and $\frac{1}{8}$ teaspoon ground black pepper. Cover and shake to combine.

15 minutes

Shopping list:

1 5-ounce bag spring mixed salad greens

2 medium pears

2 ounces Gruyère cheese

1 8-ounce bottle white wine vinegar

1 small container dry mustard

Pantry list:

Salad oil

Honey

Dried basil

Salt

Ground black pepper

Mediterranean Salad

Start to Finish: **10 minutes**

1 **6.5-ounce jar marinated artichoke hearts, drained**

1 **15-ounce can three-bean salad, drained**

1 **large tomato, seeded and chopped**

1 **tablespoon snipped fresh basil or ½ teaspoon dried basil, crushed**

¼ **cup Italian salad dressing**

Lettuce leaves (optional)

Halve any large artichoke hearts. In a medium bowl combine artichoke hearts, three-bean salad, tomato, and basil. Drizzle Italian dressing over bean mixture; toss gently to coat. If desired, serve on lettuce leaves.

Makes 6 servings

Nutrition facts per serving: 109 cal., 5 g total fat (0 g sat. fat), 0 mg chol., 538 mg sodium, 16 g carbo., 3 g dietary fiber, 3 g protein.

Shopping list:
1 6.5-ounce jar marinated artichoke hearts

1 15-ounce can three-bean salad

1 large tomato

1 package fresh basil

Pantry list:
Bottled Italian salad dressing

Greek Salad with Wine Vinaigrette

Start to Finish: **15 minutes**

6 **cups packaged chopped hearts of romaine**

¼ **cup thin red onion wedges**

¼ **cup red sweet pepper strips**

¼ **cup crumbled feta cheese (1 ounce)**

2 **tablespoons pitted kalamata or ripe black olives, halved**

½ **cup bottled olive oil vinaigrette**

In a large salad bowl toss together romaine, onion, sweet pepper, feta cheese, and olives. Drizzle vinaigrette over romaine mixture. Toss to coat.

Makes 4 servings

Nutrition facts per serving: 190 cal., 18 g total fat (4 g sat. fat), 6 mg chol., 280 mg sodium, 4 g carbo., 1 g dietary fiber, 2 g protein.

15 minutes

Shopping list:

1 10-ounce package chopped hearts of romaine

1 small red onion

1 small red sweet pepper

1 4-ounce package crumbled feta cheese

1 6-ounce jar kalamata olives

1 8-ounce bottle olive oil vinaigrette

Festive Fall Salad *(See photo on page 284.)*

Start to Finish: **15 minutes**

- 1 **5- to 8-ounce package mixed salad greens**
- ⅓ **cup dried cranberries**
- ⅓ **cup broken pecans, toasted**
- ¼ **cup crumbled blue cheese or shredded white cheddar cheese**
- ¼ **cup bottled balsamic vinaigrette salad dressing**

In a large salad bowl combine greens, cranberries, pecans, and blue cheese. Add salad dressing; toss to coat.

Makes 6 servings

Nutrition facts per serving: 110 cal., 8 g total fat (2 g sat. fat), 4 mg chol., 206 mg sodium, 9 g carbo., 1 g dietary fiber, 2 g protein.

Shopping list:
- 1 5- to 8-ounce package mixed salad greens
- 1 3-ounce package dried cranberries
- 1 6-ounce package broken pecans
- 1 4-ounce piece blue cheese
- 1 8-ounce bottle balsamic vinaigrette salad dressing

15minutes

BLT Coleslaw *(See photo on page 282.)*

Start to Finish: **15 minutes**

1   **16-ounce package shredded cabbage with carrot (coleslaw mix)**

6   **slices packaged ready-to-serve cooked bacon, torn into bite-size pieces**

1   **pint grape or cherry tomatoes, halved**

½   **cup bottled ranch salad dressing**

In a large bowl combine coleslaw mix, bacon, tomatoes, and salad dressing. Toss to coat.

Makes 8 to 10 servings

Nutrition facts per serving: 110 cal., 9 g total fat (2 g sat. fat), 8 mg chol., 201 mg sodium, 6 g carbo., 2 g dietary fiber, 3 g protein.

Shopping list:

1 16-ounce package shredded cabbage with carrot (coleslaw mix)

1 2.1-ounce package ready-to-serve cooked bacon

1 pint grape tomatoes

Pantry list:

Bottled ranch salad dressing

Chunky Mustard **Potato Salad**

Start to Finish: **15 minutes**

- 1 **20-ounce package refrigerated new potato wedges**
- ¼ **teaspoon salt**
- 4 **green onions, sliced (½ cup)**
- ¼ **cup coarsely chopped dill pickles**
- ¼ **cup chopped, roasted red sweet pepper**
- ¼ **cup chopped celery**
- ¼ **cup cooked bacon crumbles**
- 2 **tablespoons Dijon-style mustard**
- ½ **teaspoon salt**
- ¼ **teaspoon ground black pepper**
- ½ **cup mayonnaise or salad dressing**

1 Place potatoes in a large saucepan. Add enough water to cover potatoes; add ¼ teaspoon salt. Bring to boiling; reduce heat. Simmer, covered for 5 minutes. Drain well; rinse with cold water and drain again.

2 Meanwhile, in a very large serving bowl combine green onions, pickles, roasted sweet pepper, celery, bacon crumbles, mustard, ½ teaspoon salt, and black pepper. Stir in potatoes. Add mayonnaise and mix gently. If desired, chill up to 24 hours.

Makes 10 servings

Nutrition facts per serving: 131 cal., 9 g total fat (1 g sat. fat), 6 mg chol., 457 mg sodium, 8 g carbo., 2 g dietary fiber, 3 g protein.

Shopping list:

1 20-ounce package refrigerated new potato wedges

1 bunch green onions

1 12-ounce jar dill pickles

1 7-ounce jar roasted red sweet peppers

1 bunch celery

1 2.1-ounce package cooked bacon slices

Pantry list:

Salt

Dijon-style mustard

Ground black pepper

Mayonnaise

Broccoli Slaw

Start to Finish: **10 minutes**

⅓ **cup mayonnaise or salad dressing**

2 **tablespoons cider vinegar**

1 **green onion, finely chopped (2 tablespoons)**

1½ **teaspoons sugar**

¾ **teaspoon salt**

5 **cups shredded broccoli (broccoli slaw mix) or shredded cabbage with carrot (coleslaw mix)**

For dressing, in a salad bowl stir together mayonnaise, vinegar, green onion, sugar, and salt. Add shredded broccoli; toss to coat.

Makes 4 to 5 servings

Nutrition facts per servings: 172 cal., 15 g total fat (2 g sat. fat), 7 mg chol., 566 mg sodium, 8 g carbo., 3 g dietary fiber, 3 g protein.

Shopping list:

1 bunch green onions

1 12-ounce package shredded broccoli (broccoli slaw mix)

Pantry list:

Mayonnaise

Cider vinegar

Sugar

Salt

15 minutes

Pasta with Tomatoes

Start to Finish: **15 minutes**

2 tablespoons olive oil

½ teaspoon snipped fresh rosemary

1 9-ounce package refrigerated fettuccine*

⅔ cup red and/or gold grape tomatoes, teardrop tomatoes, or cherry tomatoes, halved

¼ cup fresh Italian (flat-leaf) parsley

Salt

Coarsely ground black pepper

Grated Parmesan cheese

1 In a small bowl stir together oil and rosemary. Cover and set aside.

2 In a Dutch oven or large saucepan bring 3 quarts salted water to boiling. Cook pasta, uncovered, according to package directions until tender but still firm. Drain pasta; return to pan.

3 Add oil mixture, tomatoes, and parsley to pasta; toss to coat. Season to taste with salt and pepper. Sprinkle with Parmesan cheese.

Makes 4 servings

Nutrition facts per serving: 258 cal., 9 g total fat (2 g sat. fat), 43 mg chol., 202 mg sodium, 35 g carbo., 2 g dietary fiber, 10 g protein.

*Note: Snip pasta into shorter lengths, if desired.

Shopping list:

1 package fresh rosemary

1 9-ounce package refrigerated fettuccine

1 pint grape tomatoes

1 bunch fresh Italian (flat-leaf) parsley

1 7-ounce container grated Parmesan cheese

Pantry list:

Olive oil

Salt

Black pepper

15
minutes

Heavenly Couscous

Start to Finish: **15 minutes**

1 cup couscous

¼ teaspoon salt

1 cup boiling water

¼ cup slivered almonds

1 teaspoon butter

¼ cup snipped
   dried apricots

½ teaspoon finely
   shredded orange peel

1 In a medium bowl combine couscous and salt. Gradually add the boiling water. Let stand about 5 minutes or until liquid is absorbed.

2 Meanwhile, in a small skillet cook and stir almonds in hot butter over medium heat until almonds are light golden brown. Remove almonds from skillet to cool. Fluff couscous with a fork. Add apricots, orange peel, and toasted almonds to couscous. Fluff again. Serve immediately.

Makes 4 servings

Nutrition facts per serving: 250 cal., 5 g total fat (1 g sat. fat), 2 mg chol., 163 mg sodium, 42 g carbo., 4 g dietary fiber, 8 g protein.

15
minutes

Shopping list:

1 12-ounce package couscous

1 2.25-ounce package
   slivered almonds

1 3-ounce package dried
   apricots

1 orange

Pantry list:

Salt

Butter

Garlic Bread

Start to Finish: **12 minutes**

1   **1-pound loaf French bread, cut in half horizontally**

¼   **cup butter, softened**

¼   **teaspoon garlic salt**

Preheat broiler. Place bread halves, cut sides up, on a large baking sheet. In a small bowl stir together softened butter and garlic salt. Spread over cut sides of bread. Broil about 6 inches from the heat for 1 ½ to 2 minutes or until lightly browned. Cut into crosswise slices to serve. Serve warm.

Makes 12 to 16 servings

Nutrition facts per serving: 147 cal., 4 g total fat (1 g sat. fat), 3 mg chol., 316 mg sodium, 22 g carbo., 1 g dietary fiber, 7 g protein.

Garlic-Cheese Bread

Prepare as above, except sprinkle the buttered bread halves with 1 cup shredded Parmesan cheese, Romano cheese, or cheddar cheese.

Shopping list:

1 1-pound loaf French bread

Pantry list:

Butter

Garlic salt

15
minutes

Cheddar **Garlic Biscuits**

Start to Finish: 15 minutes   **Oven: 425°F**

- 2 **cups packaged biscuit mix**
- ½ **cup shredded cheddar cheese (2 ounces)**
- ⅔ **cup milk**
- 2 **tablespoons butter, melted**
- ¼ **teaspoon garlic powder**

1 Preheat oven to 425°F. Grease a baking sheet; set aside.

2 In a large bowl combine biscuit mix and cheese; add milk. Stir to combine. Drop dough from rounded tablespoons onto prepared baking sheet. Bake for 8 to 9 minutes or until biscuits are golden.

3 Meanwhile, in a small bowl combine melted butter and garlic powder; brush over hot biscuits. Serve warm.

Makes 10 biscuits

Nutrition facts per biscuit: 155 cal., 8 g total fat (4 g sat. fat), 14 mg chol., 367 mg sodium, 16 g carbo., 1 g dietary fiber, 4 g protein.

Shopping list:
1 8-ounce package biscuit mix
1 8-ounce package shredded cheddar cheese

Pantry list:
Milk
Butter
Garlic powder

15 minutes

Quick **Apple Crisp**

Start to Finish: **15 minutes**

1 **21-ounce can apple pie filling**

¼ **cup dried cranberries**

¼ **teaspoon ground ginger or ground cinnamon**

¼ **teaspoon vanilla**

1 **cup granola**

1 **pint vanilla ice cream**

In a medium saucepan combine pie filling, cranberries, and ginger; heat through, stirring occasionally. Remove from heat; stir in vanilla. Spoon into 4 bowls. Top with granola and ice cream.

Makes 4 servings

Nutrition facts per serving: 507 cal., 15 g total fat (8 g sat. fat), 68 mg chol., 113 mg sodium, 88 g carbo., 6 g dietary fiber, 9 g protein.

Shopping list:

1 21-ounce can apple pie filling

1 3-ounce package dried cranberries

1 small container ground ginger

1 1-ounce bottle vanilla

1 16-ounce box granola cereal

1 pint vanilla ice cream

Double **Berry Delight**

Start to Finish: **10 minutes**

¼	**cup raspberry preserves**
1	**tablespoon water**
1	**tablespoon brandy**
1 ⅓	**cups quartered strawberries**

In a small saucepan combine preserves and the water. Cook and stir over medium-low heat until preserves melt. Remove from heat. Stir in brandy. Divide strawberries among 4 dessert dishes. Drizzle with raspberry mixture.

Makes 4 servings

Nutrition facts per serving: 80 cal., 0 g total fat (0 g sat. fat), 0 mg chol., 7 mg sodium, 17 g carbo., 1 g dietary fiber, 0 g protein.

15 minutes

Shopping list:

1 10-ounce jar raspberry preserves

1 small bottle brandy

1 pint strawberries

Crepes with **Maple-Pear Sauce**

Start to Finish: **10 minutes**

1 **15.25-ounce can pear slices, drained**

1 **cup pure maple syrup or maple-flavor syrup**

1 **4- to 4.5-ounce package ready-to-use crepes (10 crepes)**

½ **cup chopped pecans, toasted**

1 In a small saucepan combine pear slices and maple syrup; heat through.

2 Meanwhile, fold crepes into quarters; arrange on a serving platter. Pour hot pear mixture over crepes. Sprinkle with pecans.

Makes 5 servings

Nutrition facts per serving: 344 cal., 10 g total fat (1 g sat. fat), 36 mg chol., 77 mg sodium, 63 g carbo., 2 g dietary fiber, 3 g protein.

Shopping list:

1 15.25-ounce can pear slices

1 4- to 4.5-ounce package ready-to-use crepes

1 2.25-ounce package chopped pecans

Pantry list:

Maple syrup

15 minutes

Blueberry Cream Treats

Start to Finish: **10 minutes**

1 **8-ounce carton dairy sour cream**

¼ **cup packed brown sugar**

1 **quart (4 cups) fresh blueberries**

   Brown sugar (optional)

In a small bowl stir together sour cream and ¼ cup brown sugar until smooth. Divide blueberries among 6 stemmed sherbet dishes or dessert dishes. Spoon sour cream mixture over blueberries. If desired, sprinkle with additional brown sugar.

Makes 6 servings

Nutrition facts per serving: 170 cal., 8 g total fat (5 g sat. fat), 17 mg chol., 25 mg sodium, 24 g carbo., 2 g dietary fiber, 2 g protein.

Shopping list:

1 8-ounce carton dairy sour cream

1 quart fresh blueberries

Pantry list:

Brown sugar

15 minutes

Brownie Surprise *(See photo on page 288.)*

Start to Finish: **10 minutes**

4 **purchased brownies (each about 3x2 inches)**

1 **15.10- to 16-ounce carton cherry-chocolate ice cream**

¼ **cup dried cherries**

¼ **cup chopped mixed nuts or nut topping**

2 **tablespoons chocolate-flavor syrup**

Place 1 brownie in each of 4 dessert bowls. Top with a scoop of ice cream. Sprinkle with cherries and nuts. Drizzle with syrup.

Makes 4 servings

Nutrition facts per serving: 660 cal., 35 g total fat (17 g sat. fat), 81 mg chol., 255 mg sodium, 81 g carbo., 3 g dietary fiber, 9 g protein.

Shopping list:

4 bakery brownies

1 15.10- to 16-ounce carton cherry-chocolate ice cream

1 3-ounce package dried tart red cherries

1 small container mixed nuts

1 24-ounce bottle chocolate-flavor syrup

Bittersweet Chocolate-Orange Fondue

Start to Finish: 15 minutes

6 ounces bittersweet chocolate, coarsely chopped

¾ cup half-and-half or light cream

⅓ cup sugar

¼ cup orange liqueur or orange juice

2 tablespoons honey

Dippers (such as dried fruits; biscotti cookies; clementines, tangerines, or oranges, peeled and sectioned; pear or apple wedges; whole walnuts, almonds, or pecans)

In a heavy small saucepan melt chocolate over medium-low heat. Whisk in half-and-half until smooth; stir in sugar, orange liqueur, and honey. Cook, stirring constantly, for 4 to 5 minutes or until mixture is slightly thick and sugar dissolves. Transfer to a fondue pot. Keep warm over low heat. Serve with desired dippers.

Makes 8 servings

Nutrition facts per serving: 205 cal., 11 g total fat (7 g sat. fat), 9 mg chol., 10 mg sodium, 28 g carbo., 2 g dietary fiber, 2 g protein.

15 minutes

Shopping list:

1 6-ounce package bittersweet baking chocolate

1 8-ounce carton half-and-half

1 small bottle orange liqueur

Desired dippers

Pantry list:

Sugar

Honey

Tropical Breeze Sundae

Start to Finish: **15 minutes**

1   **quart pineapple, lime, or orange sherbet or sorbet**

   Fresh pineapple, papaya, or mango slices

½ to ¾ **cup pineapple ice cream topping**

   Pressurized whipped dessert topping

Scoop sherbet into 6 dessert dishes. Add fruit slices. Top each serving with a spoonful of ice cream topping and some whipped dessert topping. Serve immediately.

Makes 6 servings

Nutrition facts per serving: 282 cal., 0 g total fat (0 g sat. fat), 0 mg chol., 46 mg sodium, 72 g carbo., 0 g dietary fiber, 0 g protein.

Shopping list:

1 quart pineapple sherbet

1 fresh pineapple

1 12-ounce jar pineapple ice cream topping

1 6.5-ounce can pressurized whipped dessert topping

Chocolate Peanut Butter
Ice Cream Sandwiches

Start to Finish: **15 minutes**

1 **pint tin roof sundae or other chocolate swirl premium ice cream**

8 **3 ½-inch purchased peanut butter cookies**

¼ **cup miniature semisweet chocolate pieces or crushed chocolate-covered crisp peanut butter candy**

Place a scoop of ice cream on the bottom of 4 cookies. Top with remaining 4 cookies, flat side down. Press gently to force ice cream to the edges of the cookies. Place chocolate pieces in a shallow dish. Roll edges of ice cream sandwiches in the chocolate pieces to coat. Freeze for 5 minutes or until firm.

Makes 4 servings

Nutrition facts per serving: 625 cal., 36 g total fat (17 g sat. fat), 123 mg chol., 312 mg sodium, 65 g carbo., 2 g dietary fiber, 11 g protein.

Shopping list:

1 pint tin roof sundae ice cream

8 bakery peanut butter cookies

1 12-ounce package miniature semisweet chocolate pieces

15 minutes

Mocha Mousse Cups

Start to Finish: **15 minutes**

2 teaspoons instant espresso powder or 1 tablespoon instant coffee crystals

1 tablespoon hot water

4 3.5- to 4-ounce containers chocolate pudding (prepared pudding cups), chilled

½ of an 8-ounce container frozen whipped dessert topping, thawed

9 chocolate wafer cookies, coarsely crushed

In a medium bowl stir espresso powder into the hot water until dissolved. Stir in chilled pudding. Fold in whipped topping. Divide half of the pudding mixture among 6 dessert dishes. Sprinkle with half of the coarsely crushed cookies. Repeat layers.

Makes 6 servings

Nutrition facts per serving: 187 cal., 7 g total fat (5 g sat. fat), 0 mg chol., 164 mg sodium, 27 g carbo., 0 g dietary fiber, 2 g protein.

Shopping list:

1 2-ounce jar instant espresso powder

4 3.5-ounce containers chocolate pudding

1 8-ounce container frozen whipped dessert topping

1 9-ounce package chocolate wafer cookies

15
minutes

Grilled Chocolate Banana Sandwich

Start to Finish: **10 minutes**

½ **of a 3.5-ounce chocolate bar, halved**

2 **slices white or whole wheat bread**

½ **of a banana, sliced**

1 **tablespoon butter**

Sifted powdered sugar

Place the chocolate bar on 1 bread slice. Top with the banana slices and remaining slice of bread. In a skillet heat butter over medium-low heat just until it begins to bubble. Add sandwich to skillet, chocolate side down. Cook, covered, about 1 ½ minutes or until bread is golden brown and toasted. Carefully flip sandwich over and cook until brown. Remove from skillet, slice in half, and dust with powdered sugar. Serve warm.

Makes 1 serving

Nutrition facts per serving: 560 cal., 29 g total fat (17 g sat. fat), 42 mg chol., 473 mg sodium, 70 g carbo., 4 g dietary fiber, 11 g protein.

15 minutes

Shopping list:

1 3.5-ounce chocolate bar

2 slices bread

1 banana

Pantry list:

Butter

Powdered sugar

Cinnamon Toasted Pound Cake and Strawberries *(See photo on page 287.)*

Start to Finish: **15 minutes**

1 tablespoon sugar

½ teaspoon ground cinnamon

3 cups strawberries, washed and quartered

¼ cup strawberry jam

1 tablespoon lemon juice

1 10.75-ounce frozen pound cake, thawed and cut in 12 slices

2 tablespoons butter, softened

Frozen whipped dessert topping, thawed

1 In a small bowl stir together sugar and cinnamon. In a large bowl toss together strawberries, jam, lemon juice, and 1 teaspoon of the cinnamon-sugar mixture until berries are well coated.

2 Toast pound cake slices. Spread 1 side of each slice with butter. Sprinkle with remaining cinnamon-sugar mixture. To serve, place 2 pound cake slices on each of 6 plates. Top with strawberries and whipped topping.

Makes 6 servings

Nutrition facts per serving: 875 cal., 56 g total fat (31 g sat. fat), 378 mg chol., 540 mg sodium, 135 g carbo., 5 g dietary fiber, 13 g protein.

Shopping list:
1 quart strawberries

1 10-ounce jar strawberry jam

1 lemon

1 10.75-ounce frozen pound cake

1 8-ounce container frozen whipped dessert topping

Pantry list:
Sugar

Ground cinnamon

Butter

Chocolate-Coconut **Cheesecake**

Start to Finish: **10 minutes**

1 **30-ounce package frozen New York–style cheesecake**

1 **12-ounce jar fudge ice cream topping**

4 **soft coconut macaroon cookies, crumbled**

¼ **cup sliced almonds, toasted**

Thaw cheesecake according to package directions for microwave thawing. Spread top of cheesecake with fudge topping, allowing some to drip down side of cheesecake. Sprinkle with crumbled cookies and almonds.

Makes 12 servings

Nutrition facts per serving: 371 cal., 17 g total fat (9 g sat. fat), 45 mg chol., 305 mg sodium, 48 g carbo., 0 g dietary fiber, 6 g protein.

15 minutes

Shopping list:

1 30-ounce package frozen New York–style cheesecake

1 12-ounce jar fudge ice cream topping

1 12-ounce package coconut macaroon cookies

1 2.25-ounce package sliced almonds

Fruit and Cereal Drops

Start to Finish: **15 minutes**

2 **cups rice and wheat cereal flakes**

¾ **cup mixed dried fruit bits**

½ **cup whole almonds, toasted and coarsely chopped**

6 **ounces vanilla-flavor candy coating, chopped**

1 **tablespoon shortening**

1 In a large bowl stir together cereal flakes, fruit bits, and almonds; set aside.

2 In a medium saucepan melt candy coating and shortening over low heat. Pour coating mixture over fruit mixture; toss gently to coat.

3 Working quickly, drop the cereal mixture from a teaspoon onto a cookie sheet lined with waxed paper. Freeze for 5 minutes or until set.

Makes about 24 cookies

Nutrition facts per serving: 81 cal., 4 g total fat (2 g sat. fat), 0 mg chol., 21 mg sodium, 10 g carbo., 0 g dietary fiber, 1 g protein.

To Store: Place cookies in layers separated by waxed paper in an airtight container; cover. Store at room temperature for up to 3 days. Do not freeze.

Shopping list:

1 12-ounce package rice and wheat cereal flakes

1 7-ounce package mixed dried fruit bits

1 6-ounce package whole almonds

1 6-ounce box vanilla-flavor candy coating

Pantry list:

Shortening

15 minutes

METRIC INFORMATION

The charts on this page provide a guide for converting measurements from the U.S. customary system, which is used throughout this book, to the metric system.

PRODUCT DIFFERENCES

Most of the ingredients called for in the recipes in this book are available in most countries. However, some are known by different names. Here are some common American ingredients and their possible counterparts:

- Sugar (white) is granulated, fine granulated, or castor sugar.
- Powdered sugar is icing sugar.
- All-purpose flour is enriched, bleached, or unbleached white household flour. When self-rising flour is used in place of all-purpose flour in a recipe that calls for leavening, omit the leavening agent (baking soda or baking powder) and salt.
- Light-colored corn syrup is golden syrup.
- Cornstarch is cornflour.
- Baking soda is bicarbonate of soda.
- Vanilla or vanilla extract is vanilla essence.
- Green, red, or yellow sweet peppers are capsicums or bell peppers.
- Golden raisins are sultanas.

VOLUME AND WEIGHT

The United States traditionally uses cup measures for liquid and solid ingredients. The chart, top right, shows the approximate imperial and metric equivalents. If you are accustomed to weighing solid ingredients, the following approximate equivalents will be helpful.

- 1 cup butter, castor sugar, or rice = 8 ounces = $\frac{1}{2}$ pound = 250 grams
- 1 cup flour = 4 ounces = $\frac{1}{4}$ pound = 125 grams
- 1 cup icing sugar = 5 ounces = 150 grams

Canadian and U.S. volume for a cup measure is 8 fluid ounces (237 ml), but the standard metric equivalent is 250 ml.

1 British imperial cup is 10 fluid ounces.

In Australia, 1 tablespoon equals 20 ml, and there are 4 teaspoons in the Australian tablespoon.

Spoon measures are used for smaller amounts of ingredients. Although the size of the tablespoon varies slightly in different countries, for practical purposes and for recipes in this book, a straight substitution is all that's necessary. Measurements made using cups or spoons always should be level unless stated otherwise.

COMMON WEIGHT RANGE REPLACEMENTS

Imperial / U.S.	Metric
$\frac{1}{2}$ ounce	15 g
1 ounce	25 g or 30 g
4 ounces ($\frac{1}{4}$ pound)	115 g or 125 g
8 ounces ($\frac{1}{2}$ pound)	225 g or 250 g
16 ounces (1 pound)	450 g or 500 g
$1\frac{1}{4}$ pounds	625 g
$1\frac{1}{2}$ pounds	750 g
2 pounds or $2\frac{1}{4}$ pounds	1,000 g or 1 Kg

OVEN TEMPERATURE EQUIVALENTS

Fahrenheit Setting	Celsius Setting*	Gas Setting
300°F	150°C	Gas Mark 2 (very low)
325°F	160°C	Gas Mark 3 (low)
350°F	180°C	Gas Mark 4 (moderate)
375°F	190°C	Gas Mark 5 (moderate)
400°F	200°C	Gas Mark 6 (hot)
425°F	220°C	Gas Mark 7 (hot)
450°F	230°C	Gas Mark 8 (very hot)
475°F	240°C	Gas Mark 9 (very hot)
500°F	260°C	Gas Mark 10 (extremely hot)
Broil	Broil	Grill

*Electric and gas ovens may be calibrated using celsius. However, for an electric oven, increase celsius setting 10 to 20 degrees when cooking above 160°C. For convection or forced air ovens (gas or electric) lower the temperature setting 25°F/10°C when cooking at all heat levels.

BAKING PAN SIZES

Imperial / U.S.	Metric
9×1$\frac{1}{2}$-inch round cake pan	22- or 23x4-cm (1.5 L)
9×1$\frac{1}{2}$-inch pie plate	22- or 23×4-cm (1 L)
8×8×2-inch square cake pan	20×5-cm (2 L)
9×9×2-inch square cake pan	22- or 23×4.5-cm (2.5 L)
11×7×1$\frac{1}{2}$-inch baking pan	28×17×4-cm (2 L)
2-quart rectangular baking pan	30×19×4.5-cm (3 L)
13×9×2-inch baking pan	34×22×4.5-cm (3.5 L)
15×10×1-inch jelly roll pan	40×25×2-cm
9×5×3-inch loaf pan	23×13×8-cm (2 L)
2-quart casserole	2 L

U.S. / STANDARD METRIC EQUIVALENTS

$\frac{1}{8}$ teaspoon = 0.5 ml	$\frac{1}{3}$ cup = 3 fluid ounces = 75 ml
$\frac{1}{4}$ teaspoon = 1 ml	$\frac{1}{2}$ cup = 4 fluid ounces = 125 ml
$\frac{1}{2}$ teaspoon = 2 ml	$\frac{1}{3}$ cup = 5 fluid ounces = 150 ml
1 teaspoon = 5 ml	$\frac{3}{4}$ cup = 6 fluid ounces = 175 ml
1 tablespoon = 15 ml	1 cup = 8 fluid ounces = 250 ml
2 tablespoons = 25 ml	2 cups = 1 pint = 500 ml
$\frac{1}{4}$ cup = 2 fluid ounces = 50 ml	1 quart = 1 liter

INDEX

Note: Page numbers in *italics* indicate photos.

A

Alfredo Chicken Pita Pizzas, 22
Almonds
  Asparagus with Almond Sauce, 373
  Buttery Almond Salmon with Apricot Sauce, 212
  Crispy Almond Fish, 202
  Tilapia with Almond Browned Butter, 79
Apples
  Apple-Brie Grilled Sandwiches, 117
  Lamb Chops with Cinnamon Apples, 201
  Quick Apple Crisp, 387
  Turkey-Apple Salad Wraps, 167
Apricots
  Buttery Almond Salmon with Apricot Sauce, 212
  Grilled Turkey-Apricot Sandwiches, 40
Arroz con Pollo, *136*, 149
Artichokes
  Artichoke Risotto, 368
  Turkey-Artichoke Toss, 168
Asian Chicken Salad, 26
Asian Hot and Sour Shrimp Soup, 100
Asian Pork Soup, 59
Asian Pork Tenderloin with Ramen Noodle Salad, 313
Asian Salmon Burgers, *282*, 345
Asian-Style Beef Soup, 48
Asian-Style Pork Burgers, 194
Asparagus
  Asparagus with Almond Sauce, 373
  Pasta with Beef and Asparagus, 172
  Salmon with Asparagus and Mushrooms, 337
  Whitefish with Roasted Asparagus, 335
Avocados
  Chicken Club Sandwiches with Avocado Spread, 18
  Orange-Avocado Crab Salad Sandwich, 101
  Seafood Omelet with Avocado Salsa, 102
  Two-Bean Chili with Avocado, 359

B

Bacon
  BLT Coleslaw, *282*, 380
Baked Rosemary Trout with Parmesan Polenta, 343
Balsamic vinegar
  Balsamic-Glazed Sirloin Kabobs, 301
  Balsamic Pork Medallions, 57
Bananas
  Grilled Chocolate Banana Sandwich, 396
Barbecue Skillet Pizza, 186
Basil
  Basil-Lime Salmon, 340
  Ham-Basil-Broccoli Wraps, 199
  Turkey Panini with Basil Aioli, 166
Bavarian Quesadillas, 21
BBQ Chicken Burgers and Waffle Fries, *139*, 159
Beans. *See also* Green beans; *specific beans*
  Bean Burritos with Lime Mayonnaise, 108, *133*
  Italian Bean and Pasta Soup, 237
  Two-Bean Chili with Avocado, 359
Beef. *See also* Corned beef; Ground beef; Pot roast; Steak
  Asian-Style Beef Soup, 48
  Barbecue Skillet Pizza, 186
  Beef and Polenta with Red Onion Topper, 176
  Beef and Tapenade Focaccia Sandwiches, 51
  Beef and Vegetables with Spaghetti, 300
  Beef-Broccoli Noodle Bowl, 47
  Beef Stir-Fry Salad, 175
  Beef-Vegetable Pasta Toss, 174
  Beef-Vegetable Stew, 49
  Beef-Vegetable Stir-Fry, 182
  Fast French Dip Sandwiches, *141*, 184
  Greek Beef and Pasta Skillet, 173
  Horseradish Beef Wraps, 50
  Pasta with Beef and Asparagus, 172
  Roast Beef, Swiss, and Onions on Rye, 187
  Seared Beef with Orange Salsa, 294
  Speedy Beef Stir-Fry, *140*, 171
Beer
  Broccoli Beer Cheese Soup, 169
Berries. *See also specific berries*
  Double Berry Delight, 388
Biscuits
  Cheddar Garlic Biscuits, 386
  Chicken and Biscuits, 265
  Curried Tuna on Biscuits, 96
Bistro-Style Chicken and Roasted Pepper Sandwiches, 20
Bittersweet Chocolate-Orange Fondue, 392